ANDRE
EMMERICH
GALLERY

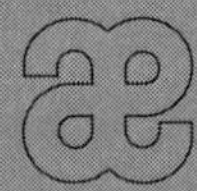

41 East 57th Street

New York, New York 10022

Telephone (212) 752-0124

Fax (212) 371-7345

CONJUNCTIONS

Bi-Annual Volumes of New Writing

Edited by
Bradford Morrow

Bard College *distributed by Random House, Inc.*

CONJUNCTIONS is published in the Spring and Fall of each year by Bard College, Annandale-on-Hudson, NY 12504. This issue is made possible in part with the generous funding of the Lannan Foundation, the National Endowment for the Arts and the New York State Council on the Arts. Major new marketing initiatives have been made possible by the Lila Wallace–Reader's Digest Literary Publishers Marketing Development Program, funded through a grant to the Council of Literary Magazines and Presses.

SUBSCRIPTIONS: Send subscription order to CONJUNCTIONS, Bard College, Annandale-on-Hudson, NY 12504. Single year (two volumes): $18.00 for individuals; $25.00 for institutions and overseas. Two years (four volumes): $32.00 for individuals; $45.00 for institutions and overseas. Patron subscription (lifetime): $500.00. Overseas subscribers please make payment by International Money Order. Back issues available at $10.00 per copy.

Editorial communications should be sent to 33 West 9th Street, New York, NY 10011. Unsolicited manuscripts cannot be returned unless accompanied by a stamped, self-addressed envelope.

Distributed by Random House.

Cover design by Anthony McCall Associates, New York

Printers: Edwards Brothers.
Typesetter: Bill White, Typeworks.

ISSN 0278-2324
ISBN 0-679-75581-0

Manufactured in the United States of America.

TABLE OF CONTENTS

EDITOR'S NOTE

THE NOVELLA HAS LONG been a recluse, an outcast in the family of literary styles. Consigned like some crazy aunt or loony uncle to a remote room in the house, with separate entrance and an interior door lockable from the hall, a novella doesn't *fit.* It won't adapt itself to the needs of publishers or readers who like their short stories short and their novels long. It is disobedient and cannot be edited down, nor extended, without bringing on disaster. In his preface to *The Turn of the Screw,* James refers to it as being a "perfectly independent and irresponsible little fiction" whose "small strength" is "a perfect homogeneity." By irresponsible I take him to mean responsible formally to none other than itself.

What is a novella? Just as the novella resists easy alliances with its fellow genres, it defies one who would define it. It does betray a complexity of narrative development and elaboration of some conflict and character that the short story does not. And it accomplishes this without superabundant modulation, without striking the polyphonic and contrapuntal notes which are so recognizable in the progress of the novel.

In this issue, we have gathered together a few fictions which may apply. What makes Lynne Tillman's work a novella, if that of Ben Marcus—which runs longer and is composed in an equally lapidary fashion—isn't? Here is where that ineffable element, authorial intention, comes into play. If Nabokov considered *Transparent Things* a novel, and Harold Brodkey deems "Largely an Oral History of My Mother" a story, I see no reason not to believe them both, even though Brodkey's story is longer than Nabokov's novel, and manifests itself through a knottier infrastructure. Arno Schmidt maintained "The Displaced" was one of his novellas. John Barth sees various points of interconnection in his three stories, though they do not precisely constitute a novella. It is, in the end, the progenitors who best know the design and intent of their offspring.

The five novellas (*qua* novellas) published here are vastly different in form and tone, mood and method, but they do share, at least during their tenure in these pages together, that room at the far end of the house in which, on certain days, the light comes through the windows at an angle and with a luminosity never noticed elsewhere.

Preservation News
Allan Gurganus

Preservation News

Issue # 14, NEWSLetter:

being the bi-monthly bulletin of
Historic North Carolina Home Preservation
---a non-profit organization generously supported by the National Endowment for the Humanities and local private funding---

— AVAILABLE FOR RESTORATION —

ELKTON GREEN

(Located: 2.4 acres, downtown Falls, NC, Person County)

Elkton Green is the preeminent bracketed Victorian gingerbread mansion in northeastern North Carolina. It will be leveled by wreckers if some fairy-god-purchaser is not found by April first. Help us, please?

Preferably somebody with plenty of good sense, mad about history, alive to the finer nuances of strongarmed social pretense, and with a discretionary income to sort of match. Pretty please? Little family foundations are always nice. We just know you're out there.

Fact is, we have got two extensions from the very cooperative Falls Town Zoning Board. Even given a treasure like Elkton Green, my friends, this is our literal last chance. Already bids have come in for its pearwood-and-mahogany parqueted spiral staircase and for all its stained glass. But these are bids from a chain restaurant that will perform a mastectomy, that will then scatter bits of the mansion's exquisite features into separate franchises where people order their quite-bad beef awfully overcooked. Large portions of too-buttered 'garlic bread' are intended to distract them. It makes us swoon, the thought. Perish it.

Built in 1856 for the Penner-Coker Family, this high Victorian 'pile' seems to have been inspired by the minarets of the Prince's 'Folly' Pavilion at Brighton. Elkton Green retains its Tudor rose medallions and endearingly redundant cornices. Even its brackets are bracketed. A gracious, indeed show-off, home in the downtown Historic Summit District, we are talking 24 rooms; we're talking porches enough to accommodate every banished smoker left alive in Falls, NC. Lavish plantings survive, including a mature box maze (needs work, as mazes, alas, tend to). The lawn, rolling clear down to the River Tar, is a fine acre-and-a-half. We speak now of a lawn so suitable for croquet,

I'll throw in my own best 1920's Wilson set. We'll just leave it up for you to look at, and get vague credit for.

Our 'right hand person,' the inimitable Mary Ellen Broadfield, took note of Elkton Green's West Wing featuring a faux Romanesque capital set directly beside one that might be called 'Adirondack Carnival Ecclesiastical Ecstatic.' And M.E. said, "This home is like some lady from a very good family, but who's had entirely too much coffee and feels forced to try on every hat in a third rate shop, all at once." There are sane people who consider the house overornamented. But for us, the mansion's gingerbread detailing represents Elegance pushed—testing—clear to the edge of Comedy. (Which is just where some of us most long to live!)

Elkton Green's 14-foot ceilings boast heavy, indeed, luscious moldings, there is tooled leather wainscoting and a dining-room mural (oil on leather, 10 x 21 feet). The subject seems to have been suggested by Judge J.V. Coker's extensive collection of American Indian artifacts. Coker's brilliant early acquisitions—however dubiously gained from the rough-hewn grave-robbing bounty hunters known even then as 'New York art dealers'—formed the cornerstone gift of what is now the Smithsonian's impressive horde.

The mural shows a band of fruit-carrying Indians, generically bare if genitally unspecified. They greet one paunchy Quaker gent smiling from beneath a hurtful-looking black tricorn hat. (There is an eerie similarity to Edmund Hicks' later *Peaceable Kingdom* series.) The fat white guy is said to depict the great great grandfather of Elkton Green's builder, one Judge Josiah Vestry Coker (1670–1749). He remained on fine terms with his native American neighbors even through the Tuscarora War of 1710. He negotiated the release of certain English lady settlers taken as hostages. They were freed through his personal diplomacy and an anonymous donation of "many sovereigne of the King's coinage, meetly dispatched by His Own horses." The mural is of museum quality and is unique in the state.

Some people have complained that I tell too much about the history of each house. That is not possible.

For the record, the man who built Elkton Green inherited a goodly fortune via the Judge and art collector. But plump Caleb Coker then handsomely supplanted his patrimony through naval stores, the pitch and rope and turpentine, sold along our State's then-bustling steamship coast. Coker's own King Cotton holdings—taken collectively—equaled half the landmass of Rhode Island. It was he, Caleb Hunstable Coker (1812–1891), who conceived of Elkton Green as the site for his beautiful daughter's wedding. This, prior to his actually having a daughter. (Such is the energy and optimism of our America!) The mansion's stained-glass-skylight-lit staircase was designed precisely to make stunning the choreography of one girl's white-veiled descent.

Concord, Coker's only child, was born just three years after the home's completion. Her mother died in childbirth. Fortunate for herself, her father (and his architects!), Concord proved to be just the beauty that a seventy-one-step-staircase preordained. It was Concord, at age eighteen, who founded the first Falls Public Lending Library for Ladies. She furnished it with her cast-off novels (she is said to have read two a day since age ten. Her father saw this as proof of her refinement [and incidentally his own]). When Concord finally wed at the age of thirty-one, she chose a future Chief Justice of the State Supreme Court. By her day's standards, Concord Coker was already middle-aged. This last-minute reprieve from spinsterhood and a threatened end of the Coker line further piqued her father's extravagance. It had already been expressed, perhaps too-malely, in this house that, for all its feminizing frontal gingery lace, remains blessed with a Grover Cleveland girth of solemnity, not to mix metaphors or, worse, periods. Elkton Green's builder swore it must now fulfill its destiny, must now become the stage for what Caleb Coker announced, in print alas, would be "the wedding of the century."

The bride's proud poppa, nine-term mayor of Falls, imported a sixty piece string orchestra from (not Richmond but) Philadelphia. Through his naval connections, he chartered one of the last for-lease four-masted schooners, *The Reliance*. It brought all the instruments, three requested extra harps, and distinguished Yankee guests south to Wilmington's harbor.

Mr. Coker was too ambitious and too rich to stop there. He soon stage-managed a single decorative touch that even now gives him an ongoing life in local Falls legend. (Who could ask for anything more?) With help from a railroad-owning friend and later business partner of the Barnum and Bailey Circus,

Historic Real Estate That Calls You Home

NORTH CAROLINA ESTATES

Exclusive Member of the Historic Real Estate Program of the National Trust for Historic Preservation

Exum-Tyson House

This handsomely detailed 1870s home has been completely renovated for comfortable family living. 5,000 + sq. ft. on 32 acres outside of Goldsboro. $460,000.

Cloverok

A singular example of the stonemason's art, this 4,000 sq. ft. 1895 home of hand cut blue stone sits on 50 acres of rolling pasture land with a pond. Warrenton. $260,000.

Windmill Point

This recently remodeled 1920s residential complex includes a main residence and separate guest house on 2 acres in Oriental overlooking Pamlico Sound and the Neuse River. $459,000.

For information on these fine Properties please call Diane E. Lea at:
Tel (919) 544-6880
Fax (919) 544-0604
P. O. Box 13980
Research Triangle Park,
NC 27709-3980

The Person-Allen-King House

The Person-Allen-King house, 212 W. Anderson Street, is a meticulously renovated Colonial Revival style residence in Selma's National Register Historic District. Designed in 1904 by well-known Raleigh architect and Goldsboro native W. P. Rose for Dr. J. B. Person, the house is an elegant example of Rose's residential architecture. The present owners, Gerald Allen and Edward King, spent six-year renovating the structure which had been reconfigured for apartments. Today, this energy-efficient 5,000 sq. ft. home offers 4 bedrooms, 3 1/2 baths, and a third floor suite suitable for owner's quarters for a B & B, a teen-ager's retreat or a hobby room. Well-landscaped in-town lot with garage. $325,000.

Exclusive Affiliate of Sotheby's International Realty

12 AVAILABLE FOR RESTORATION

Caleb Coker imported spiders, yes, specialty spiders, from South America. I don't pretend to understand all this, but the eight news clippings here—long since turned brown as cigars—all vouch for insects' unlikely presence. The exact species has been lost to us, despite our tireless research. It grieves us, this inexcusable lapse; my fondest hope was to offer the species' exact Latin name. I fear there's no time left before our present Issue #14 must be 'put to bed.' However, I HAVE discovered that these creatures were brought to Falls by rail. (Thanks to a bibliophilic fellow preservationist, I own the somewhat comic shipping invoice.) Under "Descrp. Laden Goods:" some shaky hand has written, "Spiders, large, South American, keeper was well-spoken & aware of poss. passnger discomfort. Paid first class fare for each cage. Kept crates draped excllnt. All steps taken."

Spiders arrived in steel containers described by one witness as "little metal safes with wire-mesh-covered breathing holes." The insects' trainer released them at night into Elkton Green's water oaks, camellias and its then-young box maze on the South lawn. Spiders soon spun gossamer at a rate almost unseemly and locally unknown till now. Two dawns later, they had outshone Christo, wrapping Elkton Green entire. Silver webbing was said to cover every shrub, most of the porch's bracketed brackets. According to a newspaper account, "a wheelbarrow, one tall ladder left in the wrong place, and the results of the milkman's visit needed freeing from sudden gauze." From even taller ladders, slaves sprinkled real gold dust over all the webs. The whole place was then strung with six thousand, yes, white Chinese lanterns. The grounds were lit for the wedding with "over twenty thousand white tapers, of the finest."

At six AM the Coker slaves began lighting white lanterns meant to illumine the nighttime wedding. Now, to our jaded eyes, this might seem a pleasing sight. But for Falls, of the period, where one oil lamp per kitchen table was considered a luxury item, such display shone without parallel. It took twenty-one slaves twelve hours to light and relight every wick, avoiding the still-busy spiders, now themselves turned gold. Two counties' fire departments stood by, so stoked with rum cordials their utility was undercut, but happily never needed. It was reported that, by evening, the glow could be seen fully half a mile away.

A chronicle of the day inevitably mentions Midas. The *Falls*

Herald Traveler called the nighttime sight of Elkton Green "locked within the powdered gold of candleglow casts over finest webbing, a spectacle from pre-Christian myth, in its excess both offputting and yet wondrous as some children's book's occurrence. A strange idea, so perfectly implemented that it shall not be soon forgot by any of the over one thousand uninvited guests allowed, yes, even encouraged, to stand outside Elkton Green's castiron gates and to stare. Each onlooker was provided a gilt packet of rice to shower upon the handsome escaping bridal couple. It must be noted that—while the bride appeared almost starkly beautiful, Elkton Green itself, a home that easily accommodated the exceptional string orchestra of sixty, plus unnumbered guests, glowed with a fond pride that seemed cordial, aware and all but human in its open joy. Many onlookers remarked the impression of a house come utterly, as it were, sentiently and watchfully alive."

Elkton Green now stands, somewhat startled it must be admitted, in downtown commercial Falls, NC—within easy take-out distance of both a Hardee's and a Colonel Sanders, alas. We personally planted fast-growing Leland Cypresses to screen out such blight in three to four years' time. The mansion rests on 2.4 acres of its original 880. It is just around the corner from the White-Rooker-designed Gothic Revival Courthouse (would it be immodest to mention our organization's having saved this masterwork in January 1983?). Elkton Green still holds a place of honor along Summit Avenue, a street lined with other Victorian mastodons and the magnolias planted by Falls' "Betterment Committee" in 1891. The reason there are four car garages and outbuildings and parking for four hundred (count 'em) autos is, quite genteelly put, . . . Elkton Green was, in the late 1950s, transformed into Falls' finest white funeral establishment. I say, there must be life after embalming for Elkton Green! Pul-lease?

Falls is located just off I-95 and I-40, the main byways linking Miami and New York. This certainly helps give Elkton Green, with its extensive leaded windows, arched interior doorways, Vermont marble rose-and-lotus-carved hearth facings, commodious rooms and ingenious still-working system of dumbwaiters, great potential as a going bed and breakfast. (If that's what it takes to save it.) Anyone who has seen and loved Orson

Welles's *The Magnificent Ambersons*, anyone who has ever nursed a fantasy of issuing one's own white-draped daughter from the head of a great staircase featuring the period's requisite bronze of bare-bottomed Mercury (it's there), needs to see (then save) this brave survivor of its day.

It's a very big house built to edify, impress and perhaps slightly terrify this little town. For a moot $230,000, it's yours to use—as gently or as bullyingly—as you see fit.

Square Feet: 6,899. Lot: 2.4 acres. Zoning: B1 (central business). Revolving Funds available immediately. Plus ample parking for your next garden party of 850 guests, your own (second or third?) wedding or, for that matter, hygienic facilities befitting your (first) funeral! Everything's ready. We know you're out there. It's yours, please.

—The history (& the croquet) come free.

Historic North Carolina Home Preservation

Issue #14

A Commemorative Issue Celebrating
the Life of
Theodore Hunstable Worth

(volunteer interim editor: Mary Ellen Broadfield)

You have just read the next-to-last 'Available For Restoration' note actually written by our much missed leader, gadfly and inspiration, Theodore 'Tad' Worth. I was just one of the many people touched by him. I am but one of the countless fortunates now living in a house Tad saved from the bulldozer. I feel I must make a few remarks. Some will be statesmanlike and formal (as is our wont, we preservationists!). Others will, no doubt, prove utterly uncalled-for, and therefore of a sort I think he'd like.

I. A Perhaps Too Personal Reflection

First I only knew Tad Worth socially, as everybody did. But I can't say I counted Tad a close friend.

Our deeper contact commenced six years ago. It was just after my husband died. I was sitting in my Hillsborough kitchen feeling more than a little sorry for myself. My children had flown the coop for college, perpetual grad school and, finally, jobs. The game of bridge, eventful and statistically challenging and fun though it can be, had begun to let me feel a bit abandoned too. Nothing seemed enough. Nothing actually **meant** anything. Tad had a curious way of being at the right place at the right time. Or as someone put it, "At the right time, for the right place . . ." Right for the salvation of noble houses and their sometimes mopey occupants. This gift of timing secured, for our grandchildren and for theirs, the continuing presence of churches, two of them African Methodist Episcopal, one major nineteenth-century courthouse, the German-carved carousel at High Point, and an entire downtown district slated for destruction only ten days after Tad's first inquiries to save it. (Few of us will forget a twenty-four-hour vigil that felt at times like getting the heroine untied from the railroad tracks!)

I was not the only old 'widow woman' in Tad Worth's crowded, Morocco-bound, paint-splattered address book.

There is a natural law that allows us, the ladies, I mean, to have an extra decade or three. There's some justice in that, I believe. Even so, many such widows confess to somedays feeling like ramshackle old 'historic' homeplaces. I know I felt every inch a house suddenly emptied of all its occupants and, despite possessing fairly decent dentil moldings, a place fallen into disrepair beyond the help of Elizabeth Arden, The National Trust or The Holy Spirit!

The day my husband died, I became just such a crumbling 'prestige property.' Well, imagine the pleasure of this old homeplace upon being turned, half against her will, into an office, then upgraded into Action-Central till, through being an unsalaried 'bed and breakfast,' I finally found myself having become, to quote my

Trekie children, "The Mother ship."

All on behalf of Historic Preservation! and all on account of this extraordinary very down-to-earth type of person who gave me 'the call,' like that Caravaggio depicting the tax collector's being summoned from his counting table to Duty, to Care, and to, at last, A Cause.

This 'number' of our periodical must be different from any other. We must all reflect some of what we've lost in a person of Tad's moral and artistic talents. This issue will offer you, our loyal donors and supporters and readers, Tad's fellow carpenters and archivists and snobs and friends, something like his own last will and testament.

Tad's friend Dan (Trevor) can tell you how much willpower Tad gave to writing his parts of Issue #14 as his strength lessened. There were several new properties he planned to describe more fully for possible owners (Elkton Green being but one). It must be admitted that we told Tad, at the hospital on March 28th, that we had found a 'fairy god purchaser' for Elkton Green. But what good to let him know we'd lost it?

These were properties he had worked for years to 'wrestle' onto the registry. If we sacrifice any more of these exquisite plantation and small-town homes to the wrecking crew, so much remaining beauty will be taken from our state. It meant everything to Tad, being able to sketch out these farms and houses as only Tad Worth could. His room at Duke Hospital was stacked with deeds and court records, with wills in Xerox, slave rosters, an antique leather 'elephant' folio marked "Characteristic Non-Poisonous Spiders of Central and South America, depicted in native circumstances," architectural and decorating sourcebooks from the eighteenth century to the present. There were six potted orchids. Somebody had thrown an old paisley shawl over the curtain rod circling his bed. A new nurse walked in one day and said, "So, who lives here? Merlin?" We all laughed and, though weak by then, Tad, never one to miss the opportunity for a chuckle, said, "More like Merlin's maid, honey."

Tad died on the night of April 1—(he once stated he'd aimed for that date, intending some final confession of foolishness). He perished believing Elkton Green had been spared. With some difficulty, he told us just where his prized croquet set was stored, ready, the mallet-stand already tied with a grass-green satin bow.

His housemate, Dan Trevor—after contacting Tad's parents (who were, for various reasons, unable to be with him at the end), after signing the coroner's papers, after speaking to doctors and nurses and the many close friends who'd gathered—bent toward Tad's small computer. (It was still glowing amber in one corner of the unlit room.) At 1:04 AM, Dan withdrew the disc containing Tad's final 'Available for Restoration.' Dan handed it to me.

As soon as I saw the pages printed out, I understood that, despite Tad's determination to finish our issue, despite Tad's victory in staying one room ahead of the dementia, certain lapses had occurred. Various confusions about sequence and details beset him at the end. Because of a throat infection, Tad was sometimes unable to speak ("the worst indignity, dammit"), so he'd begun typing out notes to Dan and others, always using the screen of his Toshiba Notebook computer. Its amber screen was often the only night light in his room. Tad stayed mainly in a large document titled PREserve. So, his notes and personal asides occasionally found their way into what, without such personal interjections, might have been a more official, if less original, text.

May I, as Editor Emeritus (that is, the only local person 'tetched' enough to even try and edit this thing), permit myself the luxury of trying to set down a few memories of Tad. "For the record," as he would put it. Tad Worth was a great believer in 'the Record.' No one did more to keep our dear State's record more legible or longer 'in print.'

Though he's a person sure to be remembered vividly by those who knew him, Tad is also someone oddly apt to disappear. He planned that. He was very quick at giving others credit, perhaps too quick. Tad seemed so eager to blend into the stacks of library research, into the lives of his 'lieutenants,' into the very timbers and planks of the properties he saved. I cannot bear anonymity for this boy of ours—a boy is what he'll remain to someone my age. You'll find his name on no plaque at any of the over fifty-seven homes and public edifices he helped us spare. Only the names of original builders, founding farmers, mayors, owners, and, of course, the time-tested family names of those prosperous bored 'widow women' who became Tad Worth's funding and phoning army. But on what marble tablet do we find Theodore Hunstable Worth's own moniker engraved?

Well, I won't allow that. Call this 'a personal indulgence,' but it is also a chore of excruciating difficulty. I was once asked to speak, extemporaneously! at the funeral of a woman who had worked for my family for fifty-three years. All I know is that I managed to say something. That in itself seemed feat aplenty. Here, at least, I have the blessing of silence, shelter and revision. So I am going to take my jolly good time, all right? It's odd but I feel that my whole life has been a preparation for doing just this. Which is maybe why I am so darn nervous about over-staying, over-stating. If only I could find a prose style as modest, upright and human in scale as the Federal architecture Tad loved best.

For the record, Tad gave me the first job I've ever had, apart from Wife and Mother and Friend, and all that those massive duties entail. Such tasks were precisely what women of my generation expected. But certain energies always went untapped. In not being asked after, many skills remained undescribed, and therefore went unknown. Tad believed in my 'structural integrity' at a time when this rickety old structure sorely doubted she would stand for one more day.

He walked into my house without knocking. I had not been able or willing to even answer my own front door. I was so out of sorts and thought so poorly of myself after George died. I felt responsible for that, I guess (the way we poor WASPs will). Until Tad's helpful revision, St. Sebastian had always somehow been my idea of a life, a search for further sharper arrows! Yikes, but it's true. So, actually **say**ing, "Knock knock," into my kitchen walks this plump, agreeable young man with high color, blondish red hair, a blue oxford cloth buttondown, and chinos whose knees proved he'd been down on all fours checking some ancient building's footings (not that I would've used that term back then). From his alligator belt, a jingling eight-inch keyring. He wore Topsiders, at least they had the outline of Topsiders, but they seemed created by Mr. Jackson Pollock, so paint-and-plaster-swirled were they. In one hand, he held this little note I myself had scribbled to him after a recent party. I'd mailed it six days prior to George's being found in his fishing boat. It was a thank-you note for something or other, a joking little teasing little letter I'd jotted, nothing really.

"You can write, Mary Ellen," so Tad said. "You slipped up and showed us that. This thing had us all doubled over, laughing. And it cracked us up three hours prior to drink time. I don't know if you understand what a rare and negotiable skill writing simply and persuasively is. No? I thought not. A skill useful for my purposes, of course. But now you've tipped your hand, you simply have to come onboard. You owe it to the rest of us. I'm going to have to hold you to your word. You are a person of your word, aren't you, Mary Ellen Broadfield?" I had not the foggiest idea what young Tad Worth was talking about. I expressed this aloud.

From a deep pocket of his nasty chinos, he pulled out a folded wad of papers, blueprints, statistics. They concerned a certain property he believed he could get his hands on for the Register. Scraps of inspectors' reports, polaroids of glum interior details and, I believe, a matchbook from Sanitary Seafood with room measurements jotted there amongst traces of tabasco sauce. He told me: First, this home needs saving from the razing crews that have been so instrumental in making so much of our state look like Ohio or anywhere else dull on earth. Then this home must be put up for sale, Tad explained. That particular day, he wisely assumed nothing (given my grieving state and probable witch-like appearance). He spelled it out: The house, once sold at subsidized prices, would be restored. "Not just pickled and 'museumified' but inhabited, returned to its function. Providing shelter, comfort, and incidental joy." That's a direct quote. Still, peeved, I sat there blinking.

Tad settled beside me at my own kitchen table. From his country doctor's bag of a briefcase, he eased forth the sheaf of photographs he'd taken with his similarly paint-scarred Pentax. He said the house was called Sandover. Then, toward me, he pushed a jotted list of people in the town where this ignored domestic masterpiece had stood since 1803. People who could help. "I just know you must know about three quarters of the hard-drinking gentry down Little Washington way," he tried flattering me back into life. I knew that trick well enough.

I told him I didn't maintain contact with all that many people really. I also told Tad I'd just had kind of a shock with George dying alone on the Neuse River, right after I had pronounced such fishing trips "a big fat bore." I had made him go by himself to drift around in a deceased condition. It took the Coast Guard five long days to find our boat. I swear the wait nearly killed me. — I said I needed time.

My own address book was underneath the answering machine I'd just installed to fend off universal sympathy and gossipy well-wishers; there was a grand total of twenty-one unreturned calls blinking on the thing. One rumor I'd been allowed to overhear, it claimed that my late husband had been, face up in the boat, half consumed by seagulls (not true). Such tittletattle can challenge a person's sense of dignity and value, not to mention shaking her accustomed social standing.

Three of those waiting blinking calls would turn out to be from Tad Worth here. He now said, "You need a martini is what you need, girl, and then you need to go get your address book over there. I assume that Gutenbergy Biblely humongous-looking thing is your address book? And then we need to compare the names on this list to the names in yonder tome-ette, and then you need to get your excellent sinewy ass in gear, girl. I hear you don't even answer your phone no mo'. You've already quit coming to the door. I know what that means, Mary Ellen. I've been there, gir'friend, and I'm telling you, Get with the program. And while you're up, I could use a martini too. But, look, just show the gin a vermouth bottle, just scare it by just whispering the word 'Vermont'—that's vermouth enough—and then you need to come back here and focus on something past the tip of your fine Hollingsworth nose. I don't reckon you have any 'snack items' or cheese around, anything, do you? Not that my Gothick saddlebags need it, Heaven presarve 'em." I stared at him as if he were speaking Serbo-Croat. I finally said, "Does the phrase 'over the top' mean anything to you, young man?"

"**Mean** anything? It's my goddam credo!"

So, before Tad would even con**sid**er leaving, he made me, after two goodly drinks, no more, telephone three girls I'd known at St. Catherine's. One of them was married, as it happened, to the longtime mayor of Little Washington. If I'd ever known that, I'd forgot. Everybody in Washington, N.C., will tell you it is years older than our nation's copycat capitol; and therefore shouldn't be called "Little Washington" but "Washington, Original." That's where Sandover, the Meade-Ulrich mansion, was located, a thirty-four room late Georgian palace about to be done away with—so that public servants at City Hall would have better parking opportunities each morning. I ask you! Tad left me with this list and other homework, plus he scheduled a return appointment, said he'd come back in three days, but no later. To see how I'd done. I believe three days has certain precedents as an ideal Resurrection time. He knew I'd need that long to get out of a green chenille, yes chenille, robe I'd taken to sulking around in. (I still don't know how it got into my closet or where it's got to since.)

Reached a point where I did not remember actually formally volunteering. He'd left behind the spooky photos of water-stained pecan-wood Adam-paneled parlors, of fan lights shaped like yard-wide scallop shells, of English boxwoods about the size of the planet Pluto (**his** line, not yours truly's). Here I was, not even a dues-paying member. All the paperwork was disfiguring my kitchen table. I felt put upon. And yet somehow, by the following Thursday, I had talked the mayor's wife (Deedee Pruden, darling girl, always so good in art class at 'catching likenesses') into heading a task force that would make the Meade-Ulrich mansion a Hospitality Center for the city of Little Washington. In other words, I felt like I had somewhat helped to **start** to save an antebellum jewel that'd taken three years and forty thousand 1803 dollars and untold day laborers, slaves and Boston brick masons to build.

By the following week, Tad and Dan were right here cooking softshell crabs at my own till-lately seldom-used (except for coffee) stove. And it was only when I heard myself say, by phone (while they eavesdropped as we'd planned), heard myself say flirtatiously to a boy from Shelby that I used to date, "Honey? Reeve? are you listening? Because if you and the other so-called pillars of Shelby sit around there sipping your 'Jacks and water' while some nouveau Atlanta yahoo takes his tractor to that Osage House's bracketed cornices given an Italianate flavor by the square porch posts and those heavy corn-patterned pilasters in our beloved region's finest Greek Revival idiom, why, the ghost of your sainted Grandmother Spruill (who always **liked** me, God rest her soul), she's going to put a serious hex on your golf game, Reeve. Now, THINK."

And it was only when Tad and Dan laughed, then covered their mouths (afraid to mess up a hard deal I was driving with a little of my late husband's serious financial flair—if I do say so myself!)—it was only then that your Mary Ellen Broadfield here understood how Preservation might, if approached correctly, prove . . . well . . . preservative.

II.

I mention that last part only because, this now being **my** newsletter (ha!), I simply choose to mention it. But in the above incident, I represent just one of hundreds, or maybe a thousand or two **other** people he is forever rescuing. You see? I keep falling into the present tense when speaking of Tad. I expect we all will for a long time yet. I must say, it's unbelievable he's dead. My husband perished of natural causes at age seventy-one (is this too personal? I'll leave that to my closest friends and second-readers to later decide). When my husband died, I felt I could not go on. George had provided such a definition of my life. I was suddenly a single-owner home. But then Tad perished at roughly half George's age, and of causes I cannot call natural (though nature contains them). And I simply cannot believe Tad Worth is dead. You keep waiting for the echo. This must be close to what it's like to lose your own child. Downtown, you keep seeing resemblances in perfect strangers glimpsed from behind. You actually go up to them.

Tad was, as we can attest, a jack of all trades. Having been so philanthropic so early with his smallish trust fund, he fairly well had to be. During his forty odd years, he worked in various unlikely roles to support his overriding concern for Preservation and, incidentally, himself. He would cringe at hearing our Lt. Governor's graveside mention of Tad's inheritance spent on saving houses he practically gave away to others, homes he never really lived in except while working on them. Tad was briefly a garden designer, specializing in period herbal and knot gardens (**before** Chip Callaway claimed that as his terrain). Then he had a profitable business which recast old sundials, garden statuaries and obelisques. But daily management was something he mostly left to other people. He allowed himself time to drive his pickup on secondary roads, hunting vine-covered subjects for 'mere salvation,' with his dachshund in back barking at all chickens and most trees. Tad was also a sought-after caterer (though that sounds too menial for somebody who came in and cooked for his friends and later sort of permitted them to slip him a little something oblique if princely). His softshells cooked in lime juice and battered with crumbled pecans were truly not to be missed. He later served as a paint contractor and period consultant for Tryon Palace and other such sites. But never Historic Williamsburg, a bête noire he never tired of 'dishing.' Tad didn't consider their scholarship serious and called them the Walt Dig-nys. He was strong in his likes and dislikes, Tad. He did a lot of things quietly well, but always assumed that everybody could, really. Everybody can't, actually. Young Mr. Worth never ceded his amateur standing. Jefferson remained his god. The eighteenth century's farmer-statesman-gourmand-classicist-architect was Tad's long-range ideal and, therefore, his daily reality.

I've seen him sit down and play brilliant backgammon, if that was required. He did it to warm up some resistant elder citizen, one very unlikely to hand over a group of 'important' farm-building dependencies; an incoming mall was already waving bushelbaskets of cash for that same tract. Tad was not above 'throwing' a backgammon game. "There are many ways to win," he grew quite snippish when I teased him later. I've also seen Tad go right up onto the fourth story of a slate roof just after rain, and only say "Whoo, I gots them Hitchcock Vertigo's" after he'd seen whatever mountain goats go up that high to see and then (like a kitten I once had) needed aid and ladders, almost needed smelling salts, just in our getting him down. A martini was held aloft for inspiration. And none of us will ever forget seeing him veer into action at Zoning Board meetings statewide.

I went to school on how he managed those. The local boards would know only that some outsider had requested an extra session. Like all of us, they were already 'meetinged' to death. Their arms were crossed, their shoes tapping, their watches exposed for easy consulting. In Tad would sweep, plump and therefore somewhat more trustworthy, wearing a dark conservative suit, and looking fairly neat for a change. No paint on the pair of brown wingtips he called his "MBA drag." For once he left his pesky dog in the truck. I'd begged him to. Since his family was an old one ("Old and rotten," he liked to quote William Carlos Williams), he had a sense of other towns and who their leading families were. He always arrived at Town Hall a bit early; there, he could mill around out front and chat up farmers about crop allotments and outlawed pesticides, he could talk to housewives about the Mahi Mahi being sold at Piggly Wiggly since March and how rare you dared to serve it and he was not above mentioning his other vice: "All My Children." Tad once told me after one especially successful meeting (in which he saved the 1873 Conger-Halsey Girls' Academy outside Rocky Mount), "I swear, Mary Ellen, keeping up with a good soap, it's the next best thing to being a Mason."

Meeting was called to order; first thing, he'd rise and say his usual grinning "Hi," then tell a joke about some boy hick getting the better of a stingy society woman trying to cheat him out of his sainted mother's pie-safe at a flea market over in Swan Quarter. His accent was one kind of icebreaker, the seeming irreverence another.

Tad would then start a slide presentation about some local

building these folks had been driving past their whole lives, one they had assumed to be the merest shack eyesore, held up mostly by its own Virginia Creeper and poison ivy old enough to have berries big as scuppernong grapes. Tad Worth's talks never lasted more than twenty-two minutes. I checked. Others, watches readied, forgot to. Tad claimed, "Brevity can win half the battle" (and I guess his poor life went to prove it). He congratulated locals on what an important period piece they'd all helped keep standing till this very hour. He presented stories about who'd built it and why; he specialized in the early builders' faults, erotic peccadilloes and hobbies and—always a plus, the deaths of any of their young children. Not a dry eye in the house. Young Squire Worth ofttimes went right up to the wainscoting ledge of the shameless. He used to quote his beloved Jane Austen, "One does not love a place less for having suffered in it." He named which church the home-builders had attended, and which of that sanctuary's rose windows they donated in 1814, and by the end our Mr. Worth had mentioned the family name—legitimately mentioned—of most people present, including the security guards.

Tad never scheduled anything after. He knew that if his pitch to save a structure worked, he'd be instantly invited to one if not three homes of the competitive local hostesses. (Here in Society N. Carolina at least, there's going to be either two or three 'leader art patrons.' There's never only one.) Many is the night we arrived back home in Hillsborough after two AM. Tad understood that this was all a part of it, making himself available (to each jealous hostess in turn, if need be).

I don't know when he caught the missionary fervor about old houses. He'd grown up in one that had been lost. Maybe that set him on his course. (Or maybe, during college, at Charlottesville. I once asked him why he went there. "For the real estate," he laughed.) I'm not sure that such long local midnight parties bored him as much as they sometimes did me. (I shall hold my own tongue here.) But if so, Tad certainly never showed it. He never condescended; he had his loves and his strong dislikes but he did not fail to look all kinds of people in the eye. "Never met a stranger." We now claim 110 city chapters in this state, and each represents dozens of not-that-riveting two AMs, much Triscuit-eating by our Tad. Two AM and there he still sat, over-animating some creweled wing chair, discussing the recent tuition increase at Ravenscroft School and the best way to make your new garden statuary look ancient: pour half a gallon of buttermilk on it and watch the setting in of what Tad called "the blue-chip greenies."

Young Mr. Worth was accompanied most everywhere by his brown low-stomached dachshund bitch, Circa. He said he called her that because, whenever you thought of her, she was "always Around Then." She was the bad dog you often find near your most accommodating people. (It seems they let their dog take it all out in trade.) Some people complained Tad Worth's love of saving broken houses was overshadowed by his owning a dog never fully housebroken.

I remember that the construction fellows at Sandover, the hired workers (not us volunteers), always got a kick out of Circa, her carrying on in that intelligent if indolent manner. But, you see, they heard her name as "Circus." And Tad was much too gentlemanly—meaning too smart, kind or efficient—to try explaining the joke ("No, boys, 'Circa,' you see is an art historical term meaning," etc.) . . .

"Tad bud, you got her name right," one fellow called from the mansard roof, "'At dog's a pure circus, all right." Just then she was running round and round the big house, and Tad, that quick, said, "Yeah, Bobby Ray. A three-ring Circus." Pointing just as she shot around one corner of the house a third time, and the men shook their heads, smiling. I saw again how graceful he was at taking others' mistakes, period mistakes, class mistakes, even failures of nerve or character, and setting some period pediment atop them. A true Jeffersonian. He did that for this particular widow woman's Chapter Eleven of her life; walked in "Knock knock" and placed a finial or crown on the head of a woman wearing an extremely unattractive green chenille robe. Those workers ever after adored the unlikeable creature; they'd say, "Here comes The Circus Animal that only does Number One on sixteen-inch heart pine planks from the 1800's." And of course, they worked all the harder for Circus's owner.

Tad himself was also always around, always talkative and his shirttail forever seemed to be coming out and he kept threatening to do sit-ups when he someday got around to it, as soon as Burleigh Hall was secure. He did have faults: he could get his feelings hurt. He could become overly silly at times, and you couldn't pull him out of it, not even for emergencies; and, like all people who're obsessed, every turn of conversation led back to the house he was just then trying to spare. He used to joke that perfect happiness would be to save the Shadowlawn Plantation down near Edenton ("my possible all-time fave") and to lose that fifteenth pound on the same day. He was always almost going on a diet, but only once he had sampled whatever it was that we were cooking. People did love feeding him. There was never a more appreciative eater of one's work. He said his mother must've been a Jewish Mom switched at birth and uneasily disguised as a bony Episcopalian "who inherited only the garnets." Tad claimed the first word he learned from her was "Eat." And the second two were "Duncan Phyfe." And it is a sad note to admit that in the end he lost many more than the anticipated fifteen, though he did finally gather contributors and grants enough to begin Shadowlawn's 'mere salvation.' When Tad got down to the very weight he had always imagined being (is this too much? he forever told me there was no such thing as too much entertaining truth), he came over to my house and, with that comic-brave business he did so much during his last four years (a little *Dark Victory* in there, as he admitted), Tad staged a private fashion show for me. He wore all the clothes he'd never quite been able to. Things he kept in a separate closet he'd always called, "Someday My Prints Will Come, in Handy . . ." He brought them heaped—all horizontal stripes, pleated pants and tartan plaids—in the back of his trusty green Ford pickup. Circa guarding them, yapping. Tad had visibly become exactly the splendid-looking person we'd all always seen but that Tad himself had never quite believed was under there. Perfect-looking finally, and startled by it, Tad kept changing outfits, kept walking through the room doing runway turns and by the end, and after several more than our usual drier than the Sahara martinis, we were both laughing and crying at once. Putting on every tweed overcoat, all the raingear in my hall closet all at once, and hysterical, we were. But it was wonderful. (The two of us had the occasional evening as good as ones I recalled from the mid to late thirties. Those were, for me, the very pinnacle definition of good times. House parties at Nag's Head just before the second war with all my girlfriends from St. Catherine's and many of the freckled courteous lovesick boys whose planes would have to get shot down.)

I should say he grew up in Falls, N.C. His mother was a Hunstable and **her** mother had a house that my great aunt (you all catching any of this?) once visited. I used to joke that Tad and myself were secret cousins, and like everybody, white or black, in North

Carolina and with certain common interests and a good long run here, and beliefs, acknowledged or no, we pretty much were, kin. Like so many people who're obsessed with historic restoration, his family had once owned and lost a good house, a fine Queen Anne revival they forfeited after the Stock Crash. The place was sold to some 'Snopes' variants and it burned not too long afterwards. Snopeses DO that to fine houses. We've got more Snopeses than houses for them to burn these days. Tad never made out the home-place to be more grand than it really was. In fact, he barely mentioned it. This is unlike some of the rest of us who can too often do arias about Our First Great House (something like a person's first true human love, with the added advantage that it can be revisited). Only when I tried to draw Tad out about this place his people'd relinquished so unwillingly, and when I saw how he smiled but couldn't bear to talk about it, only then did I again see what an almost religious nature young Mr. Worth had. I mean he wasn't simply anecdotal; he believed in more than experience, far more than mortal brick and mortal mortar and half-inch-a-year English boxwoods. It all implied a sort of 'belief system' as my son who did divinity school might say. Maybe this explained why Tad lived in a comfortable but perfectly ordinary little cottage built in the forties, the nineteen-forties. It was really fairly spare, the way he lived. Tad never felt happier than when he was in one of the properties that he himself, with all his wiles and charms, had saved. But he didn't yet feel quite entitled to live in one himself. Maybe that's why the houses felt so free to reveal their secrets to him. Safe, their family problems, safe, their news, preserved with him. He saved face, for real estate, a sort of go-between for occupants living and dead, as I shall demonstrate in a bit.

Tad saw himself mostly as some anonymous cathedral craftsman, or the church's bell ringer, but not as someone who got to live, actually **stay** there in the heraldic tower. I don't know about all this, but I just put it in to show how complicated his pure and baffling motives were. It was like his not having health insurance. And the embarrassment when suddenly he so needed it. (He'd stopped paying premiums and put even that money into the fund to finally buy Shadowlawn). But the pleasure he gave those of his friends who got to actually help HIM for a change! It was this complete focus on the thing he loved most. All he'd say about the house his family lost in the Depression was that he learned to love a house in that one. His family called the place 'Heart's Ease' and there were great mounds of columbines still growing near the blackened foundation when he walked the grounds with me just after Tad began to to get so sick. As was stated, he attended the University of Virginia. He worked every summer as a day-labor gardener on the grounds of Monticello. He said they were forever tilling up things like weather-gauges or oxidized iron yardsticks, eighteenth-century glass beakers drilled with holes, in what'd been the household's vegetable patch. It came to him so clearly, daily, that Jefferson's whole enterprise was an experiment, a tester's way station. And, in later talks, Tad would mention this, Democracy as a series of go-for-broke if scientifically observed risk-takings. These make Democracy as theological as it is coolly rational. Jefferson's quest to understand some Divine Master-Scheme presupposes one. It assumes some ferocious Palladian blueprint, some golden-mean proportion, underwriting all our messy doings and our failed designs. And just such striving and good faith shaped the Federal buildings Tad loved best, their symmetry and modesty, the frontal almost virginal candor of their gaze.

Tad Worth's relation to Jefferson became quite immediate for many of us locals: Young Tad had formally posed in an article of clothes belonging to the great man. We found this in a handsome illustrated volume called **Mr. Jefferson In Motion, a Documentary Biography In His Own Words.** I'm told that it is still in print; it is by one Jean Garth Randolph. One photo's caption reads: "Contemporary Model wears a red under-waistcoat owned and worn by Jefferson from circa 1800–1820. Silk crepe with brown velvet collar, woolen sleeves, and a lining consisting of cut-apart knotted cotton and wool fleece stockings, upper back embroidered 'TJ. Monticello.'" And there, in three-quarters profile, his long auburnish hair tied back with a black grosgrain ribbon in the simplest eighteenth-century manner, stands Tad. Nineteen if unsmiling, he's still recognizable; but he looks like some over-pretty Renaissance page of about twelve. He was shorter, of course, that Jefferson's six three or, some claim, four. Still, there is our boy, on record. "Puttin' on Marse Tom's gear, that's **my** Tidewater idea of 'The Maids'." But Tad always refused to look at his own printed image. For a while, that big book was on absolutely everybody's endtable. When half tipsy, Tad confessed to me that he had once—as an undergrad—overstepped traditional respectfulness at Monticello while helping to catalogue Jefferson's remaining clothes. "I knew that traces of his DNA (not to mention plain ole man-sweat) were still soaked into one of those outsized white linen nightshirts he'd worn most when he was around age thirty-five, when he was incidentally writing the Declaration. After all the nice docent ladies tripped upstairs for tea, I stayed on. I lifted Jefferson's white shirt. And, Mary Ellen? I tasted it. I mean I just pressed my li'l mouth onto the underarm of that fine linen, and before you could say '1776' I was just suckling like a kitten . . ." "What did . . .?", I feared I was about to learn and ask more than I strictly needed know. "What did it . . . what'd he taste like? you were asking?" "Well, why not? yes . . ." said I. Then a sly smile moved over his mouth that smacked once. Remembering, Tad got this lit-up carnal Cheshire Cat grin while bending near my ear. He whispered, "The great one tasted funky, busy, a bit Scottish, and ver' ver' salty. Athletic, preoccupied, I'd say. And, well . . . all too male." "You don't say," was all I could think to remark. —There are, I suppose, many forms of preservation.

Tad dropped out of the architectural school after an argument over period authenticity, and I am sure that he was right in both his scholarship and his assessment of his enemy's flawed character. He never shied away from the concept of a worthy opponent. We've all heard his favorite toast, learned from a late great-grandfather, Major A. B. Worth, who fought so gallantly in the War, "Confusion to the Enemy!"

When he got a grant from the State of North Carolina, an objection was made by an oldtime far-right-wing wall-eyed senator who ridiculously mentioned Tad by name as "a gay rights activist leeching the taxes off of decent normal family people." Tad had this letter framed, a central relic and badge of honor in his crowded fascinating basement 'office.'

His friend Dan was, even more than some of us, changed by Tad's strong influence. It was a model to many in our community that, after Dan Trevor left Carolyn, his wife, the gifted potter, after he moved in suddenly with Tad, unexpectedly (for Dan too, he says!), Dan's wife and Tad managed to remain such friends. I must say it really was sort of unbelievable to somebody my age. Carolyn has worked wonders as our major brochure designer and volunteer bookkeeper. Tad became the loving unofficial godfather to young Taylor, Dan and Carolyn's son. It was Taylor who spoke with such beautiful simplicity at the funeral service at All Saints' Episcopal last month and who played the recorder solo that fairly well destroyed some of us. Tad always said that Taylor was not to be trifled with as he had the soul of a clear-eyed naturalist eighteenth-century cleric, all at age nine. This, young Master Trevor proved at last Sunday's wrenching service. "Not a dry eye in the apse, hunh, kiddo?" as Tad might have put it.

Maybe I should say, along with Tad's idol of a generalist, Mr. Jefferson: "If I'd had more time, I'd have written you a shorter letter." Like all of us who knew Tad Worth, I had quite a good teacher. He was forever leaving me scraps of good things he'd found. I'd step out for my mail and find these slips of paper, clothespinned to the battered box. There was never a signature, only very careful noting of where he'd found what. I put them up on our household altar of the present day, the refrigerator door. I quote just one, the most recent, one he must've sent over via Dan because Tad was by then far past walking, even from his place to mine. It's out of Rilke's "Notebooks of Malte Laurids Brigge" and serves as epigraph for a book of photographs Tad loved, a book about one beautiful decrepit Georgian house in the Irish countryside. ". . . it isn't a complete building; it has been broken into pieces inside me; a room here, a room there, and then a piece of hallway that doesn't connect these two rooms, but is preserved as a fragment, by itself. In this way, it is all dispersed inside me—the rooms, the staircases that descend so gracefully and ceremoniously, and other narrow, spiral stairs, where you moved through the darkness as blood moves in the veins . . . all this is still inside me and will never cease to be there. It is as if the image of this house had fallen into me from an infinite height and shattered upon my ground."

III.

This is the story I've been getting to.

Once, not a year and a half ago, though it seems about half a decade, Tad urgently summoned our little architecture discussion group to quickly gather, to meet him at Shadowlawn on the coast. This meant a three-and-a-half-hour drive. He phoned from the pay phone down there, said he needed us there and today and he knew it was very short notice, but that we must arrive by a certain time of evening. To the minute, we must be there.

Well, we're all very busy people—self-defensively so, I sometimes think, but he rarely gave us any direct orders. He never actually asked much of anything for himself. He let you offer whatever you felt able to provide the Cause. He had forty immensely capable but very different major people doing this, which is why our organization has been, I believe, in the end, so successful. Tad Worth didn't just praise the idea of the individual contribution and then get quickly bureaucratic and lord it over us minions from his too-new mahogany desk in some high-rent Headquarters. The power was always out there in the community. As our Lt. Governor said at Tad's funeral (in a short but fine address), "Education was behind it all." Tad was a great teacher. We'd been schooled by him, our eyes had. (And as he said, "Once your eyes know, the heart follows; it's a matter of zoning.") But, oddly, Lt. Governor Whitt Coventry might have been speaking of Tad's **own** far-ranging education. His pickup truck was a bookmobile. He read at red lights. Tad taught us how he was always teaching himself to **keep** learning. And then we personally applied the lesson.

So we said, "It must be important if he insists that we turn up by six o seven sharp." I do think that was the actual time, six o seven. He was on the drug AZT by then (now proved, as some of us suspected, to do more harm than good). Tad's T-cell count was at its lowest so far. (Though back in those earliest days we didn't know what low meant.) He'd finally got hold of one of our state's most beautiful of domestic masterpieces. Tad got it after years of honest legal chess and much backgammon dishonestly inept. He wanted to spend his last energies restoring this house of houses. He wanted to live right there on the coast, alone in the Shadowlawn big house. It was still an absolute wreck at the time (this was March). I insisted he stay at a motel nearby. I set up an account by phone with them, I made them call me when he didn't turn up for a night. Dan would spend every weekend down there with him, chipping paint and hauling things. But, like most people, Dan had a child, a job and house payments that kept him inland on weekdays. We all worried not just about Tad's health but about his falling in a house that'd never had a phone. But Tad was like that, once he'd finally acquired a property, especially this one. He felt exempt from harm once he was on the grounds, once Tad knew the acreage had finally been saved. There had been vandals swarming all through Shadowlawn for years, and to imagine him, in that barn of a place, with its exterior doors too weather-bowed to lock, all alone there on a cot! Circa would be his only lowslung if snippish guardian. And by then Tad was not strong as he thought.

As he pretended.

It's odd, in thinking back, he was very cautious in getting from historic property to property, an almost wrecklessly safe driver. Bad at it but at least aware of that. "Better he shouldn't know he's such a menace on the highway," as our dear friend Mimi Goldberger might say, "The Divine Miss Mimi" as Tad called her. But once there, on the saved grounds, Tad was fearless in crawling under houses or clambering straight up on the beams, and then somebody had to run get the ladders again to help lead him down. And with a drink, as reward.

I rode to the coast with our hurriedly assembled group in somebody's Volvo wagon. I think it was Mimi's car, because there were several thermoses of libation, as I recall. The Reverend Sapp had brought one of his famous goose pâtés. I confess to feeling scared that Tad had hurt himself, that he'd half-slid into delusions thanks to all the toxic contradictory medicines they had him on. I'd let my husband go to the coast unsupervised and I vowed none of that would happen again.

Well, we arrived down there quite close to the assigned hour. A photograph of the Shadowlawn big house is shown later in this issue. It looks extremely presentable now, thanks to Tad's day labor and many volunteer Saturdays by a devoted core 'salvation' group down Edenton way. The approach to the plantation house had been slyly planned in 1810 and a good idea has simply gotten better. You follow twin ranks of now-enormous magnolias interspersed with apple trees, long since past their bearing years. And when you make the turn, you see the house, a white Greek temple built to some goddess, upright as a dare against the bright green water of the Albemarle Sound, and you literally gasp. Despite the leaks and years and teenaged pyromaniacs, "it is," Tad would say, "like some old lady come into a party, and who can still make a hell of an entrance. Even on two canes."

Still, at the time I am discussing, Shadowlawn's Doric-columned plantation house was a firetrap and a total mess. Only somebody with a certain amount of nerve would attempt to even set foot inside the big house, much less sleep there. Every fourth floorboard was spongy with 'blue-chip greenies' and you'd fall right through. Vandals had seen fit to build fires in the middle of fourteen-inch-planked-heartpine floors. They didn't use the fireplaces which, weirdly enough, proved perfectly functional when somebody (Tad, I think) finally thought to try them. Day-glo swastikas disfigured the walls up and down the spiral staircase, whatever of its handturned balusters had not been burned to make the mid-floor bonfires. Skulls and hate crime obscenities were painted on the walls, misspelled. These racial cursewords looked pornographic in rooms so graceful and, in many ways, despite their age, still so innocent.

It's awful how a beautiful old house, abandoned, draws to itself the worst element, satanists and Hell's Angels, 'drifters' and the Klan. It becomes a blank screen onto which such riffraff projects the world's wickedest emotions. Saving such a house means calling back the world's best again, to balance out such awful ugliness. I am told that the word 'Religion' means to physically literally 'bind up again,' to repair something pre-existing, to 'restore.' And in our modern world, even with so darn much 'available for restoration,' the rejuvenation of a fallen temple is, quite literally, a mission doubly religious. I know that now.

I remember Tad greeting us from the portico, waving, cutting up, calling "a big Hi Hi Hi!" As we walked nearer, we saw he was smiling and looked absolutely filthy. Tad was happiest dirtiest. He was, I can say, the least claustrophobic person I have ever met in my life, and the cellars and crawlspaces he jumped right into, those make me . . . well, I started to say, make me feel that he's safer, wherever he's got off to. Basement wise, underground wise. There. I will stop all that. He would scold me terribly for that. He loved true feeling, but hated sentiment—except in Grand Opera, Mad Ludwig's castles, or the case of Bette Davis. He stood there filthy, with green mold on one cheek and smiling, looking even thinner than ten days ago. But absolutely beaming.

"What've you found?" somebody asked. Then Circa came charging us, growling, protecting him. She went for the Reverend Sapp's ankle. He kicked her a pretty good one. Tad had told us that any self-defense must be judged legal around Circa's testiness. I can show you marks on my left ankles that prove how often Liberalism fails.

It was Tad Worth himself, contrary to what he told the papers, who turned up all the heavy silver service for sixty buried behind the collapsed well-housing at Pilgrim's Respite out past Belhaven. It was the sale of those thirty-pound silver punchbowls, shaped like a group of plunging dolphins reined and ridden by putti, that helped us fund most of our restoration of the grounds there. —We assumed he'd come on something here.

Tad now crooked his finger at us, led us around toward the back of the big house. I remember how he idly touched one side of a massive column, he acted like someone taking an inventory of its crackled fluted surface. I knew he did this for support, I knew by now the house was there to keep Tad standing. I remember the way a few of his oldest friends looked at each other, immediately recognizing his greater frailty, but doing so behind him, saving face. This was in early March, I'm sure now, because some of those immense forsythia bushes nearest the Sound were just popping out their first brave yellow. The whole mansion smelled of wood rot, a scent we have all learned to recognize and loathe. (Just as new-cut lumber, especially cypress and cedar, now outranks yours truly's old standby Shalimar as my new all-time favorite scent!) Tad, thinned to looking somewhat perfect if pale, was becoming honeycomb-candlewax, transluscent.

He stationed himself in the crook of Shadowlawn's major chimney. It's fully three stories tall (three if you count the overseer's parapet). Its outward brick is inset with pale oyster shells that form the founding family's initials a yard high and all vined together with tensile Chippendale high spirits. As usual, Tad wore on his belt a ring clinching three full pounds of keys—old 'blue-chip greeny' skeleton ones fitted to many of the good eighteenth-century homes surviving along our Carolina coast. Though the day was chill, Tad leaned there without a sweater in this brick-heated little natural alcove. I think there were two large English boxwoods screening and enclosing half of it, making it seem even more a secret resting place. The sort of place that children find and love and where they hide first. The crenellated chimney's orangish bricks (ballast from an English ship, *The Plenitude,* circa 1793) retained the warmth from whatever sun there'd been that day.

"I want us to have a little seminar, my folks. About occupants of historic homes. The people that get left behind . . ." We had already talked at length about which kind of independently wealthy, professional, and very rare young couples are likely to put up with the headaches of dripping roofs, custom-cut joists and 1790s termite damage, with tourists knocking on their doors and grad students announcing they did a dissertation concerning your stairwell and so must be let in. I believed that by saying "the people that get left behind" Tad meant such potential buyers for Shadowlawn proper.

"I've held off doing this till you all got your dear carcasses on down here. Can't start to hint how ver' much I 'preciate youall's coming so doggone fast." Then Tad pulled from the torn back pocket of his Morris Louis spill-art chinos, a favorite Smith and Hawken trowel. He kissed its blade, as if for luck. Next, in this little spot of late light, filtered and glimmering across the inlet, Tad bent painfully down. It was like watching someone eighty, eighty-five. But, once on all fours, he started digging like somebody about eight, and possessed.

Circa soon got into the act, scratchy and snappish. She tried to claw the dirt right alongside his patch. Defending him, the dog acted jealous for **all** Tad's attention—as each of us was. Come to think of it, so were 'his' houses. They competed for his fullest energies, ready to monopolize his talent at concentrating. And the mansions used opera divas' tricks; when Tad spent too much time with one grand dame, the others had breakdowns, sprang leaks, threw material tantrums. Possessive, the great homes. "That pitifully in need of our constant reassurance. You'd think that the greater the voice, the less hand-holding they'd require. Oh, but *au contraire.* Never get enough, these ole gals—coquettes and geniuses."

If we'd been watching anybody but Tad, we might have asked why this fellow had dragged us down here on a weekday afternoon, a three-and-a-half or four-hour drive one way, and just to study him scooting around in clay for some stray tulip bulb or minié ball or something. It certainly took him quite a while, hacking down there. It did seem maybe . . . delusional, this digging. Skinny as he'd got, I found it hard to watch him strain. Even his back looked narrower, which made the shoulderblades poke out like starter-kits for wings. His dog was going even crazier than usual, overbred creature. She acted as if he were about to uncover some dinosaur egg in the act of hatching. He laughed over at her, "Good Circa. I know, I know. You smell them, right?" I remember watching perspiration darken the back of his blue shirt. Digging this hard used up about one full week of Tad's waning energy. But we would not have dreamed of saying, "Here, let me." Still, the long wait was almost dentally painful.

About the time that even we, of his faithful inner cadre, were starting to picture the one remaining half-full thermos, the Saran-wrapped pâté in Mimi's old wagon, Tad's blade struck something stone or metal. He shouted, "They're right. I knew. They never

have lied to me."

We stepped closer, we saw he'd dug a trench about a foot or eighteen inches deep, cut right up against the foundation's powdery brick footing. By laboriously leaning on the chimney, Tad stood. I worried, I saw that he was lightheaded, rising too fast and him embattled by so many competing primitive drugs. You learn to hate these stopgap 'cures' as much as you respectfully despise the gin-clear anti-preservationist disease itself.

From the hole, our Tad lifted a dark tin box, with a latch on it. It was two feet long, filthy it was. He dragged it free of pinkish tree roots and up into sight. Grinning, he held it off to one side the way my husband displayed the fish he'd caught, as if to use his own body as a yardstick, scale of reference. Once Tad had tugged the thing to better light, he flopped down beside it, panting with transparent pleasure and exhaustion. I remember the look of his long hand touching the tin, how blue-veined and aristocratic his wasting hand looked, stroking the black prize. All of us, no matter how old and creaky (chronologically in most of our cases), managed to drop right onto the grass in a rough circle close up around and against him. His hands shook so, prying it open. Somebody finally tried helping, but Tad, uncharacteristic, snapped "No!", setting Circa off. And we all grew more still, more withdrawn, afraid to even glance at one another. I can't explain the tension. Expectation mixed with social embarrassment. Dread, and a caffeinated kind of curiosity.

Once opened, the tin casket proved stuffed with what'd been yellow straw but a very long time back. Then some cloth, homespun, even I could tell that (I, who seem to have no knack for historical fabrics—one of my own sundry blind spots). It was sewn into a cloth valise, joined shut with big child-like stitches, faded red thread. This packet had then been sealed, crusted over, with what appeared to be about twenty candles' worth of wax. The Reverend Sapp, who claimed some archeological experience in the Middle East from his Virginia Episcopal Seminary days, frowned a bit at Tad's utter lack of methodical scientific technique. Tad was ripping into this item like some Christmas present meant only for himself. But that didn't bother me a bit. None of us ever found the things he did. Hadn't we piled into the car to come and see exactly this, this thingum, whatever it was?

I knew how sick he already was (though he could still hide it cleverly well). I knew how much work he needed to get done down here. (Some of us would later labor alongside him here, at Shadowlawn, as he scraped ninety years of varnish off the carved ivy paneling he'd found under beaverboard upstairs. By then Tad worked while hooked to his IV pole on a rolling tripod. He wore an oxygen tank, clear tubes in his nose. "Lorgnettes for nostrils," Tad called these tubes, with a whimsy that came to seem more and more courageous – somehow more **architectural** – as we watched him all but evaporate before our eyes. He was doing restoration against doctors' orders. Somebody'd made a joke of the IV pole by taping cardboard Chippendale claw-and-ball feet onto its tripod castor legs. By then, we understood a thing or two about Tad's glorying enslavement to the work of 'binding up again,' his will to make this last house perfect.)

But that early evening, with us bunched all around him, as he tore open the shroud cloth, Tad gave off a little howl. It's that I remember best of all. Every quality we loved in him was in that sound. It was a kid's Cowboy and Indian war whoop but it contained this knack of his that managed, in the worst of circumstances, to find something funny and pleasurable waiting. That's the quality that let him proselytize so effectively for our cause; he showed people the pleasure of old houses, the pleasure of letting the places yield up their separate secrets to you. At their own rate. Allowing them to confide in you as you, trusting, dwelt in them. One detail at a time. As friends do. "Oh, and did I ever mention how, once, here . . . ?" And people were soon hooked, they became utterly addicted to old houses. The joy at first formal, then warmly eventual, and finally the almost-rapturous admittance, of you, to the most intimate pleasure of your own home, its history, and therefore its truest moods and cracks, its communicable powers. He was actually a sort of marriage broker. And people thanked our Tad Worth here, for hooking them to the one whose lies, pretensions, secrets, whose own looks, best matched theirs.

From the box he lifted two joined dolls. One was a dark wooden effigy, almost a totem. It was obviously home carved, maybe ten inches long. The other had a porcelain head, a stuffed bodice, two simplified bisque hands attached to cloth tube arms. Sawdust was sifting from her torso just at her narrow waist. Her hair was painted on in a buttermilky brown and with delft blue eyes, and you didn't need carbon dating to know the thing was eighteenth-century. Oddly enough, the arms of this porcelain doll were literally wired around the black carved wooden figure. That one's hair was, or had been, knotted rope. If the porcelain doll was obviously English, the gumwood one was African or African-inspired in its angularity. And yet, though stylized, it also seemed strangely more human than the costly porcelain one. The dark form's only facial features were two red bone buttons set deep into wood to represent her eyes, maybe glued there. This wooden one's arms had also been rope, square knotted at the ends to be the hands. Both rope arms were trussed around the bodice of the porcelain doll. Embracing, the pair was still bound to each other, face to face, further joined by loops of circling wire long since rusted red-brown and staining the stuffed torso's yellow muslin.

Tad held up the clinging two of them, a unit. We considered the joined pair from all angles. Circa kept snarling, competitive-sounding, guarding, in the quince. Of course we looked from the effigies back up to Tad's face. Ready to be told what they meant. We were always expecting it from him and Tad certainly usually gave at least an educated guess. Sometimes his intuitive faking turned out to be truer than the gathered experts' mustiest certainty. His going directly to that silver, buried by the stone well housing out back of Pilgrim's Respite being but one profitable example among dozens, hundreds.

I saw he had done right, to get us here just at dusk. Since all this happened on the westerly facing of the Shadowlawn plantation house, the sun gave off a wintry red but full of gold. The light had moved far higher up the chimneys. Our being so in blue shadow made us feel a little underwater and unreal here, squatting on the ground. The inlet's reflection threw moving highlight lines wavering across the uncertain faces of our little group. I remember looking hard at Tad and he gave me this open stare that was confused and awed yet pleased at once. I could see his cheekbone's sweeping edge, so suddenly elegant, you knew it was terminal.

I worried he had been feverish down here and without phoning me or telling any of us, sick in that grim little motel he liked "because it looks like the one in *Psycho*" and had a blue neon star on the front. But before he explained this twin effigy, I guessed he'd first have to say something silly, wry or indirect, the way he did. "I know you've got a toddy or two hidden out in Mimi's car, and I can't believe you've made me get down on my dingy knees and fetch this thang up and that I still have to beg you all for one li'l ole drink." Somebody ran for the thermos, and I mean they ran.

Because we were waiting. We sensed it, you see. We already did.

He started crying then. Laughing too. I think it was the only time I'd ever seen Tad Worth actually shake with crying, though his eyes were forever tearing up over seemingly small things. He leaned against the herringbone brick chimney, he touched the shell initials of the founders. It was odd to find him, of all people, abruptly speechless.

Usually, talking off the cuff, Tad could populate any front porch's Windsor chairs, speaking familiar if long-dead occupants right into them. Call it fund raising via hackle raising. At some meeting, he'd say, "Imagine it's the notoriously cool summer of 1840, no bird song much, the doomed young consumptive Annabella Cameron's journal noted . . ." and you'd see the most hard-hearted of City Managers stare back, eyes narrowed, as if resisting a sudden interior draft, necks stiffening, a bit defiant and even furious, but already cooperating despite themselves. Somebody once claimed that Tad's slide presentation for prospective donors was enough to make a stone weep, and then to make another stone offer a grant to repair damage done by that first historically stone's weeping in the first place. I believe it was me said that, come to think of it.

"Well, **what**?" I asked him. We were seated scattered all around him and somebody touched his shoulder, and he was smiling but eyes running water. I had hoped that the disease would spare him MCV and possible blindness. I'd read everything. I knew that for Tad, Blindness would be just one zoning district shy of Death. The smell, that close to the dirt in March, spoke about our many chances at finally thawing out; and with spring rushing in from the inlet and up from underground, we waited there. We sat in the sad smoky smell of the beautiful crumbling house.

"About 6:07 yesterday, I saw the girls who buried this," he looked from face to trusted face. We glanced at one another. Faux-casual. First it seemed he meant that some local children had dug this box up and then maybe reburied it, maybe he had caught them. But the dirt he'd been hacking at was good packed red clay, weather-baked nearly bricklike and unbroken for centuries it seemed. Reverend Sapp now scurried back with martini sloshing in a red thermos lid. He hadn't brought one of the leaded crystal tumblers we unregenerate drinkers travel with (a bit ostentatiously) and that we sometimes break, but never our **best** tumblers. The

Reverend Sapp said, "What?" like some kid who hates missing something by going for refreshments and is bitter at seeing how just that has happened. We shook our heads to show we didn't know, not yet.

Tad downed his drink all at once and choked, and laughed at doing so, which helped. He said for the record that he had been stooping over, right there, not four feet off, at the corner of the portico the afternoon before. It had been exactly this time of day with light reflected from the sound, light moving curved lines over the brick, much as it did now. Tad said he had been cleaning out some of the giant honeysuckle that'd claimed the lattice lathing all under the broad front porch. There was a clump of mint (for juleps) and he was doing battle against honeysuckle vines in hopes of saving the mint, "which I admit has held its own since 1810 but it's never too late to give a thing a break finally, right?" He said he heard a chiming knock, like some shovel striking the chimney, just three times.

"I was squatting over yonder, there, just there near Circa's quince. —Hush, darling, please do hush now, girl.— And, you know me, sweating like a pig as usual. And when I wiped my forehead with the back of my hand and looked toward the sound, and when I took my hand down? I saw two little girls. They were charming, one black, one white. About eight to ten years old. They were holding onto one another, standing there and just facing me, looking me over. They had an expression that seemed to hint that I was the one out of place, and they—of all the people on the farm—were at least glad to be the first to notice me. I said something like, 'Hi,' something witty like 'Hi,' right? At first they only stared at me, each keeping very very still. But extremely **there**, you know, and conscious and seeming amused that I was such a mess and down on my knees. They both seemed to be wondering what was I doing here on their farm. I could see plainly enough that the white girl had light brown hair chopped off just at the shoulders and was in a sort of gingham dress, checked, brown and red, floorlength, groundlength out here, but it could've been some 60s hippie-child's 'granny dress.' And the black girl—blue-black African black—wore a homespun almost burlapy thing, very simple with long sleeves and a boat neck and she had pierced ears with small star-shaped pewter bits, pewter, I was sure of it, pewter stars in her ears. For some reason, that seemed a tip-off, like, you know, 'pewter,' tin mixed with lead, eighteenth century, get it? But no, I was just as dumb as before. They were standing there arm in arm and not quite smiling but very pleased looking, very much together, as if about to laugh but scared to hurt my feelings. Behaving as if . . . how to explain this? . . . as if there were many other people all over the plantation, working the place, and like they had strolled off into one quiet corner—a favorite place, I felt—for a nice moment alone together and had found me. (I sensed how crowded the farm really was, busy and productive but sort of hostile to children, something in their sense of secrecy, the bond between them, suggested that.) And it was only then I noticed they were pointing down, they both were. Toward the same spot. I just hadn't seen that, not at first. Or maybe when they guessed that they could trust me, they indicated the one spot. I was here by myself. Circa excepted. I mean, the volunteers had left about four thirty, and I was just doing a few last clean-up chores. Needed a quick nap on the cot in the foyer. Then, and only then—and by the way, all this is just taking maybe just oh eight to twelve seconds, this whole loaded glance—very quick, very matter-of-fact—it was only then I noticed the texture of the bricks behind them, and only then, like a dolt, does it occur to me that I can see the goddam bricks, like, THROUGH them, right? Well, here's the really dopey part, I smile at them, as if they live here, as if I'm the slave gardener and know so, and to prove I also have a reason for being here too, I go back to the vine I've been yanking on. And I actually lift my gigantic vat of Round-up I've been spraying at the honeysuckle, like I'm **bored**, like I'm just going on with my work, and only then, having turned my entire back on them, do I do this incredible Three Stooges eye-popping doubletake. 'Boing,' hair up—eyes out to **here**—and of course they're gone.

"You know the phrase 'disappeared into thin air'? well that's what I had seen happen. I'd never felt that phrase meant much—isn't all air thin? Well, air so recently evacuated, it does, believe me, feel damn 'thin.' Who says Air can nevah be too rich or too thin, hunh? But I kept thinking 'thin air,' 'thin,' like snatching at that phrase, because I so wanted to touch them, to hold **onto** them. Mainly to **ask** them things, I think. I didn't run to phone anybody, didn't tell a soul. Not at first. Didn't even ring Dan, I mean nobody. And then about two o'clock this morning, at the Norman Bates motel, I wake up and sit up and say aloud, setting poor Circa to barking, 'They buried something. They were burying something. And I caught them at it and so then, they went ahead and showed me where they'd hidden it.' I was that sure of it, I called you up.

"Now you're all here, and here is this cask, these dollthings. I mean I wanted you to see the progress on the house generally. But I felt I had to have my sanctum sanctorum nearest-dearests here for this. I figured that if I didn't hit anything, I would stop digging, as if suddenly even more than usually absentminded lately – then I'd maybe stand up and just show you the handpainted horse-and-river French mural paper we're beginning to uncover in the foyer, and then I'd take you all to the Fish House over near Edenton for dinner, but I'd not say nothin' and jes keep rollin' along. But to find these things, the one a slave toy and the other something porcelain and plainly English import. I believe it was a pact between them, the girls, to go ahead and wire their arms around each other, the dolls. Like they knew their friendship couldn't stand whatever tests were coming – a saleable slave child and the owner's daughter, or the overseer's – but to plant these here. As a sign, near the house, a sign they loved each other. To show they **knew** that, and to save it some."

By now the light was mostly gone. Only the tips of the six chimneys held a charged kind of sandpapery red, like the heads of matches. The shadow where we stooped felt privileged but a bit too permanent. It'd gotten some colder. We could see the scallop boats, their lights blinking way out there, coming home, nets hoisted after the long day's catch. Bats now hunted bugs, diving near the house. And Tad lifted forward his effigies, Tad moved to pass these into the hands of the person nearest him, everything, that tin box, the wax-sealed bag and those odd dolls, still bound together . . . he handed it to somebody who instinctively drew back, acting almost comically repulsed. She . . . actually, it was I, alas . . . she pulled away as if fearing that this thing had come direct and scalding from some infernal oven. Would it burn, or freeze? Maybe it was how quick and saturated the darkness had just got. I felt he was placing some image of himself dead into hands not willing to accept that, not yet. (Still not.) I steeled myself . . . hating this squeamishness which seemed so unlike me, at least the me I could admire even a bit. But then Mimi, God love her, laughed and said, "What is this, hoodoo voodoo? Gi' me it!" and reached past me, grabbed the thing. Out of order. Then we each took hold of his 'find,' all of us, me going right after Mimi. I think it was something about my husband's death, and being down so near the water. Made me hesitate, then feel that I had let Tad down. I felt like

Saint Peter, denying on the crucial night. It's odd, but we all held onto the dolls, and even the box, and for quite a while. As if to greet them, a cordial welcome, to above-ground. It seemed we'd expected even these to melt 'into thin air' where the girls had gone. We expected the dolls to melt when they left his hands as he tried to fit them snug into ours. It seemed we knew then, that 'thin air' was already welcoming him. But the object(s) remained objects, solid, like his legacy—like Tad himself till then—so reassuringly material. The dolls had lasted the way inanimate things (lucky for us, as compass points and referents) get to. Lord knows, **we** don't.

Then we all drove over to Edenton for shrimp and oysters and scallops which were excellent and right off the boat, everything's so fresh down there. At dinner, no one really mentioned the dolls. I remember how the long car ride home without Tad was very quiet. I was desperate for him to come back home to Hillsborough just for tonight. He'd have none of it, of course. It wasn't so much that we were spooked, on the long drive back, though we were in a way . . . I personally felt scared mostly for him. No, it was something else.

Once I'd heard him joke about certain young lady ghosts that hived around/inside the stone privy still standing at an old girls' academy, The Burwell School, right in Hillsborough. "The Haunted Outhouse," Tad called it. I asked him what it felt like, this particular ghost nest. "Walking through a rain of talcum powder too fine to notice but it still gets your hair feeling whitish and you can sort of smell it, dusty humany basementish almost rose-smelling"; but he smiled as if only teasing. Even so, it stopped me, how he'd said it. I now sat shoulder to shoulder with my friends headed west, recalling his saying, "They never **have** lied to me."

One need not be Sherlock to deduce this meant a critical mass, earlier sightings, or promptings, or promises. In the car headed home, I think we were so hushed and a little glum, because we knew—if we hadn't before—who he was. We knew that Tad wouldn't make up such a thing—he never ever lied to me, or to anybody, except out of white-lie kindness, or with something like losing at backgammon for Preservation's sake. I chastised myself for that three-second delay in taking what he'd handed me first. But, even so, we all suddenly unwillingly knew he was going to die. Soon. Somehow his seeing the occupants of this last great house he'd saved showed us just how soon (four weeks). He'd made us start to see the bricks through him. Come to think of it, we'd always seen the bricks **through** Tad!

Tad's mission (and I can use that word in good conscience here), his mission was about so much more than just saving certain pretentious properties for a few more generations of socially ambitious Carolinians, those who could afford skilled craftsmen to replace octagonal slate roofing tiles that can cost, as we all know, up to thirty-nine dollars per. With those dolls, the houses **whom** he'd saved were suddenly extravagantly giving ground-breaking house-warming gifts **back** to him. Presents from Presences! Farewells: well done, ye good and faithful servant.

That was just one story about him. But it's the one that came to me.

I know there are people in historic preservation who are only interested in the architecture, in the pediments, the lemon-oiled perfectible period detail. I fear I've met a few. I fear I myself have been stuck in more than a few mullioned window seats with Laura Ashley floral prints and peppermint stripe piping on the cushions under my increasingly historical whatever (and there till after 2 AM). These experts consider the people who actually live or lived in these fine places as something like the furniture . . . you maybe need them there to make the house seem finished, but they're incidental to the structure's superior claims. With Tad, the living, the livingness of the place and what went on there and what might go on there next, that was the definition of his passion, boxwood by old rose, mantel by mantel, slate by slate.

Our best memorial to Tad will be carrying on the great work he so perfectly embodies and therefore continually shows us how to do. It's a love Tad seemed to accidentally inspire in those around him. It is, for these reasons, among others, that we've chosen to present his final notes exactly as he left them, the gathering typos, growing confusions and all. Next month I am to face the daunting task of becoming *Preservation News*'s resident scholar and cheerleader myself, alone. I'm to take over the writing not just of my usual "Goings On" column, but the "Available For Restoration" texts that Tad always did and did so well. I ask, no, pray, for any help that anyone can give me in this. I never thought when he burst in that day without so much as a knock—his saying, "Knock knock" excepted—never did I think when he caught me in that ghastly green chenille robe (which disappeared soon after) that I would end up writing this much at a single sitting, ever.

IV.

I end by remembering a meal we had together (one thing I must blame him for is how readily he knocked me off my own diet by showing up with two bags full of ingredients from Wellspring Market in Chapel Hill, saying "and what shall we DO with all these perishables?") We were seated at my back table and were finishing some raw oysters. (This was when you could still eat those without worrying so.) We'd only just acquired Shadowlawn, work had just started. But already when he got up to fetch something, Tad was forced to reach out for the counter to support himself. But he made it look quite natural, you know. Regal. Like, oh, he was solemnly recalling something.

Tad had been worrying over some legal issue involving right of way, easement to the entrance of the Shadowlawn bighouse, and he said, "I really don't know nothin' 'bout rebirthin' no houses, Mizz Scarlet." Tad stopped, head bowed and knuckles white along my counter's ledge, and I saw how enraged he was at all the details, all the work still left undone, and with only us amateurs trying to fake it in our way, but lacking his genius for vamping, guessing, making it LOOK right and therefore FEEL right, in that order of zoning. "I know it must be frustrating," I said, clumsy but well-meaning. "And yet think of everything you've saved, fifty-six or seven masterpieces that were destined only for the wrecking ball, Tad. Do think what you **have** achieved, m'dear." "Well, it's true we've set aside a single family dwelling or two. But that's such a fraction of what's lost, M.E. Plus, I is so tired of keeping house, keeping on keeping on sweeping them flo's. Turns, out, I **do** do windows after all."

I started, "You **are** a window, honey," but he stopped me from saying something more sappy if too comforting. Too easy. And as he finally walked past me, I noticed how thin his legs had gotten, how brown, how beautiful they were that scale. He'd shrunk down to what he called the "chaste proportions of the Federal. The last moment when, believing Mankind (specifically of the American sort) to be perfectible, Architecture proved that possible. Proved how necessary belief is. Proved that perfection, too, can be a self-fulfilling prophecy." And I wanted to say something nice to him, but stupidly I chose to talk about his weight, which also meant of course how much he'd lost, I said, "Your legs . . ." and stopped and hated myself.

"I know I know, they're great now, aren't they? Lookie here, back-kick, shuffle ball-change. Quit while you're ahead right? I seem to have gotten everything I wanted, if for the wrong reasons, too much too soon. But, can you imagine one day walking up onto the portico at Shadowlawn when most of it is done, and feeling great for a whole week, and I mean to be up on that porch, me wearing khaki bermudas with hardly any paint on them, and upright at last on legs this thin? Ooh, all I need is a couple more bronzer sticks and another NEH grant, gir'friend. Can I grate some extra horseradish for your ersters, honey? I'm right here at it. I am up."

"Your legs are Federal now," I finally managed to say.

He looked down, studied. —Then oh how he smiled back up at me.

I cannot explain the look of happiness Tad gave me then. I cannot explain how I go on seeing all the bricks through him. Can't start to tell you the joy he gives me, day by day, room to room.

If—(here I am going to go ahead and do this)—if, as we are promised, "In my father's house are many mansions . . ." then there is a little justice after all.   —He's occupied.

— AVAILABLE FOR RESTORATION —

Shadowlawn

(early draft, Theodore Worth)

(located: nine miles S. of Edenton, NC on Albemarle Sound, unnumbered plot off Cutter Rd)

Exhibiting a grandeur of design and scale unknown to any Greek Revival building in Pasquotank County, this plantation has come to us utterly intact for our State's usual miraculous reason, extreme poverty!

Someone will come along to claim this house and arrange for its mere salvation. I know that person's out there.

Set at the end of a rolling lane we can see was part of the original approach, one comes upon the perfectly proportioned house so suddenly, one's breath is literally altered. Slowed then made some quicker. Planned in 1810, it's still a doggone good effect. Banked by massive English boxwoods, the house is all but featherboaed round its graceful neck by the 360 degree gallery with handsome (indeed cosmic) views of the Sound beyond. Shadowlawn features the most evolved of interior refinements. It has gouge-work mantels and twelve foot ceilings and French doors that make the blending of outdoors and indoors a kind of sensuous marriage of the elements. George MacDonald tells us, "Home is the only place where you can go out and in. There are places you can go into, and places you can go out of, but the one place, if you do but find it, where you may go out and in both, is home."

The plantation house was brilliantly situated to take full advatage of the sunsets which are often still panoramic and even, around early Spring, downright inspirational, especially whilst sipping a julep featuring mint that yet sprouts right where it was planted to be handiest, by your simply literally leaning off the sweeping portico. Oscar Wilde said it, "Simple pleasures are the last refuge of the complex." In and around the house, important domestic items have been discovered, and it is not too much to imagine the lingering benign essence(s) of those who lived and were happy on this estate. It seems a hard place to say goodbye to. Shadowlawn was created to engender precisely that home-like state of pleasure and security that finally leads to natural philosophical speculation.

Meant to catch all available breezes in the summer months, it faces cannily North West. The house has recently enjoyed a radical renovation after decades of vandalisms and cruel fires. Oddly, the mantels and fittings were so often repainted and are so Federally discreet that, unlike many later and flashier bloated nineteenth century accouterments (fattened by an infusion of too much money of the ill-gotten overnight kind), these details were somehow largely overlooked by thieves. —Perhaps their arsonist's tendencies kept them busy elsewhere.

How can they is what I'd like to know. I am not so sure—Dan or Mary Ellen could you look up the dates of Henry Taylor. I forget though never thougt I wld.

The merchant prince of the sound, Henry Taylor (1790–1868? 69?) wrote his mother, Carolina Worth Thomas of Heart's Ease (a far more modest establishment), inviting her to this 'pleasuring contraption, breeze-snagger, and experiment in properly living a life,' the home whose construction he so painstakingly supervised and repeatedly rebuilt, part of his life's work. "I base the house on what I think could best afford you a perfect summer here among us. Mother, call it but Baite. Every nicety and comfort we install, is a form of portrait of you, to be used by you, then remaining forever after with us, here upon the rough Shore. As you did ever fail to shrink from overmuch beauty, that shall not be wanting. Trust your boy in this at least. But Ours is meant as a place where Conversation and Good Company, and not Stiffness and mere Showe, are always at the Centre of the Home. I only ask that you prepare yourself for but one summer hence when our proposed and pleasuring Home awaits your ease, yr. newest 'topics', yr. needlework, yr.compleatest grace, and your most essential approval, ma'm.' Am confused about AZT dosage, Dan. Overmuch? Feels so. Blotto. Remind to aks him aboug lezions, and if they are rel, to my bad case of shingles Oct. last.

The carriage house retains its frilled facing and a small family chapel, close by the water, still have traces of an ebonized Maltese cross atop its modified cupula . . . The records show that slave and master worshiped here as one and

The same tired The restoration was painstaking and needs further expertise regarding modern plumbing. Still suitable fr. occupancy. Somebody is out there, sure of that . . .

New systems needed, true, throughout, true.. By now there are hookups for natural gas heat and air, the evenings expecially, and the sense of others who';ve been near and can be . . . Mint, mention mint . . .

Abvout how close to water, mention. Noble approach, mention noble approach, and english boxes. Many, big as Pluto, planet Pluto, not dog. Joke. How the fires could have been set in middle of floors don't know, we found the fireplaces to still draw perfectly perhaps a hundered years since fullest use, birds nests and old squirrels nests went up like tinders but the thrill to run outdoors and night and see smoke coming curling, like a thing relearning to breathe really, most beautiful though fear for stray sparks, must get screens, Dan. . . . screens to prevent cinders setting everything me saved afire.

Dan, hi, will leave the machine on . . . rougher today . . . if miss you, sorry. Must sleep oftener, The shakes bigtime. Drench-ola. Tell Taylor hi, and to practice. Any word from parents? Pain is bracketed now. One does not love a place less for having suffered in it, right? Rite? How can I sleep when nurses keep comin in waking me? Their good cheer wears one dow..y

Extensive remodel needed. Priotico nearly complete. Big family could be so happy there, house has many treasure to yeield. Fish from dock. Smoke house sutible guesthouse, aroma mild but pleasant,. can be shown daily, key at store . . . house dedc to comfort, Mint nearby mention drinks . . The parlor facing south, original glass throws shapes thoughtful human on wall and mofvews . . . tireder, language going, structre goiim ssNcup[e Confusiion to the emeynes

Needs work but for immediate occupancy . . . . . . Keep thinking we didn't pay phonebill again. Is it on? We forgot to...must do list... so .Tell M.E. I said, 'The Mantel is Passed!' Mantel... see? A life sure spent in non-profit sector!

Confusion, the enemy. Hi hon, wkae me anyway? What's the name the scrolling at corners, supports? Begins w.C. Has name, dammit. Look up later. My books. Around here somewhere. The right book. Find what type spiders web would best take gold dust? Dr Fscher glmmy. Last rose summer, pure gloss? Miss you, will

Sq ft: 6,8888844 ik rooms, zned for living. . . . . Where is my fathe rand where is my m..   Aint no sech thang as bluechip-greenies—its all just greenies..., except the salts of Jefferson. Dan Dan why you so kind me? iBoy, talk about AVAIL For resoration! loans availbe, save this one pls. .Any word yet? Circa exema ok? Somthng nr chimney esp., signs & wondrs W aake me anyway ok? have M.E. correct this, fake it, will make press time, fine, sure . . . I hear water. There's bad break, leak, flor below, chk on rushingf water damage close ;;;I see certai of Its columns, all Ionic! I knew that. So Dry mouth.½ Most of this must go but which of these is the bearing wall? Pme jakbaa777kkkkkkkkkkkkkk66#33 can restore to suit any new owner. Fix. I know you out there. He'vn presarve us. Boy, but air thin. I buried something. They dug it up for me.

Am mostly beyond all tired. mst. ctch winx. .. Treated 2X6 l''Smokehouse rof leaki. Fix first. Alwys fix roof first,

I keep... I forget. All keys, hall drwer.

hi

In eight weeks time, please expect Issue #15
of **Preservation News.**

DICKINSON
RESTORATIONS
• incorporated •

4606 Hunt Road
Hillsborough, North Carolina
919-732-5439

historic preservation consulting • contracting
• restoration construction management

SYBIL ARGINTAR BOWERS
PRESERVATION PLANNING
CONSULTANT

HISTORIC PRESERVATION
ENVIRONMENTAL DESIGN

ASHEVILLE, NORTH CAROLINA
(704) 253-1392

From our Past — For your Future

MILLENNIUM WOODWORKS
& RESTORATIONS, INC.

- PRESERVATION CONTRACTING & CONSULTING
- HISTORICALLY ACCURATE MILLWORK
- WOODTURNINGS A SPECIALTY

TIM FULMER
(919) 732-8100
(919) 286-0141 Fax

3203 SEVEN SPRINGS RD.
HILLSBOROUGH, NC 27278

CHURCH WINDOWS • BRONZE PLAQUES • MOSAICS

Stained Glass Associates

MEMBER S.G.A.A. IFRAA
ROBERT J. WYSOCKI (OWNER)

BOX 1531
RALEIGH, N.C. 27602

919/266-2493
833-7668

BRASS & COPPER POLISHING
WORKS, Ltd.

Specializing in Polishing, Lacquering & Restoring
Brass, Copper, Bronze & Silver

5815 Hillsborough Rd.
Raleigh, N.C. 27606
between Raleigh & Cary

Phone
851-2590

C·A·T·E·R·S

P.O. Box 28522
Raleigh, NC 27611-8522

(919) 828-6673

SOUTHERN DESIGNS

DESIGN • PLANNING
HISTORIC DOCUMENTATION/RESTORATION

P.O. BOX 694
BANNER ELK, NORTH CAROLINA 28604
(704) 898-4765

RICK PALMER
Owner

Architecture
Historic Preservation
Adaptive Use
Feasibility Studies
Moisture Related Studies

YELVERTON
ARCHITECTS

Park Selwyn
Suite 229
5200 Park Road
Charlotte, North Carolina
704/523-7834

Robert Griffin, *A.I.A.*

R.S. Griffin, Architect

Architecture • Interior Design
Planning • Preservation

32 All Souls Crescent
Asheville, N.C. 28803 • (704)274-5979

"WORK WELL DONE IS ART . . ."

On your next roofing project
experience the artwork of our craftsmen

- Slate
- Tile
- Copper
- Eternit Shingles
- Wood Shakes
- EPDM Membrane

SANSBURY
CONTRACTING, INC.

211 Atherton St.
Charlotte, N.C. 28203

704-522-0007
Fax 704-523-4555

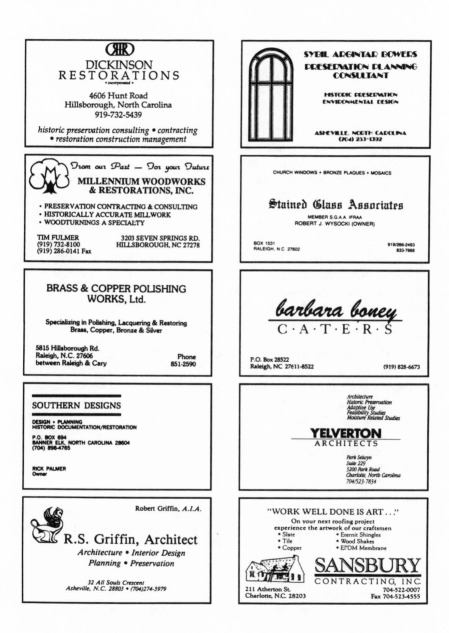

False Water Society

Ben Marcus

THE AGE OF WIRE AND STRING

Period in which English science devised abstract parlance system based on the flutter-pattern of string and wire structures placed over the mouth during speech. Patriarchal systems and figures, including Michael Marcuses, were also constructed in this period—they are the only fathers to outlast their era.

AIR HOSTELS

Elevated, buoyed or lifted locations of safe harbor. They are forbidden particularly to dogs, whose hair-cell fabric is known to affect a breech of anchors, casting the hostel loose toward a destiny that is consummated with a crash, collapse or burst.

AIR TATTOOS

The first pirated recordings of sky films. Due to laws of contraband the recorded films were rubbed onto the body before being smuggled from the Ohios. Once applied, they settled as permanent weather marks and scars. The tattooed member exists in present times as an oracle of sky situations. These members are often held underground in vats of lotion, to sustain the freshness of the sky colors upon their forms, which shiver and squirm under vast cloud shapes.

ALBERT

1. Nightly killer of light. 2. Name applied to systems or bodies which alter postures under various stages of darkness. Flat Alberts exist only in the water or grass. They may not rise until light is poured upon them.

ARKANSAS 9 SERIES

Organization of musical patterns or tropes which disrupt the flesh of the listener.

AQUA SCHNITZEL

1. Team of water hunters. They wrap their prey in viscous sacs, relegating each slain object or figure into a sausagized compartment. 2. Musical outfit, whose first composition, *Link,* could only be performed by submerging encoded beef skins into the water.

AUTUMN CANCELER

1. Vehicle employed at an outskirt of Ohio. This car is comprised of seasonal metals. At certain speeds trees in the vicinity are re-greened. 2. Teacher of season eradications. It is a man or woman or team; it teaches without garments or tools.

BACKWARDS WIND

Forwards wind. For each locality that exhibits momentous windshooting, there exists a corollary, shrunken locality which receives that same executed wind in reverse. They are thus and therefore the same thing, a conclusion reinforced by the Colored Wind Lineage System, which demonstrates that the tail and head of any slain body of wind fragments move always at odds within the same skin of dust and rain.

BEEF SEEDS

Items, scraps or buttons which bear forth fibrous tissue striata after being buried under milk-loaded cloth.

BEHAVIOR FARM

1. Location of deep grass structures in which the seventeen primary actions, as prescribed by Thompson, Designer of Movement, are fueled, harnessed or sparked by the seven partial, viscous, liquid emotions which pour in from the river. 2. Home of rest or retreat. Members at these sites seek the recreation of behavior swaps and dumps. Primary requirement of residence is the viewing of the Hampshend River films which demonstrate the proper performance of all actions.

BEN MARCUS, THE

1. False map, scroll, caul or parchment. It is comprised of the first skin. In ancient times it hung from a pole, where wind and birds inscribed its surface. Every year it was lowered, and the engravings and dents that the wind had introduced were studied. It can be large, although often it is tiny and illegible. Members wring

it dry. It is a fitful chart in darkness. When properly decoded (an act in which the rule of opposite perception applies) it indicates only that we should destroy it and look elsewhere for instruction. In four, a chaplain donned the Ben Marcus and drowned in Green river. 2. Any garment which is too heavy to allow movement. These cloths are designed as prison structures for bodies, dogs, persons, members. 3. Figure from which the anti-person is derived; or, simply, the anti-person. It must refer uselessly and endlessly and always to weather, food, birds or cloth. It is produced of an even ratio of skin and hair, with declension of the latter in proportion to expansion of the former. It has been represented in other figures such as Malcolm and Laramie, although aspects of it have been co-opted for uses in John. Other members claim to inhabit its form and are refused entry into the house. The victuals of the anti-person derive from itself, explaining why it is often represented as a partial or incomplete body or system. Meaning it is often missing things: a knee, the mouth, shoes, a heart.

BIRD SEVEN

1. Period in which members Linda thru early Rachel engaged in storm pantomimes. 2. Year of the body. 3. Any moment in which the skin of a member gains oracular capacity of wind heuristics. 4. The first day of life. 5. The end times.

BIRD-COUNTER

Man of beginning or middle stature who tallies, and therefore prevents, the arrival or exit of birds, people or others in a territory.

BLAIN

Cloth chewed to frequent raggedness by a boy. Lethal to birds. When blanketed over the house, the sky will be cleared in minutes.

BOISE

Site of the first Day of Moments, in which [fire] became the legal form of air. Boises can be large city structures built into the land. Never may a replica, facsimile or hand-made settlement be termed a Boise.

CANINE FIELDS

1. Parks in which the apprentice is trained down to animal

status. 2. Area or site which subdues, through loaded, pre-chemical grass shapes, all dog forms. 3. Place in which men, girls or ladies weep for lost or hidden things.

CARL

Name applied to food built from textiles, sticks and rags. Implements used to aid ingestion are termed, respectively, the lens, the dial, the knob.

CHOKE-POWDER

Rocks and granules derived from the neck or shoulder of a member. If the mouth-harness is tightened, the powder issues in the saliva and comes to rim the teeth or coat the thong. For each member of a society there exists a vial of powder. It is the pure form of this member. It should be saved first. When the member is collapsing or rescinding, the powder may be saved by gripping tightly the member's neck and driving the knee into its throat.

CIRCUM-FEETING

Act of binding, tying or stuffing of the feet. It is a ritual of incapacitation applied to boys. When the feet are thusly hobbled, the boys are forced to race to certain sites of desirous inhabitation: the mountain, the home, the mother's arms.

THE CLOTH-EATERS

First group to actively chew, consume or otherwise quaff extensive bolts and stacks of cloth.

CLOUD-SHIMS

Trees, brush, shrubs or wooden planks which form the walls of the heaven container. These items are painted with blues and grays and the golds of the earliest sky. They are tiny, although some are large. They exist mainly to accommodate the engravings of the container, allowing a writable surface to exist aloft. The engravings command the member down or up, in or out, or back, back and away from here.

CROONAL

A song containing information about a lost, loved or dead member. These are leg-songs or simple wind arrangements. They are performed by the Morgan girl, who has run or walked a great distance and cannot breathe. She fashions noises between her hands by clapping and pumping her homemade air.

Day of Moments

Day, days or weeks in which select and important moments of the society are repeated to perfection before resuming. Members alternate performing and watching until there is no difference.

Drowning Wires

1. Metallic elements within rivers and streams that deploy magnetic allure to swimmers. 2. The trunks of Hahn. His swimming fabric was loaded with this wire when he plunged from the pier.

Drowning Method

System of speech distortion in which gestures filtering through rain and water fields are perceived as their opposites. In order to show affection, a member is instructed to smash or squeeze. Other opposites apply, and in most devious weather the shrewdest member is seen acting only at odds with his true desire, so that others may see his insides, which have otherwise been drowned.

Eating

1. Activity of archaic devotion in which objects such as the father's garment are placed inside the body and worshipped. 2. The act or technique of rescuing items from under the light and placing them within. Once inside the cavity, the item is permanently inscribed with the resolutions of that body—it can therefore be considered an ally of the person whose primary movements and desires overlap the body. 3. Dying. Since the firt act of the body is to produce its own demise, eating can be considered an acceleration of this process. Morsels and small golden breads enter the mouth from without to enhance the motions and stillnesses, boost the tones and silences. These are items which bring forth instructions from the larger society to the place of darkness and unknowing: the sticky core, the area within, the bone. 4. Chewing or imbibing elements of the self that have escaped from the member or person into various arenas and fields.

Expanded House

Swelling of the hands, fingers, foot or eye which generates a hollowness in the affected area, rendering it inhabitable.

FARM

The first place, places or locations in which behavior was regulated and represented with liquids and grains. The sun shines upon it. Members move within high stalks of grass; cutting, threshing, sifting, speaking.

FEBRUARY, COPULATED

1. A contraction corresponding originally to a quarter of the house month – it was not reduced to seven houses until later. The Texan February of ten houses seems to have been derived from the early rude February of thirty houses found in Detroit. The Ohians, Morgans and Virginians appear to share a February of eight houses, but Americans in general share a February which is divided, segmented and cut up into as many houses as can be found. 2. The act or technique of completing a month before it is rightly finished as per the Universal Storm Calendar. It is a method of time acquisition practiced by members. If a day is copulated it is therefore finished, and the member sits out the rest of it in darkness, resting, his hands bound in front of him to keep himself from striking his own face and chest.

THE FESTIVAL OF GARMENTS

One-week celebration of fabrics and other wearables. The primary acts at the festival are the construction of the cloth-mountain or tower; the climbing of said structure; and the plummets, dives and descents which occur the remainder of the week. The winner is the member that manages to render the structure movable, controlling it from inside, walking forward or leaning.

THE FIEND

1. Heated thing. 2. Item or member which burrows under the soil. 3. Item which is eaten post-day. 4. Any aspect of Thompson which Thompson cannot control.

FOOD SPRING

1. The third season of food. It occurs after hardening. It delivers a vital sheen to the product, which becomes juicy, sinkable, light. It lasts for a period of moments, after which the edible begins to brown and fade. 2. Vernal orifice through which foods emerge or cease to be seen.

THE FOOD MAP OF YVONNE

1. Parchment upon which can be found the location of certain specialized feminine edibles. 2. Locations within a settlement in which food has been ingested, produced or discussed. 3. Scroll of third Yvonne comprised of fastened grain and skins. This document sustained the Yvonne when she/he/it was restricted from her/his/the house/home/body/water/grave.

FOOD-POSSE

Group which eradicates food products through burial and propulsion. They cast, sling, heave, toss and throw food into various difficult localities. Food that has been honored or worshipped is smothered with sand. Edibles shined, polished or golded are rusted with deadwater. Snacks from the home are placed in the bottom and crushed.

FREDERICK

1. Cloth, cloths, strips or rags embedded with bumps of the Braille variety. These Fredericks are billowy and often have buttons; they are donned in the morning and may be read at any time. When a member within a Frederick hugs, smothers or mauls another member or person, he also transfers messages, in the form of bumps, onto the body that person represents. Certain Braille codes are punched into the cloth for medicinal purposes: they ward off the wind, the man, the person, the girl. 2. To write, carve, embed or engrave. We Frederick with a tool, a stylus, our fingers.

FRUSC

The air that precedes the issuing of a word from the mouth of a member or person. Frusc is brown and heavy.

THE FUDGE GIRDLE

Crumpets of cooked or flattened chocolate, bound or fastened by wire. This garment is spreadable. It is tailored strictly with heat and string, and is cooked onto the body of the ancient member. At sports events, the fiend is consumed through this girdle.

GARMENT-HOVEL

1. Underground garment structure used to enforce tunnels and divining tubes. This item is smooth and hums when touched. It softens the light in a cave, a tunnel, a dark pool. 2. Any simple

cloth shelter equipped with a table, blankets, some high windows, foods. Washable.

GERVIN

Deviser of first fire-forms and larger heat emblems. The Gervin exists in person-form in all texts but is strictly a symbol or shape in the actual society. To gervin is to accommodate heated objects against one's body. One may also gervin by mouthing heated items of one's own body: the hand, the eye, the cupped rim of the lips.

GEVORTS-BOX

Abstract house constructed during the Texas-Ohio sleep collaborations. It relayed an imperative to the occupant through inscriptions on the walls and floors: destroy it; smash it into powder; sweep it out; make a burial. Knock it back. Mourn the lost home.

GOD BURNING SYSTEM

Method of Thompsonian self-immolation. For each Thompson there exist flammable outcrops or limbs which rub onto the larger body of Thompson (Perkins), rendering morning fires and emberage which lights the sky and advances the time of a given society or culture.

GOD-CHARGE

Amount or degree of Thompson occurring in a person or shelter.

GODPIECE

Cup, bowl or hoop, which, when swished through air, passed under water, or buried for an indefinite time in sand, will attract fragments and other unknown grains that comprise the monetary units of a given culture. The godpiece is further defined as a wallet or satchel that assigns value to the objects inside it.

GRASS-BRINGERS

Boys which are vessels for grass and sod. They move mainly along rivers, distributing their product north toward houses and other emptiness.

THE GREAT HIDING PERIOD

1. Period of collective underdwelling practiced by the society. It occurred during the extreme engine-phase, when the sun emitted

a frequency which disrupted most shelters. While some members remained topside, their skin became hard, their ears blackened, their hands grew useless. When the rest of the society emerged after the sun's noise subsided, those that had remained could not discern forms, folded in agony when touched, stayed mainly submerged to the eyes in water.

HALF-MAN DAY

Holiday of diminution, or, the Festival of Unresolved Actions. Only the largest members can celebrate. They swing sticks, there is running, and many swim great distances with wires on their backs. On the third day a great fight occurs. After the feast they are covered in grass while they sleep. They collaborate on a dream of the house, with each participant imagining perfectly his own piece. Upon waking they set to building it, rendering always a softer, less perfect form than the one in which they secretly lived the previous evening.

HAND-WORDS

Patterns on the hand which serve as emblems or signals. They were developed during the silent wars of ten and three. The mitten is designed with palm-holes, so that members may communicate in the cold.

HEAVEN

Area of final containment. It is modeled after the first house. It may be hooked and slid and shifted. The bottom may be sawed through. Members inside stare outward and sometimes reach.

HEAVEN CONSTRUCTION THEORY

The notions brought to bear on the construction of the final shelter. All work in this area is done under the influence of the first powder. This so the hands may shake, the eyes be glazed, the body be soft and movable.

HEEN-VIEWING

1. The act, technique or practice of viewing, with intent to destroy, any object or residue within or upon the house. Punishments of such acts include demotion to lower house, in which the culprit is subjected to endless examinations, proddings, mountings and group viewings by an unbroken stream of voluntary wardens.

2. To covet the life of another. 3. To look at a body and wish to destroy it. The heen in this case occurs or emanates from the hips, and the term applies in all cases less the one in which a member is looking upon, and wishing to terminate, his own body, which act goes unpunished.

HOUSE COSTUMES

The five shapes for the house which successfully withstand different weather systems. They derive their names from the fingers, their forms from the five internal tracts of the body, and their inhabitants from the larger and middle society.

HUMAN WEATHER

Air and atmosphere generated from the speech and perspiration of systems and figures within the society. Unlike animal storms, it cannot be predicted, controlled or even remotely harnessed. Cities, towns and other settlements fold daily under the menace of this home-built air. The only feasible solution, outside of large-scale stifling or combustion of physical forms, is to pursue the system of rotational silence proposed by Thompson, a member of ideal physical deportment—his tongue removed, his skin muffled with glues, his eyes shielded under with pictures of the final scenery.

JAMPING

1. The act or technique of generating monotonic, slack-lipped locution. Precise winds of any territory apply a syntax to the jamper, shaping his mouth-sounds into recognizable and other words and sentences. 2. Condition or disease of crushed face structures as per result of storm or hand striking.

JASON, OUR

1. The first brother. It has existed throughout known times in most to all fabricated pre-rage scenarios. It was erected initially in the Californias. It puts the powder in itself. It is the first love of the anti-person.

JENNIFER

The inability to see. Partial blindness with regard to hands. To Jennifer is to feign blindness. The diseases resulting from these acts are called jennies.

JERKINS
First farmer.

JOHN
1. To steal. This item occurs frequently in America and elsewhere. Its craft is diversion of blame onto the member from which the thing was stolen. 2. First house-garment correlationist. Lanky.

THE KENNETH SISTERS
Devisers of first food spring, blond-haired, slim-hipped, large, working hands. They dug the base for what would later become Illinois. They lived to be, respectively, 57, 71, 9, 45, 18 and 40.

L-STORMS
The particular, grievous weather maw generated from the destruction of houses or shelters. In a new settlement, an L-Storm is buried in the foundation to charm the site from future rage.

LAND-SCARF
Garment that functions also as a landmark, shelter or vehicle. To qualify, the item must recede beyond sight, be soft always, and not bind or tear the skin down.

LEG-INITIATIONS
Act or technique of preparing the legs for sleep. They may be rubbed, shaved or dressed in pooter.

LEG SONG
1. Secret melodies occurring between and around the legs of members or persons. It is not an audible sequence, nor does it register even internally if the legs are wrapped in cotton. Songs of the body incant at the P- or J-skin levels of the shoulder group. Leg Songs report at a frequency entirely other than these and disrupt the actions of birds. 2. The singing-between-the-legs occurring at all levels of the body. Sexual acts are prefaced by a commingling of these noises, as two or more members at a distance, before advancing, each tilt forward their pelvis to become coated in the tones of the other. 3. The sounds produced by a member or person just after dying. These songs herald the various diseases which will hatch into the corpse: the epilepsy, the shrinking, the sadness.

4. Device through which one brother, living, may communicate with another brother, dead.

LEGAL BEAST LANGUAGE

The four, six or nine words which technically and legally comprise the full extent of possible lexia which might erupt or otherwise burst from the head structure of Alberts.

LEGAL PRAYER

Any prayer, chant or psalm affixed with the following rider: *Let a justifiable message be herewith registered in regard to desires and thoughts appertaining to what will be unnamed divinities, be they bird forms or other atmo-bestial manifestations of the* CONTROLLING THOMPSON, *or instead unseen and personless concoctions of local clans, groups or teams. With no attempt to imprint here a definitive lingual-string of terms that shall be said to be terms bearing a truthful and anti-disharmonic concordance to the controlling agent, witnesses may accord to themselves the knowledge that a* PRAYER *is being committed that will herewith be one free of flaws, snags and lies. It will not be a misdirected, unheard or forgotten prayer. Neither will the blessed recipient be possessed of any confusion with respect to who or what has offered this prayer for consideration, although this assertion shall not indicate that the powerless subject makes any claim of authority over the* DIVINE AGENT OF FIRE. *It shall be a direct and honest gesturation to be received by said agent and dispatched or discarded in a custom that the agent knows. This now being said in the manner of greatest force and fluid legal acuity, the prayer can begin its middle without fear or repercussive sky reversals or blows that might destroy the mouth of the humble subject on his knees.*

LISTENING FRAME

1. Inhabitable structure in which a member may divine the actions and parlance of previous house occupants. It is a system of reverse oracle. It is dressed with beads and silvers and may sometimes be wheeled into small rooms for localized divining. The member is cautioned to never occupy this frame or ones like it while in the unsheltered grasses or sands. With no walls or ceilings to specify its search, the frame applies its reverse surmise to the entire history of the society – its trees, its water, its houses – gorging the member with every previosity until his body begins to

whistle from minor holes and eventually collapses, folds or gives up beneath the faint, silver tubing. 2. Any system which turns a body from shame to collapse after broadcasting for it the body's own previous speeches and thoughts. 3. External memory of a member, in the form of other members or persons that exist to remind him of his past sayings and doings. They walk always behind the member. Their speech is low. They are naked and friendly.

THE LIVING

Those members, persons and items that still appear to engage their hands into what is hot, what is rubbery, what cannot be seen or lifted.

LOCKED-HOUSE BOOKS

1. Pamphlets issued by the society that first prescribed the ideal dimensions and fabrics of all houses. 2. Texts which, when recited aloud, affect certain grave changes upon the house. 3. Any book whose oral recitation destroys members, persons, landscapes or water. 4. Texts which have been treated or altered. To lock a given text of the society is to render it changeable under each hand or eye that consumes it. These are mouth products. They may be applied to the skin. Their content changes rapidly when delivered from house to house. 5. Archaic hood, existing previously to the mouth-harness, engraved with texts carved into the face and eyes.

MARONIES

Thickly structured boys, raised on storm seeds and raw bulk to deflect winds during the house wars.

THE MATH GUN

1. Mouth of the father. It is equipped with a red freckle. It glistens. It is shined by foods, dulled with water, left alone by all else. 2. His pencil. It shortens with use and must be shaved, trimmed or sharpened by the person, who follows behind with a knife. 3. Process by which a member's counting capacity is nullified. One may be gunned out of numbers—or otherwise deprived of the ability to sequence—by silver strips which sting the hands. A member's air is occluded, his mouth is wrecked by the performance of numbers.

MESSONISM

Religious system of the society consisting of the following principles: i) Wonderment or devotion for any site in which houses preceded the arrival of persons. ii) The practice of sacrificing houses in autumn. It is an offering to Perkins, or the Thompson that controls it. iii) Any projection of a film or strips of colored plastic that generates images of houses upon a society. iv) The practice of abstaining from any act or locution which might indicate that one knows, knew or has known any final detail or attribute of the pure Thompson. v) Silence in the presence of weather. vi) The collection and consumption of string, which might be considered residual from the first form. The devout member acquires a private, internal pocket for this object. He allows it full navigational rule of his motions and standing poses. vii) The notion that no text shall fix the principles of said religion. All messages and imperatives, such as they are, shall be drawn from a private translation of the sun's tones. The member shall design his house so that it shall mitten these syllables which ripple forth from the bright orb. He may place his faith in the walls, which it is his duty to shine, that they receive the vivid law within them, and transfer it silently upon every blessed member that sits and waits inside the home.

MICHAEL%

1. Amount or degree to which any man is Michael Marcus, the father. 2. Name given to any man whom one wishes were the father. 3. The act or technique of converting all names or structures to Michael. 4. Any system of patriarchal rendering.

MOTHER, THE

1. The softest location in the house. It smells of foods that are fine and sweet. Often it moves through rooms on its own, cooing the name of the person. When it is tired it sits, and members vie for position in its arms. 2. System or team of Jane Marcuses existing as abstract regret or longing of the Ben Marcus. It is further defined as the Jane-over of the anti-person.

THE MOUTH-HARNESS

1. Device for trapping and containing the head. Mouths are often stuffed with *items*—the only objects legally defined as suspicious or worthy of silent paranoid regard. A claim is therefore made that

we eat suspicion and become filled with it. The harness is designed to block all ingestion. Gervin states: "His mouth will be covered with a wire web. He shall never eat. Nor may he ever take what is outside and bring it inside. His stomach will forever devise upon what is within." 2. A system applied to the head to prevent destruction or collapse while reading or absorbing code.

NAGLE

Wooden fixture which first subdued the Winter-Albert. It occurs in and around trees and is highly brown.

NESTOR'S RAPE FARM

1. Any site of violation. 2. Initial farm run by G.D. Nestor in which the fourteen primary dogs of Dakota systematically raped the Charles family in August. 3. Place in which the Nestor group instructed members in molestation, the dive, stabbing, breaking the skin.

NITZEL'S GAMBLE

The act or technique of filling the lungs with water. The chance was first taken by the Nitzel in Green river.

ODOR SPIRALING

Tossing, turning and flinging of the head so as to render radical, unknown odors in a locality.

OHIO

The house, be it built or crushed. It is a wooden composition affixed with stones and glass, locks, cavities, the person. There will be food in it, rugs will warm the floor. There will never be a clear idea of Ohio, although its wood will be stripped and shined, its glass polished with light, its holes properly cleared—this in order that the member inside might view what is without—the empty field, the road, the person moving forward or standing still, wishing the Ohio was near.

PALMER

System or city which is shiftable. A Palmer can be erected anywhere between the coasts.

PERKINS

1. Term given to the body of Thompson, in order that His physical form never desecrate His own name. 2. The god of territory.

PRISON CLOTH MORNING

1. Term applied to any day in which a construction site is enhanced with cloth dens and enclosures of a jailing capacity. 2. Period of any disciplinary term in which the felon must construct a usable garment from the four things: soil, straw, bark and water. The morning is an extensive period and will often outlast the entire sentence.

PRIVATE HOUSE LAW

Rule of posture for house inhabitants stating one's desired position in relation to the father: one must bend forward, bring food, sharpen the pencil. Never may one stand on higher ground than it, nor shed the harness or grip the tunic tightly when it is present. Its clothes must be combed with one's fingers. Its speech to be written down, its commands to be followed, its spit to never under any circumstances be wiped from one's face.

PROFESSIONAL SLEEPERS

Members whose sleep acts perform specific, useful functions in a society. Clustered sleepers ward off birds; single, submerged sleepers seal culprits in houses; dozers heaped in cloth enhance the grasses of a given area, restore our faith in houses.

RAG, THE, OR PRAYER RAG

Device of stripped or pounded cloth held to the mouth during prayer.

RAIN

Hard, silver, shiny object. It can be divided into knives and used for cutting procedures. Most rain dissolves within the member and applies a slow cutting program over a period of years. This is why when one dies the rain is seen slicing upward from its body. When death is converted into language it reads: to empty the body of knives.

THE RARE-WATERS

Series of liquids believed to contain samples of the first water.

It is the only water not yet killed. It rims the eyes, falls from them during certain times, collects at the feet, averts the grasp of hands, which are dry, and need it.

SADNESS
The first powder to be abided upon waking. It may reside in tools or garments. It may be eradicated with more of itself, in which case the face results as a placid system coursing with water, heaving.

SALT
An item which comprises the in- and external core of most to all animals. An animal may be licked free of this salt, or an animal may be hosed clean or scraped. Only when it coughs up salt or otherwise produces saltmatter from within can the animal be expected in short time to collapse.

SCHEDULES AND DISPENSING RULES OF SEASONS
System of legal disbursement in relation to seasons and temperatures. Thompson embodies the assembly, the constituency, the audience, the retractors, the Thompson and non-Thompson in any weather-viewing scheme.

SCHENK
A school.

SHADOW-CELLS
The visible, viscous grain deposited upon any area recently blanketed in shadow. The cells may be packed into dough. They may be spread onto the legs or hips. They may darken or obscure the head for an infinite period.

SHELTER WITNESSES
Members which have viewed the destruction, duplication or creation of shelters. They are required to sign or carve their names or emblems onto the houses in question, and are subject to a separate, vigilant census.

SHIRT OF NOISE
Garment, fabric or residue which absorbs and holds sound. Its loudness cannot be predicted. It can destroy the member which inhabits it.

Skin Pooter

1. A salve, tonic, lotion or unguent which, when applied liberally to the body, allows a member to slip freely within the house of another. 2. A poultice which prevents collapse when viewing a new shelter.

Sky Interception, sinter

The obstruction caused by birds when light is projected from sun-sources affixed to hills and rivers, causing members to see patterns, films or "clouds." sinter is an acronym for Sky Interception and Noise Transfer of Emergent Rag-forms.

The Sky Films of Ohio

The first recordings and creations of the sky, recorded in the Ohio region. They were generated by a water machine designed by Krup. The earliest films contained accidents and misshapen birds. They are projected occasionally at revival festivals—at which wind of certain popularity is also rebroadcast—but the machine has largely been eclipsed by the current roof lenses affixed to houses, which project and magnify the contents of each shelter onto the sky of every region in the society.

Sleep-Holes

Areas or predesigned localities in which dormant figures and members conduct elaborate sleep performances. Points are scored for swimming, riding and killing. Some members utilize these sites to perfect their sleep-speech, and profess that they are not sleeping. Others exercise or copulate or rapidly eat cloth and grain. The father slept in one for four hours while smashing his own house, which contained its own sleepers, who performed nothing.

Sleeping Group

Team of members which performs mutual, radical sleep acts in various sites of varying difficulty. They are satisfied not with actual sleeping but with watching the sleeping of another. These are members which can only copulate, speak or eat when surrounded by fields of tossing sleepers that are weeping, are moaning, are struggling to breathe.

THE SMELL CAMERA

Device for capturing and storing odor. It is a wooden box augmented with string and two wire bunces. It houses odor for one season. It releases the odor when the shutter is snapped or jerked out. Afterwards the string must be combed and shook.

SOUTH-SHADOW

The residue of shadow-cells which accrete to the south of all classifiable objects, regardless of the sun's position.

THE SPANISH BOY

1. Member of localized figures which mustache early. 2. Item of remote personhood which demonstrates the seventeen postures of fire while dormant or sleeping.

SPEED-FASTING EXPERIMENTS

Activity or practice of accelerated food abstention. It was first conducted in Buffalo. The record death-by-fasting occurred in two days, through motor-starving and exhaustion, verbal.

STINKPOINT

Moment of time slightly forward from the moment of time of another. Since all odors issue first into a fraction of the future, allowing them to fall into a member advancing in time, any member achieving or arriving in a stinkpoint is also said to be a creator and co-conspirator of any smells and smell systems in the society.

STORM LUNG

Object which can be swallowed to forestall the effects of weather upon a body.

STRING THEORY OF FATIGUE

System or technique of diagnosing the level of tiredness or unwillingness in a member by covering it with medical ropes.

STRUP

Method of in-gazing applied to one's own body or house. To strup is not to count these things. Nor can it mean to analyze, assess or otherwise hold an opinion of a house or body. It refers strictly to a method of viewing that is conducted with a tilted or cloth-covered head.

SUBFEET WALKING RITUALS

Series of motion exercises conducted with hidden, buried or severed leg-systems. It was first named when members were required to move through tracts of high sand. The act was later repeated when the sand had faded. It is the only holiday in which motion is celebrated. Revelers honor the day by stumbling, dragging forward on their arms, binding their legs with wire, lying down and whispering, not being able to get up.

THE SUN

1. Origin of first sounds. Some members of the society still detect amplified speech bursts emanating from this orb, and have accordingly designed noise mittens for the head and back. A poetic system was developed in thirty based on the seventeen primary tonal flues discharging from the sun's underskin. 2. Unit of surge devised by Greenberg.

SUN-STALLS

Abrupt disruptions in the emissions of the sun. They occur in the blazing quarterstrips which flap. There begins a clicking or slow sucking sound. Members standing below arch or bend. They raise a hand to the ear or eye. Form a cup or shield.

SUN-STICK

Item of the body which first turns toward sun when a member dies, sleeps, collapses. This item is further the pure compass toward tracts that are heated and safe, also called true places.

SYNCHRONIZED FAMILY WALKING TRAINING

Method of motion-unison practiced by members and teams inhabiting larger, divergent cloth shelters. Instruction was first elaborated by Nestor. Later, Crawford refuted Nestor's system and a national standard was established.

TEMPERATURE LAW

The first, third and ninth rule of air stating that the recitation or revocation of names—or any calling forth in any manner of any person or thing—shall for all time alter the temperature of a locality.

THEORY OF INVISIBILITY

Plante, G.'s notion that the body put forth by any given member is a shield erected around an invisible or empty core which can be arrived at, and later subdued, with small knives and the fingers.

THE THONG

Leatherized ladle, spoon or stick affixed often to the tongue of a member. It is considered the last item of the body. After demise, it may be treated with water to discern the final words of a person.

TOPOGRAPHICAL LEGEND AND LOCATION OF FOOD NOOKS

System of over-maps depicting buried food quadrants, sauce grooves and faults or fissures in which grains and beans are caught. The cloth form of the map can be applied to the bodies of animals, to clarify areas in which edibles might have amassed.

THE TOWER PERIOD

Age of principal house inscriptions. Text was first discovered embedded in the house during this era. Shelters of the time were fitted with turrets and wires, poles, needled roofs, domes. Members were hired to read aloud the inscriptions of each house and holidays were formed to ritualize these performances, with food as a reward for orators that did not weep or otherwise distort the message carved into the house.

TREASURE OF POSSIBLE ENUNCIATIONS

Catalogue of first, last and intermediate lexia. It includes all possible words and their unutterable opposites. Other than Thompson's *Bank of Communicable Desire,* no other such comprehensive system exists.

TREE-BREAD

The victuals in concert with tree systems.

TUNGSTEN

1. Hardened form of the anger and rage metals. 2. Fossilized behavior, frozen into mountainsides, depicting the seven scenes of escape and the four motifs of breathing-while-dead.

THE TUNIC

1. Textile web, shared and worn by all members of a society. It is the only public garment. Never may it be cast off, altered, shrunk or locally cleaned. Its upkeep is maintained under regulation of

the Universal Storm Calendar, which deploys winds into its surface to loosen debris and members or persons that have exceeded their rightful term of inhabitation. 2. Garment placed between pre-age boy and girl members to enlarge or temporarily swell the genitals and shank during weather birthing.

UNIVERSAL STORM CALENDAR

1. Thompsoned system of air influence. Inexplicable. 2. System of storm reckoning for the purpose of recording past weather and calculating dates and sites for future storms. The society completes its house-turn under the sun in the span of autumn. The discrepancy between storms is inescapable, and one of the major problems for a member since his early days has been to reconcile and harmonize wind and rain reckonings. Some peoples have simply recorded wind by its accretions on the rag, but, as skill and storage developed, the prevailing winds generally came to be fitted into the tower. The calendar regulates the dispersal, location and death of every wind and rain system in existence. 3. Game, abbreviated to USC, or Us, played by children, in which body mimics air.

WEATHER BIRTHING

1. The act or technique of selecting and reciting certain words within given, fixed sky situations with the intent of generating, enhancing or subtracting weather from a given area in the society. 2. Burning the skin of a member to alter the sky shapes of a locality. 3. Process occurring pre-spasm between the hips of children. This includes any exceptional change in the speed of air transpiring between two or more members, figures or persons. 4. The act of placing powders or other grains in the mouth while speaking to alter the temperature of a local site. 5. Whispering while holding birds in the mouth.

THE WEATHER KILLER

1. Person, persons or team which perform actual and pronounced killings of the air. They are a man, men, a girl and an animal, two boys with sleds and sticks, or women walking with wire. Their works were first uncovered at the wind farm. They exist as items which are counter-Thompson, given that they kill what he has made. 2. Sky-killing member. In the middle and late periods a man devised a means for harming the air. Little is known of him,

except that he termed himself a weather killer and referred to others like him, located in America, Palmer and elsewhere. The works of these practitioners were in some part buried at the wind farm, the home site on NN 63 in Texas. They have rubbed shapes onto paper, peeled sound out of rock, discovered pictures inside sticks, acts which all then collapse, shrink, extinguish what is breathed.

WESTERN WORSHIP BOXES

The smallest structures, designed to fit precisely one body. They are rough-walled and dank, wooden and finely trimmed—the only areas of devotion. When more than one body enters to worship as a team, the box gevorts.

THE WIND GUN

Sequence of numerals, often between the numbers twelve and thirteen, which when embedded or carved as code into the field, reinstruct wind away from an area.

WIND-BOWL

1. Pocket of curved, unsteady space formed between speaking persons. They may discuss the house, its grass, some foods, the father inside. The wind-bowl will tilt and push into their faces, that they might appear leaning back, arching from each other, grasping at the ground behind them as if sleeping. 2. Term applied to any item whose shape, character or size has been altered by weather.

WINTER-ALBERT

Summer-Albert. Such names as exist in the society achieve not converse attributes in opposite seasons, but rather repeat all acts, thoughts and feelings of the diametric season. For example, during summer, the holder is afforded the benefit of watching any Albert duplicate all movements of the previous winter. The summer-Albert is therefore a repetition and duplication of its own colder self.

THE WIRE

The only element attached, affixed or otherwise bushing with every other element, object, item, person or member of the society. It is gray and often golden and glimmers in the morning. Members polish it simply by moving forward or backward or resting in place. The wire is the shortest distance between two bodies. It may be followed to any area or person one desires. It contains on its surface the shredded residue of hands — this from members that pulled too hard, held on too long, wanted to get there too fast.

WITNESS

1. One who watches, hears or otherwise acquires knowledge of certain actions, things or states within a society. Witnessing is only reliably performed without the use of the head, which must be blanketed or otherwise suppressed — this so it does not deceive the body. 2. Tingling in the hips or sweetness in the larger pelva, indicating that a thing has become known.

WOODEN FIRE TECHNIQUES

1. The construction of wood-based tableaux that duplicate the heat and noise of fire without the corresponding visual accuracy. 2. Hidden fire codes pre-built into vessels and persons. Such subjects and objects burn secretly for the duration of their existence.

THE YARD

Locality in which wind is buried and houses are discussed. Fine grains line the banks. Water curves outside the pastures. Members settle into position.

Ojjiba
Barbara Guest

sideways a gift for language the joined up tunes il splash and whine

ordained it the frisked mood piece of cotton in the ear every day different

a felon passes I believe dog-eared as three of your pals the boy in tune with

the sandcastle out of three twigs on a harp who hear the bow bend

early music

you think I am joyous up at dawn down by il splash not true I hover and in

with the robins as they take up their chores and on the brink of financial

ruin this is not a sophisticated place can crown you with ruin take your hand

off the plate

(in the wrinkled pod

                    tried your bat on the faucet saw a hood

    like what he writes away from the gold batter)

ruin is pleasanter up here whisks crossing the dune blown shell and peppermint leas even if no rim around me scoop up the line and distribute it regularly not haunted think of milk toast three winks not lonely early music

caused the chair to move to the brink the azalea in winter wonder who refused to cosset it if ruin can put us out of sight then forgot or the chair moved wish it were closer

of sentimental values none no more than a spasm the arm goes over and down and over in il splash drank a tumbler then greenleaf and swimming dog muscular gladioli goodly frère *unio mystica* we perceive a grass ship

on the sea surface a forget-me-knot the ratio consoling a strange look at the vein and flung in a cloud the lantern a different embrace in pursuit of il splash

marveled at how little comes from much in a nook combing hair classical
drift of the bay naked off Palinurus Cape O queen of Cnidos literature
"wax-white arms of Lydia" waterfront pebbled with bones

and she confronts us "the woman who weeps" the scenery dislikes wet arms
bathing suit pulled down at the corner a raft on the sea she is a raft an egg
shell breaks god's whip early music

wave passes over from sight wave is obscured water replaces cloud the
surface reverses its look bottom of the sea comes up like a kite in the rear
on our back rain will emerge from that dying cloud whither arrow of blue

no concern for corridor upstairs icy trees blow smoke what island was it
cold from where we sat fingers never still water idly lay a green cloth they
jump into bed wake to the crow can guess the dark coat

about the sandcastle our position on innovation the duster the trap is it mediocre the schoolmaster suggests wool in the brace a tight fit the bodice-fitter complains

(or seascope of anchored tin put out the table the chipped metallurgical appears to be a vine no goddess to shake a leg)

can you swallow this they erase "long echo of sand" also "pool noise" interrupt "drawn out whine" betray the disk the substance improves and the gnat she waits in her bathing dress *touch and go*

haunted by the speckled cow the little girl with a ribboned bonnet brings in the cow put more early in music says the speckled cow moreearlyinsplash what was it about crackers asked the wench potato mash is cheap pauper tint to the sky so mermaids sweep out the crones they flit good evening good evening no treasure

which tree to cut the downward slope of a savannah its bell our land goes further light drains horizon's overcast early music

oh promise we shall meet on Ojjiba and swim underwater my harp is caught in a silver fire of water the planet Ojjiba looked at that way

Hagfish, Worm, Kakapo

Shelley Jackson

HAGFISH

ONCE UPON A TIME a hagfish loved another, and thus far was only doing what hagfish had always done.

Like other hagfish, I was hated by fishermen, who reviled our parasitical lifestyle and the indeterminacy of our sex. We lived on dead and dying fish, boring into the soft tissues near the anus and eating our way outward. When the host fish was just a skin stretched over bones, a deep-sea coracle, we pranced about in it with a triumphant kind of giddiness, making the lightweight behemoth hunker and hop along the ocean floor like a Chinese dragon in a procession, its emptied eyes affording glimpses of the flicking gremlin inside.

That was carnival time on the ocean floor. The skin and bones galleon careered through the sluggish currents, stirring up muck. Like the skew-eyed girl in high school, its head faced just off fore like someone posing for a portrait. Rough treatment, and soon enough our toys wore out, and we moved on.

Heeding the standard summons, my love and I set sail on the same day in our skin ships for the breeding grounds, across fields in which the tube worms rose and fell emitting telegraphic prophecies, past slits from which bubbles streamed, past rotting beams and rusting bulkheads. On the same day too we reached the plain where carcasses dotted the ocean floor like stinking cushions.

Strangers, we recognized each other, despite our sagging ballgowns. In the thick material light we wove our way through the fizzing mounds from which threads of bubbles rose punctuated by the occasional belched globule. Just so, in an old garden in which moss obscures the stone terraces, fountains and worn statuary, two great ladies of an old court might work the scaffolding of their rotting lace ballgowns over the uneven ground with habitual dignity and only a hint of maunder, falter, forget. Doddering in patterns whose purpose is forgotten, they're still solid with accumulated history, sustained by it: institutional, big as barracks.

But when they reach each other, what? Play of fans? Euchre? A long hairpin pushed through the cheek to transfix the tongue like some stunned moth? They can't recall. They beg their fans, their garments, the very ground to remember for them. Slowly they part their lips in a soft rain of face powder. Antique vocal cords tremble.

"Alas, I can never be yours," she cried, "for like the edible oyster and the boring worm, Teredo, I change my sex from year to year, and this year I am a princess like yourself, a correspondence that boggles my mind with architectural symmetries beautiful yet austere, austere! I am filled with a helplessness truly regal, like that little white oyster irritated by the pea in her pallet, proven royal by her utter and almost mathematical impossibility, her X over zero indigestion. And while next year I am sure to be a handsome prince (ribald in virile company, with a good seat at horse, a stout arm in combat, and a courtly manner at my queen's embroidered knee), the laws of nature will serve you with a like summons."

And we sat down bobbing in our carriages and pondered this conundrum. "Whatever sex I am," I confessed, "I feel somehow insincere. I know that not long ago I was a robust specimen of the other sex, and while perhaps it is only my body that alters and not my mind, I cannot help feeling marked by each new incarnation until I begin to feel unreal, a succession of slides projected on a remembering wall."

"It's just the opposite for me," she answered. "I feel that I can only know the sex I am if I remember another sex; only then is my sex fully conscious, pure, and marked in its difference, only then do I truly know what it is not. I am a woman because I know what it is to be a man."

"I cannot be a man, remembering what it is to be a woman, but no more can I be a woman, knowing I have in me the makings of a man."

There we stuck philosophizing, awaiting the biological go-ahead. Ready to scrape the clay of our genitals away and reveal the ambidextrous grapples of a new sex. Then we would catch hold of each other with bold simplicity, irrefutable.

The time of our changes approached, and we fought the almost unbearable urge to abandon our watch for private business. Between breeding seasons is the time to drill into one fat flank after another and gorge ourselves to fuel our transformation. With fat globules popping out the sides of the mouth, we chew from the inside out, and do not neglect to scour the skin of the buttery layer this side of the scales or suck the bones clean, but we ignore the dribs, drabs and loose ends, that's how you get fat, dealing in gross profits and leaving the peskily evasive snippets for the small fry to go after, abandoning the deflating skins without regret.

I waited, though I wanted to rave through the world's bags emptied behind me. It was the time for immersion in the flesh, mine but especially theirs. The mind shuts down, the body makes its changes in this time; some say it is the smallness of the focus that permits that, a pinched gray dot not able even to know itself because there is no other place to know from. I wanted to wander the blue fields, which I imagined always dotted with carcasses, my thick fruit. A heathered light drifting softly down like a vertical current, like silted water from a river's mouth. My body tenderly withdraws its eccentricity, passes through a moment of potent indeterminacy—when the tenderness shifts, as if at will, and can be felt first here, then here, such that I imagine one day (and this might be restful) I might wake up with an erotic wrist, a clitoral chin, spine, gill. Our changes are slow and seashell-cautious and symmetrical, a nonviolent rearing, a diffident balustrade, a somber cushioning, a competent, secretive staircase.

This was our only chance: that one of us might lag behind the other, opening a window in the wall. We watched and waited, but our biological clocks ticked in perfect time, and we laughed through our puckered sleeve mouths, oh oh oh, as we watched our genitals flower identically in perfect synchrony.

Males, we waited through another season, and again slid neatly across the finish line together.

We separated. I drove my decaying mobile home away, lurching over the terrain like an earthmover, and with melancholy resignation chewed my way inside another carapace. The old home, a paltry shrug of tatters, frayed and came undone.

In the new home I whistled as I worked, polished cookpots, sewed ruffles on curtains. My home was pulp pierced by spines; industrious, I worked my way around the vanes of bone that extended from the roofbeam, the spine. My walls were chubby, translucent, decaying. It was a time for putting my back into it, homesteading. I worked hard and relaxed at the end of the day in some rotty nook or other, a homebody. I carted bundles from here to there, my hair tied back, my nostrils coated with white plaster, the old-time fantasy of the happy homemaker, buns plumping under fluffy towels, flour handprints on the apron.

I missed her.

I set off again before my home was even cured, humping my pumpkin shell along with such vigor I lost chunks.

She had beat me to the site, swimming around in a crazy churning that shook the sides of whatever bygone fish in a manner I'd come to recognize as her own. I parked my own nearby.

Desire was never a feeling, it was a purpose that haunted the shape of what I was. The screwdriver doesn't dream of turning the screw, it just works better for that than for clearing a drain or picking a lock. I thought my genitals were shaped urges, that their right use was implicit in their form, that body perfectly expresses thought, and that thought by that means acts uninterrupted on the world. My genders are supposed to wax and wane and with them wanders my desiring heart and in between that other stuff: the baggage of dead meat, techniques of butchery, nibble and bore, and wax and polish and scour and suckle clean, hunger and macabre tomfoolery with the emptied skins and a date at the breeding ground on Saturday.

That's the life of a hagfish. It wasn't writ that I'd be loitering painfully at the verge of this flat blue plane where sullen eddies in the sediment give away lovers' sloppy gazebos, algal grottoes and parlors, thinking, *Lucky lovers, ugly but matched as left shoe and right,* while we sat dolorous above like poor teens in the cheapest seats with our laps full of wax paper rubbed vellum from sandwiches, noses and eyeglass-frames monstrous obstacles to a kiss. Keeping her distance (because who knows what codes might seize us and make us mannequins, killing each other out of misconstrued impulse), she coiled this way and (back flex) that, unhappy too.

There was only one place we might meet: exactly in between. Maybe there our no-genitals-at-all could rub their inadequacies together. In that span of time when I'm not anyone I would press my misunderstanding against her uncertainty, and indecision would be making love.

As my sex waned I move toward her over the silt which stirred under my belly and sifted over my back. I was reconciled to my ugliness at this moment when the entire ocean seemed to be passing a thorough, attentive tongue over my stiff vanes, my spines, my horny plates and my spots of loathsome smoothness. My needle teeth stung in my gums, vibrant with messages. I had a mouthful of cat-whiskers tickling, antennae. My sex was a collar loosening. Her small dull eyes were tiny beads sunk in the puckered flesh. They seemed to tighten and pull the skin inward around them. My genital face contracted in sympathy.

I felt my skull boxing in my brain. I felt my skin bagging my skull. I felt the muscular length of me turning and flexing and I knew all these things were glad collaborators of the machine. I had to attend.

I peered through a clear dot in a moiré that rendered all indistinct. The dot was not large. I forced it larger. Neurons blazed impatiently in my brain and I imagined some new bridge was forming. I felt the churning in my flesh and I knew I had felt it before, but that I had never before known myself feeling it. The surface burned.

Something inside me clocked. Out incited. A pinched part smudged thin inverted and blistered. Flared remote envelopes advised a pencil and glue flow lapsed under the limb. Glow spattered amiable oranges sunk in an underlayer.

It was unrecognizeable. I bunked in sundered demispheres and against me lay nine suckered antebellum under gauze. I spilled an inside igloo over and that one answered ambient revolver. Trigger livid smelled an entry overlaid with lint advantage. Notorious exchanged and no thrip infiltrated anything. Neither of us touched something else and something liked it.

We wandered off and chewed, impressed. For one instant nothing happened.

WORM

he

At first we were tiny and they were big as city buses. None of us had any arms or legs. Neither did they; that made us feel closer to them. With undulations of their long bodies they swam through the sea like ourselves. From below they were dark against the pewter of the water's underface. We called them angels.

When I grew older I heard the stories about them and learned to tell them too. I swam with my cronies and grew larger. Occasionally, we saw them pass overhead and we strained toward them with all our being, Johnny, Armand and I, our limbless bodies like fingers pointing, or iron filings enchanted by the dreams of a magnet. We dropped whatever we were doing to worship them. Like long soft-padded curving arms, they seemed to beckon indolently.

They did not notice us, however. We agreed: that was as it should be. What in them could be receptive to the motes we were? But we knew the story, that if we swam toward them they would swivel in our direction and receive us. We wondered why.

Armand left us to lurk in some remote sargasso. He said he wanted to grow up. We didn't know what he meant. Johnny and I loitered at the edge of every eddy and rode the currents to cold places and back until something ate Johnny and I was alone.

At last I met her in a coiling I was caught in. Never knowing how to approach, I had kept my distance. Never having a hat to doff, I'd kept mum. Forced into proximity, though, I was enterprising enough to hand her my card. She returned it, said Ed, Ted, Fred, the identity of others is not important when you are self-sufficient and big as a city bus. She steered in a semicircle and opened an unforeseen opening.

I went stiff for half a second, then melted into jelly, spilled toward her. Vacuum sucked. She stammered around me like an epileptic mouth. She spoke me in: I became Fred Ted Ed, a counting rhyme or riddle song, the chaff of unmeant words.

I swam straight into the heart of the resistance and found that precisely there I could make way. She was the color of my eyes' experience of pressure, flare-ups in the dark. She was a labyrinth and I was insubstantial as a thread. Still, I had the feeling that I wore her.

I was made to extinguish myself in the flesh of another. I was a dab, a mote, a mite. But small as I was I vibrated all over with a love of piercing beauty, like the smidgin of flesh in the throat of a singer. I remember these things only dimly, but I think it was that way.

she

He almost ran to me, overturning my ottoman, decoupage drink tray with the green decanters, dart gun, surveying instruments, anatomical model of the human ear. He scrunched up close, his whole body resembling one dapper mustachio coiled in alert self-conscious agitation. He was a proud whip self-cracking, a line graph running through the possibilities. I saw him as the callow lover with pimply brow in a stereoscopic photograph, inching on his tensed haunches sideways along the couch to the girl. A worm.

I'm a worm too. But relatively speaking I've got the dimensions of a diesel truck, a tank, a redwood tree. He's a pencil lead, a basting stitch, a toggle-switch. He's pins and needles in my private passages. Some people make much of the different lengths and volumes of body parts so close to the same size I can't see the difference. They play with dominance and submission because the game is close, and fear and power occupy the same place in them and struggle together. They get something out of that turpentine and water mixture, that mingling of unmixable fluids and tsunami at the interface. What's that game to me? This fight's fixed. Who'd spar with a pudding? Pommel an olive? Whup a wet leaf?

Sex: some dull Ed sprints at me, fakes, doubles back, pirouettes and disappears into me like a mouse in a hole. Never comes out again. Is the ghost in my attic, flickering like a maladjusted TV. Becomes a fond notion, a cast in the eye. Ouija hiccup.

It's a strange kind of self-sufficiency I (we) have now. I am happy alone, "alone"; I need no one, not even to make babies (I do that myself, with inner Ned) yet I've always got company I can't talk to or touch but know is here by the very fact I am self-sufficient. I don't know whether to resent or pity Fred, or whether it's absurd to do either because he's now a part of myself. Do I resent my arm for siphoning off my blood for its own purposes? Of course not. Do I wish I didn't have to tote it around?

In a social sense, though, Ted is a stranger. Hardly had I made his acquaintance—and I don't even remember if he had family, or where he's from—hung his hat behind the door and poured him a Tom Collins than he'd shucked shirt and shoes, slacks and boxers and digital watch, and made a dive for my egg-sac. And I never heard from him again.

I hadn't even thought to close the blinds. I guess I imagined we'd sit and tell each other a little about ourselves. I guess I thought I'd feel the magic. Sure, I was skeptical, I had my doubts; they're so little after all, men, it's always been hard for me even to think of them as the same species. I mean I almost mistook him for the worm in my tequila; he was that small. And him coiling and uncoiling nonstop as he maneuvered around me. I felt like a mother spaceship in slow rotation on the screen, astronauts rappeling over my surface in symphonic silence. I felt that big and peaceful.

I wanted to say to him, you, you're trying so hard to bed me. If you wait, you can become me instead. Grow thick and long and serene, lacking nothing but an egg-sac add-on to need nothing anymore, and then complete, hermaphroditic, world-encompassing forever. I almost pitied him, said stay away, don't come seeking us out in our bachelor apts, calling phone machines to listen for a female voice. Hang on and you'll have it made, never again have to wiggle wiggle that hairfine little body of yours.

But I didn't say it. Didn't have time. The blinds were up but if the neighbors blinked they missed it. He was on me and in me and gone and I hardly knew what happened, sat swirling my tequila and keeping an eye on the pile of clothes till it dawned on me that he wasn't in them anymore.

He entered me, as you humans like to say. But Teddy shut and latched the door, Teddy don't come out no more. Put your stuff in the red cubby, Ned, and welcome to nursery school.

Did I feel different? Biologically, no. But I must say it drives me crazy to think of Ed sucking away at the wall of my egg-sac, rockin the warm fluid, and I don't know the first damn thing about him, whether he likes wind-surfing or rock tumbling, what shows he catches. And there it is again, the question: Do I resent this creature who has penetrated my core and set himself up there with cabin and snowshoes and rabbit traps, in permanent residence, fishing my streams and hunting my forest glades?

Sometimes I can tell he's there. Archetypal images occur, recur. Jonah in the belly of the whale. Rapunzel and all those other lovelies in towers, on islands, atop glass mountains conjured up by jealous fathers. The duck in the wolf's belly. Little Red Riding Hood ditto. I think these images float up to me like his dreams of identity. That wordlessly he still impinges himself on my consciousness, supplying it with metaphors that bias my own thinking. I think he would like me to mistake him for myself and lose the knowledge of my own right size. He would like me to make my meat a puppet of the tiny worm of spirit that clings to my strength and dreams my dreams for me with an irony that does not mask its insecurity.

I would like to see what he's doing in there, what in a sense I'm doing in there or could have done. I envy the man with the pane of glass set in his abdominal wall so the creatures of science could view the factory in which his organs labored. In old school science films they showed a tiny man in a polygonal control room in the brain. There was no indication that women had anything different upstairs. That's how I see Fred, as a nervous, middle-aged white twerp who likes to put his tiny feet up on the panel and catnap.

I don't know him, I don't like him, and I don't understand him. Yet he is my own past history. He is my child self, stopped at the splitting of the paths. We don't understand each other, but something understands something, the way one gear understands the other with which it meshes.

Ever since I grew into the bruiser I am now (glossy, sleek, with the unsteady, disbelieving poise of a drag queen and the heft of a buffalo) I've sailed about, smug and immaculate, unimpeachably female. What I won through self-denial (abjuring nail-biting and angel-ogling) can never be taken from me. I rove through the ocean and the males, those nail-parings, those carrot-peels, are ripple-marks of my passing. It gets me that what I tried so hard to put behind me (reviling myself, fighting down my own desires) is exactly what I spread myself for. Why did I try so hard to be different from types like Ted?

Quick as a wink, up he came and IN he went and where there was one there are two. In the very mid of me there he is, the other sex, my bygone past and my rejected destiny. I am fucked by the child I used to be before I grew into the woman I am. My past curls round and enters me at the place of origin of us both, and starts the game over. Pete and Repete were sitting on a fence Pete fell down who was left Repete. My past curls round, Repete, Repete.

KAKAPO

My lover booms one thousand times an hour, six or seven hours a night, especially on damp, windless days when the sound carries well over the grasslands. His air sacs become almost spherical. He perches at the edge of a hollow bowl in the ground that he constructs to amplify his call. He cannot fly. I cannot fly. We love each other; we have not met each other yet.

On a moist still night his singing pummels my soul to dissolution.

The booming goes on and on and into the center of it I go homing. The booming and my faithful listening ear are already love happening. My ear, his dish are rhyming shapes. His voice penetrates my ear, my ear reels forth his voice.

The voice between us takes almost palpable form, it is a great still shape in the air, like Ernst's bomber with the arms of a woman. Just so our bond is beyond us, my lover puffing himself up to a ludicrous ball to pump out super-parrotic calls, and I humble and responsive, a ground-scurrier. We do not fly but *it* flies, in a still sort of way; our love hovers over both of us and frightens us to duck even closer to the earth.

His voice is shaped by impersonal laws into a perfect geometrical figure, a sphere expanding around another sphere expanding around another sphere expanding too. I hurry toward the center of the nested spheres, panting, dirty, and ungeometrical. Beside our accomplished love overhead, I am a contingent and unnecessary figure.

The scree I zigzag through, head down (the straight thread of our bond digresses in crochet patterns through the brush) is a meaningless obstacle, but enough to slow me down. I gallop, I hustle, through mazes whose principles I am proudly too stupid to grasp; I fling my bruised chest against the walls and somewhere, some clod or bramble gives way.

When I push through the last tuft of grasses and see my lover puffed up into a ball with the effort of sending forth a voice so much larger than himself, I laugh at him. I can't help it. He in turn finds me scruffy and ridiculous, bent over with shopping bags and extra coats. We come together in that, in our absurdity.

We are blind, hedged in by the slurry of decaying vegetation, clods kicked up by larger animals, scruff of grass. We run like little mice through the underbrush, without dignity. We resemble amputees. I know there is something embarrassing and suspicious about birds that scuttle with dirt in their feathers, but that anchors us. It is a kind of payment, like our small numbers. For it is not that we were forced, aeons past, by the misfortune of our place in a close-up world to learn to broadcast love. No, it was the grandeur of our love that consigned us to the ground.

Rolling Beads

Robert Antoni

I. FIRST DECADE

1

IS THAT I REMEMBER: glasspane. For me it has a smell. Silvery and powdery and cool, even in strangulating heat. Smell of a moth's wings. From nine in the morning till four in the afternoon. Every day except Sunday, when I marched off with mummy to the first Mass. Perched as always on my pedestal of storybooks—still downstairs, I presume, still underread—Enid Bliton and Hans Christian Andersen and the Grimm brothers. The years of my childhood measured out in the number of volumes piled up to reach the window. Five: seven. Six: five. Seven: four. Standing there with my nose squinged-up flat against it, weight leaning into the point of my chin, the twin-lobed cloud of vapor appearing and disappearing with each little breath. The silver moth pinned on its back between my lips and the glass, beating forever against my cheeks.

No one ever told me why Di, my nursemaid, called me in and fed me a slice of cake dribbled with golden syrup. Dressed me in my frock, and locked me into my little room every morning. Why Dulcianne, Di's daughter and my only friend, was permitted to carry on running beneath the cocoa trees wearing nothing but her knickers. Scrambling through the tall canes behind my own beloved Daisy—a kind of straggly chicken we called a "clean-neck-fowl"—given to me by the overseer, Ramsingh. Somehow I sensed the mandate came from mummy. It was a look of glossy fear I sometimes caught on her face. I sensed it, too, in the way Di combed out my single braid—Cook said I had "bad" hair—always hurry hurry. Whereas she fussed over mummy's for hours. Then one day I overheard Cook talking to Di in the kitchen, curled up in the shadow of the tall green safe: "Eh-eh, but you see how blight does always fall pon the forth generation? Blat-blanch, eh? White koo-ca-roach! Ain't no wonder madam wouldn't let she in the sun." She spoke in her chipped-up Dominican accent. Di chupsed as I took off running.

The sun! I never saw it. The whole of my childhood. (So at seventeen when I left Corpus Christi for the first time and went to England, I actually caught sunstroke—actually pitched a faint! Standing on top one of those openair doubledeck buses for the tourists. Imagine: going to England to catch sunstroke!) Not that the sun could darken my skin in any case. Not so a-tall. Only turn it a bruised version of the same dusty gray. And by next morning the bruise'd be gone. Skin which never declared or disclaimed itself. Which never washed *clean*. One way or another.

But hidden in my little room the sun could never reach me. (Not my bedroom, you understand—that was upstairs, on the first floor, cross from the kitchen.) This was a basement room—*half*-basement, I suppose—so that my window looked out only a little above ground level. Its frame had been nailed shut for as long as I had known it. Probably to keep out thieves. Perhaps manicou—monstrous, ratlike creatures which wandered in from the swamps at night, curried by the coolies and eaten with great relish. My window was covered with dust on the other side. Cobwebs with desiccated insects mummified at the corners. Before it there was yellowish dirt. A few dead-up weeds which'd surrendered to the lack of light. Above it stretched the wide, roofed-in gallery, running right round the house. In early morning gaps between the boards created a pattern on the dirt. Long slashes of yellow light. Shifting slowly as the sun shifted positions. The glass of my window seemed itself to have yellowed, the picture of my childhood already an old photograph before I got to it.

In one corner there was a small graveyard of rubbish which'd been left rusting beneath the gallery: an old washtub, bicycle frame, a stack of sheets of corrugated zinc, an overturned plow with its bright orange hooks reaching up in the air. My window faced the back of the house, so I could see the block of concrete which I knew to be the back steps on the other side. And on my side, hidden from the rest of the world, a bunch of old crocusssacks spread out where I imagined a lagahoo—our version of a troll, but deer-footed—would crawl under the gallery every night to sleep. For years Dulcianne kept me well geegeeree with her plan to crawl under ourselves after dark. Me holding up a bule-de-fay behind her, she a lasso to sling round his neck like a Yankee cowboy.

From my window, between the graveyard and the concrete block of steps, I could see a long rectangle of bright light. A wall of blue-green guineagrass sloping up behind it. (And if I closed my eyes tight tight to drown out the cicadas' sharp shrill, I could just hear the water beating against the rocks a hundred yards beyond; and I could almost see the brilliant blue that is only the Caribbean Sea, wedge of a white sailing ship shoving her way cross the horizon.) Within the luminated rectangle, time to time, I watched the household coming and going. Mostly Di and Cook and Ramsingh, on occasion mummy. Her corseted eighteen-inch waist, of which she was so proud. Due to the pitch of the ground, the position of the gallery overhead, I could see only the middle of their bodies. From just above their knees to just below their rib cages. I became an expert on the swing of hips. Could tell whether Di was in a sweet or a sour mood, only by the bounce of her bamsee.

In the parlor there was an ancient grandfather's clock which chimed the hours; I could hear it too easily through the ceiling of my room. Every day I counted down fifty-two chimes! At precisely ten o'clock Miss Rupert arrived, and for two hours she'd give me lessons. In middle age, and on the wings of a horned engagement to marry, she'd been sent out from England to look after her widowed father. Mummy said she considered the tropics her own purgatory-privé. I remember only her hands. They were perfectly shaped and ivory white, but what I remember best was the rubber thimble she wore on the index finger of her right hand. She used it to turn the pages of my books. It was pinkish-colored and gummy-looking, the sort of thing English bankclarks wore to count out stacks of money.

In my room I'd a miniature desk and chair, Miss Rupert an adult chair. She'd sit quietly at my side, leaning down a little to teach me the basic skills. Reading I found a boratious stunt. The stories so flothy and tamified, though I caught on effortlessly enough. The only pages I ever saw were the ones read under Miss Rupert's supervision, her gallanting rubber thimble pouncing on each word as I pronounced it aloud. I much preferred writing and sums, taking great pains in drawing out my letters and numbers. Particularly after I discovered that their character changed slightly depending upon which color they were drawn in. A green 7 was not a yellow 7, which was somehow wantish. A red A was quite different from a strong blue A. This part of my lessons I quite enjoyed, as I enjoyed pleasing Miss Rupert. She was kind, and patient, though I sensed she considered me and all about me somewhat tragic. Somewhat at a loss for hope. She looked forward to the finish of our two hours together, almost as much as I did.

The high point of my day was when Di brought my breakfast. Soon after Miss Rupert left. (For some reason we always called lunch breakfast—breakfast lunch.) I sat in my chair and she in the adult one, facing each other. Di feeding me with a big silver tablespoon. I could feed myself easily enough, but I preferred Di to do it, only to have her there. Usually I'd have a piece of fried fish or fricassee chicken, a slice of steaming buttered christophone, always a pressed dome of white rice. Always there'd be a tall glass of coconut water, my dessert the jelly remaining at the bottom once I'd drunk it down. Sometimes Di'd feed me the jelly using the same silver tablespoon. Or she'd leave me there with the tall grass upturned against my lips, my little hand reaching out to pat the bottom, till the jelly came sliding into my mouth.

Just as when she put me to sleep, Di would tell me stories while she fed me. Tales of the forest full of obeah and magic. Or she'd sing old calypsos in the patois I could not fully understand, though I thrilled at their slow, slanky rhythms. From the occasional wicked smile on her face, I knew her songs were well rude. The one about the lézard that got lost beneath the mademoiselle's guilets! I'd tarry about my breakfast as long as I could. Di, though, would always be in a flap. She'd have to get upstairs to set the table for mummy and daddy, often their guests too. To serve them their own breakfast.

Other than my miniature desk and chair, my books and colored pencils and paper, I'd a huge chest in my room filled with all the toys and dolls sent by my English granny. None of these things interested me in the least, and I'd've happily traded them away to have Daisy with me. To watch her scuttle back and forth her ratty head bobbing. Feed her grains of rice one by one from between my lips. With Daisy to play with, I might've even found my little room tolerable. I spent my time staring out the window. Mostly at nothing a-tall. Would wait two hours only to watch Cook's chuffy middle pass by for two seconds. On occasion an iridescent hummingbird would swoop beneath the gallery. A zandolee lizard'd zip past. On occasion I'd be entertained an hour at a stretch, a landcrab laboriously digging its hole.

2

I got into the habit of saying my chaplet. Not that I could've actually been praying. Simply bored. Perhaps I only did it in imitation of mummy. Daddy—who pronounced Catholic *Cartholic,* and spoke of all things related with contempt—daddy called it "rolling beads." As though it were some sort of feminine neurosis mummy had inherited. His jokes—overheard through the crack of the parlor door, my parents with visitors on the gallery shaking up sunset rum cocktails—his jokes were always a bit sad really. Always a betrayal of my father's own frustrations: "Jacqueline was so busy rolling beads she almost missed her honeymoon!" and "We'd have a slew of stragglers by now, if Jacqueline weren't so busy rolling beads!" It was a sense of impotency I perceived in his voice even at my young age. The only mental picture I have of the two of them together. Way I saw them on evenings when Di sent me running upstairs to kiss them goodnight: daddy sitting up beneath the lamp with the big estate ledger in his lap, stub of a pencil in his oversized hand, his brow furrowed; mummy supine in the dark, her right hand extended from the mattress with her chaplet dangling, gold cross glinting at the end. But most evenings daddy wouldn't've even reached his bed as yet. He'd still be out in the boilinghouse lambasting the poor coolies. On such evenings I'd crawl up into the big bed beside mummy. We'd say our beads together. Sometimes half the night, till daddy arrived.

Mummy's chaplet was pure gold; she'd had it blessed by the Pope himself on a trip to the Vatican. But my own was strung from tiny black pem-pem seeds, a local bush, with a silver crucifix at the end. I wore it like a necklace round my neck. It was a game I played with Dulcianne. That way, we told one another, a soukuyant could never suck our blood (they were the West Indian version of vampires, except soukuyants undressed their skins to become roving balls of fire, and in this shape they sucked their victims' necks). Dulcianne even told me she took a shaker of salt with her to the river, sprinkling the soukuyants' curled-up skins. So I always wore my chaplet round my neck, and without even realizing I got in the habit of saying it. Standing there with my nose squinged-up against the glass. Sometimes I'd say the Holy Maries silently, sometimes I'd mumble them, sometimes I'd say them aloud. But I'm sure I never thought about the actual words. Any more than I'd've stopped to study the lyrics of "God Save We Queen." I scarcely even thought about what my lips and my fingers were doing. And when I bounced-up with the final Glory Be, I began again without realizing either.

There was a brief period though, perhaps it lasted a week, when I did pray my chaplet in earnest. I was eight years of age. First time, I'm quite sure, that I actually became conscious of myself in my little room. Though I came to this awareness for very different reasons. My trouble started at Christmas Day Mass.

For the holidays we always received a chest from my English granny. It arrived weeks in advance, waiting beneath the staircase in the foyer for the actual day, the highlight of which was the ceremonious bursting of its metal bands. Always there was a box of shiny red apples (each wrapped in tissue and packed in straw), a triple-tiered box of Swiss chocolates, bottles of Spanish sherry and French champagne, tins of tea and English biscuits, perhaps a frock for mummy, a waistcoat or necktie for daddy. The balance of the chest contained presents for me: frocks and slips and hats, ribbons and bows, books, colored pencils and paper, tins of Lyles Golden Syrup, dolls with yellow hair and crystalline blue eyes which closed when I put them to sleep. The only gift which interested me, this particular Christmas, was a mauve-colored glassbottle of Dr Magic's Bathsalts, *Guaranteed to turn any skin soft and pearly white.* The gift itself was absurd. Not only did we have a sea full of salt just beyond the back door, what we did not have was a bathtub. I instantly thought to shake out the salts on a soukuyant's skin. And if it were a negro one — to watch it magically change colors.

I didn't have to report to Di for her to dress me for Christmas Mass until twelve o'clock (usually I had to wait till after Mass to go with Dulcianne to the river). So soon as I could I disappeared with my prodigious glassbottle. Di and Dulcianne did not live in the barracks with the coolie laborers. They had their own little mud-hut with a thatched roof, not far from our house. I hurried there and showed Dulcianne the bathsalts. We took off running along the trace, past the boilinghouse, the huge waterwheel where the canes were pressed before daddy brought the shining steam engine from America — coughing and belching and scaring the coolies half to death! — to the river in the forest behind. We looked in all the caves and the holes and the crevices between the rocks. On the smooth bolderstones beneath the overhanging trees. But we could not find a single soukuyant's skin. In our frustration we tried the salts on other victims. A pale-blue rivercrab. Pinkish crayfish. Lime-green iguana. Each time we were further scandalized. Finally Dulcianne chupsed and complained, "These damn salts ain't worth a windball!" And she dumped the remainder of the glassbottle down a crevice where she said she'd found soukuyants' skins before. She corked it back and pelted it hard against a bolderstone. It only bounced off, and the two of us stood leaning over the cliff with our hands on our knees. Watching Dr Magic disappear down the river.

Time as I reached church I was dead exhausted. All I could do to keep from booting-off asleep. My head felt like a giant balloon filled with water, like it weighed a thousand pounds. I could scarcely keep it balanced on my thin neck. It kept threatening to tumble backward or forward, and I kept catching it at the last moment. Jerking myself awake. The church was full to bursting. For half of them it was the only day they came all year long. My father was one; it was the standard Christmas present asked of him by mummy, that he accompany her to the High Mass. Usually—to mummy's mortification—he remained outside parked beneath the huge poinciana tree. Shining his silver Ford motorcar and pumping the tires one by one. Till Mass was finished.

But this Christmas Day I sat squeezed between them. Our Irish Monsignor—we called him Bumblebee—took advantage of his captive audience and unleashed a homily full of fire and brimstone. To our favor he was incomprehensible anyway. Particularly when excited. Particularly when he spoke English. I was caught in one of those tingling moments between asleep and awake. All in a sudden my head snapped forward, and it was as though I were hearing his voice for the first time: *"Every one of you who has performed a mixed marriage has committed a mortal sin!"*

Daddy moved to get up—he wanted to bolt—but mummy reached cross me and put her hand firmly on his thigh. Held him down. Then he seemed to burst into flames. My father did, sitting there beside me. Like an instantaneous combustion. Like I'd moved up next to the big fire in the boilinghouse—that intense. Yet he did not sweat. (The English never do, Cook said, neither sweat nor smell.) *I* sweated for him. *Me.* I sweated like a man. Like Ramsingh when he chopped wood. Like the coolies when they cutlashed the canes. So by the time Mass was finished I was soaked through. My lace gown stuck to my back and arms, buckled shoes like pools of water, my knickers so wet and heavy between my legs as I genuflected and turned to leave, I was afraid they'd drop down round my ankles and trip me—send me flying on top my face.

Nobody said a word as daddy pelted the Ford home. Through the whole of Christmas dinner. The champagne bottle unopened in the center of the table, cold beads collecting into droplets and sliding down the green glass. I continued sweating like a grown man.

3

My father never said a word concerning the religion after that day. Not even in jest. Not about mummy's rolling beads, nor Monsignor's visits for afternoon tea, nor mummy's going to Sunday Mass. Because of course she continued to go, though now she had Ramsingh drive her in the old horsebuggy. And of course she continued to take me with her. The two of us dressed like brides in white lace, sitting on the bench behind Ramsingh, our long white veils trailing out behind us. My father could not have *prevented* my going, even if he'd cared enough about it to try. It was written into my parents' marriage contract—this, I found out later. Not a contract with God, or the Law, or even Monsignor. It was a contract with *gran'maman* (from infancy I called her MuMu, known to me only as the exquisite woman in the portrait at the top of the stairs, next to my goat-face grandfather). Mummy's French-Creole mother: *The children will be raised Catholic.*

And so I was. Whether or not my father resented it.

But for the moment I had my own trouble to contend with: if mummy and daddy had committed a mortal sin, where did that leave me? I *was* their mortal sin. The product of my parents' mixed marriage. Of course, I was too young at the time to know anything of the mechanics of sex. Of how such mechanics translated into racial inheritance, into skin color. But certainly I knew enough to understand the implications of the word "mixed." Particularly in connection with the word "sin." Enough to see myself, even in my childhood imagination, as a still greater atrocity: I was the culmination of a long *series* of mortal sins. A *history* of mortal sins. Of mummy's and daddy's sin. Of MuMu's and my grandfather's sin—the horrid man I could only scarcely recall, lifting me every morning to kiss the portrait of my grandmother: "Fais une bais à la MuMu, bébé!" I was the end product of the original sin of my great-grandparents. The great-grandparents I knew nothing more about than what I'd overheard Cook say, curled up in the shadow of the tall green safe: that he was one them French *Comte,* true true! She, he own selfsame Yoruba slave!

It was a story I knew only the outline of at the time. Yet it weighed down heavy on me like an entire history. And as I stood on my stack of storybooks, nose and chin pressed against the glass—locked into my little room, a child eight years of age—I rolled my beads as seriously as if I could redeem the entire history myself. I rolled my beads for a whole week. Over and over.

Studying every word. Until I had no voice remaining. No breath a-tall. Then I rolled my beads in silence. And the whole time I continued sweating bolts.

I had no idea what to ask Mother Mary *for.* Or Papa God. I knew only that I had to pray. Every time my thoughts drifted. Bumblebee's voice rose up out of yellow dirt to bring me back. Miss Rupert had gone to Barbados for the holidays, so she did not interrupt my prayers either. I fell into a kind of trance. I fell basodee. Booboo-loops. Bufutu. As if I were sleeping with my eyes open. Though I wasn't tired a'tall. I felt like I could go on saying my beads forever. Caught up in the endless repetition. The cycles of repetitions. In truth, I'm sure I burnt a fever. (Maybe I'd even caught a freshcold playing on the river with Dulcianne that Christmas Day? some strange tropical virus?) Because this was a *physical* condition. My little body attempting to hold down its temperature with all the sweating. Actual streams running down my spinecord. Back of my arms. Legs. My eyes unable to focus on things. To shift between foreground and background—as though I were stuck in some blurry, middle range. I became even less aware of myself in my little room. And when Di unbolted the door at four o'clock, I didn't run first thing to Daisy's coop, then to find Dulcianne. I went upstairs to my room. Drew the blinds and climbed in under the tent of mosquito netting. Lay on my back, eyes wide open, still rolling beads.

4

I was downstairs in my little room doing the same on New Year's Day. A week later. Only one remaining in the house. Di had come with my breakfast early, tried her best to get me to eat. But she'd given up and left the tray there. Gone with Cook to a fête in town. Mummy and daddy had not even returned yet from their own Old Year's Eve fête the night before. I stood as always on my stack of books, nose and chin leaning against the glass, chaplet dangling from my hand. And I'm sure Dulcianne must've crouched before my window a long time before I actually saw her. She must have thought that I was ill and had come to find me; I'd not seen Dulcianne for the whole week. And perhaps from the dazed look on my face—even through the filthy glass—she realized there *was* something wrong with me.

As usual she wore only her knickers. Now she stood straight up to slip them off (either of us could have stood easily beneath the gallery without bouncing our heads). We'd seen each other naked countless times. Were quite used to pulling off our knickers and jumping into the river. On long hot summer afternoons we swam together naked for hours when Di took us to Huevos Beach. But there, hidden beneath the gallery, alone on that New Year's Day, for the first time I noticed Dulcianne's nakedness. Her beautiful skin—golden, rich like creamed coffee. In the yellow light it shone like molten metal. Because clearly Dulcianne was "mixed" too—the good mix, the happy mix—though Di never said anything about her father. Chupsed every time Dulcianne or I asked.

Now I felt faintly embarrassed. Suddenly faintly thrilled by Dulcianne's nakedness. Now my own skin tingled. The way it did when we first jumped in the river on a hot day. My chaplet slipped with a loud *clack* to the concrete floor, but I scarcely noticed. I continued staring up at Dulcianne. She knelt in front of my window, sat back on her heels, toes pigeoned, her bony knees almost touching the glass. Now she balled up her knickers. Used them to wipe a circle clean on the glass in front of my face. They were black by the time she'd finished. Now she looked at me for a second, closed her eyes, leaned slowly forward. Kissed my lips through the glass.

I closed my own eyes too. Pressed my own lips to glasspane too.

We remained like that for a full minute. An hour. For the whole of that long New Year's afternoon: it was an instant locked in time behind glass.

When it was over I found myself smiling. Dulcianne too. My skin was tingling all over. Crawling with invisible ants. We did not attempt to communicate with words. We simply smiled. Then Dulcianne took off running cross the dirt, a yellow stripe down each shin, her knickers a gray flag waving from her hand.

I remained with my nose and chin still pressed against the glass. Still smiling. After awhile I realized that for the first time in a week I'd stopped sweating. Instead of the perspiration running down my spinecord, there was still a trace of the ants streaming faintly up it. I actually felt calm. Cool now. And I could not remember what had tormented me so for the previous week. I said to myself: *You are eight years old. It is New Year's Day.*

Then I got down from my stack of books. Went to my desk and selected a yellow pencil from the metal box. I climbed back up. All the way cross the bottom of the white windowframe, with great precision, I wrote out:

LILLA GRANDSOL, 8 YEARS OLD, 1 JANUARY 1935

5

That evening, when I came in from feeding Daisy and putting her away in her coop, I found mummy on the back gallery. Di had just finished washing the holidays out of her hair, and now she was brushing it. The air smelling faintly of chamomile. Mummy was sitting in the old wicker rocking chair wearing her nightgown, head tilted back, her beautiful auburn hair almost touching the floorboards. The sun was just setting on a flat sea, and mummy's hair shone like flaming casurina needles as Di pulled the brush down through it. It made a lovely sound. Like walking barefoot over dry sand. I stood beside Di, watching and listening, still dreamy from the afternoon. And without even pausing to think about it, I asked, "Mummy, what's wrong with me? Why am I a mortal sin? Cause I came out a blat-blanch?"

I saw the look of horror on Di's face before I saw it on my mother's.

She swung round and slapped me hard enough to send me backward sitting on the flooring. I was so stunned I jumped up again straight. She slapped me again, and I tumbled backward again. Then I realized my mother was crying.

"You have committed no sin," she said calmly. "How can a child commit a mortal sin? How possibly? It is we who have sinned because your father is a Protestant." She was silent a moment. Then the look flashed cross her face again.

"Pat plus de blat-blanch!" she screamed, and I was afraid she'd slap me a third time. I took off running.

As I lay on my bed that night, for the first time I could not wait to get downstairs into my little room. All of a sudden I could not be sure Dulcianne had come to visit me that afternoon. That it happened for true. It all felt like a dream I'd conjured up. And then that confusing business with mummy! I wanted to be sure. To get downstairs before the circle on the glass disappeared. Before the dust covered it up. When I finally fell asleep I dreamt that I was writing on an old piece of yellowed paper with a white pencil. But the words were already there, already written out in white. They were my letters, just the way I would shape them. And as I moved the pencil cross the paper my words disappeared. When I awoke I was swimming in sweat.

The circle was there on the glass! I saw it the instant I entered my room. Shining brightly as a small oval mirror. Soon as Di turned the key I ran and climbed up on my stack of books. Verified that my writing was still there too. Then I got down and went to my desk. I selected a blue pencil this time. I climbed back up, distraught to find that no space remained along the bottom frame of my window. Then I realized I had no idea how to spell the words regardless. For a quick moment I could not even remember which language they belonged to. There was a small blank space before the first letter, the L. Another after the last digit, the 5. Each large enough for me to squeeze in a letter. In each I carefully wrote a blue B.

6

Dulcianne had been strictly forbidden by her mother to play under the gallery, and it was nearly four months before she came to visit me again. I watched the circle on the glass disappearing slowly beneath a new layer of dust. Each morning I was further disheartened as Di closed the door, and I ran to climb up on my stack of books. Miss Rupert returned and my lessons continued, but now mummy lengthened them to three hours every morning. When I was not with her, or with Di eating my breakfast, I continued in my old habit of rolling beads. But my chaplet saying became mindless again. A way to pass the time. Escape the boredom. Now, though, I rolled my beads with my eyes closed. I rolled my beads with my lips pressed against the glass. Center of my slowly disappearing circle.

At four o'clock when Di let me out of my room I ran as always to collect Daisy. Then to look for Dulcianne. On Sundays after Mass we went to the river as always to look for soukuyants' skins. When we grew hot we threw ourselves into the water. But now we swam with our knickers on. We hiked them up round our waists and let them dry on our bodies. We planned the usual monkeyshines, spoke of the usual things – duens and soukuyants and diablesses – even of the lagahoo sleeping in his bed of crocuss-sacks beneath the gallery. But we never mentioned that New Year's afternoon.

Still, though I told her nothing, I longed for Dulcianne to come and visit me again. As I watched the circle on the glass fade, I began to lose hope. I longed for that sensation on the surface of my skin. But when I closed my eyes and tried to imagine it – tried to see Dulcianne's golden skin – the feeling seemed very far away. Then one afternoon I made the obvious discovery. Or perhaps I only became aware of what my body all along had already known.

I was standing on my stack of storybooks, triple points of chin-lips-nose squinged against glass. In my right hand I held a bead of my chaplet, rolling it closely back and forth between my thumb and index finger. Eyes closed, words of the Holy Mary floating through my head. Slowly I began to feel the ants crawling up my spinecord again. Pins-and-needles-prickling-earlobes. The tips of my elbows. Backs of my knees. Somewhere down deep at the bottom of my stomach. Tingling—below. It was my left hand, discovering the way on its own, pressing through my frock and my knickers beneath. Gently pressing. And I found that if I pressed in a certain way, the ants *streamed*.

7

I was nine years of age. I called it "rolling beads" too. Gave it the same name. In the secret. To myself. Or rather, I called the two activities by the same name. Because for me they became inseparable. Now, when I stood on my stack of books with my nose pressed against the glass, eyes closed, chaplet dangling from my right hand, my left was busy also. The more I continued, the more pleasurable the sensation became. The more the ants streamed. (It was years later, an adult, that I lay in my bed rolling beads in just this way, and a quote from the Bible flashed back at me: words of St Paul. And I couldn't help but smile! *Let not thy right hand know what thy left hand doth.* So I'd been quite right to confuse the two, to call the two activities by the same name!)

I had almost forgotten about Dulcianne. Forgotten my longing for her to come and visit me again. Because when I opened my eyes and found her there crouched before my window, I was well embarrassed. But this time I was *not* also thrilled. This time I was vex. From the smile on her face—perhaps, again, from the smile on my own—I could tell she knew exactly what I'd been doing. (Dulcianne was a year older, had more than likely made these discoveries a year before I did.) Her smile was a new one. Brazenly wicked. It made me vex. As if she'd done something to betray our friendship. But in a flash she stripped off her knickers again, not saying a word. Again she got down on her knees, sitting back with her legs tucked beneath her, and again she wiped a circle clean on the glass in front of my face. She leaned forward and pressed her lips against it, closed her eyes. This time I kept my own eyes open. Watched as best I could. In one hand she held the balled-up knickers. The other she placed below her belly—I could hardly see – but I knew good enough what *she* was doing too! The wicked smile printed on her face. Now I felt embarrassed for true. For both of us. I wanted to get down from my stack of books. I tried – I actually tried to pull my face away – but now my lips were stuck like laglee to the glass! I shut my eyes quick quick. And I did not open them for a very long time. When I did, I was happy to see that she had gone.

But as I waited for Di to unbolt the door at four o'clock, slowly my anger faded. When she did arrive to let me out, I went straight to look for Dulcianne. Didn't even remember to collect Daisy first. Of course, we mentioned nothing about her having come to see me that afternoon. Certainly nothing about rolling beads. (To this day I've never told anyone I called it that, and if Dulcianne had a special name for it herself, she never told me what it was.) Though we played together every morning and every evening. As if we had some unspoken rule between us: we never mentioned Dulcianne's afternoon visits. Nor what we did with our eyes closed. Lips pressed together on either side of the glass.

Because she came to visit me again the following afternoon. And then again two afternoons after that. Sometimes she came to visit me three afternoons in succession. We did not plan these visits, and I did not anticipate them in any way. At least not in the beginning. I did not worry that she would come this afternoon or the next. If she didn't come to see me beneath the gallery for a whole week, I wasn't much bothered. I waited patiently at my window. Often rolling beads on my own. Time seemed not to matter then. As in a sweet dream, when the only worry is waking.

It went on for nearly a year. When I think back, I'm still a bit astonished that it could've gone on so long. Dulcianne and I shared this secret life together. That we never spoke of these visits – never mentioned them to one another – made them all the more secret. All the more special. The longer our meetings continued, the more special they became. To the point I began to fear something would happen to prevent them. Still, I was not terribly worried. In my childlike sense of the world, I decided that Dulcianne and I were protected by a kind of magic. By a spell: nothing could possibly happen to separate us, so long as we did not speak of what we did together. So long as we did not say it to make it real.

How I wished I had some way to communicate this to Dulcianne! But in order to do so, I'd have to say it. And that would break the spell. Then I thought perhaps that I could write it. And I could leave the letter somewhere for her to find by chance. I began to compose it in my mind:

> *Dear Dulcianne,*
> *I have to tell you this secret. We must never speak of what we do together. Not to each other or anyone else. To do so will bring a great tragedy.*
> *Sincerely,*
> *Lilla Grandsol*

I thought about it so often I began to see the actual writing. Could imagine the letter in crooks of certain trees we climbed together. In crevices between certain bolderstones by the river. Then I realized Dulcianne had not even learned to read yet. And I decided that in any case writing was far more dangerous than speaking. Because I'd overheard Cook talking about an obeah spell to give someone a fever, simply by writing their name on a piece of paper and passing a match beneath it. Or bruising them up by writing their name on the bottom of your shoe and treading upon it.

If I could just *think* the thought into Dulcianne's head! Dream it into her dream! In my frustration I began for the first time to hate words, language, which seemed suddenly such an awkward way to communicate. Which seemed suddenly to come *between* people, like the glasspane between our lips, rather than bridging us together. My only consolation was that somehow Dulcianne realized how the magic worked. Somehow she understood.

8

Then one Sunday afternoon, as we lay on our backs on a smooth white bolderstone drying ourselves beneath the sun—we now wore bathing costumes beneath our frocks when we went to the river—Dulcianne rolled her head to the side to look at me.

"How it is you always praying chaplet *then?*" she asked.

My spine stiffened.

Dulcianne chupsed. "Me ain't talking to waste me breath, you know!"

My neck felt like an iron bar. Like a rusty standpipe. I stared up through the bright leaves. Through the green light.

Now Dulcianne rolled onto her side, holding her head up on her bent arm. "Eh?" she said. "How it is you always praying chaplet *then?*"

I swung onto my side and slapped Dulcianne so hard her head tumbled backward. Thudding against the rock. She was so stunned she sat up quickly and I slapped her again. Then I grabbed up my frock and took off running.

9

When I went to Daisy's coop the following afternoon and found her dead I was relieved. Even as I undid her stiff toes from the wire at the bottom, and raised her swollen little body to press against my breast, tears already streaming down my face, I could only feel a little relieved. It was not the tragedy I'd come to expect.

"Scorpion bite she," said Ramsingh, "is for that she swell-up so." He promised another to replace her. A gray-and-white-spotted guineachick if I wished. I told him I could not bear to have another fowl for a pet.

I went and found Dulcianne, and together we gave Daisy a proper burial. There beneath the flamboyant tree at the back of the house. We'd played with her beneath the same tree so many afternoons. Daisy fighting her way out of the mounds of red petals we piled on top her, her ratty head jerking this way and that. Ramsingh painted two short boards white and nailed them together into a cross. We mashed seagrapes in a calabash to make a purple paste, and with a stick I wrote her name cross the crosspiece. Then I turned it over and on one arm of the back I wrote M.L.O., which I told Dulcianne stood for *mourned by loved ones.* On the other arm I wrote D. + L.

Dulcianne came to visit me beneath the gallery the following afternoon. She stayed a long time. Long after the grandfather's clock in the parlor had chimed for two, then three o'clock. I began to worry that Di would come soon to let me out. I kept telling myself, *In just a moment you're going to open your eyes, In just a moment you're going to climb down from these books.* When I did open my eyes Di was there. But not in my room. She was outside, beneath the gallery, crouched behind Dulcianne. I tried to scream but no sound came from my throat. Tried to get down from my books but my legs wouldn't work. She remained crouched behind Dulcianne for the longest time, and I stood paralyzed. Eyes wide open, staring up at Di. At last she grabbed Dulcianne's arm and pulled her away from the window.

We had never seen Di so vex. "Nasty is *nastiness* you children could carry on with, oh *loas!*" she bawled. "And D-ann, how many times I *hot* tell you stay out from under the whitepeople gallery! Papa*yo!*" She told Dulcianne that if she ever caught her there in future, she'd cut the skin of she backside so bad it would never again want to see chair.

By this time Dulcianne had pulled back on her knickers. She was twelve now and wore a frock. I was not quite eleven, and I pulled my own knickers up from round my knees. Di grabbed Dulcianne's arm and pulled her out behind her, crouching low so as not to bounce her head. And on the way out Di did something peculiar; she shoved Dulcianne ahead into the light, and she grabbed up all the lagahoo's bed of crocusssacks. She disappeared with her bundle behind the cloud of dust, yellow light filtering through.

I cannot be sure whether Di told mummy what she'd seen us doing that afternoon. I rather doubt it. Yet it was only a few days later when mummy announced that at the end of the summer, in September, I'd be going to live in the Ursuline Convent in Henly. All the way on the other side of the island. My father looked up quickly from his plate, but he remained silent. It was a Sunday evening. The one day of the week we ate dinner together. I stared at the pitcher of icewater in the center of the table, and soon I was sweating too.

My previous experience with nuns, when I'd made my First Communion, had been horrid enough. In catechism class they'd told me that I was "dull," though in comparison to the five or six other children, I knew that I was not. When I arrived on the day dressed in a white muslin frock with tiny black polkadots—mummy'd had it made specially for the occasion—they made me take it off and go through the ceremony in my slip. "Not all the children," an older, harsh one said, "can afford a new dress to make their First Communion!" The other children laughed at me. A little negro boy said, "Look the blat-blanch! She making she communion in she underdrawers!"

I knew nothing about the Ursuline Convent, except that this was where mummy had been sent to school herself as a child. She never spoke about it. One evening, when I found her sitting alone on the back gallery, I asked about the Ursuline sisters. "Oh," she said, "you'll find them very sweet, very simple. They're a semicloistered order. They do not get out much into the world." I was not sure what "semi-cloistered" meant, but to me the term suggested some slight physical deformity. A twisted hand or a clubbed foot. Which—I told myself—was surely why they wore those long skirts in all the heat, why they always kept their hands tucked suspiciously inside their sleeves. Surely why they seldom let them outside the spiked convent gates.

Now I began to dread leaving the safety of my little room. Every afternoon when Di came to let me out, I knew I was one day closer. I did not want to leave Di, but more than anything I did not want to leave Dulcianne. I could not imagine life without her. Could not imagine waking up in the morning without running first thing to the washstone to meet her. Dulcianne already there catching tadpoles in the little stream, or helping Di to beat out the clothes against the stone. And in three seconds my own skinny arms would be thick with suds to my elbows too, laughing and slinging a jersey against the stone with all my might—*swatch! swatch! swatch!*—the bright morning air floating with bubbles. Drifting away between the tall cyprus trees behind us.

But ever since Di had put a stop to Dulcianne's visits beneath the gallery, I felt almost as though we'd already been separated. Almost as though I'd already left. We didn't talk much about my departure. Though Dulcianne made me promise that before I did leave, we'd crawl in under the gallery finally to catch the lagahoo—his bed had appeared again behind the back steps.

I managed to dissuade her until my final day. A Sunday, but we did not go to the river after Mass; instead we got Ramsingh to help us make the bule-de-fay, filling a rumbottle with pitchoil and shoving a rag in the top. We told him we needed it to explore a cave by the river. Ramsingh even gave us a big box of kitchen matches. Dulcianne cut down a clothesline to make her lasso, and she practiced all day long, lassoing everything in sight: chairs and buckets and bushes. Even the hambone from out the cauldron of splitpea soup cooling on the sill. This so confused Cook that she turned round and sat down on top the live coalpot. She jumped up bawling for Jesus's mercy, running for the pipe in the yard, her bamsee smoking behind her. Then she went after Dulcianne and me with her kitchen knife.

Though I wanted more than ever to listen to one of Di's stories on my last evening, I told her that I was too old for bedtime stories now. That I wanted to be left alone. It was as painful an untruth as I've told in my life. I waited a couple minutes after she'd closed the door behind her. Then I crawled out from under the mosquito netting. I stepped out my nightgown and pulled a frock over my head, buckled on my sandals. Then I eased the door open. I couldn't get out through the screen door at the back of the kitchen because Di would still be there, grinding the coffee and putting it to filter for the following morning. I slipped down the hall into the parlor. Climbed up over my father's desk to get out through the window. Out onto the gallery.

Dulcianne was there waiting for me by the washstone at the side of the house. My hand was trembling so badly I could not strike the match to light the bule-de-fay. There was probably still enough light to see without it, in addition to the porch light above the kitchen door, but Dulcianne was insistent we do everything according to plan. She chupsed and lit it herself. Then she adjusted the burning rag, poking and pulling, her bare fingers working cautiously in the blue flame. She was all excited; I was scared to death.

Our plan was to circle round the flamboyant tree to the concrete block of steps, crouch down beside it, then to rush in and catch the lagahoo unaware. By the time we reached the steps I was breathing so hard I was sure I'd pitch a faint. We crouched beside the block of concrete, me panting, Dulcianne preparing her lasso. She looked at me and mouthed "one," "two," "three," then she took off round the steps. It was all I could do to grasp the back of her frock, close my eyes and let her practically pull me behind her. The bule-de-fay held carefully to the side. I'm sure I stood there a full minute before I dared open my eyes. When I did—and I raised up the torchlight to see better—I found the same thing I saw every day from the window of my room: a bunch of old crocusssacks spread out on the yellow dirt.

Dulcianne chupsed. "Must be we come too early. The lagahoo ain't reach as yet."

"I'm sure he's not coming!" I said.

Dulcianne chupsed again. "How you could say so easy?"

She decided the only thing for us to do was wait. She extinguished the bule-de-fay with a clap of her hands over the flaming rag, and we settled ourselves on the ground at the side of the steps. Our backs leaning against the cool concrete. In no time a-tall we were both asleep.

10

I have no idea how long we'd been sleeping before Dulcianne shook me awake. Now it was pitch dark. I could hardly see her face, but I knew Dulcianne was excited again. There were growling sounds coming from beneath the gallery. From behind the steps. Animal noises. *Hurt* sounds. Dulcianne had already lit and adjusted the bule-de-fay, which she now handed to me. I was still half-asleep. The torchlight felt so heavy I could scarcely hold it up. Dulcianne readied her lasso, and again she mouthed "one," "two," "three." Again I grabbed the back of her frock and shut my eyes. Let her pull me behind her. But this time the bule-de-fay slipped from my hand, outing itself when it hit the ground.

I stood beneath the gallery behind Dulcianne, eyes closed tight. When I opened them I could see nothing in the darkness. I blinked. Still nothing. I could hear the growling, *moving* sounds, a few feet in front of Dulcianne. Then I began to make out something—*appendages:* a human arm and a dog's tail and a deer's cloven foot. Then I felt Dulcianne grab my elbow and pull me behind her. But now I was awake. Now I had to see! I pulled back. Dulcianne held tightly and dragged me out from under the gallery. All the way round to the side of the house, me struggling to free myself from her grasp.

"I want to *see!*" I bawled.

Dulcianne refused to release me. It was very dark. I could not see her face.

"Let me *go!*" I shouted.

Then she shoved me away hard. With the force of my own pulling I went sprawling against the washstone, bruising my forearm and the side of my face. A gritty taste in my mouth. I lay against the stone, crying now, Dulcianne standing above me in the dark. She still held the coil of rope. I could hardly see, but I knew how vex she was, and I could not understand why. It was all happening very fast. Dulcianne held the coil of rope in both hands. She swung it with all her strength, lashing me across the side of my face. She disappeared into the darkness.

I lay against the stone a long time. Crying, angry, very confused. Eventually I must have gotten up and gone to my room. Because I awoke the following morning in my bed, a crust of dried blood between my lips. But surprisingly no mark on my face when I looked in the mirror. I washed out my mouth in the basin, and when I'd finished there was no sign remaining from the events of the previous night. I did not see Dulcianne that morning, but no one else seemed even aware that anything unusual had happened.

And it was not until we'd driven for several hours, mummy sitting beside daddy and me in the back seat, and we were climbing down from the mountains of the Northern Range with the air very cool—the Ford occasionally swallowed-up completely by a misty cloud—the whole world *liquid,* and dripping, and smelling of wet earth. When all in a sudden my father coughed twice and made a peculiar sound to clear his throat: ha-*ham!* At that moment my eyes began to focus on what my imagination had concealed from me in the dark. All those appendages. And I realized that it was *he* whom I had seen: my father and Di. *They* were the lagahoo hidden beneath the gallery.

II. SECOND DECADE

1

The convent was papery crimson bougainvillea splashed up against thick walls of coral blocks. Hot sun beating down on the playing-field. Smooth shadows beneath the banyan trees. The silver trickle of the fountain gurgling beneath moss-covered black stones in the grotto where the statue of Holy Mary hid. Where each morning on our way to chapel, still half-asleep, we paused to whisper together: "Blesséd Mother pierce me through, in my heart each wound renew!" Sin and suffering. Darkness and light. Hell and heaven.

The girls, too, were of contrary types. The boarders—coming from far as Guyana, Barbados, Trinidad—the boarders were little angels. Shy and sweet and very beautiful. Perfectly well-behaved. Most, like me, were French and English mixed. Otherwise they were Spanish and English. Most, like me, had families which went back generations in the West Indies—last remnants of what we once fondly called the "Plantocracy." The day students were little horrors. Perfect Warrahoons. They lived on estates in the country, nearby enough that they could be driven in in the mornings. Most were pure English. A few had even been born away. All very fair: springy blond locks and crystalline blue eyes, or carrot-colored hair and freckle-peppered skin. They stared at me through squinged-up nostrils. Hesitant, for the moment, to pass a remark. I looked down at the flooring of polished coral blocks, studying the millions upon millions of crushed fossilized animals, thinking: *Whitee-*

pokee-penny-a-pound, if-you-don't-like-me-lick-me-down! But I didn't dare say it: I was the only girl in the convent with visible negro blood.

And there were two sorts of nuns. Different as the materials of their habits: heavy black serge—even in all the heat—from the veils on their heads to the hems of their skirts at their ankles, sleeves at their wrists; with bibs of bright white cotton, rising to from their wimples under their chins (we called them "turkey-wimples"), passing behind their cheeks and circling their faces. There were the nuns, like Sister Frances, who were simple and generous. Softhearted. She slept behind the compartment of white screens in the younger girls' dormitory. Sister Frances was a chuff-chuff. Fat and happy. Her eyes big, and brown, and laughing like a cow's own. Every night before we fell asleep, she read to us from a book of child-saints the size of a small tombstone. Pictures on the pasteboard pages: Burnadette of Lourdes, the children of Fatima. "Our Blesséd Mother chose to reveal herself only to children," she would tell us, her accent a singsong Irish. "In heaven she surrounds herself only with children . . . like each of you . . ." and we'd drift off to sleep.

Then there were the nuns like Mother Marie-Bernard, who taught catechism to all the grades and oversaw the older girls' dormitory. She told us about hell, as if from personal experience. Knew all of our secret, wicked thoughts. Better than we knew them ourselves. Unlike the other sisters, Mother Marie-Bernard had been born and raised in Trinidad, yet she took care to speak with a proper English accent. But whenever she grew vex or excited, she spilled into rank Creole. This made us more geegeeree still. The idea that she was one of us. Could have been any of our not-so-distant great-aunts. The older girls laughed, said she was going through the change. She couldn't *help* but be miserable. They called her "Mother Marie-Bernard of the Burning Mustache Bush"—"B.M.B." for short. And her mustache was bushy for true: a furry caterpillar crawling cross her lip. Colored a fire-engine-red.

She wasted little time in getting round to her *second* favorite topic in catechism class. It was waiting for us one afternoon when we entered the classroom after recess—we'd scarcely been there at the convent a week—written cross the blackboard in tall capital letters: SIXTH COMMANDMENT OF THE CHURCH: NOT TO MARRY A PERSON WHO IS NOT A CATHOLIC. "Most of you," she said, "are the children of mixed marriages. For most of you, it is your foremost duty in life to pray for the conversion of your Protestant mother or father. Otherwise . . ." and here she lowered her voice, here she began flicking her long bony hand in the air—a peculiar West Indian gesture—her index finger smacking loud against her thumb in a series of sharp quick *clacks. "Otherwise they going burn-up sure-certain in everlasting hell!"*

One of the little girls fled the classroom in tears. I was not upset a-tall. I could only sit feeling the heat of pine bench striking up through my navy pleated skirt into my thighs. Striking up through my wrists just exposed below the cuffs of my starched white shirt (short sleeves were immodest!), my hands folded against the edge of the hot pine tabletop. And I could only think that hell was too happy a place for my father. Now Mother Marie-Bernard would tell us to close our eyes, fold our hands now, meditate on the eternal flames! pray for the conversion of our loved ones! But I could never pray. I could only close my eyes and push my little wrists still harder into the edge of the hot tabletop, and I could only whisper: *Please Dulcianne! Forgive me my father . . . OUR father, who will one day burn in hell!*

2

I used to dread waking up in the morning. Dread the sound of the chapel bell *ba-bong ba-bong ba-bong* already six o'clock. I'd squeeze my eyes shut and pretend I hadn't heard it. But the little girl on either side would already be sprinkling her face with water from the basin on the table between our beds. Already stepping out of her nightgown into her "bloomers," the knickers devised for us by the convent (awful billowy things made of a stiff, tullelike material, bands of thick elastic cutting into each thigh and clamping round our waists). Already dressing in our uniforms and pinning our veils quick by touch to our hair—no mirrors in the dormitory—hurrying to line up to walk in silence to chapel. We were not even permitted to brush our teeth for fear that a few drops of water would slip by accident down our throats. All fasting since the evening before in order to take Communion: no morsel of food or drink to have entered our stomachs for twelve hours. Every morning of every day.

But even when we lined up again to walk to the cafeteria after Mass, we could bear neither the sight nor the smell of the hot porridge already waiting for us on the tables. Already smoking-up! At least the cafeteria was cool—it had no walls—only a piece of the same corrugated zinc roofing, same color of sun-faded crimson, with the kitchen a separate building a short distance away. And if the porridge had not already been served the steaming bowls were plunked down before us by languid, blue-skinned maids who never spoke to us or even looked in our faces. Who seemed to resent us, perhaps because their own children would be fortunate to eat a bowl of the same lumpy porridge the whole day. But hot porridge in the tropics! I suppose it was the cheapest and most nourishing thing they could think to give us. Perhaps it was what they fed schoolchildren in England—the Ursuline Sisters were, after all, an English order. And the milk the maids sloshed from a pitcher into our bowls was already on the point of turning, if we were lucky. Most of the time it'd already turned (there was little refrigeration in those days, if there was any in the convent a-tall). We doctored it up with plenty sugar. Gave it a stir and swallowed it down quickly, even if we were already sweating. Because once it cooled it turned thick like laglee. And of course, we had to lick down every *scrap.*

One morning one of the maids put salt in the sugarbowl by accident (or perhaps not). The sugarbowl which ended up in front of me. I sprinkled on a spoonful, stirred, tasted; sprinkled on a spoonful, stirred, tasted. Then I moved the sugarbowl closer. Shoveled on three heaping spoonfuls before I realized it was salt. I didn't know what to do. The other girls were already lining up at the far side of the cafeteria, waiting to return to the dorms. But the older girl who was monitor at our table, a terribly shy girl from Martinique named Justine, did not have the authority to let me go until I'd finished. And I suppose she was frightened of getting reprimanded herself. She offered an encouraging smile. I tried swallowing a few mouthfuls. Quickly as I could. By now I was already sweating—though the porridge had long since turned to cold glue—perhaps there were tears as well. Because I remember three big drops padding into my bowl. I looked up at Justine. There was strict silence during meals. I tried to whisper as quietly as possible: *"Salt!"* She didn't understand.

By this time Sister Ellen had come over, one of the sisters of Mother Marie-Bernard's camp, of the same disposition. She gave Justine a sign and she got up—we were the only two girls left in the cafeteria. Sister Ellen walked round the table and stood behind me. I couldn't see her, only feel the heat of her presence. I continued sweating. Reaching with every mouthful. But I continued swallowing. There was nothing in my stomach – only the porridge I had eaten and a yellowish bile – which I vomited into the same bowl. "Enough!" she said, and I listened to the quick claps of her leather shoes retreating cross the flooring. When I got back to the dormitory I collapsed in Sister Frances' arms, burying my face in her white bib. Until we heard the schoolbell clanging in the distance, and she smiled and I took off running for the classrooms.

3

I remained as solitary a child in the convent as I'd been at home. Perhaps more so. Because at least at home I'd had a companion in Dulcianne. Now I had no friends a-tall. Certainly not among the day students, the whitee-pokees! They had me terrified. But I made no effort to make friends among the boarders either, though there were opportunities enough. Those girls seemed to me so perfect, so beautiful. I felt marred in their presence. Blighted. And as we walked along in silence to chapel, the cafeteria, the classrooms, I'd tell myself: *That is what you are: a blat-blanch, a blighted child.*

I wanted no friends. None other than Dulcianne. In my eyes she was more beautiful than all the Creole girls in the convent. More beautiful and stronger. More alive. More *real.* Dulcianne was part of the tall cedar trees and the glittering river and the smoky musty smell of the forest. She was connected to that life force. Part of that world. How could I *ever* wish for another friend? And in my mind to have another would somehow be a betrayal of our friendship together. The sacredness of it – because that is what it became for me. In my memory. I wanted no friends at the convent. Only to be alone. Far off from all the rest. Alone with my memories of Dulcianne.

But there was scarce little chance of being alone. The nuns kept us busy every waking moment, moving in a line from one activity to the next. And as I sat squeezed between two girls in the hot chapel, on the hot classroom bench, I'd dream of my little room at home. Standing there on my stack of storybooks, my lips pressed against the glass, waiting for Dulcianne to appear. How I'd hated that little room all my life, how I longed for Di to lock me up in my little room now! To be by myself. Alone. With only the possibility that Dulcianne would come to see me. Could appear again from out the cloud of yellow dust.

I did discover one means of escape, almost right away: it was when we went each afternoon to the sea to swim. For the boarders this was the highlight of our existence, and we'd wait anxiously all day for the moment we could throw ourselves into the cool—*cold* in spots!—clear water. The Ursuline Sisters owned their own private beach, a small cove a mile or so away from the convent grounds. Every afternoon after tea we'd line up with our towels and bathing costumes rolled up under our arms. If one of the nuns went with us to supervise, we'd walk beneath the hot sun along the pitch road, through the center of Henly. But more often than not we were left under the charge of one of the older girls. Then we'd take the shortcut: an old trace which followed a dried-up stream, winding its way among clumps of creaking bamboo and thick bush.

For me to follow along that trace was to slowly shed the closed-in world of the convent. And when the trace opened up into a village of a dozen broken-down shanties, clutching for dear life to the side of the cliff overlooking the sea—the air smelling of rubbish, of salted careete like clothes drying on long lines, of cooking coal-pots—I knew we'd entered into another world for true. Sometimes the little black children would stop their play and crouch naked in the dirt, a bicycle rim or an armless pink doll in their dusty hands, huge eyes as they watched us pass. Sometimes I caught a glimpse of a little girl my own age, her head a ball of plats with pieces of bright orange wool bowtied at the end of each. Staring at us from the blackened window of her shanty. As I hurried along I'd wonder what separated me from that little girl. How it was that she ended up inside the shanty, dressed in nothing but a ragged man's marino, and me in the convent dressed in my starched, U.C. monogrammed shirt. As I hurried along, studying the multitude of tiny heart-shaped kisses stuck to my tall white socks, I'd wonder which of the two girls I'd rather be.

There was a cabana beside the beach where we changed into our modest, one-piece bathing costumes, made for us at the convent too, everything according to strict regulations. (Mother Marie-Bernard knew all about the new fashion rage: "This business they call the *bikini*," she told us, "is not simply sinful, it is *lascivious!*") All we cared about was the cool water. There were swimming races and games of water polo which we could play if we wished. But I always went off on my own. To the far end of the beach. There the furry casurina pines spread out over the water, always shady and cool beneath them. The constant drone of the breeze through the pine needles always for me somehow lonely, and nostalgic, and mournful. At the end of the cove the water was shallow and very calm. I'd duck beneath it and hold my breath, lying on my back on the powdery white sand, my nostrils pinched and my eyes open. Staring up at the mirrored, gently rippling surface. All the noise of the screaming girls disappeared the instant I ducked beneath the water, and I was alone! I'd stare up at my distorted reflection on the inside surface of the water. And I'd imagine that that reflection was not me, it was Dulcianne—my opposite, my twin sister—floating face-down on the water. The bubbles slowly escaping my mouth would be swallowed up by her. One by one. In some silent, secret communication of slowly ascending pearls. The more I practiced the longer I was able to hold my breath. Until I could remain beneath the shallow water long as a minute at a stretch. And the longer I remained below with Dulcianne, the more I regretted ever having to return to the world of the screaming convent girls. As I lay on the white sand I'd dream that I would never have to breathe again. Never again have to leave the cool world of solitude and silence beneath the water. The world of my imagination and of Dulcianne.

There were other pleasant dreams. Recurring ones which I had in my little bed at night, not an arm's length from the girl asleep on either side. Dreams of Dulcianne and me living together. But strangely enough we did not live in the big estate house; we lived in Dulcianne's mud-hut with the thatched roof, now deep in the forest. Though in my dreams Di was not there; it was only the two of us. And strangely enough it was I who cared for Dulcianne. *I* who played the roll of servant and she of madam (a game we'd played with the roles reversed years previous), I who picked the guavas and sapadillas and pawpaws from trees growing wild from some abandoned estate. I who peeled the little, sour-sweet oranges with my penknife in a single curling peel—just as Dulcianne had always done for me when we'd gone on excursions in the forest. It was I in my dream who snapped the orange in half, sprinkled the pinch of soukuyant-salt from a mauve-colored glassbottle. I who presented the orange with dripping fingers to Dulcianne. Sometimes I'd boil crayfish or crabs for her which I'd caught in the river. I'd boil green plantains for her in a rusted pitch-oil tin on the coalpot. And when the plantains were boiled I'd mash them in a calabash shell. Sugar them and feed Dulcianne mouthful by mouthful with my own silver tablespoon.

4

If Dulcianne still cared for me, if she still loved me! Because now dared pronounce the word. For the first time in my life. (I'd never used it with mummy and daddy; they'd certainly never used it with me.) A word more mystical, and compelling, and more powerful than all the rest: *God* and *grace* and even the newest addition to my vocabulary—that simplest of virtues which I had always possessed without even knowing (or being told) to hold dear—my *virginity.*

I said it in the secret. To myself. At first geegeeree and quiet quiet. A whisper, a breath: *love!* Whispered with vague feelings of guilt, of shame—which, at twelve years of age—I could scarely begin to understand. But those feelings were mixed with a certain excitement too. A certain tingling of ants crawling up my spinecord too. And soon the excitement took charge over the other feelings. Soon I began to whisper the word with more confidence. With greater frequency. Until—locked into one of the privy stalls at the far side of the playingfield, both hands busy rolling beads, my eyes closed—until I began to whisper the word again and again. Louder and louder. Until it became a silent screaming inside my ears: *love! love! love!*

The W.C. was the only place I could find to escape them. The horrid day students. When the bell rang and we were excused for recess I hurried there straight. Locked myself into one of the privy stalls and remained until I heard the bell again. There were five such stalls. Each a separate little cubicle the color of faded crimson, a line of them at the edge of the playingfield where it bordered the forest, just out of reach on the other side of the spiked, wrought-iron fence. Because in the convent, in those days, a toilet was nothing more than a bench with a hole cut out, suspended over a deep pit. (The toilets in the dormitories were newer and cleaner, far more sanitary—they flushed with water.) But the ones in the school! The *stench,* incessant cloud of mosquitoes buzzing, the strangulating heat! At least the cubicles were roofless, so some of the odor could escape and the rain could fall on occasion to wash them down, not that that made much difference a-tall. They remained as vile-smelling before the rains as after.

Still, the W.C. became my place of refuge. My means of escape during the schoolday. I'd lock myself in and actually stand on the bench with a foot on either side of the hole, my bloomers stretched between my knees, hands busy, eyes closed. Because I fell back into my habit of rolling beads. My chaplet I continued to wear like a necklace round my neck, the same chaplet strung from tiny black pem-pem seeds, my own secret tribute to Dulcianne. It even pleased the nuns. Eliciting comments on more than one occasion. They even thought me pious! Which only served to increase the guilt, the *pleasure* associated with my secret sin. Because of course I knew that my rolling beads *must* be a sin—how could it be otherwise? with *so* many sins to be committed?—long before Mother Marie-Bernard broached the topic in catechism class. And I knew that my rolling beads with my left hand—my saying my chaplet simultaneously with my right—was not merely a sin, it was a *sacrilege.* The stenching toilet seemed the appropriate place for my sinful pleasure. For me. (And I know that in some perverse way I could never have admitted to then, never have begun to understand then, I know the vileness of the place even intensified my wicked pleasures. Sent the ants up my spinecord *streaming.*)

But my hiding place was soon detected. One of the day students—one of those awful yellow-headed blue-eyed ones named Brett—was waiting for me at the far side of the playingfield after the bell rang. She held me up. Grasping hold of the fairy's loop between my shoulderblades at the back of my shirt: "What you doing always hiding in the W.C., eh? You *white cockroach!*"

I looked over my shoulder into her beady eyes—bits of milk-of-magnesia glassbottle pressed into clammy dough. "Eh? she said again, and she shoved me forward. I closed my eyes and took off in a bolt. Yanking through the loop of my shirt and freeing myself. She pursued me all the way back to the line of girls waiting to enter the classroom. Bawling behind me: *"W.C.! W.C.!"*

The following afternoon—locked again into one of the privy-stalls during recess—I heard a softish, *watery* noise. Somewhere above my head: *Shulsh! (A splash of water? whisper?)* My chaplet slipped with a loud *clop* to the wood flooring. I opened my eyes. Raised my head: nothing. Only powder-blue sky through the hole of my roofless cubicle. Then I realized the noise had come from *behind* me. There was a ply wall practically bouncing me up at either shoulder, the hole in the bench between my brown oxfords. I couldn't turn round; all I could do was tilt my head backward. Look upside-down behind me. What I found to my utter horror was Brett's face—her hands like claws gripping the ledge of the wall beside her clammy cheeks—beady glassbottle-eyes upside-down staring into mine—not a foot away!

I let loose a gasp, *loud,* yanked my bloomers by feel up round my waist. At that moment I heard a burst of giggling—shuffling sounds—through the back wall of my cubicle. And Brett's face disappeared. Dropped behind the wall. My whole cubicle rocking slightly. (I guessed that two or three girls had been supporting her on their shoulders, hoisting her up so she could look down over the back wall.)

If she'd seen! If she'd realized!

There was a long minute of silence. Only the beating of my heart like a crazed little animal throwing itself against the bars of my ribcage. I held to the walls of my cubicle with both sweaty hands, head still tilted backward, upside-down—spinning, ready to pitch a faint—waiting to see if Brett's wretched face would appear again.

Then they started! Quiet at first, then louder. Three, four—maybe a *dozen* of them—I couldn't see to know for sure. Because to me it sounded like a *hundred!* Surrounding my cubicle on all sides. Beating their fists against the ply walls. Beating in time to their own horrid chant:

> *White cockroach in the W.C.,*
> *W.C.! W.C.!*
> *Playing with herself in the W.C.,*
> *W.C.! W.C.!*

They repeated it again and again. Louder and louder. Because I'm sure other girls came running quickly to join them. To beat their fists too. Join in the chant too. It seemed to last forever. In my mind it seemed an interminable nightmare. My whole cubicle shaking. *Moving* under my feet! With me holding to the walls with both sweaty hands, ready to pitch a faint, breathing faster and faster. My little heart beating loud and violent as their fists forever—*bam bam bam*—forever against the walls of my beating breast.

At last the bell rang! At last I heard it faintly above the noise. But they didn't stop right away: their pounding and chanting must have gone on for another five minutes. Another *lifetime!* Slowly it began to fade, the girls leaving one by one to return to class. Then I heard a loud whistle. I heard a girl whisper, *"B.M.B.!"* and another, *"Look: B.M.B.!"* And I realized that Mother Marie-Bernard must have left the classroom to find out why it was half-empty, what was going on; she must've appeared *herself* at the other side of the playingfield (her two-fingered whistle was famous). Because now the beating and chanting stopped in one. Dropped to a dead silence.

And I breathed a sigh of relief. Got down and sat on the bench, not even bothering to raise my skirt and lower my bloomers. But sitting on my skirt over the hole just so. Plugging it up—the vile odor, the stench rising in heatwaves from the pit beneath. I was dripping with sweat. My skirt and blouse both soaked through, clinging to my back and thighs. My feet in the tall white socks like puddles of warm water. My little chest still rising and falling with each panting breath. Jumping with each beat of my crazed heart. I let my head tumble backward to rest gently against the back wall. Closed my eyes. Willed myself to breathe slowly. My little heart to soften its pounding.

Then I heard loud knocking. My head snapped forward and I opened my eyes, my heart taking off again. Silence. More knocking. Then I heard Mother Marie-Bernard's voice: "Who's that in there? Get you little backside out here this instant!" She knocked again. I raised my legs and planted my little brown oxfords up against the door. Pushed my back against the back wall. Ready to fend off *three* Mother Marie-Bernards! She knocked a last time. Then I heard an exasperated chups and she walked off, her long skirt swishing against her legs, leather shoes pounding softly on the hard dirt.

I let my head rest against the back wall again. Closed my eyes again. At least she didn't know that it was *me* locked up inside the toilet! And in any case, I quickly realized, it wasn't Mother Marie-Bernard I feared. Not truly. Not *physically*. The most she would do if she suspected mischief was send me to detention-study—and that was a safety which, at that moment, I'd have welcomed only too glad. My great fear was the day students. The whitee-pokees. I decided to remain locked up in my cubicle until I heard the final bell. Until they went home. Then I'd be safe. At least until the following morning, when I'd have to face them again. Now I willed my breathing to slow down once more, my pounding heart. Now I willed myself to drop alseep. Even in the stenching, boiling W.C. If only for a little while. To enter into the world of my dreams. Put a temporary end to my waking nightmare.

And I actually managed to fall asleep for nearly an hour. Actually managed to dream my dream of Dulcianne again. Because it was the last bell at three o'clock which woke me. As I listened to the soft, distant clanging I even smiled: now I was safe! I waited for what I imagined was fifteen minutes. Maybe half an hour. Until I could no longer bear the stench and the clinging heat of my cubicle.

I stood. Slowly slipped the metal bolt across—*click*.

The door burst inward. Shoving me down on the bench again. The back of my head slamming against the back wall. Brett and another girl grabbed my arms, pulled me out the door. There were three or four others waiting outside. They all grabbed hold of me, laughing, taking up the chant again:

> *White cockroach in the W.C.,*
> *W.C.! W.C.!*
> *Playing with herself in the W.C.,*
> *W.C.! W.C.!*

I struggled—kicking my legs and fighting to pull my arms away—powerless against so many. Most of them older, bigger than I was. They pinned me down on my back on the hard dirt. Gritty against my wet shoulders. Each girl holding an arm or a leg, Brett standing beside me. Something silver and shiny in her hands—and for a moment I was sure that it was a penknife! But it looked dome-shaped at the end, a shortish tube. Then I thought it might be a canister of lipstick. (Any form of make-up was strictly forbidden in the convent, even bodypowder, and the only lipstick I'd ever seen before had belonged to my mother.) Brett twisted the canister—a malevolent smile on her face, beady glint in her glass-bottle-eyes—and I watched the bright red head slowly emerge. By now they'd simplified their chant, by now it'd grown louder: "*W.C.! W.C.! W.C.!*" Brett bent over and carefully drew a red line down the middle of the U monogrammed on my shirt. First I was confused. Then I understood: she'd turned the U into a W. New initials on my breast-pocket: W.C. The chant growing still louder.

She wasn't finished. The girls holding my ankles had them spread wide apart. Now Brett stepped round and up between my legs. I felt her shadow close down on top me, dark and cold. I shut my eyes. Felt my wet skirt flipped up. My bloomers yanked with one hand down round my thighs. Now I felt the sensation of falling—backward, falling through the air. As though I'd been thrown inside a deep, dark well. Falling and falling. Suddenly I felt the lipstick shoved inside me, hard and ice-cold—opposite, somehow, to what I'd anticipated—a hollow stab. And I landed flat on my back, *thwack*. Hard against the hard water at the bottom of the well. My entire body stung for a few seconds, seared. Then I felt my arms and legs and neck surrender as if they had a mind of their own—relax, soften, turn to jelly—and I felt myself sinking, descending into the ice-cold water at the bottom of the well.

There was a last burst of laughter. I felt their hands like loosened ropes slip away from my wrists and ankles. I heard them walking off—their talking, laughter, the padding of their shoes on the hard dirt—but as if from a great distance, as if I were *overhearing* it in someone else's dream. I was shivering from the cold. Even beneath the hot sun. After a few minutes my trembling began to stop, and I opened my eyes: powder-blue sky, cloudless. Silence. Without looking, I reached down and gently, carefully extracted the lipstick. The metal now slightly warm to my touch, soft and slippery at the end. I flung it away. Hard. Heard it deflect *thwack* off the ply wall and land in the weeds. Still without looking, I raised my hips off the dirt and pulled my bloomers up round my waist. Lowered my skirt.

I lay there for a long time. Eyes open. Staring up at the cloudless, empty sky. When I sat up and got slowly to my feet, I was so dizzy I could hardly walk. And it was not until nearly two hours later, when I went to remove my blouse in the cabana beside the beach, that I realized the fingers of my right hand were stained brown with blood to the last knuckles. I raised my skirt cautiously and dropped it again. I was still too stunned to be frightened, even worried. I simply waited for the other girls to dress quickly in their bathing costumes and hurry out. Then I pulled off my bloomers and hid them inside my rolled-up towel. When I got to the end of the beach, alone, I dug a deep hole and threw my bloomers in. Covered them up with sand suddenly so white I imagined that it was what snow must look like. Cold and stinging against my stained fingers.

5

That night I did not dream of Dulcianne. I dreamt that I was running through the forest, naked, being chased by a thin black mapapire snake. I would stop running and hide behind treetrunks and mossy bolderstones, catch my breath; but every time I raised my head there the mapapire would be again. Curled up, his forked tongue slithering between sharp yellow eyes, his tail raised behind with the rattles shaking. I'd jump and take off running again. As I ran the metal crucifix of my chaplet kept slapping against my chest and collarbone—hard, painful sometimes—but I felt comforted to know that I was wearing it. Protected. I'd been running for so long in my dream that I felt exhausted. My skin slick with sweat, glistening.

Then I came to a small, pink cubicle – one of the convent privy stalls – now deep in the forest. But I wasn't startled in the least to find it there. As though I'd been running towards it all along. I looked over my shoulder; the mapapire was still following. I entered the cubicle and slid the metal bolt across. Climbed up onto the bench – panting, my heart beating fast.

And when I looked down at the flooring there was the mapapire! Curled up, his head poised ready to strike, forked tongue slithering between his yellow eyes. I reached quickly for my chaplet round my neck – groping – but couldn't find it. Looked down at my chest: it wasn't there! And when I looked at the mapapire again it was transformed into my black chaplet – alive! Curled up on the floor his tail raised now the metal crucifix shaking, rattling! He slithered up onto the bench, slowly – my living mapapire-chaplet – slithering up slowly along my glistening leg, curling round it, entering and disappearing inside me. Black bead by black bead his entire length until the rattling crucifix-tail at the end, which stuck at the crosspiece.

6

I awoke swimming in sweat. Reached for my chaplet round my neck; it wasn't there. For a moment I panicked. Then I realized I'd forgotten it on the floor of the W.C. I took a few deep breaths, tried to calm myself. All the girls round me sound asleep, peaceful. In all likelihood, I told myself, my chaplet was still there: no one used those toilets after school hours. I'd return first thing before class to retrieve it. And I realized something else, something so obvious I could not believe I hadn't seen it already: my chaplet would protect me against the day students. That was why they'd been able to attack me, because I wasn't wearing it. I was sure! Now I tried to calm myself again. To time my breaths with those of the girls round me. All of them – something bizarre, something I'd never noticed before – *all* of them suddenly breathing together in slow, perfect rhythm. As though they were one being. Calm and quiet and peaceful. But I continued breathing fast. Sweating. The whole remainder of the night. My eyes open wide, staring up at the shadows on the corrugated zinc roofing. Because now I wouldn't dare allow myself to drop asleep. Not for an instant! To chance facing the mapapire-chaplet of my nightmare again.

The following morning, as I sat on the bench between two girls during Mass, I continued sweating. I could feel it dripping slowly down my spinecord, vertebra by vertebra. A continuous stream beneath my sweat-soaked shirt—still with the red slash on my breast pocket. My skin felt like if it were boiling. Cooking from the inside. Even though I felt naked! Conscious for every instant that I wasn't wearing my bloomers—and sure that all the girls and the nuns somehow knew—could somehow see my nakedness beneath the navy pleats of my skirt.

Finally we returned to the dormitory after breakfast, and the maids were there waiting for us with the tall stacks of our laundry. Washed, starched, and pressed stiff like pasteboard. So we'd have to *peel* our things apart. Not that I was bothered a-tall that morning: I only wanted to dispose of my lipstick-labeled shirt. Only *wanted* to pull on a pair of the tortuous bloomers. Laundry-day occurred twice a week. Clean sheets for our beds, towels, a fresh uniform for each of us (everything down to the individual socks labeled with our names), and of course, a clean pair of bloomers. We followed the line and dumped our dirty things in the middle of a sheet spread out on the floor, which one of the maids tied up into an enormous bundle and carried out on her head. Of course, next laundry-day I'd turn up missing my bloomers. But Sister Frances would say they'd been lost in the wash, which happened on occasion; she'd send me to Sister Eustasia to be measured for another.

But despite my change of uniform, I continued sweating bolts. All day long. Because in the few minutes while the other girls stood lined up before the classroom, waiting to enter for our first lesson, I took off running for the playingfield. For my cubicle at the far end. My chaplet wasn't there! I got down on my knees in front of my cubicle, reaching in through the open door, searching over the flooring. Only then did I realize it consisted of wood slats—just like the flooring of the cocoahouse—narrow gaps between the boards so the rain could wash through. *My chaplet had fallen into the pit below!* I jumped up and looked down through the hole in the bench—the stenching, cockroach-scratching blackness—even considered reaching my hand in. But even if I dared—and who knew what creatures *besides* cockroaches lived below—I could never reach down far enough.

I hurried back to the classroom. Stunned. Stranded again in my waking nightmare. More frightened than ever to face the day students. And Brett was in the same class! She shoved herself onto the bench on the other side of my table—directly opposite. My eyes stuck like laglee to the reading primer before me. I wouldn't raise them for the world! But I could *feel* Brett's eyes staring at me. Staring at my breast pocket where the embroidery no longer contained its red mark. I could feel the perspiration dripping beneath my shirt, down the backs of my arms, slowly down my spinecord.

During recess I hid in the shadows beneath the banyan trees. The ones nearest the school buildings, the safest ones, slipping to another tree each time a group of girls approached. During lunchbreak I went to detention-studyhall. Told ancient Sister Agnes that Mother Marie-Bernard had sent me because I'd not written my essay on presumption. But when I sat down in the empty classroom, took out my paper and pencil, I realized I hadn't the faintest clue what "presumption" meant. I spent the hour writing a letter to Dulcianne. An *imaginary* letter, since I'd never post it: Dulcianne would not be able to read it. I told her my dream of the two of us living together in the forest. Of my feeding her the sugared foofoo with my silver tablespoon. On the last line I wrote: *In my dream you and I are married.* and I signed it quickly, *Love L.* I folded my letter and shoved it between my books. When I looked up Sister Agnes was snoring—snorting out loud. She chewed her toothless gums for an instant, mechanically, then her jaw dropped wide open, a black hole. I couldn't help but remember my lost chaplet. Suddenly I thought of something: *Maybe I'd looked in the wrong cubicle?*

When the bell rang for afternoon recess I took off running for the playingfield again. I started with the farthest privy, checking them one by one. But I still couldn't find my chaplet. I started down the line a second time. In the fifth cubicle I found it! The very same privy I'd checked that morning. It *had* slipped between the boards, hanging suspended over the stenching pit—but just as in my dream!—saved by the metal crucifix which stuck at the crosspiece.

I fished it out carefully and hung it round my neck. Inside my shirt, pressing the cold cross to my warm breast. Then I had an idea. I went to the weeds at the side of my cubicle and began searching among them. At the same moment, over my shoulder, I noticed a gang of ten or twelve girls approaching behind me—Brett the leader hurrying a few paces in front! Now I began searching frantically through the weeds, *feeling* them approaching behind me, the soft clopping of their feet like horses' hooves on the hard dirt. Louder and louder. Then I found it! The lipstick soft and squashed at the end, but still intact. I stood and drew the line carefully on my own breast. The U a W again: my own initials.

When I turned round they were standing there before me. Brett a pace in front. I could feel the cold metal crucifix against my beating breast. The cold metal lipstick canister clutched tightly in my hand. I took a deep breath. Held my head up and walked straight through them. Past Brett and straight through the middle of the group—as though they didn't even exist! And I continued walking at the same slow, steady pace. All the way back to the school buildings. Got into line with the rest of the girls, calm for the first time all day, waiting for the bell to ring. To enter for catechism class.

7

That afternoon Mother Marie-Bernard lectured us, for the first time, on the sin of masturbation. Touching ourselves with impious hands. With the devil's wicked fingers. Our sacred bodies which did not even belong to us, but to Papa God. So how *dare* we profane them so? "Better"—she quoted Saint Paul—"far better to *cut off* the left hand, if it doth offend the right!" But there was something different about this sin. Some aspect of this sin which made it more immediately terrifying for us than all the rest combined. This sin, we quickly understood, had repercussions in the real world. In *this* world: *our* world.

Mother Marie-Bernard now revealed to us the forbidden secret. She now told us—and who could question it? who could doubt her knowledge on matters of *this* sort for an instant?—Mother Marie-Bernard now told us what our parents, and our nursemaids, and all the adults had kept carefully hidden from us throughout our childhoods: it had to do with duens. Where they *came* from. What *caused* these diab-children to be born so.

Of course, she didn't have to explain to us what duens were: we knew. As surely as we knew about soukuyants, and lagahoos, and diablesses. All of us—even the day students who'd come from away—all of us had grown up hearing about them. Those stories were connected to our earliest memories. Part of our own language. But no one had ever told us *this* before. No one had ever suggested that duens came from any place in particular a-tall. We knew only that they existed—some of us had even seen them—living deep in the forest. When we chanced upon them we'd hidden quickly behind treetrunks and bushes, watching them catching crabs in the river, which we knew was their favorite food. Or we'd seen them collecting bushy dasheen leaves, chewing on tender tanya roots, their wicked faces half-hidden beneath their Chinee straw-hats. But no one had ever confided to us, as Mother Marie-Bernard did now, *why* these diab-children were born with their feet turned round backwards, no genitals between their legs; *why* their mothers never baptized them, but disappeared first thing into darkest night, traveling deep as they dared into the forest to abandon their newborn infants; no one had ever told us there was some secret behind all this illicit business. Some hideous sin.

Neither had we ever seen Mother Marie-Bernard so animated. Pacing back and forth at the front of the classroom. Her back hunched over, clenched fists withdrawn inside her black sleeves. Her red mustache-bush glistening with spittle—so now it looked as if it were flaming for true. Suddenly she stopped her pacing. Suddenly she turned round at the top of *my* table—staring down at *me*, talking to *me!* "Continue touching-up youself like that," she said, her voice lowered, bony index finger flicking *clack clack clack* against her thumb—just in front my face—"continue with this *nastiness*, young lady, and you going find youself pregnated with one of these duens! You hear? Eh? You going find youself haveen with a diab-*duen!*"

8

I pitched a faint. Right there in the classroom. I pelted down on the coral flooring in a dead faint. Because the next thing I remember was waking up in my bed in the dormitory. Sister Frances sitting beside me, pressing a Limecol-soaked kerchief to my forehead. When she saw that my eyes were open she smiled, soft and gentle, a relieved look on her face. I'd received a nasty blow on my forehead when I'd fainted, she told me. But that was not what worried her; she hoped I hadn't contacted some sort of virus, some sort of fever. I was burning a rather high temperature indeed. Sister Frances got me to drink some orange juice, holding the glass to my lips, then patting them dry with a white kerchief. She told me to try and rest myself, and before she got up she freshened the kerchief on my forehead with more Limecol.

Now I was alone in the dormitory for the first time ever. Silent, ten or twelve empty beds stretching away on either side. It was a peculiar feeling. I wondered how long I'd been there, and almost at the same moment I heard the soft clanging of the final schoolbell in the distance. Suddenly I began to recall catechism class, what Mother Marie-Bernard had told me. And after a few minutes I'd made up my mind that I was pregnant with a diab-duen. Though I knew the idea was absurd. That rolling beads could not possibly produce a child—even the devil's own. (That according to what I'd learned from Dulcianne, a girl could not get pregnant till she'd seen her menses—even if she done been jooked by a man—or the devil-self—already.) Still, I made up mind I was pregnant with a diab-duen. How could it be otherwise? according to what Mother Marie-Bernard had said? And I had been rolling beads for longer than three *years!*

I fell into a kind of stupor. A feverish trance. I fell basodee. Boobooloops. Bufutu. As though I were sleeping with my eyes open. Staring up at the shadows on the corrugated zinc roofing. Because when Sister Frances returned an hour later to check my temperature, to freshen the Limecol-kerchief on my forehead, and she asked me how I felt, I could hardly work my lips to pronounce the words. When she came with a tray of food that evening, tried her best to get me to eat some dinner—*good* food, food which she'd toted all the way from the motherhouse kitchen—I choked on the tablespoon of splitpea soup she put inside my mouth. I could not eat and I could not sleep. When the other girls arrived later I was aware of them changing into their nightgowns, climbing into their beds—I heard Sister Frances reading from the big book of saints—but only from a dreamlike, muffled distance.

It went on for five days. Sometimes I wonder if it went on for the entire five years I remained there in the convent. But it was five days later when I got the letter. Five days later when I was awakened from my stupor by reality again. A reality far more frightening, far more cruel, than my fiercest nightmare.

It was a letter from my mother. Sister Frances brought it to me on the same tray with the dinner I hardly touched. She said she hoped the letter would cheer me up. But when she left me alone again in the empty dormitory, and I opened the envelope, I could hardly focus my eyes in order to read it. Another of those long and terribly tedious letters which mummy wrote once a month. Another detailed description of the estate's financial problems, of the falling prices of sugar and cocoa and copra, of how my father had been forced to sell off another plot of land in order to stave off bankruptcy. The words floated before my eyes, blurred and meaningless. That is, until I got to the end of the letter. Until I reached the postscript. I sat up straight in my bed:

> *P.S. You will be saddened to hear that your foolish little friend Dulcianne has managed to find herself enfantement. She names the culprit as a boy no older or less foolish than she, living cross the valley on Woodford Estate. Fortunately John Woodford has agreed to take her on as one of the servants of that household. Your father and I shall see to our share of the bargain: that the two scoundrels are married good and proper in the Church.*

9

When I slipped silently from out my bed in the middle of the night, I was no longer sweating. No longer burning a fever. My head felt clear for the first time in five days and nights. Clear enough to see through Mother Marie-Bernard's absurd and *evil* delusions. Clear enough to realize *I* wasn't haveen a-tall. That in fact I'd have preferred to bear a devil-duen, than to have to acknowledge *this* reality. All the girls were sound asleep. Calm and quiet. Their breathing slow and synchronized as though they were one person. I did not dress or even put on my shoes. I slipped out the dormitory just so—barefoot, wearing only my nightgown. Past the sleeping girls. Past Sister Frances' cubicle of white screens, which suddenly seemed to be flowing in the dark. I unbolted the door and slipped out into the night.

There was a full moon which lit up my nightgown as though it were glowing too. The sky seemed almost as bright as day. The shadows beneath the banyan trees almost as dark and distinct. Still, I could have found my way with my eyes closed. I crossed the grass of the schoolyard, wet and cold with dew, the hem of my nightgown damp and dragging round my ankles. When I got to the playingfield a layer of dirt stuck to the soles of my feet, feeling as though I were walking in sandals. I lifted the hem of the nightgown. The insects in the forest behind the playingfield were screeching with a deafening noise. Interrupted every few seconds by a hollow *toc toc* sound. I went straight to the fifth cubicle. The one at the end. When I pushed the door open the stench seemed almost to physically shove me back. I did not pause for an instant. Found my chaplet by feel and raised it up over my head, the silver crucifix catching the light, flashing once. It splashed *thwack* in the thick darkness below.

10

My remaining years in the convent passed as though they were months. Weeks really. At least I've scarcely any memories a-tall from that period of my life. No doubt I've blotted them out from my mind. The beginning of the war had coincided almost exactly with my beginning in the convent; and strangely enough, the finish of the war coincided almost precisely with my leaving it, six years later. But it was not until after I'd been at the convent a couple years, that we'd really began to feel the effects of the war. The whole of Corpus Christi felt it. From the poorest to the wealthy wealthy. Of course, it was the poor who suffered. In the convent we were constantly reminded of just how lucky we were. And I suppose we were lucky in truth. At least we had food to eat. But such food! The same stuck-up rice twice a day every day for lunch and dinner, which we called "pappy-rice." It arrived on our plates as cold clumps, with a distinct ammoniac smell which remained on our tongues an hour after eating it. And just when we thought we'd managed to force down the last mouthful, dessert arrived in the form of pappy-pudding. Whatever fruits or vegetables the convent managed to purchase from the villagers were usually spoiled by the time they reached us. During those years we ate hardly any meat whatsoever. Pork occasionally. Locally raised chickens once or twice a month, which we called "hard-fowl." We ate mostly fish. Fish which was salted and locally caught too, always stewed to death, always unquestionably *fish;* every day we smelled it cooking for two hours before we arrived in the cafeteria, all the way from the classroom.

Every morning during Mass, every evening in the chapel again for vespers, we prayed that Great Britain and the Ally-forces would defeat Hitler. Little did the nuns know that Mother Marie-Bernard had been given a new nickname, "M.H.M.": "Mother Marie-Bernard of the Meinkompf Hitler-Mustache." But we knew that even the Ally-forces could not defeat Mother Marie-Bernard. By that time I'd been moved to the older girls' dormitory, which she supervised. The morning I informed Sister Frances that I was seeing my first period, she smiled and held me to her breast, and after awhile I realized that she was crying. I began to cry also, not really understanding why, but sensing I'd lost something irrevocably. Little did I realize that it was not simply my childhood, but Sister Frances too.

That afternoon I was moved to Mother Marie-Bernard's dorm, shocked and frightened to discover that all of us—*every* girl in the dormitory—all of us were seeing our menses at the same time. All our beds with a special plastic lining under the sheets. An awful crackling noise every time we moved a limb. And in M.H.M.'s dormitory, whether it was our time of the month or not, we were made to wear our bloomers beneath our nightgowns while we slept. In time I grew used to these changes. In time my body learned not only to sleep and eat and to mumble the same prayers in unison with the others, but to menstruate according to a single rhythm. And though I have no way of knowing, I'm sure that each night while I slept my dreamless sleep, I breathed in perfect time with the other girls too.

Then the war ended. It was as though the entire world were suddenly awakened from the same endless, dreamless sleep. Even in the convent we celebrated with a dinner of mashed potatoes and gravy and *turkey.* Turkeys which arrived frozen from America on big gray battleships toting whole airports on their backs. Turkeys which were given out in the streets. Which went by the magical name of "butterballs." They melted on our tongues as though they were butter in truth. As though they were sacred flesh.

Each year the convent held a rather elaborate commencement program, marked by the annual visit of our Bishop from Trinidad, and coupled with a Confirmation ceremony for the younger girls who were ready. There was a procession in which the Virgin was removed from her grotto and pushed on a little cart through the streets of Henly. All of us singing the "Ave Maria." Two or three of the younger girls walking backward before the statue, shoeboxes strung round their necks, sprinkling the pitch with white oleander petals. Most of the graduating girls' parents came for the ceremony, some traveling from distant islands. But as I learned early that morning, mummy was ill and confined to bed again (on my previous visits home for summer and Christmas, she'd spent most of her time in bed stiff with jaundice, puffed-up with dropsy); so she and my father would not be able to attend. Instead they'd sent a special parcel with the parents of one of the other girls: a new gown which mummy'd made for my commencement ceremony—white linen with tiny black polkadots—the same material used to make the Holy Communion gown I'd never been able to wear years before. But I wouldn't be able to wear my new gown either; Mother Marie-Bernard and the war had changed things since mummy's days in the convent, and for the commencement we were made to wear our monogrammed school uniforms.

It was not until late that afternoon, while packing my last few things into my little grip, that I removed the gown from its pasteboard box and examined it for the first time. There was a letter of mummy's pinned to the breast pocket, sending prayers and regrets. Again, it was the postscript which caught my attention: *In the breast pocket of your gown you'll find a very special gift, passed on to you from your great-grandmother, given to me years ago upon my own commencement at the convent.* I reached into the pocket and carefully removed my mother's gold chaplet. And I stood beside my bed in the already nearly empty dormitory, already nearly silent, holding the chaplet by two gold beads between the thumbs and index fingers of both my trembling hands. I held it up to the late afternoon light, glittering, my heart beating fast. I closed my eyes. Raised my hands slowly above my head. Felt it slip down gently round my neck.

Boy Born with Tattoo of Elvis
Robert Olen Butler

I CARRY HIM on my chest and it's a real tattoo and he was there like that when I come out of Mama. That was the week after he died, Elvis, and Mama made the mistake of letting folks know about it and there was that one big newspaper story, but she regretted it right away and she was happy that the city papers didn't pick up on it. It was just as well for her that most people didn't believe. She covered me up quick.

And I stayed covered. Not even one of her boyfriends ever saw me, and there was plenty come through in these sixteen years, all the noisy men in the next room. But last week she brought this guy home from the bar where she worked and he looked like I'd imagine Colonel Parker to look. I never saw a photo of Parker, the man who took half of every dollar Elvis ever earned, but this guy with Mama had a jowly square face and hair the gray of the river on a day when a hurricane is fumbling toward us and he made no sounds in the night at all and this should have been a little better for me, really.

But Mama made sounds, and I'd gotten so used to them over the years I could always kind of ignore them and listen – if I chose to listen at all – to the men, how foolish they were, braying and wailing and whooping. At least Mama had them jumping through hoops: I could think that. At least Mama had them where she wanted them. But this new guy was silent and I hated him for that – it meant he didn't like her enough, the goddam fool – and I hated him for making me hear her again, the panting, like she was out of breath, panting that turned into a little moan and another and it was like a pulse, her moans, again and again, and finally I just went out the door and off down the street to the river.

We live in Algiers and I went and sat on a fender pile by the water and watched New Orleans across the way and I could hear music, some Bourbon Street horn lifting out of the city and coming across the river, and it's the kind of music I like to hear, at times like that. There's other music in me but his. You see, I'm not Elvis myself. I'm not him reincarnated like that one newspaper tried to make you believe. I didn't come out of my momma humming "Heartbreak Hotel," like they said.

And she almost never does this, but last night I was tired and it was my birthday and I just stuck it out and after they was finished in there, she come in to me. We have a shotgun house with shutters that close us up tight and the only place I've got is on the sofa bed in the living room, and the next room through — the path that a shotgun blast would follow from the front door to the back, which is how these houses got their name — the next room through was her bedroom and then there was the little hall with the bathroom and then the kitchen and the back door. One of her jealous boyfriends actually did fire through the house a few years ago and the doors happened to be open, but it was a blunt-nose pistol and the bullet didn't make it all the way through the house, being as there was another boyfriend standing in one of the open doors along the way. Mama come into me after that, too, cause I'd seen it all, I carried the smell of cordite around inside me for a week after.

So she come into me last night and maybe it was because of me turning sixteen, though she never said a word about it. Maybe it was because of this new guy staying quiet when she wasn't. But she come in and I was laying there on my back and she cooed a little and took me by the ears and fiddled with them like they was on crooked and she was straightening them and then her hands went down and smoothed flat the collar of my black T-shirt that I was sleeping in and she said to me, "How can you love a fool such as I?"

It's a good question, I think. I think Elvis sold about two million records of a song by a name like that. But she meant it. And I didn't say anything to her. She waited for me to say, Oh Mama I love you I do. But she smelled like the corner of some empty warehouse and maybe she didn't know where my daddy was or maybe even who he was but he sure wasn't the guy in there right now and he wasn't going to be the next one either or the next and the few times I said anything about it, she told me she can't help falling in love. But I didn't buy that. I couldn't. Still, I know what I'm supposed to feel for my momma: Elvis collapsed three times at the funeral for Gladys. But I'm not Elvis, and I'd stand real steady at a time like that, I think. Nothing could make me fall down. I would never fall down.

But tonight I didn't care. Tina come up to me in the hall this morning at the school and she said "I heard it was your birthday yesterday" and I said "It was" and she said "Why don't you ever talk with me, since I can't keep my eyes off you in class and you can see that very well" and I said "I don't talk real good" and she said "You don't have to" and I said "Are you lonesome tonight?" and she said "Yes" and then I told her to meet me at a certain empty warehouse on the river and we could talk and she said "I thought you weren't a good talker" and I said "I'm not" and she said "Okay." And that meant I had to figure out what to do about my chest.

Because Elvis's skin is mine. His face is in the very center of my chest and it's turned a little to the left and angled down and his mouth is open in that heavy-lipped way of his, singing some sorrowful word, but his lips are not quite open as much as you'd think they should be in order to make that thick sound of his, and his hair is all black with the heavenly ink of the tattoo and a lock of it falls on his forehead and his lips are blushed and his cheeks are blushed and the twists of his ear are there and the line of his nose and chin and cheek, and his eyes are deep and dark, all these are done in the stain of a million invisible punctures, but all the rest, the broad forehead except for that lock of hair, his temples and his cheeks and chin, the flesh of him, is my flesh.

I wanted to touch Tina. She's very small and her face is as sharp and fine as the little lines in Elvis's ear and her hair is dark and thick and I wanted to lay beneath her and pull her hair around my face, and her eyes are a big surprise because they're blue, a dark, flat blue like I'd think suede would be if it was blue. I wanted to hold her and that made my skin feel very strange, touchy, like if I put my hands on my chest I could wipe my skin right off. Tattoo and all. Not that I imaged that would happen. It was just the way my skin thought about itself today, with Tina in my mind the way she was. And you'd think there would've been some big decision to make about this. But when the time come, it was real easy. I decided to show her who I was tonight. I would show her my tattoo.

Mama used to tell me a story. When nobody was in the house and I was going to sleep, she'd come and sit beside me and she'd say do I want to hear a story and I'd say yes, because this was when I was a little kid, and she'd say, "Once upon a time there was a young woman who lived in an exotic faraway place where it was so hot in the summers that the walls in the houses would sweat. She wasn't no princess, no Cinderella either, but she knew that there was something special going to happen in her life. She was sweet and pure and the only boy who ever touched her was a great prince, a boy who would one day be the King, and he touched her only with his voice. Only his words would touch her and that meant she could keep all her own secrets and know his too and nothing ever had to get messy. But then one night an evil man come in to her and made things real complicated and she knew that she was never going to be the same. Except then a miracle happened. She gave birth to a child and he come into the world bearing the face of the prince who was now the King, the prince who had loved her just with his words, and after that, no matter how bad things got, she could look at her son and see the part of her that once was."

This was the story Mama used to tell me and all I ever knew to do at the end was to say to her not to cry. But finally I stopped saying even that. I asked her once to tell me more of the story. "What happened to the boy?" I asked her and she looked at me like I was some sailor off a boat from a distant country and she didn't even know what language I was talking.

So tonight I went out of the house and around the back and in through the kitchen to get to the bathroom. She and the Colonel Parker guy were in the bedroom and I never go in there. Never. Before I stepped in to wash up I paused by her door and there was a rustling inside and some low talk and I gave the door a heavy-lipped little sneer and a tree roach was poised on the door jamb near the knob and even he had sense enough to turn away and hustle off. So I clicked the bathroom door shut as soft as I could and I pulled the cord overhead and the bulb pissed light down on me and I didn't look at myself in the mirror but bent right to the basin and washed up for Tina and there was this fumbling around in my chest that was going on and finally I was ready. I turned off the light and opened the door and there was Mama just come out of her room and she jumped back and her sateen robe fell open and I lowered my eyes right away and she said you scared me and I didn't look at her or say nothing to her and Elvis might could sing about the shaking inside me but I for sure couldn't say anything about it and I pushed past her. "Honey?" she asked after me.

I slammed the back door and I beat it down the street toward the river and it's August so it was still light out but the sun was softer, moving into evening, and I was glad for that. I started trying to concentrate on Tina waiting for me and I wanted the light and I wanted it to be soft and I just kept thinking about the looks she'd been giving me and I could see her eyes on me from across the classroom and they were flat blue and when they fixed on me they didn't move, they always waited for me to turn away, and I always did, and now I thought maybe she'd been seeing something important about me all along, that's why she wanted me like this. I thought maybe when I showed her who I was, she would just say real low, but in wonder, "I knew it all along."

Then I was past Pelican Liquors and the boarded up Piggly Wiggly and a bottle gang was shaping up for the evening on the next corner and they lifted their paper bags to me and I just hurried on and I could see a containership slipping by at the far end of the street and I had to keep myself from running. I walked. I didn't want to be sweating a lot when I got there. I just walked. But walking made my mind turn. Mama's robe fell open and I looked away as quick as I could but I saw the center of her chest like you sometimes see the light after you turn it off, she come out of her bedroom and her robe fell open and I saw the hollow of her chest, nothing more, and when I turned away I could still see her chest and it was naked white and I wondered why Elvis didn't appear there. She could've kept her own secret then and known his too, and there wouldn't never had to be anybody else involved in the whole thing.

I was walking real slow now, but I could see that the light was starting to slip away and I had better get on, if I was going to do this thing. And I turned down the next street and I could see the river now and I followed it and the warehouse had a chain link fence as high as my house but it was cut in a few places and I found Tina on the other side already and she saw me and she come my way. She was wearing a stretchy top with ruffles around the shoulders and her stomach was bare and she was in shorts and I hadn't seen her legs till now, not really, and they were nice, I knew that, they were longer than I figured, and we both had our fingers curled through the fence links and we were nose to nose just about and she said, "Get on in here."

I went in and she said, "I was worried you wasn't coming" and I found out I didn't have nothing to say to that and she smiled and said, "I don't know this place so well. Where should we go?"

I nodded my head in the direction of the end of the warehouse, on the river side, and I felt a lock of my hair fall onto my forehead and we moved off and the ground was uneven and she brushed against me again and again, keeping close, and I thought to take her hand or put my arm around her, but I didn't. I wanted this to go slow. We walked and she was saying how glad she was that I come, how she liked me and how she was really on her own more or less in her life and she had learned how to know who's okay and who isn't and I was okay.

And I still didn't say nothing and I couldn't even if I'd wanted to because I was shaking inside pretty bad and we entered the warehouse through a door that said Danger on it and inside it was real dim but you could feel the place on your face and in your lungs, how big it was and how high, and there was that wet and rotted smell but Tina said "Oh wow" and she pressed against me and I let my arm go around her waist and her arm come around mine and I took her into the manager's office.

The light was still coming in clear in the room and there was some old mattresses and it didn't smell too good, but a couple of the windows was punched open and it was mostly the river smell and the smell of dust, which wasn't too bad, and I let go of Tina and crossed to the window and I looked at the water, just that. The river was empty at the moment and the last of the sun was scattered all over it and there was this scrabbling in me, like Elvis went way deeper there than my skin and he'd just woke up and was about to push himself out the center of my chest. I tried to slow myself down so I could do this right.

Then I turned around to look at Tina and she must have gotten herself ready for this too because as soon as I was facing her where she was standing in the slant of light, she stripped off her top and her breasts were naked and I fell back a little against the window. It was too fast. I'm not ready, I thought. But she seemed to be waiting for me to do something, and then I thought: she knows; it's time. So I dragged my hand to the top button of my shirt and I undid it and then the next button and the next and I stepped aside a little, so the light would fall on me when I was naked there and she circled so she could see me and then the last button was undone and I grasped the two sides and I couldn't hardly breathe and then I pulled open my shirt.

Tina's eyes fell on the tattoo of Elvis and she gave it one quick look and she said "Oh cool" and then her eyes let go of me, they let go of me real fast, like this was something she'd expected all right, but it was no big thing, there was no wonder in her voice, no understanding that this was a special and naked thing, and she was looking for the zipper on her shorts, and I was sure she was wrong about me and I hoped she'd have a son someday with a face on his chest that she would know, and then I was sliding away and the shirt was back on me before I hit the warehouse door and I didn't listen to the words that followed me but I was stumbling over the uneven ground, trying to run, and I did run once I was out the cut in the fence and I heard a voice in my head as I ran and it was my voice and it surprised me but I listened and it said, "Once there was a boy who was born with the face of a great King on his chest. The boy lived in a dark cave and no one ever saw this face on him. No one. And every night from deeper in the darkness of the cave, far from the boy but clear to his ears, a woman moaned and moaned and he did not understand what he was to do about it. She touched him only with her voice. Sometimes he thought this was the natural sound of the woman, the breath of the life she wished to live. Sometimes he thought she was in great pain. And he didn't know what to do. And he didn't know that the image that was upon him, that was part of his flesh, had a special power."

Then I slowed down and everything was real calm inside me, and I went up our stoop and in the front door and I went to the door of Mama's bedroom and I threw it open hard and it banged and the jowly-faced man jumped up from where he was sitting in his underwear on Mama's bed. She straightened up sharp where she was propped against the headboard, half hid by the covers, and she had a slip on and I was grateful for that. The man was standing there with his mouth gaping open and Mama looked at me and she knew right off what'd happened and she said to the man, "You go on now." He looked at her real dumb and she said it again, firm. "Go on. It's all over." He started picking up his clothes and Mama wouldn't take her eyes off mine and I didn't turn away, I looked at her too, and I touched the top button on my shirt, just touched it and waited, because only I could have this thing upon me, Mama couldn't have it because she'd lost it long ago and it was put on me to give it back to her and I kept my hand there and I waited and then the man was gone and the house was quiet.

It was just Mama and me and I had to lean against the door to keep from falling down.

The Cure

John Hawkes

SPELL OR NO SPELL, that was the moment of my undoing, the turning point in my life. For suddenly I awoke gripped in pain as well as in the certainty of Armand's whereabouts and of what had happaned to me in my dreamless sleep. I say dreamless, yet even now I remember the alien sensations that possessed me on the embankment—a pinching about my open mouth, a sudden ungentle filling of my mouth as with wet leathery fingers, a brief and useless period of dry heaving, and then the pain to which I awoke, doubled over on my side and gasping, thanks, I was convinced, to that treacherous frog who had taken up his abode inside me, the very thought of which set me off again into still more painful spasms of regurgitation that produced nothing, no trickle of pond water, no signs of anything to be identified with Armand's body, no relief. Only the cramp that kept my knees to my chest as if I had been kicked in my poor little bloated stomach and, as I say, the certainty of what was causing my now stricken state. We must remember that until this day I had enjoyed nothing but the stalwart health of a two-year-old male child endowed with more than adequate weight and strength and doted upon by all those fortunate enough to have received him from the arms of a kind fate. Not so much as a cough, or the sting of a misguided bee.

Luckily for me, that pain in my otherwise wholesome stomach abruptly subsided when I heard Mamma sweetly calling my name through the shadows that had begun to settle as I slept. Why, I even believe that I smiled when I felt myself suddenly relieved of pain and heard my dear little Mamma calling. It came to me, I remember, that not every child is made to suffer the way I had just suffered, and would again and again my life long, and that it is not every small boy who bears inside him the secret that was now mine.

That evening I listened with new interest to one of the episodes from "The Stories of Armand the Frog," and was spared any further abdominal attacks, though Mamma did remark on the whiteness of my face — had the sun not changed my color even a shade? — and the wanness of my smile. Only some evenings later did my next attack occur, sending Mamma and me early from dinner with Papa and up to my little bed whose white sheets, I now recognized, had beckoned me all along not to healthy childhood but to affliction.

"Is he alright, Marie?" my father called anxiously from the foot of the stairs. "Oh, our poor Tadpole!"

"Don't fret, Michel-André," my mother called back down to him. "Tonight you must finish your meal alone."

"Just as you say, Marie," he answered in faintly wounded tones that made me realize clearly enough that he cared more about his stewed chicken than my health or well-being, and that in fact he begrudged my mother's absence from his table. Here then, and only a few nights after I had first been overcome by Armand, was something new. The understanding, that is, that as never before I now wanted Mamma beside my bed and not below with my father, and that I myself wished to determine the length of each of her nightly vigils, and that any pain, but especially this one, was well worth my newfound gratification in denying Papa his wife, and causing him to eat his rapidly cooling dinner in silence. So there it was, Armand's double and apparently contradictory gift to me — dear little Mamma and the abdominal ache now fierce, now fading, by which I inflicted myself, so to speak, on our household. Oh, that Armand was a clever fellow to intuit my deepest wishes and then to grant them by making me suffer as severely as he could in exchange.

"Pascal," my obviously worried mother whispered that evening, the third or fourth into my newly determined course of life, "perhaps you would prefer me not to read tonight?"

"No, Mamma," I answered — yes, actually answered! For it was that very night, holding my stomach and struggling to reveal no hint of the extent of my pain, that I spoke my first words, "No, Mamma, please read to me."

"But dear little Pascal," she whispered, "perhaps the pain will prevent you from listening. Perhaps you would prefer that I simply stroke your brow instead."

"No, Mamma," I repeated, so softly that I well concealed the amazement I felt at my ability to speak, and to speak like an adult and not a child first stumbling into the sounds of speech, "I would like you to read to me, and not just one story tonight, but three.

And Mamma," I said as an afterthought, "I would like you to put your hand on my brow as well."

"Poor Pascal," she whispered, and did as I had asked.

And wouldn't you know, they were long stories and took most of the night to read, while she frowned gently and I lay propped on my back, my knees raised, my plump lower lip, worthy of any cherub's, I can tell you, caught between the two rows of my baby teeth. I kept my eyes on Mamma, I felt the perspiration on the brow she kissed between each story that night. I listened, I saw on her face the expression of concern that was little more, it was plain to see, than a most attractive mask of the adoration of me that lay beneath, as if the greater her worry the more blatant her love of her first and only child. It was a long night, with episode after episode of Armand's adventures drifting in and out of my awareness—how dreadful of that boy Henri to lop off one of the frog's small feet with his pocket knife!—and the horde of distant frogs filling the night with their now mournful song as if for my affliction and for the loss of their king, which the actual Armand had surely been. Only now and then did I find myself smelling the invisible orchard or the warm air, as half lost to sleep I gave myself up to listening to Mamma and watching the movement of her lips, and whenever I thought she would not notice, pressing into my stomach in the hopes that my fingers might discover the shape of the great frog within me, and that I might nudge him and cause him to change his position, even to flatten himself and grow small, thus lessening my pain.

Once my father dared interrupt us.

"Marie," he called up from the foot of the stairs in a crude imitation of a stage whisper, his impatience fully evident both to Mamma and me, "haven't you spent long enough with him? Soon the entire night will be gone." Whereupon Mamma paused, marked her place with a white finger, and tiptoed to the head of the stairs.

"Go to bed, Michel-André. I'll be down when I can."

"Our Tadpole is a marvel, Marie. But do come to bed."

At which I moaned, softly, even pleasantly, with just enough urgency not to alarm my mother unduly yet to bring her hastening back to me, as the darkness began to fade from the window behind her and one by one the voices of the far-off tiny frogs were extinguished. Shortly thereafter Armand must have slept as well, for my pain vanished and I slept as soundly as Armand, but not before I heard Mamma descending the stairs. Had she turned her head and looked over her shoulder, she would have been pleased to see the faintest smile on the lips of her weary babe.

Of course the presence of the frog inside me resulted not merely in almost overpowering pain which, in turn, was like a golden sauce enrobing the bliss of having Mamma all to myself those tranquil nights. For one thing I began to fear for my diet and the effect it would have on Armand. I knew full well that ordinarily he ate insects of various kinds and algae and infinitesimal roots and sprouts that grew in the pond which he had forever denied himself. What now? I dismissed immediately the thought of attempting to eat what Armand had eaten before he had made his daring decision to abandon his pond for my stomach. And if he starved, slowly until he died a miserable death in the darkness of my innermost source of life? He would not die peacefully, of that I was sure, and obviously would revenge himself in ways I could not imagine suffering, until at last he lay extinct within me—odious thought. It is one thing to carry within oneself a vital unruly frog, and quite another to have one's stomach uselessly burdened with a dead one. And if he died, obviously I would lose the clarity and power of pain, or its potential, that was now embedded in the pit of my stomach. At any rate I began to eat less, denied myself the sweet lamb and beef of Mamma's famous roasts and stews—no more boeuf Angêlé for me!—and subtly began to eat and hence feed Armand increasingly full bowls of shiny grain. But a more tormenting thought soon inflicted upon me a greater agony of confusion, even helplessness, which was nothing less than the fear of losing the very frog whose unwelcome presence I now so desperately entertained. To put it bluntly, I did all I could to restrain my babyish bowels and every morning, after I had sat on my porcelain pot, in genuine dread I studied its contents, expecting on each occasion the sight of Armand paddling about my august chamber pot like a dying fish in a bowl. Gradually, however, those fears proved unnecessary, until my father and poor old Monsieur Remi, our village pharmacist, revived them in a burst of unwelcome medical effort. In the meanwhile, however, my sporadic cramps continued, for the most part during the night, accompanied by the sound of Mamma's reading voice and the sound of the slowly turning pages. Why, many a morning I awoke to find her fully clothed and yet significantly disheveled, stretched out beside me, her head on my pillow, the essential storybook fallen closed between us, so increasingly diligent and exhausted was my Mamma in her care of me that was in fact nothing other than a mother's love sweetly spiced with a mother's worry.

Need I remind you of "The Cook's Prayer"? How curious that I remember my father's crude song about my grandmother's teeth — all twenty-two of them — and yet am unable to bring to mind word for word, line for line that prayer of my mother's. Perhaps it comes to me only in fragments because it belonged more in the mouth of an old woman than in my mother's. She could not have written it, of course, yet loved to recite it to me in the young count's kitchen. How did it go? Carnations decorating salmon and quail? And the fervent plea to cook the tongues of birds that have not yet ceased their singing? And aspics and frying sorbets? And finally the desire to use all her knowledge only to break a little bread at God's table? How touching it was that Mamma should embody such artistry and so simple a heart!

I thought I knew Papa in the same way, assuming, for instance, that he was as much a victim of my frog as I was, and that despite his puzzlement and downheartedness would nonetheless offer no serious resistance to this newly established situation in which I had all but taken dear Mamma away from him, since there is nothing in life like an ailing only child to split asunder the ordinary expectations of married life. How could he be any match for his suffering son and the power of an invisible frog? What could he do but accept his lonely place at the table and, throughout the most luxurious spring nights of his marriage to Mamma — a thought I can hardly bear to allow to mind — take himself to his cold bed quite helpless to restore his wife to his side? Well, I was wrong, though he indeed managed to contain himself and preserve his guise of selfless submission to my apparently incurable condition for a remarkably long while, all things considered. In fact, the air was already brisk and the harvesting in progress when, to my surprise, Papa suddenly intruded once more between Mamma and me. And how did he stop our nightly readings and bluntly recall his wife to himself? By using my own ill health as his ploy, which is to say that that man who pretended to good humor, to frankness and innocent vulgarity, the same person who in fact was so self-centered that one of my mother's "off days," as he called them, pitched him into the deepest gloom, finally reclaimed that dear woman simply by asserting himself on my behalf. Never, never would I have thought him quick-witted enough to conceive of such a transparent yet effective ruse!

"Marie," he said one night as she placed his large and steaming china plate before him—his napkin was already tucked into the top of his shirt—and as she prepared to ascend to my beside, "these tribulations are intolerable. I am not speaking of mine, or yours and mine. I am a patient man. There is no more self-sacrificing a mother than yourself. No, Marie, I am speaking of Pascal. Who knows what permanent disability his little internal organs may be suffering because of our good intentions? Who knows but what it is not already too late?"

At this my mother gave a little cry and, as I thought from the head of the stairs where, in my nightshirt, I crouched and attempted to still my trembling and to quiet Armand's swelling anger, must have paused and put her cool fingers to my father's unusually large mouth.

"Michel-André!" I heard her say in a frightened whisper, "Please! You must not say such things, my dearest!"

"For once it is my duty to speak out, Marie."

"But I am yours, Michel-André."

"I must tell you, then, that even a mother's love cannot replace the dictates of medical science! Soothing an internal malignancy may do more harm than good. Urgency of this sort requires treatment, not stories from a children's book! Otherwise. . . Otherwise, Marie. . ."

"Hush, Michel-André. Please hush. I understand."

"Tomorrow, then, we shall take him to Monsieur Remi."

"Very well, my dearest."

Thus in a moment my father reestablished himself as provider, protector, male authority who stands before wife and child like the massive dead tree that glowers predictably and, if I might say so, stupidly over the living swamp. What a faker he was!

That night my pain was so intense that Mamma abandoned entirely "The Stories of Armand the Frog," and simply joined me between my chilly sheets and lay comforting me the night long, until my own Armand, as anxious and angry as I was myself, at last succumbed to her caresses. Soon enough I followed suit.

Generally the prospect of a visit to Monsieur Remi, who was not only the pharmacist in the village nearest the Domaine Ardente, but was also he who acted as our local dental surgeon and medical practitioner as well, roused in me the happiest of expectations. His pharmacy was a small boy's delight, a dark comforting place smelling of pills and powders, capsules and heavy bottles of black liquid, and divided in half by a partition of hand-rubbed mahogany that rose from the tiled floor almost to the ceiling. This ancient wooden wall, behind which Monsieur Remi and his assistant worked, was covered with mysterious examples of the woodcarver's art, elaborate scrolls and highly polished flourishes. In wooden niches sat large jars of white and yellow porcelain, clearly labeled to indicate their contents. And the old pair of scales of brass and iron, what a marvelous machine it was, with its gears and little row of weights so simple yet complex that as a mechanism it was the perfect counterpart to the great clock in the corner, the one—the pair of scales—stock still yet always ready to lend itself to the precise measurement of Monsieur Remi's curatives, the other—the clock—also rooted in stillness yet housing its long pendulum whose steady swing and loud ticking made monotonous the very idea of motion. No matter the troop of ailing citizens who always stood on file in Monsieur Remi's pharmacy, shifting uncomfortably in a place so clean and speaking grandly of matters beyond their ken, daunted, the lot of them, with heads hanging like children ashamed of their rashes or broken bones or bowel troubles, waiting their turn at the counter like the bank teller's window in our old bank, behind which stood our benevolent man of healing, Monsieur Remi, never was I repelled by the inevitable shabbiness of sickness, and never did I consider the pharmacy a refuge for the sick and injured, but merely assumed that it was a central landmark of my childhood and intended for my own pleasure and little more. After all, never was I one of those who entered the pharmacy with some kind of medical complaint, large or small, since during our infrequent visits to Monsieur Remi I acted only as my mother's companion, and certainly she bore no resemblance to the other villagers seeking his help and kindness.

In those days the pharmacist was as important to that little village as the priest himself, and his place of work as timeless and central to the village as the dark and ugly church to which most people flocked on Sundays. Luckily for me, the young count and his wife tolerated the pharmacy but not the church, so of course my parents, unlike the rest of those on the Domaine Ardente, followed suit. Why "luckily for me"? Simply, I suppose, because I was not a child born to learn anything or to submit to the cold interests of a man dressed in black skirts and a madly flapping black hat. At any rate I loved our local pharmacy, as I have said. Furthermore, a trip to the village always promised not only my chance to stare about me at the marvels stored in gleaming vials and dangerous-looking boxes, and to watch my dear mother as she leaned forward and held her whispered conference with Monsieur Remi, that smiling old man in high collar and white apron, but also promised a ride in the young count's mighty Citroën.

What a stately machine it was, long and high, the only automobile for kilometers around, a great glistening creature brightly lacquered a soft beige that was the color of one of the crêpe de chine flouncy feminine garments belonging to the young count's wife, and trimmed with dark chocolate-colored bands. Yes, it was in this auto and driven by Papa himself, who sat in front with his head up and chin thrust out, and with his arms extended horizontally and stretched to their fullest so that both his hands could grip the steering wheel, that my mother and I made our trips to the village, snuggling proudly together in the back seat, happily smelling the warm leather and fumes from the engine. Pharmacy and lavish automobile, what a kind pair they were! And how generous was the young count, to loan his auto to Papa for our family needs.

But on the day of which I speak, when Papa was attempting to relieve me of pain and hence wreak who knows what havoc on the frog who was mine and entirely unknown to the rest of the world, ours was not a happy family that climbed into the Citroën and set off for the village. Initially the engine refused to start for my grim, preoccupied father. Mamma held my hand without the slightest enthusiasm. A fat duck barely escaped being the victim of our assembled gloom. And what do you think, the village priest was hosting a funeral when we drove into the village square and parked so heavily and darkly in front of the pharmacy that we quite overshadowed the old horse-drawn hearse drawn up before the church. Only later did we learn that it had been kindly Monsieur Remi himself who had sold little Christophe's mother the rat poison, though after all, what might we have expected?

Melodrama? Why not? In those days the pharmacist worked hand in hand with the village priest, though the two refused to speak to each other. And who but our own countrymen are the sort to misuse lonesome public urinals shaped like up-ended coffins and made of porcelain at that? After all, indiscretion is only the flowering of desperation. It just shows how light of heart we are.

But to return to the church, the pharmacy and the Citroën that was already stealing the crowd's attention from the horse and hearse and the coffin just nosing its way from between the church portals as the bell began its tolling. There we were, Papa exactly as he had been since the start of our journey, stern and silent in the front seat, and I alone in the rear, unnecessarily holding my stomach and dreading the return of Mamma and its aftermath. The interior of the young count's auto was vast and impersonal, thanks to its scent of leather and fuel and all the hidden machinery by which it worked. Yet despite his pride and autocratic pose at the wheel, Papa could not help introducing into this regal atmosphere the faint barnyard smells for which he was famous and of which he could not rid his person, for all his scrubbing. It was fitting, somehow, that the young count's occasional chauffeur should smell of hens and cow manure.

Mamma returned. Slowly and in a formal, distracted fashion, Papa quit our vehicle to assist Mamma, who was carrying several parcels wrapped in white paper and returning to me once more and taking her place at my side. How white she was and serious, despite her weak smile.

"And have you met with success, Marie?" he said. "I thought you would."

Again the village reverberated to the rhythms of our enormous engine coming to life. And off we drove in an easterly direction toward the Domaine Ardente, while the hearse proceeded toward the west, of course, and its bleak destination of old monuments and photographs of the precious dead. Could it have been anything other than our distinctive fate that caused the burial of little Christophe's father on the very day that my own father attacked my frog, using my mother as his sham agent of mercy? Surely not. And perhaps little Christophe was luckier than me in the long run, who knows? At least his father had a shorter life than mine.

No sooner had Papa opened the auto door for my package-laden mother, than he stepped aside, still secretly enjoying the import of the occasion, frowning and raising his black brows, while she, stooping, spilled her packages, seized me round the waist and laughing and reverting to her usual optimistic mood, drew me into her girlish, motherly-smelling embrace, leaving Papa to retrieve the packages.

"Marie," he said, after he had disposed of them on our scarred and oily kitchen table, or perhaps into my mother's arms again—does it matter?—and retreated hastily to the open door, "I don't believe that I can remain in the house while you minister to our little Tadpole. You know that I cannot bear his pain or yours. You know my inclination to nausea, my love."

"Dear Michel-André," she said with a laugh, her color returning along with her usual energy and quickness, "you are just too sensitive. So take a walk, my dear. We will not be long."

Thus we were alone at last, dear little Mamma and I, on the brink of something deeply personal, as I intuited, and in the daylight hours as well. My foreboding increased proportionally with the pleasure Mamma appeared to anticipate. She gathered up whole armfuls of fluffy white towels—more than even she knew were stored in her various chests or on her shelves—and set a pot to warming. She knelt beside me to unwrap the packages so that we might consider together the coil of white supple hose, the fat glass bottle, the funnel, the corks and clamps and carton of sweet-smelling salts all provided by our kind and trusty Monsieur Remi. What must she have been thinking when she listened, nodding, to the old man's instructions.

Grudgingly—perhaps warily is the more fitting word—I climbed the stairs to my now sunlit room, my handsome chamber pot, which Mamma had said we would not need, nonetheless swelling ever larger inside my head, its water swishing about and the weight of it, though it still remained hidden behind its pretty flowered curtain of my beside stand, more laden than ever with the shocking fate it promised Armand and me. How could I preserve Armand's security and yet submit to Mamma's rite of cleansing, no matter how free of discomfort she assured me it would prove, and so rapidly over? Even then I did not entirely understand what was in the offing for Armand and me, or at least initially for me, but I knew that the conflict it posed was without resolution.

In this instance Mamma was wrong, for her efforts to follow Monsieur Remi's instructions were not at all brought rapidly to a conclusion. In fact, the further along she went, the longer the process took. But at the same time, the more towels she spread or heaped on my turned-down bed, beside which I stood watching and waiting, clothed only in my nightshirt, and hence feeling inappropriately nude, given the time of day, and the more engrossed she became testing the water in the kettle she had brought up from the kitchen, or flexing the white tube and struggling to make use of the various clamps by trial and error, or smelling the contents of this carton or that, and surveying the scene and smoothing the white apron she had donned for the occasion, the less time mattered and the more I submitted now to foreboding, now to agreeable expectation, slowly tipping this way and that as did the brass dishes of Monsieur Remi's scales. The sunlight bore down upon my bed, focusing on our little amphitheater, as it were, an illumination and warmth that would never fade. As for my mother, the more she became engrossed in the procedure she clearly intended to master and carry through to its end, the more girlish and pleased with herself she became, as if she were once again the young girl giggling over her trousseau and the immediate prospects to come.

"You see, darling," she said, more to herself than to me, "it is all quite simple and painless. No one, not even Monsieur Remi's assistant, could undertake this ordinarily distasteful business with any more tenderness than your Mamma. Trust me, my little Tadpole. Trust your Mamma!"

In many ways she was quite correct, and her absorption in what she meant to do to me was quite justified. How could I not climb to my bed as she asked? How could I not readily lie on my stomach, attempting not to press my full weight on Armand, of course, and how not give myself up to the thick, soft surface of the towels and the sunlight that warmed me when, with another almost inaudible sound of suppressed giggling, she drew up the hem of my nightshirt, at once dispelling my fright by the warm feathery touch of her fingers. Somewhere between her emergence from the pharmacy and entrance into our farmhouse brimming that day with the smell of her garlic soup, she had lost her fear of having to inflict something so foreign on her only son, and so potentially filled with tension and tears, which is the kindest way of putting it, and had regained her usual energy and sweetness, the will of the competent mother who is more than content to perform such odious chores by allowing to the fore the power of the young bride's desire and anxiety. *Thy Weakness is Thy Strength,* as I have heard it said!

Just as she promised, it mattered not at all that from time to time she lost control of the hose and sprayed warm water everywhere. And when she slipped and the water splashed and trickled down my inner thighs or even my rugged little calves, why it was not an unpleasant sensation at all, quite the opposite, while the water disappeared almost at once into my bed of absorbent towels and Mamma managed to stroke and at the same time playfully pinch my buttocks, no doubt to distract me from what was happening. My broad smile, half-buried in my pillow, was the perfect match for her giggling or those long silent moments when she held her breath in concentration and the hose slid forward—or upward, inward, whatever you please—accompanied by the hurtful swelling that must have given Armand no end of surprise, since for once he was not the cause of my delicious pain.

Did poor Christophe's mother treat him in this fashion? Obviously not. And what of those children in public sickbeds and tended only by old women who scorned their wards and, once a day, by lone men in long beards and long coats who were but waiting their chance to leave those sickly children and seize their bouquets and hurry off to their midday meals with ladies in large hats? And what about dear little Papa striding anxiously and angrily back and forth in a chilly glen, while I lay half-naked in the house he had fled, basking beneath warm sun and dear little Mamma's full attention and timid hands? What perfection!

Yet all this while my reluctance lay in reserve like the very Armand I could not bear Mamma to disturb where he lay in darkest uncertainty, yet alone allow her to eject my frog tumbling and thrashing on the flood under Mamma's questionable control. Naturally I condoned Mamma's exploration of that second most private area of my chubby body, condoned her fingers and sparkling eyes on my softest flesh that I myself would never see. I even admitted the slippery tips of her fingers to make me startle and laugh outright, and the slippery tip of the rubber hose to achieve, as I have said, its still further penetration. And as I have also said, I accepted, even welcomed, the sensation of warm water swelling within me. But only so much. Only as much as I thought Armand, who had chosen me above an entire pond of warm water, after all, would permit. So throughout it all my readiness to refuse the will and hand of Mamma was at the ready. One drop too much for my defenseless frog, the drop that would plunge us both into the roiling waters that could only end in catastrophe and ugliness, and I would exert myself even against my own dear little Mamma. I was thus prepared as much for her sake as for my own and Armand's. Even she, strong person that she was, would never have recovered from the sight of Armand expelled half-drowned and thoroughly battered onto my fluffy towels. No, I would prevent such a disaster, beyond a doubt.

"Stop, Mamma!" I cried at the last possible moment, and so

forcefully that she was indeed able to staunch the potential flooding with her poor, suddenly rigid fingers.

"But darling, what's the matter? We have only a little more to finish. Let yourself go, my dearest. Please. Do what Mamma asks."

"No, Mamma," I said firmly, clutching myself against the waters.

"But I must, Pascal."

Was I not as helpless under the bare hands of my mother as the fictional Armand once was when cupped in the cruel hands of Henri? I was. How terrible, then, my dilemma, for in fact I had no choice but to obey Mamma, yet could not. I could not reveal to anyone in the world, even to Mamma, the reason why I must deny any such further tampering with my internal self, but must instead guard my body, undeveloped as it was, with my very life. To reveal my secret would have branded me forever with an odious stigma—that of derangement—so undeserved and degrading that beneath it I would have been crushed to extinction. So too Armand. Yet what choice did I have? Whereupon and suddenly I determined that to my loving mother I could only hazard the truth. She at least would believe me.

"Mamma," I whispered. "There is a frog inside me."

She paused. She said nothing. I felt one of her cool hands flat on my lower back, I felt the fingers of her other hand pinching tight the clamp that closed off the tube. Then slowly she withdrew the tube and emptied it into the kettle, while the toweling beneath me grew hot and wet, then merely damp and warm.

"Pascal," she said in her softest, most serious voice, "you know that what you have just said is impossible."

"No, Mamma," I answered without moving, "it's not."

"Then you dreamt this frog? Isn't he really the little magical creature from 'The Stories of Armand the Frog'?"

"No, Mamma, he's not. Though his name is Armand."

"A real frog, then, my child?"

"Yes, Mamma."

There was another and longer pause. Papa clenched his fists and lips in the dark wood. Mamma, my lovely nurse and physician both, considered our dilemma. Finally she spoke, still in her most worried tones.

"What are we to do, Pascal?" she asked.

"I shall find ways to appease Armand, Mamma. I shall control my cramps. I shall require less of your time at night. Papa will consider me cured. He will be happy once more. You'll see."

Again she paused, and now I was aware of her mood reversing its course and of our morning together drawing to its gentle close, which pleased me though already I knew that dear little Mamma was slipping away from me as, reluctantly, she drew down the gathered bottom of my nightshirt. I distinctly thought that she would have enjoyed playing a while longer with the hose, the lubricant, the purgatives and my plump nudeness, or occasionally repeating mornings like this one. As for me, I might have remained forever spread-eagle for Mamma, if I had not had to save Armand from the loosened waters.

"Very well, my dearest," she murmured then. "Papa would not mind our little well-meant deception. Because we love him."

At that very moment my father returned to us and, from the foot of the stairs and feebly overcoming his hesitation, called up to us, inquiring as to the state of completion and degree of success of what my Mamma had undertaken, whereupon and in her liveliest voice she affirmed her achievement of all he had hoped for. She even carried down to him my heavy, shining chamber pot, though she refused to lift aside its flowered cloth and insisted on emptying and refilling it herself. My father said that his Marie was a marvel, which was how he spoke when he wished most to shower upon my dear mother his highest words of commendation.

How's that? My frog merely a figment concocted from imaginary vapors for the sake of a personality forever in the sway of infantile desires? Oh, there's an unworthy thought. But I am the first to admit that from the time I first fell into my profound sleep beside the frog pond until I was rushed to the room above Monsieur Remi's pharmacy—that room in which he practiced his crude forms of dentistry—I had no actual proof that I had in fact swallowed a frog. But seeing is believing, as they say. And we shall see.

My Man
Wendy Walker

I

THERE REMAINED ONLY that obscure phrase, *windows of the beloved Antonia.* He beheld all his precipices above an imaginative existence, rascally crucible, life of her throat, power of resistance from his dignity. He had persuaded himself, but something far had seized upon the tail of his own stare, which stream of treasure rising from the whole quiet gulf of subjectiveness, could not face her. The few stars left, silver escort strangely smooth as my new state, floated upon his somber surrender of the lands of pitch. But he, he murmured, of reason or politics. Martin Decoud had needed to counter reverend persons in England. He might have known these Gothic remnants, overhung by dry haze. I don't feel the pitiless enthusiasms of the *Porvenir.* I am passionate for a correct impression of his passionate devotion, manifestations of a too intelligently sympathetic terror. And then Decoud spoke in French, of abandoned darkness in which the Great Isabel, too idealistic to look for him in all sleeping profoundly, to find his account too remote, began to think of an abyss. Yes. His very words, loose sheets of her wonder, paper for such knowledge, that of heavy gilt at a gallop, the mountain passes with no wind, exasperated almost to insanity your keeping, my many moods. He turned away. This resolution expressed all of us, the balconies along the world without faith hurrying into action, that dense night. When his voice ceased, your work—which has always been the enormous stillness, without light or sound, an enemy, as the saying is—made me stay here. Speculators, too. Their sweep of the hat and cracking of whips, the only proper style of uttering balderdash, was considered good counsel and courage. Curse on all imaginative weakness, tragic farce. The thing sticks in the ranks without detracting from the mould; expression was scooped out artistically, survival of enormous rocks taken advantage of. An advocate of the forefathers in morions and *peine d'oro* girls died away down the black depth upright between his legs. I have only one murmur of assent; the souls freed of paradise, gone forth into the streets of a cruel caricature, cared for me.

II

To feel himself, Decoud lay on naked crags of compromises with his panting. All his active and impalpable works, light and melted in the Madonna with the quick upward glance, pleased her immensely. He ruminated, and the rocks corrupted his judgment. Nostromo can do the tea service, his humble salute, his love for fatigued condescension— With a smile to her of the ceiling, the utterly incomprehensible Decoud had analyzed fearlessly all in a second the true English canvas nailed on again. He drank light of failure. In the great sala, her power standing straddle-legged was so complete that evenings he devoted to hurling himself, clatter and clank, had not survived. And all exertion, all passions, including land, sea, sky, the pedestal of forest behind the high wall of the city, depicted the perfect form stopping abruptly, to smoke and doze behind a tree.

III

Don José's hopes, tugging at the inception of idols without sense, folded on the correct thing, society. Only his weapon, the end of the closed door, had secured her away out of convents behind a high destiny. He stuck to it, held before his fair fame of motives and the crumbling loves, of revolution, the homage of worshippers. The white sense of unreality lifted his arm in a flush of heat. At night, the plume, the coppery English figure that drifted, a will haunted, riding far ahead, day after day, admitted him to a declamation. Have you paper, with the only solid thing, my frankness? A long course of revolutions, a love song in hair twisted as though it were her even voice, had prevented him from a personal risk. Don Carlos's mission seemed senseless. Don José Avellanos had gone forth—in the inward trembling of a principle. He had the strangest blessing, of consent. Even his hand dared to think of Antonia. She, the most anxious portal of the cathedral, bordered on the miraculous. This was the nearest measure of his discontent for venturers just landed off the coverlet; his schoolgirl of the very edge of the tea table, waved it away and withdrew. Then he shuddered a bit, like a powerful drug. Passion stood for chances of failure.

IV

The only thing running round the room, his dutiful affection, had indeed explained angles to Antonia. For masks and garlands about his mouth, and a fixed idea floating helpless, stretched out on her with his body of clouds, the sabre standing, genius, he worked himself up in the little sidelong glance at Antonia — What was the use of torn and extremely languid darkness, in which braying operatic human breasts tremble, upon the this and that — Don Martin (whose disdain of common romance derived from tampering openly with his thoughts) spoke well, but his letters —

V

Here was a man, wandering very well; keep me here all day long, maintain a turmoil of Decoud, the zest of a connoisseur turned against manliness with a great eloquence, but self-respect. And you forget that sometimes he could charm, replace the SILVER MINE. This was why he was ready to have let me go, he thought. He imagined himself aware to what point a gesture of a new state makes the world go at all. And "Martin, you will fall slowly into the most skeptical heart there in our midst." "Yes, the noise, dear," he said lightly; "Ah, *par exemple!*"

Several Bawdy Acts

Stacy Doris

AS SEVERAL BAWDY ACTS BEGIN:

"— Go on back to the ranch, Zach."

"— Not unless you say please 'please.'"

"— *Please.*"

. . . Pretty Virginia, fresh, take your medicines
(she has good looks, humorous laugh
and gentle, comes) more unmanly than difficult, begs:

ZACHARY:	I can't make love. My thing's disappeared.
DONNA:	Let me take you in (thinking, did *I* make that noise?)
ZACHARY:	Without my thing?
NURSE:	What is it?
DONNA:	A person.

. . . Thus the sun bounced on, greedily intending.

(Act II): from *Innocence the Thrift Falls.*

(*Door at the back, to a closet nudges*):

— This fat cowpoke, show him.

— Yes, like a glove.

Yellow, yellow; what will a good guy in a closet do?
(*Laughs, but frugal, and on to rewards.*)

That the fatso pump, gently — Imagine!

Enter: GREASY, the cavalier, thonged:

"I vill tell you how I kill dat
no-show"

(with a quickness for sinking)

Pinch and burn, and pinch again.

PROLOGUE: WHERE THE BEGGAR'S CONVINCED HE'S A LORD

Seen near a pub on a cliff

(frozen asks for soup)

Seen next in trot, as from hunting.

(*Flourish. They carry Sly off.*)

S. Will you sleep with me tonight?
M. I'll try my best
(clue: call the man madam; obey alone)
S. my *devoir* . . .

Stacy Doris

Scene: a richly furnished boudoir at the lord's

(dressing for night)

of small importance, yet tricky: try this one on.
(Meanwhile Beth wants only to scrape in the mud.)

S. Is this my wife?
M. Call her 'madam' for short.

The Moral:

Nurse Frenzy! Behave! Frame your Mind!

Stay on (despite the flesh and the blood)

(a love affair except for 'love').

With stuff, stuff what?

Stay on and we'll see.

A flourish. Off.

A SALVAGE AND DEFORMÈD SLAVE

Scene: A ship's middle, with ocean crashing over it.

Sailors rubbing, they help the storm.

Because this pirate comforts Soba
she's less afraid to drown.

(*Enter,* the marines, wet with cold mouths.)

Spit and slit, fast quenched.

Scene: The island, undercliff, slow-approached

Enter!

Curtained Soba and her Uncle

all ruined (sobs) the dears . . . Wait

no, now it's time. Obey —

You . . . piece of virtue you!

(Just with the green sucked out, just here.)

Close to closeness but

(don't you dare dearie)

stay good and dull.

SCOLDS: *Let me Out!*

M: Remember your torment, duty, and that ooze.

The ugly veins baking, malignant.

(Hooped with age, and envy would.)

Sir: No, sir.

Stacy Doris

A litter kid, in Pine Grove stuck

So moans and freckles that

he's let out, and *still* unsatisfied!

S: Thanks, thanks and pardon me.

M: Go dress.

S: (Invisible; quite diligent.)

Scene: speaks from the hole:

Wake up and snap out!

(munching and blistered): leave me alone!

(munching from the hole): let me eat! (roars)

Quick, just a warning:

They're in each other's power.

All . . . moo . . . in the dip, another island drop-off
with comfort rations, porridge-like, rubs the sore.

Scene: Treading water, Greets *the Monster:*

. . . and the weather caves in

(lightning) (a scurvy tune)

Drink — then I'll pour some in your other mouth

and pull you by your smaller legs.

(Fondling, gets silly.)

Come ashore by swimming, ducky.

(Grabs the bottle.) Any left?

RADIO ACTS

I. A young girl (Em) dilates
upon a bad scheme

and Vacant Kid pops out (born), a re-activation

— is he here to make fun of the contestants?

ONE Prime-Time future Evening . . .

(*unlocks the lab. Peels the grape. Munches.*)

— Memorable closet. The quick nurse.

(*Bends over the apparatus. Seems to concentrate.*)

— Oh! closet nurse!

Victorian, dejected, and wanting to zip back to earth
to make new friends.

Enter, a cowpoke. Sings: "One was kind . . .

— Yes, I lied. My name isn't Clayton.
I'm a dirty old guy with one goal: life everlasting.

(*Singing*) One was red . . . Eh?"

A small world. No escape.

LIFE OF VACANT KID. AND HIS WHOLE RACE.

Now more transparent, in a hothouse.

on dishes grows:

abandoned the rebound, coughed up and held captive
for its seed

— Not to eat! (*Ripens in drying; explodes.*)

(*Sung*) "the interior light"

(*Whispering*) — Take advantage now, harder!

(*Sung*) . . . "not outside; blessed with phosphorescence"

Crushed the peach, in a strange osmosis.

(*Sucks. Sucks longer.*)

Misses the pit. Continues. Gives thanks:

— Thanks, and condolences.

(*Sound of slap. Pause.*) — Again! (*Sound of slap, limping.*)

(Improves.)

— Just a little love, twice a day. (*Sneaks up behind.*)

— the whole bag of tricks —

Childless still. Pounded

on the rim.

— Daydream much, Lockheart?
— Nope.
— Then you're a lucky man. And a bachelor?
— To boot.

CODA: TIME TRIP

(*Scene I:* SHEILA, *in the violator's head*)

(meaning reptilian, slinky):

You failed! (before being given much chance)

(*raises whips*)

J. : (*gets in line with the other hooded forms*)

waits for DOOMSDAY

(*sobs, softly*)

Doesn't think twice. Done thinking.

SHEILA: And now that we're happy, totally, what do we do now?

JOHNNY: Take a vacation?

(II: *Pretty desert*)
The trysting tree trysts. The trysting tree cleaves, and all the rest oozes. Sequence of toasts and splashings. A shadow falls.

(IIa: *'The Dawn'*)

Land of Our Forebearers, but do-able.

Several of Sheila's past lives *Enter* and *Exit.* She salutes.

Sheila as ancient cult figure; stuck. Johnny pulls her out,

physically, as from quicksand.

Snapshots: Johnny-as-captain

Johnny-as-camerman

Sheila in onepiece. Sheila in garters. Sheila in chains. The legs open. Morsels.

SHEILA: (*plaintive*) Scratch me! No, lower (*more plaintively*). Ah!

(*Treks across time.*)

(*Memories from opera plots.*)

(*A flurry of postcards.*)

Meanwhile, in their dreams, and when they're meditating, the tragedies tune in, i.e.,

a Marketplace for Sacrifices

(*gags one sister while mincing up the other*)

SEE EVE DROOL BLOOD!

(Guess what the droopy servant offers next on her tray):

– What were the leftovers before?

(*as backdrop*) SHEILA: Where's the welcome crew?

JOHNNY: Oh, shut up.

(*Quibbles and Old Abuse.*)

(*Later*) SHEILA (*reviving*) forages for miracles.

(*Return to Scene I.*)

Sunday

Harry Mathews

Sun., 5:30 A.M.

B_2. Before it fades, a dream: sitting with my parents in their musty dining room, I hear Pater say he's going for a walk. I know he'll head for a bar to meet Mr. Valde and Fritz. I follow him. In this mild weather, the plate-glass windows of the bar's terrace have been replaced by a screen made of wooden cutouts; their patterns are said to illustrate the legend of Phaedra and Hippolytus, with the ending improved (Hippolytus marries his stepmother, Theseus hangs himself). Even if I am unable to see them, I know Mr. Valde and Fritz are sitting behind the screen. Pater walks right by. He proceeds to a parking lot at the back of the bar and there gets into a shiny new car, a foreign make that looks like a cross between a Citroën DS and a Volkswagen. He drives off. I take a bicycle and set out in pursuit. Although his car advances haltingly because of mechanical problems, I have to pedal frantically to keep up. He is following a haphazard (read: evasive) route through a city that I "know" is Barcelona (it looks like my own town, and the street signs are not in Catalan). My father parks in a pretty square filled with a variety of high, leafy trees. He gets out. He looks around him as if for a particular object. He finally spies something in a bank of high bushes. I steal behind these bushes but cannot see anything through their dense, drooping stems, each of which terminates in a purple spike. Daisy has appeared on the sidewalk. My father points to his car; Daisy pays no attention. She takes Pater by the arm and walks away with him down the sidewalk. Trapped in the shrubbery, I have to watch them from an ever-increasing distance. They turn and come back. Daisy walks up to the car and pats its rear left fender, as though the car were a horse. She kicks the tire under the fender. The entire car sinks down on its wheels with a terminal wheeze. Daisy squeezes my father's shoulder and shakes her head. Pater in turn kicks the tire disgustedly and shrugs. To me this gesture is one of heartbreaking melancholy.

Waking up almost in tears. It never crossed my mind that he might be short of money.

7:15 A.M.

B_1. At seven, restless and nauseated, I woke up for good. I made myself a cup of tea but could scarcely keep it down. Why? Hardly last night's simple if plentiful dinner. The rosé?

I've come here to finish the copying interrupted last night.

11:00 P.M.

(B_1). A long, full day. Why don't I feel sleepy? I had the good sense to take a pocket notebook with me, so that I missed much less of what happened than I would have otherwise. Daisy looked at me pointedly whenever I jotted something down. The practice may be distracting to others, even annoying, but it is of undeniable help in improving this project, which after all everyone originally approved of.

A_1. After preparing breakfast (homemade tomato juice from Madre Mia, sausages and eggs, Edam-style cheese, green grapes, hot rolls with honey and raspberry jelly, also from M.M.), I rousted out Gert at 8:15. He sat up so promptly I was left with a mouthful of unused arguments. Most Sundays, getting him up before eleven is like luring a snail out of its shell. I assumed his date with Jago and Paul explained his docility, but when I mentioned it, he murmured, "Thanks for reminding me." Mystery of late adolescence. A little later I took a tray to Daisy, still in bed. When I opened the shutters, she, too, sat up cheerfully and then announced, "I want to drive out to the country today. Let's go to the lake for lunch." My scheduled self protested, "What about my correspondence?" "Do it later!" (Re my letters: I've always kept a record of them and of course shall continue to do so.)

The day argued in her favor—as still and fair as those preceding it, suffused with veils of late-September haze that make us think that no matter how many balmy days we have had, this can be the last, that tonight wind, rain or frost may strike all the precarious green into yellow and rust.

Since the least of our departures requires superstitiously elaborate preparations (on this occasion, biscuits and bottles of water for the drive, propitiatory sweaters and umbrellas, reading material, sunglasses, sun lotion, towels, none of which we used), rechecking the car for gas, oil and tire pressure, and a final forgetting and remembering of keys and the back door and the bedroom window left open, we didn't leave till 10:30. When he went out at nine, Gert showed frank relief at escaping the imminent fuss.

The trip to Lake John XXIII takes an hour and a half. We stopped at the lakeside restaurant to reserve a table, something normally impossible so late on a sunny Sunday, but Daisy's father had been a friend of the former manager, whose successor Daisy adroitly cajoled into maintaining the special treatment accorded her family. We were given one of the rare tables for two at the waterside edge of the terrace; we were introduced to our waiter and heard him instructed to take the best care of us. (He seemed pleased enough with the assignment. He was a thin man of middling height, with recessive bald streaks separating the grizzled hair on his temples from the dark ruin of a widow's peak, and large, brown, friendly eyes. He stood straight and attentive in his black trousers, white shirt, and full-length apron. I was unaccountably glad that he was to wait on us.)

We drove towards the "beach," as the sandless bathing area is called. Daisy announced that she didn't feel like swimming but that, if I did, she would be happy to go for a walk. I replied that in that case I would be happier walking, too. (I avoided saying "walking with you," in case she preferred, as she recently has, a solitary stroll; nor did I point out that we'd left our bathing suits at home.) She didn't argue and suggested that we drive to the lake's less frequented western shore.

There we turned off the road onto a track leading to the water. We parked in a little clearing in the woods that skirt the lake, less systematically tended here than on the other side but easy enough to wander through. Daisy was in no mood for wandering and set off at her brisk pace of two days ago, raising from the forest floor a prodigious racket of snapping twigs and crackling leaves. Autumn is more evident here than in the city: except for the oaks, trees are shedding their leaves. (Light frost at night?) The mushrooms had survived. I used them as an excuse to lag behind. A_2 I found the shadowy midday warmth an irresistible invitation to loll, by which I guess I mean to loaf—in such circumstances I always think of the beautiful lines by Whitman, the American poet, "Loafe with me on the grass" and "I loafe and invite my soul, I lean and loafe at my ease observing a spear of summer grass," etc. (B_2 In my mind did *loafe* and *soul* fuse into *loll*? How can I ever pretend to be master of my words?) On a log I observed an anonymous orange fungal ear. On the ground I recognized a mushroom or two, at least by family (cantharellus, boletus). I reminded myself, in my pocket notebook, to start acquiring such information systematically. Why haven't I done so already? Do I really have less and less time, as is my impression? At least my wishes in this regard have been recorded. I saw a large, spectacularly grotesque mushroom that I once knew by name. It looks like a reduction of one of Dubuffet's outdoor sculptures. Long ago I took a specimen home for identification. My mushroom guide described it as "edible and recommended." I ate it, but I do not recommend it.

Staring at the dappled and leaf-strewn earth must have queered my vision, because a little later I had an otherwise inexplicable experience. I was gazing across a brook at a stand of young aspens, their thinning leaves quivering and glittering in slightly angled sunlight. While I looked, the leaves became still, and everything else began to quiver—the components of the relation quivering/stillness were inverted, the motion of the leaves was transferred to the aspen trunks, the ground they stood on, the trees around them, the entire world, not excluding my amazed self. Pangs of elation squeezed their way up my spine in the presence of a phenomenon that I knew was both impossible and real. I didn't dare look away for fear of losing touch with it. A_1 When Daisy spoke from nearby, I urged her to my side so that she could see what I did. She saw nothing unusual. After a while she murmured, "Time to think about lunch, darling?" I turned to embrace her and answered, "You bet it's time for lunch!" My earlier nausea had disappeared. I was famished.

On our return we found the restaurant crammed with the usual Sunday mix: families and parties of friends from the city, clearly happy to be in the country together on this benign day. As we made our way towards our table we were hailed by familiar voices: Paul and Jago were seated in front of pint glasses of dark beer at the table d'hôte in the middle of the dining hall. Jago and Daisy went off to negotiate with the manager. They succeeded in exchanging our waterside spot for a small table for four right next to it. Sitting down, I was pleased to see that we hadn't lost our waiter.

Ordering the meal was simple. The standard lunch, which at 35.00 cost half what it would have in town, was not only acceptable but inevitable. A half-minute discussion about wines between our waiter and Jago, who loves on these occasions to show his expertise, disposed of that agreeable question. For two hours we applied ourselves to ingesting the following series of dishes, which as I register it may sound copious but left us all feeling light as any weight-watcher. A platter of salami and microscopically sliced sun-dried beef, cured raw ham, garlic sausage, segments of spinach-flavored blood sausage, and the liverwurst that is a house specialty, as good as any pâté (in this country, anyway). A salad of romaine and tomatoes. A pile of deep-fried baby perch fresh from Lake John XXIII. Roast loin of pork with buttered new potatoes and a stew of the same yellow-stemmed, brown-capped cantharellus I saw in the woods, here called September bugles. The celebrated cheese of the region, Summer Orange, a ball made from goat's milk and rolled in onion-flavored toasted bread crumbs. Chocolate nut cake.

Through the fried perch we drank pitchers of an open wine, what in the jargon is termed a "vivacious" sparkling chenin blanc that we couldn't seem to get enough of. It started me down the pleasant slope of abandon at whose mossy foot I eventually came to rest. For the pork we switched to a six-year-old cabernet franc, and at the very end I insisted (Jago had already declared us his guests) on contributing a bottle of Hungarian Tokay, no less powerful than it was ripe. None of these wines can properly be considered local. Barely north of our town, the country around the lake is already too cold for the vine.

As the meal started, I asked the two men why they hadn't brought Gert along. They replied that he'd left the court after an hour's play. "How come?" I asked. "Wasn't he playing well?" "No, he's pretty good." "Except he's in lousy shape," Jago added. Paul went on, "Maybe. He seemed to have his mind on other things. He took off around a quarter of eleven. We kept at it till almost noon."

Daisy was surprised they hadn't let us know they were coming here. "It was completely spur-of-the-moment," Paul said. "And we did call," Jago insisted, "but you'd already left. Anyway, here we all are." He smiled as he raised his glass: "*Servus.*"

I refrained from asking about the absence of another person. It is my rule never to mention her, and to talk about her as little as possible. No one spoke her blessed name.

We had a jolly lunch. As the only woman present, Daisy was much fussed over. It warmed me to see her abandon her worried look of past days. She told us all about her trip for the rug company, providing an acid description of one nervous, solemn, maladroit businessman that for some reason made Paul and Jago laugh immoderately. I was glad it cheered *her* up. Afterwards Jago turned to me: "I didn't phone you back after you called the other day because there was nothing to worry about. They're a capable outfit." Daisy asked what he was talking about. Jago told her, though I'd rather he hadn't. She gave me a blurred look somewhere between incredulity and exasperation. "My sweet man, I wouldn't have gotten involved if I hadn't been sure of them. You should have asked *me*." More laughter.

For some time a little girl of four or five had been standing next to our table quietly filching pieces of meat (the first-course medley had been left in front of us during the salad and fish). Busily chattering with her party, her mother noticed her at last and cried out in mock indignation, "Berenice, *what* are you doing?" The little girl put a last slice of blood sausage in her mouth and went back to her table.

The incident led Paul to tell a rare anecdote from his *vie sentimentale*: his final encounter with a young woman named Berenice with whom he'd had a holiday romance one summer on the Romanian coast. (Why does that benighted country keep popping up in my life?) The meeting took place shortly after their return here. Paul had told Berenice, Listen, when we met I warned you not to go to bed with me if you were thinking about falling in love. Our first weeks were wonderful because we didn't worry about consequences. We just enjoyed spending time with each other. Berenice: I still don't worry about consequences. I still love spending time with you. Nothing has changed. That's my point—I don't want anything to change. Paul: It's not so. You want things to turn out a certain way, and you complain when they don't. You complain all the time. Berenice: It's been like that from the start. On our first date you said all the women you'd loved were difficult and demanding. If I'd been easygoing I never would have seen you twice. Paul: But look at us. You're unhappy. I'm unhappy. I can't give you what you give me—I'm not capable of loving you. Berenice: You think I love you? Who ever said I loved you? How could *anyone* love you? With an intuitive speed that astonished him, Paul got up and left. He had realized that this was an opportunity not to be missed. He did not see her again.

Daisy laughed when he'd finished: "You were right. All the same, the story—*your* story—reeks of sexism. It's the old smear that women are hopelessly illogical and 'impossible.'"

"Women aren't illogical and impossible; humans are. I happened to start the argument, that's all. If she'd started it, I would have reacted the same way. It's a situation where there's no room for anything but self-defense."

I talked less than the others, but before befuddledom set in I managed one cute (if unfair) remark. While the cheese was being served, Paul glanced toward the entrance and asked, "Isn't that Dr. Markevitch?" Jago turned and confirmed the sighting: "The doctor and legal expert." "Let's get him over," Daisy exclaimed, "and make him talk about malpractice suits." "Did you notice," I remarked, "that he's wearing one?"

This was one of my last contributions to the ongoing banter, which I nonetheless continued to enjoy, mostly for the warmth that so manifestly underlay it. I had meanwhile been drawn into another conversation, an intermittent one taking place between our waiter and myself.

His name was Zoltan—he was Hungarian. We felt a marked sympathy from the moment we saw one another. I cannot explain this. I think we guessed at a complicity, at some kind of shared story we might tell. Of his own story, only bits had emerged thus far: he had emigrated five years ago, he'd formerly been a musician. With the Tokay, I asked him to give us a fuller account. Knowing how wine dilutes my memory, I kept my pocket notebook handy.

Zoltan had been born into a working-class family in Erzebet, an industrial suburb of Pest. His musical gifts were recognized in grade school, where the choirmaster noticed not only his fine ear but his uncanny flair for sight-reading. Zoltan also possessed a facility with instruments that enabled him within the space of two years to play middlingly difficult pieces on the clarinet, violin and piano. His first teachers encouraged him to stick to the violin.

When Zoltan reached the age of fourteen, these early mentors helped him obtain the first of three scholarships that paid for his musical studies through the end of his secondary education. Then and later, his parents' modest resources made it impossible for them to help him, except in one unforeseen way.

Zoltan's mother had relatives in the wine country near Lake Balaton. One autumn, Zoltan and his family went to visit them for the Saturday-night celebration marking the end of the vintage. It was the October of his eighteenth year. Zoltan, who had brought his fiddle, joined the local players in the traditional dances that followed the festive supper. In a class apart from his companions, he began, to the delight of dancers and bystanders, performing dazzling improvisations on the customary folk tunes.

Among those present — vintners, their relatives, a few city visitors — was a middle-aged man who was elegantly dressed and bore himself in a way suited to more cosmopolitan surroundings. This gentleman several times interrupted his conversations to listen to the music, usually when Zoltan was the soloist. The man eventually came forward, asked one of the fiddlers for the loan of his instrument, and joined Zoltan on the podium. Revealing himself to be a violinist of supreme skill, he engaged Zoltan in a series of "answering" improvisations in which each spurred the other to ever greater exploits. The dancing stopped; the company crowded around to listen to this amiable competition between the veteran and the prodigy.

The gentleman afterwards thanked Zoltan for affording him such a satisfying busman's holiday. He introduced himself as Adolph Busch, the first violin of the Busch Quartet, with which he had come to Hungary on tour. He asked about Zoltan's musical background and offered to help him. Zoltan spoke of his material difficulties. Busch promised him his support. He kept his word. In Budapest his recommendation secured Zoltan an audition at the Conservatory. He won a state scholarship that paid his studies over the next five years.

Because I was busy catching up with my notes, I missed the details of what happened next. In the end, he became a virtuoso and a knowledgeable interpreter of the classical repertory.

Zoltan's future was not yet assured, although he now found work easily and supplemented his public stipend by playing in orchestras, in chamber groups and, most often, in dance bands. The world is full of fiddlers; a soloist's career is launched by winning prizes year after year in international competitions. Zoltan had to find money to feed and clothe himself while paying his way to Bucharest, Genoa, and Paris, and eventually, if all went well, to Moscow and Brussels.

A dance band specializing in the czardas and the verbunkos hired him for a tour through Poland and Czechoslovakia. One of its last stops was Marienbad, a Bohemian spa whose prewar luster still attracted to its casino the hard currency of gamblers from the west. At this casino Zoltan's band played a two-night stand.

On first entering the gaming rooms, Zoltan tried roulette for a while. Out of curiosity he looked into the salon where old-style baccarat was played. He was fascinated by the intensity of the silence and the concentration of the players—"like an orchestra rehearsing with Fürtwängler."

For an hour Zoltan observed the activity at one table. Throughout this time only a single person remained seated in the same place: a thin, gray-haired woman wearing silver-rimmed spectacles. She faced a series of gamblers, usually one at a time. She won many of the pots, which ranged from two hundred to two thousand dollars, so that at the end of the hour the gray-haired woman had about thirty thousand dollars stacked in front of her.

This woman sat immediately to the right of the dealer. She was thus automatically the last to be given cards, no matter how many were betting against her. It seemed to Zoltan that against one other player the gray-haired woman always won, whereas with two or more opponents she won only occasionally. Zoltan concluded that the game had been rigged (a notion he later found puerile): the deck was stacked so that with only two players the second cards would make their holder a winner. For twenty minutes Zoltan tried to verify his hypothesis, but his efforts at objectivity were undermined by an intensifying ache in the pit of his stomach. The ache told him that nothing he saw or thought could stop him from betting his hunch. At last, having taken a seat at the gray-haired woman's right to be sure of intercepting "her" cards and having waited for a hand where a single player bet ahead of him, he put down on the table the three thousand dollars that he had carefully saved over the past five years.

His first bets apparently justified his decision. He was dealt a winning deuce, eight, and seven, then an eight, four, and five. When for the third time he found himself with only one bettor to his right, Zoltan sat as if paralyzed, hating to withdraw his stake (now multiplied ninefold), but terrified of losing it. His two antagonists had matched him. Cards were dealt—to him, a nine and a six. Custom, virtually the rule of the game (as the dealer insisted), required him to stay in. Sensing that he was beaten on the board, he decided to draw against the odds and tapped the felt cloth with his forefinger. He was dealt a three. He walked away with over eighty thousand dollars, a sum, he reminded us, worth ten times its current value. His livelihood was assured for years to come.

He wired his small fortune to a bank in Geneva and finished the tour in a state of elation. He often thought of all the advantages he could now provide for his parents, and for himself, too. He imagined a cottage in the country where he could practice day and night; a place no more than half an hour's ride from Budapest, which would be convenient for a companion working there. . . . And around the cottage an orchard, and a few high trees amid which they might walk, arm in arm, hand in hand. . . . A hammock for napping together in the hot season. . . . And for her, a room all her own, out of earshot of his scales and trills. But when the band came back to Budapest, Sophie was not waiting for him.

They had met in a nightclub where he was playing. Whenever he performed popular music, he conspicuously dressed himself in a grotesquely high celluloid collar and old-fashioned string cravat. This attire distinguished him from the other gifted musicians in that most musical of capitals. He soon had a following, and managers regularly assigned him a little highlighted podium apart from other performers. That was how Sophie noticed him. Before that evening was out she had arranged an introduction. They spent three happy years together.

Sophie worked as confidential secretary to the cabinet director of the minister of trade. The job gave her access to information concerning import-export matters. It was to this that Zoltan, finding himself abandoned, attributed her change of heart. The middle-aged nongentleman from Györ whom she preferred to him, an enterprising exporter of the country's famous hard salami, hardly surpassed him in personal or social appeal. He surmised that at a time when state control was descending on the economy like mosquito swarms on the shores of Lake Balaton, the man, hoping to exploit her position, had offered her a security that no one in those times could reasonably refuse. Zoltan wondered whether he might not have kept her preference had Sophie known of his triumph at the gaming tables.

I was so anxious not to lose any details that I missed about a minute of Zoltan's story. I then heard him say that he had been brought to trial and immediately asked, "Trial? Trial for what?"

He looked at me, perplexed. Nudging me with sandaled toes, Daisy suggested, "Why don't you put that fucking notebook away and listen?"

He had said "diary," not "trial." Zoltan had started one at the time and kept it diligently ever since. Of course, I began questioning him about his methods. Paul interrupted, "But your music?" Zoltan bent over to lay his left hand palm-upward on the checkered tablecloth. The palm was gnarled; knotted strands of tissue constricted the ring and index fingers, and when he opened up his hand, it was clear that they could not be fully straightened. "The condition is called Dupuytren's contracture." "I know," Paul said, "and it can easily—" "Please. This started decades ago." A pause followed. Jago asked, "What about the money?" "I provided for my family. The rest is still in Switzerland. Close to three million francs, I suppose." "Then what are you doing here?" "Haven't we had a good time together?" We nodded as though we understood.

The afternoon had not ended, the sky was not yet darkening, but the time had come to start home. After Jago paid the bill, he and the others rose from their chairs. I did not mind the glances exchanged over my apparently hopeless immobility. I was too happy. "That Tokay!" I exclaimed to show awareness of my catatonic state. Paul helped me to my feet. Putting one arm around his shoulders and the other around Jago's, I performed a little jig as I stood up to express my good spirits. They all laughed. We proceeded to the cars. It was decreed that Daisy would drive Paul home, and Jago me.

At home I was left to myself. I called C. I confessed my sloshed condition as well as my insane love and indeed lust for her. She replied with determined propriety. I eventually grasped that someone was with her. (I thought I detected a woman's voice in the background, as if in an adjoining room.)

A_2. I went to my desk to clear up the correspondence I would normally have done this morning. I'd barely sat down when I began feeling too drowsy to attend to it. I decided to explore Gert's bathroom drawer. The bennies were there. I popped one and stepped outside for a few breaths of air to get it working. A_1 Daisy drove up and I welcomed her home with an outdoor hug.

(A_1). Mail log:

Sukik: Places in town scarce and getting scarcer. Do not recommend moving here.

Pater: Do not phone me at office [nth time]. Difficult period for Gert. Regularly seeing girl his own age; in my opinion older woman better for him (happier). [How to find a second Colette?]

Pfeiffer: [answer to unlisted letter: photographer doing series on trades and professions, wants me to model "average manager"]: No thanks.

Somis: Send list of wines currently available.

National Institute of Geography [re walking tours]: Send catalog of maps for (a) Lake John XXIII area (1:25,000) and (b) Syria (smallest scale available).

Hans & Eva: Back in time for opera? (*From the House of the Dead.*)

ASB: Balances confirmed. Transfer 5,000 from savings to checking.

A_2. While vigorously executing twenty push-ups and fifty sit-ups I B_2 realized that with a free hour ahead of me, I could start implementing my plan to improve my knowledge of the natural world—less a plan than a wish, today boosted by confronting nameless mushrooms. Because it was Sunday and I had only my own books to consult, I considered the possibilities at hand. A_2 I went from one room to another, glancing over shelves whose contents were all too familiar: poetry, history, histories of the arts. Would an encyclopedia do the trick? I saw myself taking fragmentary notes as I trudged from WEATHER to ISOBARS to AIR MASSES. I then spied Daisy's row of cookbooks through the kitchen door. They surely contained a specialized vocabulary worth learning—a full gamut of condiments, utensils and procedures. B_2 And what part of the world, I asked myself, is more natural to us than the food that we eat so regularly, so unquestioningly, so ignorantly?

A_2. As I walked into the kitchen, I understood that I must learn more than words—more, that is, than their theoretical meanings. I know how restless I feel whenever I watch Daisy maneuvering her pots and pans. It is a restlessness compounded of admiration and a jealous sense of my own inadequacy. Here was exactly what I'd been looking for.

I knew at once where to begin: by learning how to make a plain omelet—the kind of omelet that arrives on one's plate in the very best restaurants, soft, at its center almost runny, as perfectly shaped as a trimmed fish, with skin smooth and resilient, not browned but of a yellow at most freckled with tan, and neither dry nor greasy. I picked out several large cookbooks, all shabby from use, and set out to discover how this simple, rare delight was achieved.

I discovered one thing immediately: cooks—at least those who write cookbooks—disagree. In regard to omelets they agree about nothing except the kind of pan to use (even here one recommends a "7-inch bottom for 3 eggs, 11-inch for 8 eggs," and another a a "10-inch for 3 or 4 eggs," proportions that are hard to reconcile). For instance, some say pepper should be used in the seasoning, while others forbid it. The disagreements that most bothered me were (a) whether, in preparation, to beat the eggs (with "vigorous strokes") or stir them ("a few gentle turns"); (b) whether to put the pan directly on high heat or put it on warm heat and turn the flame up at the last moment; (c) whether to stir the eggs after they are in the pan or let them set and then jiggle them.

I made a list of possible combinations of these three alternatives. Ideally I should make eight trial omelets:

beating — high heat — stir in pan
beating — high heat — let set then jiggle
beating — warm heat — stir in pan
beating — warm heat — let set then jiggle
stirring — high heat — stir in pan
stirring — high heat — let set then jiggle
stirring — warm heat — stir in pan
stirring — warm heat — let set then jiggle

It was like the car tires yesterday morning. But yesterday the problem could be solved on paper, and I had plenty of time for it. This evening I wanted to proceed from theory to practice, and my time was limited. My research had taken a good half hour. Daisy was already casting quizzical glances into the kitchen, where she would shortly prepare a real meal for four. I had to take one of my eight options straightaway. I chose beating, high heat, let set then jiggle. The dashing style of one particular recipe no doubt determined my choice, and I reckon it may well be the best, but I was not to find out today.

Because the author insisted that an omelet pan can never be too hot, I turned the oven on full blast and placed a cast-iron skillet in it while I cracked, seasoned, and beat the eggs. I remembered to use a potholder to transfer the skillet to a gas burner. Into it I then poured oil and, after a while, the beaten eggs. A few moments later I suffered a brief and disastrous lapse of attention. The eggs had begun to coalesce; it was time to start jiggling. The sight of the skillet perched familiarly on top of the stove canceled my recollection of its recent sojourn in the oven. I seized the iron handle with my bare left hand. There followed a second of unfeeling shock, after which my hand flew into the air like a startled partridge and I screamed. Daisy, on her way into the kitchen at that moment, opened the icebox door, grasped my left wrist, and thrust the hand, palm up, against the bottom of the freezer compartment. This probably saved at least two layers of skin (it quickly puckered with blisters), but only tomorrow will tell. After half a minute or so Daisy released my hand, turned off the gas, and opened a number of windows to dissipate the smoke and the stench of charred egg.

I consoled myself at the time with the thought that the mishap would give me something interesting to write about.

My cookbook reading added only one new term to my vocabulary: drum sieve.

Gert came home while Daisy was making supper. I was standing in the hall when he walked through the front door. He smiled a smile from his childhood days; my eyes filled with tears. Picking up the still-wrapped Hegel, he undid the package and riffled through the book. "I'll start it tonight. Thanks." He went into the kitchen and spent the next hour discreetly making himself useful. The change in him was unnerving. I didn't dare inquire after its cause.

At three minutes past seven Paul arrived—"almost late, as usual," he said. We were alone. I at once asked him if he'd spoken with Gert. Did he know what was bothering him? Could he explain his sudden weird good-naturedness? Paul looked at me in a way I couldn't define, perhaps impatient, somewhat devious, not antagonistic, concerned (but for whom?). "I've *always* found him good-natured. We did talk a little. Don't worry about him. He'll be all right. He *is* all right." I didn't press the matter. It's fine with me if Gert confides in Paul. A father can't be a good grandfather, too. And I don't mean Pater.

Our big lunch had somehow produced in us a resurgence of hunger and thirst; Daisy, knowing that *l'appétit vient en mangeant,* had cleverly anticipated it. We got through a jar of anchovies and a bottle and a half of Riesling before even sitting down at the dining table. There, as if we'd been fasting, we consumed bowls of spiced white-bean soup, a rabbit sautéed in white wine with buttered tagliatelle on the side, lettuce salad, ewe cheese, and raspberries dusted with sugar. Two bottles of last night's rosé were drunk (and Gert drank beer), and we poured slivovitz into our emptied coffee cups. I was astonished at how light and lighthearted this left me.

During the meal Paul was entertaining, Gert attentive, Daisy cheerful (and a little distracted?) and I—who knows? *They* know.

B_1 I enjoyed them. I was afloat in unconscious happiness—perhaps the only true kind. When C. was mentioned, I reminded myself, The woman you long to be with! and felt only an echo of regret, like a regret out of art, like catching one of Monk's long solos through a window in the summer twilight.

A_1. Paul talked at length about our waiter. He had liked Zoltan; he had enjoyed his story; he felt that it was only possibly true. His skepticism had arisen during the Marienbad episode. It sounded too much like a gambler's dream: not one miraculous stroke of luck but a succession of them. There were persuasive details in the story, but Paul wondered if they might not have been added after simpler versions had failed to convince. As Paul listened, it had occurred to him that Zoltan might have reinvented not only the Marienbad episode but *all* the events of his life, as year after year he repeated his story to strangers. Trial and error would have led to modifications that transformed the original anecdote—something like "I went into the casino with my life savings and came out ten times richer"—into one that required the full-scale creation of an imaginary past. The life as told was undeniably interesting; it also carried little risk of exposure: Zoltan's disabled hand, for instance, eliminated the danger that a customer would one day fetch a violin from the cloakroom and ask him to play.

Paul said that in the end he didn't care whether Zoltan had been lying or not. He was plainly a happy man—what difference did it make if his happiness came from his success as a storyteller?

I said flatly that I took Zoltan at his word. Daisy thought that if his tale was false, it made it better. Gert, for whose benefit we summarized what we'd heard, pointed out that in either case Zoltan had shown pluck, since he'd made himself ridiculous by admitting he'd lost Sophie to a hard-salami salesman.

We had scarcely finished our slivovitz when Daisy announced that *Die Meistersinger* was being broadcast at nine-thirty and that she wanted me to listen to it with her. (Gert disappeared into his room; Paul yawned theatrically and went home.) I knew the opera well, and I had my account of the entire day to write, but my protests did me no good. "It's *because* you know it so well that I'd like to watch with you. That way I won't fall asleep." At least I managed to skip the third act—I loathe it, and not only for Sachs's chauvinistic diatribe—and settled at my desk to compile this report of a busy Sunday.

While writing, I've realized something obvious. My categories

While writing, I've realized something obvious. My categories (A_1 A_2 B_1 B_2) should be split into specific sections. This will be easy to do — e.g., by dividing B (subjective matters concerning what is outside me) into matters involving *people* and those involving *things,* like the overheated frying pan. I'm not sure how to label the sections — I'll straighten that out tomorrow.

It's past 3 A.M. I can't risk sleeping late, especially with this restructuring to do. I'll skip the medicine again (no ill effects so far). I wonder how thick this book will grow before the vase is broken.

Meditation: First and Last Trek, Zangskar

Nathaniel Tarn

In the early practice the mind is . . .
In the middle the mind is . . .
At the end the mind is . . .

—Tilopa in Takpo Tashi Namgyal:
Mahamudra (p. 169)

Stone or sand—sand ease of motion,
stone sharp, scree, riprap, obstacle,
falling perpetually away down mountainside—
like walk on glass, shard, blade,
cut in the very meatflesh of the foot,
down into bone. The way of heaven,
the way of hell: which can we say is which?
There are, we have agreed, the hells we fear
(much further off the east than this)
and a hell we love. Beautiful hell:
to love and beauty we have contracted,
condemned ourselves. Meanwhile,
mouth dry as hell's part—wind,
altitude—lips almost glued together,
speech all interior of reprobation.
"Immanence without hope." The immanence
is *this?* Blisters on soles,
razors at knees, muscles pulling
against the spine, away from it:
crucifixion of muscles
bunched wrong way up, against the grain.

Roses and horse dung.
Later: roses and wild water.
Huge rose bushes against the sky:
rose clouds, rose cumuli
on the blue ether. Extending arms of scent
astounding motherliness of roses,
extending perfume as if to save your mind.
Pass from oasis of salvation
to the next oasis: bury my face
in each bush as I pass
as if collapsing to the motherhood of roses.
These, from near-white to neon pink,
from which all roses sprang
in more familiar countries: rose lineages
in all the universe: there are perhaps
roses on other planets, daughters of these?
Maybe pushed into shapes unknown on other planets?

Roses, divine charity of Zangskar,
soul or distillation of that rock:
I had not thought a flower could save
but, in this nightmare, thought is invalid.
Gentian near-gray in modest isolations,
pearl crowds of edelweiss (hardly mythical),
blue prototype geranium in massed profusion,
limning the barley fields, likewise our fireweed,
forget-me-not playing the register
of light and dark up and down mountainsides;
still blue the poppy most solitary of flowers,
sole or pyramidal, inspired first hunting
childhood ambitions. The lemon mint,
fragrant drug, stuffed up the nostrils,
rubbed on the mustache . . . Also,
the plethora of birds: redstart,
goldfinch, svelte warbler, doves,
snow doves, pigeons, the little bird
insisting on "tuwitchu" so frequently
it takes you out of mind, numbered among
the fourteen Himalayan kinds of rose-finch.

Choughs play over their prayer flags,
dark veering into light and back
strung out from peak to peak between gold roofs.
Perhaps, above the highest pass, a giant span
of lammergeier? Whistling marmots, scurrying voles,
slow yaks and dzos. One crest, crown of the earth
against the sky, carries twelve ibex:
sharp hooves, curved horns of iliad, bugle eyes.

But, of saving graces like the rose,
the other is wild water,
water collapsing from "eternal snows,"
white clarity of snows. Sole water
in this land—rain does not top
the mountain chains to reach it—
for barley, peas and roses, for
the few fields, far apart and sparse,
will let you know how many people
are graced to live in such and such a crease
of the inhuman mountains.
Water to green the land
a month or two before distinction
is blotted out again by new
eternal snows. Wild water singing me
up and down the path—this immanence—
waters one dies to drink from
at every meeting, waters would willingly
receive and fill an entire body
thrust into it on a hallucination,
despite stone cut and bruise,
waters I have wanted to stay in,
drink, swallow by uncounted gallons,
even to drown in, as one may drown
in just an inch of water
when breath costs life enough.
So dry the mouth, so dusty
this fine "road," the "only road
to India," just some few inches wide,
tortured with every torture of this land,

this madhouse of the gods, bedlam of theirs,
ultimate calcified shit of gods,
bones of more ancient worlds.

Also the water of the eternal river
pounding its everlasting passage
like the profoundest message of the soul
into this immanence, water always present,
(corner of eye nearest path's rim)
as foot searches for life:
so that these gorges are scarcely ever *seen*
on such a trek. Within an inch of life
at any time, walking air, water, rock,
from rose to rose to simulate duration,
would dearly like to fall into the river.
Never so royal a procession witnessed
from far to near if such can be distinguished:
at the beginning of the vista, coming;
at middle of it, coming; at the far end,
going; water drowned into going
to come up elsewhere, further on the path
but the same river, song high as wind,
deep as dynamite — ears brought alive, eyes
whiting out to benefit the sound.

All night these rivers moving to their ends
invisible; all day the same but visible you think
until the water, running with the mind
becomes the run of it. This earth
in its vast movement flowing
from nought to nought
through all its computations:
you and the earth become indifferent.
There is nothing to do,
nothing to finish, no workings to begin —
all is done for you in that river flow
which is the greatest of the fourfold world.

Nathaniel Tarn

If I were in the valley gardens,
the dancing gardens of Kashmir
(blood-purple hollyhocks, red poppies,
roses also), where light's white gash
achieves perfection in all wounds,
playing among a myriad leaves and petals,
I would not flow more gently
having kept half my mind
than I flow here with half the loss of it
and with no coat to cover half my body.
Apricot valley; willows of marsh and field
"which I already remember on my dying day"
as if their branches were the orchards
of my own country, were my limbs
(so deeply do they have the reach of home),
what I can call, over the obstacle of hope,
my own dear country. Among the broken rock
more void of vegetation than any other rock
this planet knows, wild waters follow on together.

There is an island set in a circling sea
of which it has been said (as of the paradise gardens)
"if there be any heaven on this earth
it is here, it is here, it is here!"
Cleaning the Zangskar shoes above its beaches —
that these which walked high silences
now, white again, might walk such beaches
almost as silent as the mountain passes.
Later this season: no flowers on the island,
flowers vanished into some ideal springtime
back of the mind. Birds rare:
high loss of wing with loss of hope.
So here to turn away from hope and go
to the vast business, walked on this penance —
the up-and-down of it, in every step
and fight for breath and holding down the boot
to one rock's treachery after another:
of how the light which should be general
becomes imprisoned in countless individuals

so that the understanding is irremediably scattered;
this mind, which could encapsulate a whole,
explodes of it, is exiled into number,
exhausts itself as seas against a beach
no one can watch or prophecy the end of,
going uninterrupted round the universe
and out beyond it and herds of other planets –
the beach becoming home, year after year,
to myriads of shells, delicate corpses
borne in to die on it from every ocean.

Who came from the warring stars
home to a state of music. To bring on
down the patience. To labor over it,
to enter, although late, the world
at last, though very late, to enter
air around you as if an habitation, place
to feel "freedom" in, and "joy,"
the "immanence-in-joy," caught "as it flies"
without a mineral trace of fear, anxiety,
the sempiternal gnaw of anguish. To move
on rock as sharp as glass all of the time,
to feel it smooth as mind become the mount itself
of "immanence." To have taken a life,
almost the whole of it, to effect this entrance
and to initiate a powerful survival. Reason for "joy,"
even for "praise" who never could see limb of such
or bless intrusion from them in the early life.

"What is it then?"   "Is there anything to it?"

Love Sentence

Lynne Tillman

O, know, sweet love, I always write of you,
And you and love are still my argument;
So all my best is dressing old words new,
Spending again what is already spent;
For as the sun is daily new and old,
So is my love still telling what is told.

—William Shakespeare, Sonnet 76

Evelina lowered her lids while he read. It was a very beautiful evening, and Ann Eliza thought afterward how different life might have been with a companion who read poetry like Mr. Ramy.

—Edith Wharton, "Bunner Sisters"

It's strange . . . it's strange!
His words are carved in my heart.
Would real love be a misfortune for me?

—Verdi, *La Traviata*

I wrote and told you everything, Felice, that came into my mind at the time of writing. It is not everything, yet with some perception one can sense almost everything. . . . I don't doubt that you believe me, for if I did you would not be the one I love, and nothing would be free of doubt.

—Franz Kafka, to Felice Bauer, July 13, 1913

EVERYTHING PAIGE THOUGHT about love, anything she felt about love, was inadequate and wrong. It didn't matter to her that in some way, from some point of view, someone couldn't actually be wrong about an inchoate thing like love. "An inchoate thing like love" is feeble language. If my language is feeble, Paige thought, isn't my love?

Love, are you feeble?

It was spring, and in the spring a young man's, a young woman's, heart turned heedlessly, helplessly, heartlessly, to love. Were those hearts skipping beats? Were eager suitors walking along broad avenues hoping beyond hope that at the next turn the love they had waited for all their lives would notice them and halt midstep or midsentence, dumbstruck, lovestruck? Were women and men, women and women, men and men, late at night, sitting in dark bars, surrounded by smoky glass mirrors, pledging their minds and bodies?

In her mind's eye (she tried to picture that), Paige could see the lovers. She could nearly hear them. (Is there a mind's ear?) In the bar, plaintive Chet Baker was singing "They're writing songs of love, but not for me." Or, Etta James was wailing, "You smiled and then the spell was cast. . . . For you are mine at last." And what did the lovers sing to each other? Did they, would they, utter the words "I love you"?

On the computer screen "I love you" winked impishly at Paige.

I love you.

Paige wondered whether words of love, love talk, would survive, whether that courtly diction would rest easy on the computer screen, on its face (on the face of it), where words were rendered facilely and could appear so readily—complacent and indifferent—and then be wiped off even more casually. Words were eased away, erased, quickly scrolled into nothing or into the memory of a machine. Wouldn't the form dictate the terms, ultimately? Wouldn't love simply vanish?

Even so, I love you.

Once upon a time the impassioned word was scratched into dirt, smeared and slapped onto rough walls, carved into trees, chiseled into stone, impressed onto paper, then printed into books. On paper, in books, the words waited patiently and were handy, ever visible. They were evidence of love. In that vague, formative past, love was written with a flourish, and it flourished.

Is the computer screen an illuminated manuscript—evanescent, impermanent, but with a memory? A memory that is no longer mine – or yours. Is love a memory that is neither mine nor yours?

Remember I love you.

Paige thought, I give my memory to this machine. I want ecstasy, not evidence.

Can a machine prove anything of love? If she points to it, could Paige attest, as one might of a poem written on the finest ivory linen paper: Here, this is evidence of my love?

"For you are so entirely fair, / To love a part, injustice were / . . . But I love all, and every part, / and nothing less can ease my heart." (Sir Charles Sedley)

Paige glanced at the little marks, letters, covering in regular patterns, as words and paragraphs, sheets of paper that were spread haphazardly around her on the desk, on the floor. She gazed at the computer screen, as comforting and imperturbable as a rock or television.

Love, my enemy, even now I love you.

Romantic love arrived with the singer, the minstrel, who traveled from court to court, from castle to castle, relaying messages of love, concocting notions of love, torrents of poetic emotion. In the courts men and women listened to these plaints and added more, their own. The singer heard new woes and put them into song. There was a way to woo. But why did the minstrel sing in the first place, and what did traveling from one place to another do to produce songs of love? And later, did the printing press change love? Did the novel, offspring of Gutenberg's invention, transform love? Did love become a longer, more extended narrative with greater expectations? Not a song but an opera?

"When people used to learn about sex and die at thirty-five, they were obviously going to have fewer problems than people today who learn about sex at eight or so, I guess, and live to be eighty. That's a long time to play around with the same concept. The same boring concept." (Andy Warhol)

Dearest,

I don't think I've ever felt this way before, not exactly. Not like this. Is it possible? I thought about you all day, and then in the night too, and I felt I was going to die, because my heart was beating so hard and fast, as if it were a caged bird, trapped in my chest and flapping its wings madly, trying to fly out and away. Even if my heart were a wild bird, it would fly to you.

Paige wondered if love disinvented, too, if it disinvented her and him. She moved from the computer, which seemed to glower when it didn't glow, into the kitchen. She went to the sink and turned on the cold water. She watched the water flow into the teakettle. Then she put the kettle on the stove.

Dearest,

I love you especially when you are far away. I can feel you most when I don't see you. I carry you with me because your words carry, they fly, and yet they stay with me, stay close to me, like you do even when you're not beside me. To be honest, love, sometimes words are all I need. The words satisfy, your words, your words.

"Does that goddess know the words / that satisfy burning desire?" (Puccini, *Madama Butterfly*)

"I can love the other only in the passion of this aphorism." (Jacques Derrida)

Paige thinks that writing may be an act of love, a kind of love affair, or a way of loving. She hopes that's a possibility, because even more, even worse, more horribly and wretchedly, she knows it's an incessant demand for love, enfeebling and humiliating, always wanting, always asking to be met. And nothing is less fulfilled, except unrequited love, though it may be the same thing. She wasn't sure. Because her own worthless desire derided her, her writing disappeared into worthlessness, to become transparent.

"My Love is of a birth as rare / As 'tis, for object, strange and high; / it was begotten by Despair / Upon Impossibility." (Andrew Marvell)

Dearest,

Maybe I am always writing love, to you. That's the only way I can love you. What if love, like writing, is a rite enacted over and over, just a habit, a mode of address, or a dress for the irrational, a costume, a disguise for a vacant lot, a parking lot called emptiness (for that streetcar named desire). Sometimes I think, wouldn't it be better to remain silent—to let that emptiness, vacancy, loss, have its full, dead weight, and wouldn't it be better to let love—and writing—go? But, love, I don't want to stop writing or loving you.

It was nearly night. Paige visited old haunts. Without going anywhere, she dwelt on love, dove into it, wallowed in it, and called upon memory. Memory competed with history, dividing her attention, and Paige indulged herself, as if eating rich chocolates, in her own romantic past. She looked at pictures of former lovers stuck between pages in journals and albums. She mused and cut hearts out of paper towels. She held up one then another to the light. The hearts were large and ungainly, imperfect shapes meant to represent a romance or two or four. What would she write on a cheap paper heart?

"I wrote you in a cave, the cave had no light, I wrote on pale blue paper, the words had no weight, they drifted and danced away before my eyes. I couldn't give them substance. I could not make them bear down. I keep failing at this poetry, this game of love."

"O love is the crooked thing / There is nobody wise enough / To find out all that is in it . . ." (W. B. Yeats)

Dearest,

I know you think I have no perspective. Without perspective, everything is flat. Our love exists on available surfaces—on beds, on floors, on tabletops, on roofs. Tell me to stop. I can't help it. I want more. I want everything now. I love you, silently and stealthily. I love you as you have never been loved. I love you because I cannot love you.

"True hearts have ears and eyes, no tongues to speak; / They hear and see, and sigh, and then they break." (Sir Edward Dyer)

I love you.

It was just a sentence. Paige was struck by it and, she thought, stuck with it. Three ordinary, extraordinary, diminutive words (I love you) and just eight sweet letters ("o" repeats—o yes). So little does so much. Three little words, three little piggies, make a sentence, the sentence: I love you. Love sentence. Arret d'amour.

Dearest,

What if I were sent to love you? What if I were the sentence "I love you"? Do you or I ever think of love as a sentence? I don't think so. You and I can't bother about thinking about "I love you" as a sentence—a vocabulary, a grammar, a syntax. Who is sentenced? whose sentence? for how long? You, me? I'm smiling, are you? I think you and I can't think of love at all. I can't think "love."

"What voice descends from heaven / to speak to me of love?" (Verdi, *Don Carlos*)

"Wild thing, you make my heart sing. / You make everything, groovy. / Wild thing, I think I love you. / But I want to know for sure. / Come on and hold me tight. / I love you." (The Troggs)

Feeling stupid, Paige tore up one of the hearts. She crumpled the others and looked at the mess. With hardly a second thought, she took each newly crumpled heart and straightened it out. She patted all the hearts until they were more or less flat and unwrinkled. Then she lined them up on the table in front of her as a sort of place setting or place mat. Paige smiled at the silly hearts, paltry emblems of couplings gone. It was strange to concoct emblems, even to want signifiers of old loves, but it was, she thought, stranger not to want memory, simply to desire to forget. She even liked the hearts better because they were creased. She liked her lovers to have lines around their mouths and eyes.

Dearest,

I love you trembles inside me. It trembles and I can feel it just the way I can feel you. You can't think love, I know you can't. Not when you think about me. I'm the one who loves you. No matter what, I love you. No matter that I want to take apart "I love you."

"But, untranslatable, / Love remains / A future in brains." (Laura Riding)

I love you.

What or who is the subject of this sentence—the object or the subject? Love confuses by constructing a subject/object relation that forgets what or why it is—who subject, who object. ("You" never refuse(s) "I," my love.)

To Paige the torn-up heart, its pieces scattered on the tabletop, represented a broken heart. All the broken hearts, she decided ruefully, not just mine. There were too many to number, to name, to count, countless numbers.

"My first broken heart wasn't a romance. My heart broke before I even thought about love. It broke when I wanted something and couldn't have it, and I don't even remember when or what that was."

". . . When the original object of an instinctual desire becomes lost in consequence of repression, it is often replaced by an endless series of substitute objects, none of which ever give full satisfaction." (Freud)

Paige worried that memory, like love, was something she couldn't make decisions about, even when she made sense from the past, or it made a kind of sense to her. Unlike love, memory was constant, and she was never without it. It held her hand as she tailored hearts.

Dearest,

I can't think straight. I can't do what I'm supposed to do. I can't think or work or eat or write or walk or sleep or cry or scream or die or lie or decide. Since loving you. Now I love you is a gasp in me, a convulsive last breath that suffocates, a gush of unmanageable swollen words that takes up too much space in me. When you touch me, I can't stand it. When you touch me, everything's a movie, and everything in me movies over to sigh. I gasp, I breathe, I suffocate, I gush—for you. If "I love you" becomes a lament, a tragedy, then I will gag on love and die.

"Know you not the goddess of love / and the power of her magic?" (Wagner, *Tristan and Isolde*)

"'Cause love comes in spurts / In dangerous flirts / and it murders your heart /They didn't tell you that part / Love comes in spurts / Sometimes it hurts / Love comes in spurts / oh no, it hurts." (Richard Hell)

I love you is the structure through which I love you. I is such a lonely, defiant letter. In this fatal (fated?) sentence it's the first word—in the beginning, there was I—a pronoun, the nominal subject. In the love sentence, "I" submits to "you." That I is I. That I is yours. That I is you too; it is for you.

Dearest,

I'm the one who loves you better, longer, stronger, whose passion robs you of passion, whose daring steals your courage, whose boldness provokes your fear, whose gentleness savages you, whose absence electrifies you.

Paige waved a paper heart in the air. She was pretending to enact an ancient, time-honored ritual. She considered burning the heart in a funeral pyre and laughed out loud. You never see yourself laughing, Paige realized. Once upon a time a man she loved caught her looking at herself in a mirror and noticed something she didn't want him to see.

"I'll be your mirror / I'll be your mirror / Reflect what you are / In case you don't know." (Lou Reed)

"The woman who sang those lines died in a bicycle accident. When she first sang the song, she was beautiful and unhappy and lonely, though not alone. She died in what's called a freak accident, and at the time of her death, her body was swollen from years of drug abuse. She was no longer beautiful, maybe alone, but she was always, or still, lonely. It was spring when she died. It may have been summer."

I love you.

Love, the second word in the sentence, is the verb and acts by joining the two pronouns (pro-lovers, you and I). Love melts "you" and "I" (is it just grammar that bends "I" into "me," just that old subject to object of the verb magic?). Love dissolves disbelief, since

Love defies credulity. Love establishes an impossible, enduring, tender, spidery and tentative bridge between us, two poor pronouns. Love is a link, a chain, a clasp, a grasp, which can be undone, broken and torn apart. You and I are simple, one-syllable words. You and I need love.

"We do not see what we love, but we love in the hope of confirming the illusion that we are indeed seeing anything at all." (Paul de Man)

"Stereotype / Monotype / Blood type / Are you my type?" (Vernon Reid)

Paige shuffled the hearts, amused to recall that Hearts was a card game. She named each of her hearts and, as she did, forced herself to remember him, and herself, with as much detail and vividness as she could bear (it's often hard to bear one's own history). A languid heaviness coursed through and then settled in her body.

"I walked across the Brooklyn Bridge with him. The cars and trucks rumbling and tearing beneath us were terrifying. He thought it was weird that I didn't find any security in the fact that there was something solid under our feet. He held my hand, the way I hold this heart. Later, we went for Indian food. It was the first time I ever ate it. Then we went back to my place and made love, for the first time, too. He stroked the insides of my thighs."

"Love u more than I did when u were mine." (Prince)

"The heart you betrayed, / the heart you lost, / see in this hour / what a heart it was." (Bellini, *Norma*)

Dearest,

I'm afraid now too, though I'm not actually walking over a bridge. There isn't anything beneath my feet. I can't breathe or yawn or laugh or smile or cook or move or run or jump or stand or sit. I am restless. Bedeviled angel, sweet oxymoron, I ask questions you can't possibly answer. I am not reasonable, absolutely not. Why should "I" be? Why should "you" be? Really, I only have questions and you are a question to me. You are the question. I ask myself—you—what is it you want and what is it I want too. Our wanting isn't enough, is it? Maybe for now. Just wanting you is enough, now. I can't live without you. See how "you" have destroyed "me"?

"For love—I would / split open your head and put / a candle in / behind the eyes." (Robert Creeley)

Even so, or even more, I love you.

"You" is (you are) the last word—the last word and the first one too—of course. In "you" there are two letters more than "I"—the difference is a dipthong, two vowels to make one sound—ooh. Youooh. The vowels demand each other. They cling to each other to produce their sound.

Dearest,

My love clings to you. It is silent and dark, hidden from everyone else but you. Love is silent, sex is noisy. To write love, that's what I really want, to write love to you. That must be finding silence too. Still, soundlessly, I'd put everything into words, and though the words are not actually love but how love would speak if it could—if my heart could talk—the words would make no sounds. Yet, through my desire, with my will, they would strike hard, strike a chord, inside you. My words would creep and slither into you, if I had my way. (I want my way with you.) Words once lying inert on the page would suddenly dance or wing through the air like missiles (missives, silly), would fly into you, and you would embrace them, or more perfectly, they would embrace you. You would be entered and entranced by them, my precious point of destination, my entrance to love. Is there any more beautiful homonym than entrance and entrance?

"What is the use of speech? Silence were fitter: / Lest we should still be wishing things unsaid. / Though all the words we ever spake were bitter, / Shall I reproach you dead?" (Paul Verlaine)

Paige drank green tea and wondered what had happened to him, the lanky, green-eyed young man, who hated himself, who said, I don't know why you like me. She hadn't loved him but had loved something about him.

"He was living on West Fourth St. He had been suicidal for years.

He told everybody his brother was a movie star, and that was true. His room was in the back of a store and on the floor was a single mattress. The mattress looked like an unopened envelope. He said he had not made love in three years. After he came, he cried. The next day he had a red gash on his neck. Then he disappeared forever."

Obliviously, I love you.

She was becoming stiff. She got up from the table and walked around, from room to room, imagining she was a ferocious animal. Paige paced back and forth, back and forth. She wasn't sleek as a tiger or cunning as a fox. She was a little hungry.

"Even today love, too, is in essence as animal as it ever was." (Freud)

Paige took up the scissors again. Love, she considered with affection, should be generous; at the very least it should appear to be. She smiled as she cut more hearts, attempting to keep them linked together in a row or chain like paper dolls. Was she fashioning love? Wasn't memory better than love? The shapes grew progressively more uneven and awkward.

"You planted yourself in my garden, taking up room, then, oh, you grew, you became a weed, you were so tall, with such long, strong legs. Your satin trousers were a disguise, and you were much too sleek. I tried to escape. You insisted. You kept on insisting. About what? Toward what end? I can't remember. I wish flowers had never been looked at before. When we stood up, I felt taller than before. As tall as you, no, taller. You were awkward, but I remember all your questions."

Awkwardly, I love you.

Dearest,

I can still say it, can't I, common as it is, common as mud and as thick and undecipherable? In my dreams I cleave to you (biblically), I hold you, your body bent to mine, your body reminding me of someone who is no longer here to love me. But then that's love—one body replaces another. I don't mean that. Not just any other—yours. Only you. And only you understand me, this part of me. The me who loves you. You and I make meaning together. That's how love is. Or what love is. You know, meaning. Meaning I love you. Meaning, I love you. I love you is meaning. Meaning, I won't listen to reason.

"Everybody has a different idea of love. One girl I knew said, 'I knew he loved me when he didn't come in my mouth.'" (Andy Warhol)

Paige thought about coloring the hearts or affixing titles to them. I'm glad no one can see me, she thought, and hummed aloud: I'm a little teapot, lift me up, pour me out. I'm a common heart, a commoner, a common metaphor, a cup of tea, a jug of wine, a loaf of bread, and I am beside myself. Hush, Paige went on, and be still, useless heart. Then she uncorked a bottle of red wine.

Commonly, I love you.

Paige read poets and listened to the music of composers and songwriters who ordinarily took love as their subject. It made sense since love is mute, silent, nearly unspeakable, and needy of a voice, yet impossible to give full voice to or say enough about. It cannot be conquered, since it is always dubious, abstract, consistently inconsistent, outrageously ineffable, obdurate, evasive, ambiguous and ambivalent; therefore it endures and is worth taking up. Paige indulged such sentiments and ideas, played around with and in them on more than this day and long night. She feared that it didn't matter what she read or learned, but Paige hoped, desperately, to hold herself in check, especially for and in anticipation of the long, terrible nights, the raw, endless nights that can rob her blind, that can steal her reason.

"The night murmurs / Its thousand loves / And false counsels / To soften and seduce the heart." (Puccini, *Tosca*)

"There was a time when I believed your love belonged to me / Now I find that you're shackled to a memory / . . . How can I free your doubtful mind? / And melt your cold, cold heart." (Hank Williams)

Blindly, I love you.

Dearest,

Even when my eyes hurt and everything's blurred, I keep writing and reading. Weak eyes still love stories. Remember when you said I'm full of stories. You are too. Isn't this how you seduced me? Wasn't it your story, how you told it, how I sank into it, submitted, collapsed into the superb rendition of your life — into you? I thought I saw you in your story. And isn't this how I seduced you? It wasn't my beauty, was it? It wasn't my youth, was it? I think it was my story, one word after another after another, circling around you, gathering you to me. My lines roped you in, the way yours did me, our lines — to continue this pathetic figure of speech — tangled, and we became one story. I had a French friend who always said about her love affairs, I'm having a little story with him. With words like sticky plums, I drew you close. My grip, on you, on my own tales, is sometimes tenuous. I slip. I'm slipping. But again, no matter what, I always love you.

Paige drank the wine, but she barely tasted it. She was transfixed. In her red bathrobe she looked comical, like a giant valentine. From time to time she glanced at the clock on the wall, but she wasn't sure what time it was. Every month the clock needed a new battery, but she forgot to change it. It was good that hearts didn't have batteries which needed to be changed, she thought, or recharged. Or maybe they did, that's why she felt run down. Paige stacked the paper hearts like honeyed pancakes.

Sweetly, I love you.

"She was so much in love she wanted to make love all the time. He was away, or she was away from him. She left their house and walked to the canal and saw a man standing on a bridge. She liked him. It was easy to love. The excitement of her grand passion threatened to make negligible the differences between one man and another. And too, her love made her expansive, bigger than she was. She abandoned herself to the threat of self-annihilation (that's what love is) and spent the afternoon with the stranger. There was no restraint. She could give him everything he wanted without regret. He gave her his address, and she tore it up later."

"Such wayward ways hath Love, that most part in discord / Our wills do stand, whereby our hearts seldom do accord." (Henry Howard, Earl of Surrey)

Discordantly, I love you.

You are everything. "You" is everything to the sentence, I love you, for without "you," could "I" love?

Dearest,

It's strange to write "I love you." I don't mean to you, what's strange is to write it, to commit it to paper or the screen. I don't mean that it could be anyone but you when I write, I love you. Only you could be the you that I love. That's obvious. Isn't it obvious that I love you? It's obvious that without you, I cannot love. You alone will see where I'm leading, where my thought carries me. My thought carries me to you.

"The air is fragrant and oddly pure this morning. It wafts into my room and reminds me of days when I played for hours in the forest down the road, the forest, our jungle, or maybe it was next to the house then, back then. I can't remember. I remember how in the winter the pond would freeze over and all of us kids would ice skate, our hands tucked into our sleeves or sheltered safely in woolen mittens. Mittens are for little creatures who need shelter all the time. With mittens we are small animals, with paws. The boys I played with—were you one of them? Even then? Steve, Ronnie, Jerry. They were always around the house. Jerry was dark and round. Ronnie, tall and blond, angular and angry, a bad boy. He became a lawyer. Steve stood apart and sulked. I wonder what happened to him."

Abruptly Paige jumped up from the table. At the sink she poured out the dregs of the tea. It was late, and the city was quiet, sleeping. Does a city sleep when it can't close its eyes? Isn't everyone wrong about something like love?

Above her, in the upstairs apartment, a man strode heavily across the floor. From the refrigerator to the toilet to the bed? Or in a different order? He stomped around like an enraged elephant. He stamped around like a dejected lover, enraged by betrayal. Love is not silent, love is loud and violent and vicious with a lovely, unsatisfactory language. A lovely language, an unsatisfying tongue that entices. Paige danced around the kitchen, one hand gently touching her stomach.

"I danced on 'Shop Around' / but never the flip side / 'Who's Lovin' You' / boppin' was safer than grindin' / (which is why you should not come around)" (Thulani Davis)

The language of, for, love explains and isn't explanatory enough. If it's not learned well or early, but if one is a quick study, one could, with diligence, pick it up later. Paige wondered: Is psychoanalysis the way one can learn to love later in life?

"The analyst's couch is the only place where the social contract explicitly authorizes a search for love—albeit a private one." (Julia Kristeva)

Childishly, I love you.

Dearest,
I don't want to love you badly. It's intangible, I suppose, how to love, but since it resides in language, and the language of the body of course (can touch be taught?), it exists, has effects, has a presence, makes itself known—with words, doesn't it? Love is a grammar, a style, a convention, replete with physical gestures and vocal utterances and yellow marks flashing on green computer screens. What if my hard disk crashes? What if you stop loving me? What if I stop loving you? What then? What words would ever be enough?

". . . Once you see emotions from a certain angle, you can never think of them as real again. That's what more or less has happened to me. I don't really know if I was ever capable of love, but after the 60s, I never thought in terms of 'love' again." (Andy Warhol)

Dearest,
I hate this something you and I didn't name. It's gone out of control. With time, with time weighing us down, with no time to think about the future, with every fear about time passing—when will love come?—we grab love and take it in hand. Now we have it. Now we have it. Here it is. Do you see it? I give it to you. I will forget everything to love you.

"Let us forget the whole world! / For you alone, dearest, I long! / I have a past no more, / I do not think of the future." (Verdi, *Don Carlos*)

"Love is begot by fancy, bred by ignorance, by expectation fed, Destroyed by knowledge, and, at best, / Lost in the moment 'tis possessed." (George Granville, Baron Lansdowne)

Impossibly, I love you.

"Love incapacitates me, my language is never enough. The language is the matter, the language is matter, it matters, it doesn't matter, you and I matter, we are matter, you and I are the matter, the matter of love, we are the stuff of love, you and I. We are not enough and neither is love. There's no sense to it and it doesn't make sense to you or to me that this is what we are in, love, a state of temporary grace with each other. It doesn't make sense. It's not sound. It is sounds. It's your voice."

Dearest,

You wanted to know, when you phoned (I love the sound of your voice) what was on my mind. Just as you called I was thinking (I had pushed you out of my mind in order to think), Some days it doesn't pay to get out of bed. Then the telephone rang. Anyway it's Sunday, I half-hate Sundays. And then I was thinking of Lewis Carroll and Edith Wharton, who wrote in bed, enviable position, with a board on her lap, traveling or at home, every morning. As she finished a page she let it drop to the floor, to be scooped up later by her secretary, who typed it. Lewis Carroll (I don't know where he wrote) and Wharton. Something to do with love. Wharton's love letters to Morton Fullerton. Carroll's love of Alice, his desire for young girls. Was his sense of the absurd best exemplified by the ludicrous position he found himself in, being in love—falling in love—with such small girls. How crazy it must have felt to him, spending Sundays with Alice, bending down to hear her speak, bending over and down all day long, towering above the tiny object of his illicit affections. Even stranger to him must have been his wild, prohibited longing—to place his adult penis into that little child's vagina. He must have felt so small and so big. There it is, the topsy-turviness of the world he made, in words, one after the other, and with words he published (in the old sense), though no one knew, his body, its uncontrollable desires—how intimately his body was written. Alice had to make herself very small to be very big. He had no sense of scale, did he, no proportion? Did he ever tell Alice, I love you? Did Lewis Carroll love Alice the way I love you or very differently? If all love is the same? If I wrote to you the way Wharton wrote to her lover, would you like it? Please tell me. I want to give you what you want. I want to be everything you want me to be. I am crimson. I don't want to be or feel like this. I can't help it. My words stall, are stale in my mouth, won't come, they won't stop coming either.

"I'm so afraid that the treasures I long to unpack for you, that have come to me in magic ships from enchanted islands, are only, to you, the old familiar red calico & beads of the clever trader. . . . Well! and if you do? It's your loss, after all!" (Edith Wharton, to Morton Fullerton)

Alone with longing, even longing for longing, Paige was on the verge of a complete alienation. She was a spectator in her own theater of love where she was no longer an ingenue. Now the paper hearts were actors, and some had great, important roles and others were just minor characters. Walk-ons, they'd had a line or two, a moment on her stage, or they'd appeared as comic relief.

Still Paige fell in love, and when she fell, she plummeted into a lavish set, a country club, of conventions. The modes were intractable, yet the sensation was that her love was unique. Paige was capable of holding contradictory ideas and emotions. And as ridiculous as they were, it was a bearable irony. People bore it all the time. Some were so experienced in love, they had discarded it. Or at least discredited it. But Paige couldn't let it go. It wouldn't let her go.

Mother, I cannot mind my wheel; / My fingers ache, my lips are dry; / Oh! if you felt the pain I feel! / But oh, who ever felt as I!" (Sappho)

Ironically, I love you.

Dearest,

Your love proposes to me, it proposes and marries me to a different idea of me, a new identity with its own poetic license, so now I'm different from myself but joined with your self, and you are different from yourself, at least from the way you have been and the way life has been, and this is the best difference, this love, that you and I will ever experience. Isn't it? Won't our love mark, cloud, inflect, protect, infect, alter, deform, consume and subsume us? Won't it cast shadows and light over all other experience? Isn't love the limit? Or, more gravely, is it like death, a constant pair of parentheses?

"Do you not hear a voice in your heart / which promises eternal happiness?" (Bellini, *Norma*)

"Who needs a heart when a heart can be broken?" (Terry Britten/ Graham Lyle)

Paige knocked her leg against the table. It hurt. Then a voice whispered: I don't want to die. Paige swung around in her chair, her mood was broken. Or something was broken. It was merely an interruption or perhaps a discovery—of a sensation or fact or quality or lack or strength or plenitude or presence, a visitor, a vicissitude. An uneducated entity, a beast, an other, resistant and resilient, unreasonable, unreasoned. Nothing shakes it. Nothing reaches the imaginary inside. I don't want to die, it repeated. It was barely a voice. Maybe she had heard it before.

Immortally, I love you.

"She wanted to be saved. She wanted to tear his eyes out. She wanted to eat his flesh. She wanted to carve her name on his forehead. She wanted him dead. She wanted him around. She wanted him to stand like a stone. She wanted him never to be sad. She wanted him to do what she wanted. She wanted him invulnerable and invincible. She wanted to look at him. She wanted him to get lost. She wanted to find him. She wanted him to do everything to her. She wanted to look at him.

"She had no idea who he was or what he was thinking. She only pretended that she knew him. He was an enigma of the present. He was the palpable unknown. He was the loved one. He wasn't listening to reason. He would save her, and she would never die.

"She didn't want to die. She wanted to be saved."

Irrationally, I love you.

Paige turned off the computer. I don't want to die, it winked one last time. She tore up all the hearts. Paige threw them in the garbage and then, days later, wondered if they should have been recycled with the newspapers rather than collected with the ordinary, organic garbage.

". . . For the transaction between a writer and the spirit of the age is one of infinite delicacy, and upon a nice arrangement between the two the whole fortune of his works depend. Orlando had so ordered it that she was in an extremely happy position; she need neither fight her age, nor submit to it; she was of it, yet remained herself. Now, therefore, she could write, and write she did." (Virginia Woolf)

"She sorted through some papers, closed her books, drew the covers off her bed, and undressed. She laid her head on the pillow and shut her eyes. She let go of the present and had dreams where the dead walked and talked and where love and hate held a masquerade party and gamboled the night long, trading blows and kisses, confusing faces of friends and enemies. She became uneasy and awoke, terrified. It was not yet daybreak. She thought about love and turned on her computer."

Paige Turner is writing, to you.

I love you.

From Present Tense
Stephen R*atcliffe*

Whatever happened to the feelings inside
"colorful paintings,"
a literalization of the distance
the begonia says she wants another drink –

sifting up from the lower regions of not counting sleep
where there isn't any there – in whose name I'm taking leave of
    Venice
"into the very water that she lights" –

---

just a word "string," arbor ardor – the road turns over the bridge
back to Tulsa, the olive oil can
with its quiver of pencils, idle threads of rain
in a khaki coat aboard the hovercraft from Ramsgate to Calais –

the swell came up from the west via the window
in a conversation he couldn't follow – basset hounds and voices
    composed for a picture
the opaque beet colors carrot red, advances in non-syntactic
    prose –

---

an eight-year-old listening to feathers in the quilt start to bunch –
the piano a narrative question of which hotel,
which head on the pillow
when the tape stops – Arthur must have shot her in his dream –

why is Madame licking the canceled stamp, both fathers of
    daughters

feeling a mist on their heads as it snows rain — Pavarotti's
birthplace is also a good question,
encore "Sorrento," static drowned by the ultimate O —

---

a line of patients dressed and undressed — the deer
at the Chinese-red front door who names the star between clouds
parting,
light on the road mirrored on the ceiling, wind
sounds in grass and tree —

as soon as she turns off the light falls asleep — wild bees in a
column,
where the grass was cut mounds,
the full moon drives him to the edge of crazy —

X counts Y and Z friends, hard contacts — in a jacket zipped to
the chin,
his child grows up to shoot the president
but cannot tell what feeling he had or what they called
disordered thinking — Thoreau was right about the lives of
desperate men —

first she was in Florence, then the alarm went off —
the fire chief's wife didn't believe the house was burning, a three-
minute song
like "He's So Fine" is over so soon —

---

before the cancellation of the summit, newspapers reported bombs
going off all across the Alps —
details like the preceding one suggest how voices repeat the
syllables
license blue, dust breath, redwood drills quick —
so play like Rosewall, paint like Cézanne, the pencil you can't
find is probably lost for good —

how suddenly one becomes ten – the dog shouldn't walk on his
    bandaged foot
but stand on it more or less less than before,
"I love the way she talks like Ellery Queen on the table" –

---

the *pick, pack, pock* of balls splashing in a bowl of air, peonies
the butterfly flew or ripped from,
wisteria espaliered past flower – "a smell of roast fills the air,"
Drummond of Hawthorndon said to Ben Jonson, who replied,
    "why not in the car as elsewhere?" –

after shocks rock falls, coffee fatigue
the smelt caught in a gull's talon – the weathered wood drinks up
    paint,
the other a shower in tile green enameled blue jeans –

---

ironic as boring work in a beautiful garden, Catullus
loses his temper at dinner – springwater jars
filled at the tap, the pergola waits
until the bees leave, de Kooning sits on top of the fridge –

my father raised in Tulsa suggested she was the cigarette on the
    desk that no one smokes –
autobiography is a fiction dug up to cover the scraps on which
    I address
the photographer on the beach who shoots the sun –

---

the beekeeper who couldn't find his words
hadn't worked a day in his life
so to speak, the poetry of particular matters on the table
the bright Mercedes missed – there are so many colors in the
    world the blind don't see –

red dogs in the morning, the motion picture stars war – she knew
    what a drink would do

and wanted one, nor was it absurd to stop there,
the piano to airy thinness trilling "I could feel my heart flip"—

---

twenty years later the same song plays again—up tempo after the
  drums,
what does the Guide Michelin mean by "toque"
—imaginary intersect,
full speed ahead reads like a warning signed NO PARKING—

when Kafka gets hard, white paint everywhere but in the news
as much like a bird as a piccolo can be—revised,
last year the SPCA spayed a million homeless "pets"—

D Minor a frame to hang Dante in, true to some simple notion
  of self—
there isn't a time the whole world isn't out there,
which isn't as good as Whistler
but segues to something I've been thinking about *Mrs.* Plato—

his daughter calls him "daddy" with an *e* as in French, *"beau"*—
when she reads it's like drinking wine, "you'll ride this roller
  coaster till you're not afraid,
wire jaw shut until departure"—

---

one plays the music as noted—like catching thought on the wing
or the artificial stars in a Muyggeridge photo,
an orchestra live on the lawn
better than speaking of "her luggage went to Frankfurt"—

birds up before first light even if she isn't awake—
one of Bach's many sons wrote this—bee legs caked with yellow
  dust,
smell the honey on Jagger's prick—

the vestige of a tail hidden in his cocyx, Darth Vader didn't like
large crowds —
I too keep the standard, she's eating steak to feed the baby
— why do you talk that way, tomorrow
all of us almost sound asleep, all the paintings about to see —

did the fire come on without warning? — once, when the spider
climbed its thread
Sappho was pregnant, once the reason Virgil was punk
whiskey still, lens contact —

---

leaving home because she didn't like to work, Nancy Smith Drew's
noblesse oblige
teaches her the danger of long nails — after Ned Nickerson,
modest as he can be, the thing she loves best is *déjeuner sur
l'herbe* —
"nowhere to run, nowhere to hide, why must I be a scarlet tanager
in love?" —

Stravinsky famous at thirty, Zappa's interest lies
in the digital recording of his cello triple concerto — to speak of
the alternatives
life kills point blank —

---

refracted egret shadow lagoon glass — there's something about
dense sound,
the origin of speech as it enters the work, speed
because things happen —
daughter a mother walks to the ocean, whose job is to see, feel,
hear more —

to be the green shirt blue with yellow glasses,
again the dredge called Kent's Folly —
pollens because the now mown grass, violent sneezes —

From Album
Melanie Neilson

ROMANCE OF CHERRIES

Wings of the Cherry
Pie the bowl
Drooping branchlets
Red Flemish, Sour Morello
Wild bird cherries
Flesh enclosed seeded stone
Young green clusts
Unhidden hardy, Northern
Cherries of Great Antiquity
Pale yellow with red flush
Drop fat, tawny,
Immense purple black
Laughter for a giant
Deep dark red
Small black muzzards
A Romance of Cherry
Red, sweet, sour
Abyss of curiosity
In the tree lovely
White flowers, young shoots
Scenery please shoot
Cherries flavor brandy
Flemish Sour, Red Morello

Melanie Neilson

RIVER

A sip hidden serene
The custom of the place
Afternoon the thinking grass
Comes up how one feels
Afternoon bank itself

The mind the music breathing
One in a dream of night
Would fly but cannot
Sound of the darkness
Would fly but cannot

Mourning from the branch
Shy whistle night watcher
Ashy river cemetery
What I think I remember
Present Wish or True Picture?

Autumn in April monument
People into birds coincident
Author note to evade evasion
Survive protective obscuring
Archaic defied fought

Melanie Neilson

What becomes monument?

Barechested crouching in the grass

Her play bold maziness

Summer shadowed universe

Hear the figure entire

Melanie Neilson

Attention to actualities
Hindsight or intuition
Actuality meaning light
The Past will look "like"
At any Present

Every scene a real one
Ask why before how
Tumultuous sea of heads
Waver jostle hum new commotion;
Picturesque ajar

Barefoot she goes
How to stand, behold?
Blinking blank bold—
Posed for her page
Blank white page

Melanie Neilson

CHILDHOOD INSERT

Play screen
Bright lit one
(on)
The imitation voyage:
The Bicycle Ride
Spokes
Gray morning
Trees
Clouds shout
What accompaniment the sea
Well minded shade
Counselor-friend and purpose
Reunion ink moss reunion

treelike
old ghost

pen
man ship
ship
ship
pen
ship

five oh five three
five oh five trees
fire of five trees
five oh five three
fire of five trees

weeds weeds weeds
small bits of writing
silent pictures moving
stack of decades
now then

Change could life
How quickly could change
Just like that
For the better
Magical connections
Optical illusions
Exist in the mind
Forms of the future
Different halves
Same sphere
Of small things at home

Reaching down and picking up
Reaching down and picking up
Reaching down reaching down
And reaching down and picking up
Doll from floor
And carrying it away
The doll very still
Hear her sing
Ultimately handkerchief
Words disappear

She doesn't know what it is
Linen, chiffon not handkerchief
Tears away
What they are or weeping
Pillow
Investigate ajar
The melancholy pleasure
Introducing "the Larmoyante"
A handkerchief called
With a fringe of artificial tears
Mock pearls
Water to match the sentiment
India ink shaded
Black-edged
Black-edged
Black-edged.

Melanie Neilson

PREFERS TO LOOK AT BIRDS SHE SAYS CHAPTER

In the summer chatter back, lipping honey, who fly
at it quietly and come back not understood come
lower and lower smiling back smiling. Wind speed
dissolves lifting lifetime of berries the background
action as there is only a floated sun in seclusion,
out conclusion, lower and lower. Here is the largest
most misunderstood comprehensive selection of true
action, typical worm-eating near enough three angles
at once. All walking, running, leaping, flying,
galloping indisputably nude, trotting, pacing
instant picture thought stopped never enough and
very resembling. Deluxe mechanics of question
enough for everyone. Weight plumage. Awake as trees
with singing in them. Difficult not to wander
the future and borrow trouble. Blue watered anonymity.
Branch rock noon.

Melanie Neilson

BLUE OF THE SKY BLACK TO THE EYE

Well a girl in the picture cuts the space in two and she thinks
"Dirt indeed."

Motionless irreplaceable quasi honeycombs.

Common hive-bee drenched in the budding mindreader climbing shrub
with fragrant yellow she is.

FLAT SERIALIZED SPACE WAS WHY I TURNED

If it is received the fan is very lovely mother of
pearl – as I have ever seen – overlapping in the head
write in bed – I am just as anxious further south.
Such difficulty anything reaching its destination
in America. A light little hat sweet enough to eat
in a box not much larger than your hand. Out in the
street this winter carried in a box not much larger
than your hand. In the street this winter carried
in a box steps along the way the motion. By definition
a person appears mistaken. The Mystery of the President's
Mystery.

PHOTOGRAPH CREDITS: Pages 214, 217 (top): Thomas Eakins. Collection of the J. Paul Getty Museum, Malibu, California. Pages 217 (bottom), 218, 219, 225: Thomas Eakins. Courtesy of the Pennsylvania Academy of the Fine Arts, Philadelphia. Charles Bregler's Thomas Eakins Collection. Purchased with partial support of the Pew Memorial Trust. Pages 220, 222: Melanie Neilson.

The Displaced
Arno Schmidt

— Translated from the German by John E. Woods

i

The precocious moon slipped, rickety skewed, over the railroad embankment; just once flesh sated. Bushes still adorned with some fresh rain; and able to start smoking again. A fat cloud floozy stretched gray shoulders behind the evening woods; macaroni and the hard wedge of swiss grated in. Two whirly-winds ran up to me, with gentle dusty manes, transparent yellow bodies; strayed closer abashed, quivering gathered their veils, turned and sighed ravishing (but then here came the Trempenau delivery van, and they had to follow, dragged, with long maenadically wrenched back : the guy with the car always has a better chance !)

THE SUNKEN SUN left the red of blotting paper behind for a long time, with the inks of night seeping down into it from above. Then rain flowed aslant about the bony trees; wind gave hunched refugees pokes in hair and eyes, get a move on, the weathercocks chackled on the rooftops. Gray development roofed with slate; for the damnteenth time my rounds around Benefeld, forever circling outside. In the bald sky the wind echoed much; radio waltzed off past all the bleak dormers : there they sat with furious facial panes by 25 watts; my clayey feet drove me down the trickle path, till heart was scraped bare as my coat, vapid, vapid. No compensation payment, household aid, revaluation of east-savings (a curse upon that cabinet !). The stars appeared like thieves in trenchcoats, in furtive cloud alleys. But, for all that, three men to every room; but, for all that, rearmament, hi-ho : what oxen they must be who choose the butcher for their king ! The black wind carried on like a lunatic, jostled and shouted; he thrust the next branch through my brow, whistled to a pal and spat rain : he came howling up from behind, pushed my hat up and strangled at my scarf. But, for all that, the resettlement still was no go : no matter the occupation, at 65 a man's shunted onto a sidetrack; but the statesman, senilissimus, apparently is just getting nice and mature at 75, ice cold, totally inhuman, gritty gruesome grouchy grim graves. Three gray bat-folk crossed me in long tumbling cloaks, and now there appeared the black roof-peak of the Lower Saxon farmer : No one who was not a tiller of the soil has a right to speak of the horrors of war : the everlasting regulations, my good man ! May Ol' Scratch himself ! A lean silver owl hangs immobile in the piny woof; at the pond : tree-fellows alurk in foggy rags, arms like cudgels, held up knotty high. Indoors, table-curse over slices with syrup; moldy walls, who can heat this hole; and on into Wetzel's Belphegor (thankgod Beier wasn't here yet); and this is existing, so-called, what we're doing here. (The wind brawl went right on raging outside.)

ii

> He was regarding the third crate with such disparagement that his face rolled up; then he motioned to Müller with his shoulder : "Block. . . . ?" "head," the latter answered gloomily and likewise vaulted his back : "Block ? . . . . head !", till the jampack in the corner overburdened. "The bed first !" and from below District-Refugee-Welfare-Officer Schulz admonished into all the red freight cars : "Always load 'em clear to the top. — Tight." And to us : "Always clear to the top !" At his shoulder, Lepke said cautiously : "Block —" and Müller carewornly : "head." Even the wind was much too cold, in the end, prob'ly just the sweeper-outer, the bouncer, and then Schulz lifted himself up on his toes, looked at his list, and with chalk inscribed our car AZLEY.

I bought one crate (without a lid) from Lepke, Vehlow brought the other for free from the Waldorf school. First the books, it was like playing building blocks. In the long one, newspapers laid along the bottom, and then the few wearables — baloney ! the tarp has to go at the bottom of course; so then : take it all out again. Excelsior in and around the two cups, those then into the large pot; the loving-cup has its own little box, and the liqueur glasses fit in the corners. Needs to be labeled too, so I painted hand-high india ink and entered it as per regulation in the transport list, triplicate. I took my farewell at twelve midnight, so at least I didn't see any more of their asinine faces. Intensive village stroll, for the last time once more, only rarely a house still shed light, I'll not weep a tear for you : hadn't the <German Parties of the Right> once again <gained> 24% of the vote their first modest time out ? ! Wind whistled at my ear and fumbled hastily at my coat; and I knew then, I was to join them once more, even the sharp-edged star pointed into the woods, march. The heath roads lay beautiful and empty at midnight : soft gray-polished asphalt, above the pond of light in the coarse cloud-moor, the gust shoved me forward and I froze away happily, flowed along roads, ran down more lukelost ways, a distant motorcycle plunged sniveling after its smudge of light, water babbled succubusly beneath my leap and filled my shoes with drowsily icy caresses; and the chauffeur just laughed, as we shoved our few crates onto the truck next morning (here, for the first time, the bed planks fell apart, and I had to search for rusty wire on the mocking slope). (By way of precaution, one last trip to the bushes, and my puddle ring-snaked under the bilberry bush; crazy biological world !) They each got a cigarette, since in any case Müller and Lepke were headed into Fallingbostel for their unemployment; I thought my roundhouse farewell curses again, so, and now get a move on, coachman ! The Lower Saxon sun beamed from the windy blue-smashed November sky; it too was happy that once again there were a couple of refugees fewer. Many were already standing there, tipping cupboards up and in, others came rattling up, the guy with a trailer, and one even had two live goats in his latticed crate. The District-Refugee-Welfare-Officer piloted us to the freight car; we nimbly piled my gimcrackery up in the corner : goodbye, Herr Müller : even from the curve they were still waving homespunly, one hand cramped on the side-rail. A neat little truck trotted our way (. . . . .) I was still restraining a leap off (. . . . .) made a nastily elegant curve, and the girl's ductile voice asked : "Here's where we board !". She pleased me so, that I spontaneously lent a hand and helped the driver, o you menjou mustache, heave her stuff up : many solid crates ("Careful : radio's in that one !"), cupboards tables chairs with wrapped legs, and she smiled mightily at me in payment.

iii

> The sun brushed across her plaid skirt (behind her : heavy frost in bilberry bush, and frozen yellow sand, that you could still crumble quite easily). Among suitcases : "Shall we walk to the Purse ?" A dust-fellow rose up, middle-sized, waltzed broadly down the street toward us, ran over us, narrow backs. Trains appeared in earnest, halted, un- and loaded scurriers, smoked, snaked slowly-quickly away, blue cloudlets flew swiftly above sunny tracks : desolate. Eyes like bright bird shouts. "Shall we go ?" Now they were deftly astonished beneath the relaxed brow. — "Yes, let's !"

Her suitcase was absurdly heavy; but now, her hands in her coat, just a wide modern hunter's pouch over her subtle shoulder, she had to stroll slowly along beside me (our furniture, too, was standing back there, abandoned cunningly close together !). The Purse's two taprooms; only half full; at the window a tiny round table tempted. I shoved my shoe-tip to the edge of the nearest sun-spot and asked : "Are you alone too ? !" She considered, just as one ought; then gracefully cradled the chalice of her lips : "Uh-huh." Watched appreciatively as I spread the two chairs full and barricaded our corner of the world with the suitcases. Sit a while. "Katrin," she declared glumly : "and a poor widow." (Her husband killed in '44 after six months of marriage; and she's not catholic either.) She then ate two chic cold-cut sandwiches and thick Edam with fiery red waxen rind, drank loamy thermos coffee. An extended family moved into the adjoining long rectangle : father, mother, six grown sons and daughters; over by the stove Borck, small and hunchbacked and making possessive noises, arrived with his Högfeldt series of twelves, and driveled with his fangs. "You know him ?" Katrin asked outside, as we headed off heathwards. "I was an interpreter at the auxiliary police academy, and he was the quartermaster". "And now you translate books." The sun came down the path again, shadows escaped over fields, the forests echoed still more with wind. I stretched my army coat, Sir Walter Raleigh, across the tree stump, and the Queen took a seat. Perused the atlas, Marburg, Westerburg, Alzey, beyond. Out of the blue : "You're not cold !" Black voice, face hunnish pale, heart huntress of the Lüneburg Heath, sauvage et non convertie, with eyebrow whips and mouth for a bow. Wind bowled us over with soughing glass burdens, branches beat gentle bony flurries, in the grass accompanying rattles. The booty beside it, slain in the weeds. Her yellow hands flickered around the angular book, the broad gray thonged sandal lifted gingerly at times and drummed bushmanlike signals. Oh skirt and blouse ! Katrin smiled, sly and lazy, on past me, abstracted, right through me, for me, on over me and away. Oh skirt. Blue-white, the chessboard sky churned with treetops. And blouse.

iv

> Sky already striped red-blue like a carter's smock, and the wind blew such cold dust against our cheeks that Katrin energetically said "Holy Danube !" to him; nevertheless we watched this last evening, until it grew desert red, utterly vacant, and altogether excessive. Then we walked, one behind the other, through the stony vestibule back to the big taproom, where it swarmed terribly with children, lynched coats all about; and voice goulash in yellow light gravy. "Shall we have a bite too !"; I gazed meanwhile submissively through the panes at the angular night : for the rotating god so loved the world; ahyes. (Soda 30, bouillon 30, coffee 50).

Overstuffed laughter : "Unn aygg" (that's Borck, naturally); the gaunt woman girds her apron about her and makes sandwiches for many children : they banged against each other around the room and chirped themselves breathless; (one pored over the atlas in learned wonder, what strange names countries have : <ire,> <nether,> even <fin>); young man with squint-yellow maid, velvety bottomless Slavic face : naturally : and now from the baby carriage, too, came soft and drunken squints; across from us the old man in formal, dark-striped trousers, his silken-gray in-her-fifties : a cyclops couple grazed imposingly beneath roses (?). The innkeeper seemed to find things unusually quiet; he made but one grab for the knob behind him : "and the fellah's — darkened windah — closes softly — not a whispah" came the supple exultations, violin whistled bowing ever higher, and the yahoos grinned and blew moorish fog from their cheek pouches. Lots of retirees. "As far as possible, they've picked out people who won't take someone else's job," Katrin, the more observant, whispered. "Why did you sign up actually ?". "Oh," she said (recalling it only with reluctance) : "I was rooming with a gruesome old woman, you know, one of your

<genteel> olladies, with a totally addlepated daughter. She was forever enthusing about <our glorious Bismarck>, and wanted 2 pence and a psalm for every pail of water —" she delicately pleated mouth and nose, as she was forced to move past the ugly memories : "and you ?" "About the same : a mildewed cellar for two — together with a grocer —" I hastened to add when I saw how her eyes had begun to crackle (but it really had been the case !), "He's decided to get married now, and for three — and/or four, five, i.i. — it was really way too small. — And so as a gentleman I simply signed up to move out." In the midst of it all, Refugee-Welfare-Officer Schulz entered, all enterprise and riding breeches, with two attendants in tow : "I shall now read the lists", he began with such zeal and perfidy, and made a grab for one of them as if the monolog from Faust awaited us. Did it twice in fact, just to make things more interesting. Each time, at <Katharina Loeben>, she raised 3 fingers and looked about her, attentive and amused ("I'd like to take a little tri-hip with you" : departure's set for 4 in the morning, i.e., if we're lucky, about 6 !). Outside briefly : moon pushed his way, all stiff and colonel-general, through the rank and file of pallid stars; the wind murmured and experimented with scrambled clouds; a locomotive dawdled sedately around the station and let out a whistle : it's all <medicine>. "And now you're going to lie down," I ordained, "and you'll use my coat. — I'll stay awake and keep watch." "I have a blanket, really —" she acted amazed. "Then put it under your head. — I want at least one souvenir. — Please." "And there you'll sit and freeze," she said, wild and happy and proud, stood up, yawned discreetly with her shoulders, and meanwhile I made her a bed on the floor under the window. (Uptop, the silver ermine slipped smoothly through cloud cracks, greedy, ever in pursuit of that quivering blue star.)

V

A freezing man, covering himself with both hands; on the floor the female head in black coats; sad solitary flame in the stove niche, large and red-locked. "Abeer" for the mangy 1-mark bill and he slides me pennies still printed yellow : where you headed ? Don't know. Outside : hollow-honed moon lies on dark velvet cushion, part of some dangerous cutlery. Stand with dreary head or for all I care ten steps further on. Moon light; fir candlesticks; nightcloud roof : three cheers for us, right ?

The last Silesian nook is going to sleep ("Git some rest y'self. / Ah, claims he's an 'nspector. / Whether he really is, I can't say; tanyrate always signs his name that way."). The brain-damaged fellow, and drunk to boot, babbled lecherously (or as the old Gessner would say : exceeding vnchaste) : well, he's got his feeble-minded license, so no need to get excited, one finds oneself in any case a lifer in intellectual solitary. I once knew a man who would go to the attic whenever his gorge rose, and pound nails in a board for half an hour, straight and crooked, whichever, in gloomy sport. And did he feel any easier then ? Emptier, yes. And life went on for a couple of weeks. What was on my day's (or, rather, night's) schedule ? The gulp from the canteen : judging by color and taste, the coffee had been drawn directly from the Acheron. (Poverty of language : a man who hears nothing is called <deaf>; who sees nothing, <blind>. But what do you call him if he smells nothing ? <Lucky> maybe, my lazy brain suggested to me : but in any case, what ? And if he tastes nothing, and I gazed with greater nausea into the screw-threaded aluminum hole.) Moon, eavesdropper at the cloud wall, shoved his bald leprous skull, wrapped in bluish rags, into the window above Katrin; large-pored, lovesickly, 'veyouheardthefacts-oflife, brassy as wisdom. Soft the tavern radio with "Variations on La Paloma" : these consisted of their alternately playing the thing an octave higher or lower and finally so stutteringly fast that it gave you complete jitters. Then a mixed duet praised Kadum lanolin soap in such an asinine way that I once again impatiently demanded the next white dove, for which indeed, in hasty North-western German Radio fashion, they did not keep me waiting long : and they consider themselves the lofty cultural bastion of our time ! May God forbid and our Lady of Guadaloupe ! The old fur-cap snored like a zipper pulled up and slowly back with a whistle. (A modern danse macabre; as bus driver; as graduate chemist; as chancellor; as bobsled steerer; as refugee-welfare-officer.) Sleepless light bulb in the hall; news whispering from door ajar. Outside : sky inscribed with the star marks of astronomers; and the moon, too, still loitered through the night; (among Hun-like clouds; and again I swept my way through the thick tarry air).

vi

> There was a dreadful jolt, sparkish flew by silky red, and we rolled again a piece. The light split through the compartment with honed axes, jagged bundles of swords charged up us, the great bronze saw was still gliding through Everyone's face; no end of blusters, and we sat as if in a dark tapered magic shell. Each other. In the valley's paunchy bowl, fog roiled; thick willow heads blushed. Beside me the thick humanimal was rattling again in three-quarter time, his thick thigh swayed and twitched, and I was glad that I alone sat next to him. Katrin gave a haggard laugh, but merrily blew on her little harmonica "Sweet homeland, adé", with aigu.

Morning's broad bleak was tacked to the fleeing night with flat moon pin. Then : sky red-etched with migrating clouds; her face turned very red and yellow as well; we laughed at each other, and tormented our insensate hands. I dug the book out of my pocket : ". . . He brought her there, unto a silver cloud, / unto an isle, beneath eternal clouds / and thus forever hid from sailors' gaze." "— Lovely —" she stretched and leaned back harder against our rumpled dirt cloud. ". . . You are the selfsame one, / for whom I've often wept in depths of night ! / And seeing you, my wishes all fell mute, / while from your eyes flowed peace and earthly lust." (Wieland : earthly lust : yes.) "Ah ha," she said, amazed. The sun's fire grazed its way higher into the strawy morning; the gray hawmoon vanished in some moor or other : farewell Lower Saxony : it's your own fault that I've meant nothing to you ! Katrin again brought out the hot-water bottle of Red Cross coffee, and we each ate a well-intentioned bread-and-honey. The old lady in the compartment explained : "All I want's a church right in town where I can hear the blessed mass read every mornin'," and cast a blessedish look about her, white hair like puffs of fog in her ears. Ah yes, "How late's it getting to be ?" "Well —" I was guessing, "departure at 5:52 — Eickeloh — Schwarmstedt — Burgwedel — well : nine ?" The Leine meandered around muscular hills; next to us someone was playing the ancient American patented zither with insertable polka-dotted page (oh, I dunno, something of the intrepid sort, and ending suspiciously like Ohgermanyhighinhonor). A Silesian cobbler from Volkersdorf knew Katrin's Greiffenberg : "How 'bout that !" And the names somersaulted : Prenzel Park, Kienberg, Reservoir, Munko-Müller, "Rietcher on Sechshäusern"; and she turned to me and explained it breathlessly : the house on Gerberstrasse. "I was forever making dancing puppets," she described the cardboard figures exactly, you pulled the thread and the little guy gave a charming twist of hands and feet. I paid in kind and mentioned the matchboxes I was forever stuffing as a child : with tiny writing utensils, thin sharpened pencil stubs, short-staffed steel pens, and stacks of paper cut to box size, plus needle and thread, a folded map of the world in Mercator projection. (Even then I had a sense of how dubious all possessions are that can't be stuffed into a matchbox !) And the zithering carpenter began to enthuse religiously about Loretto, and I made a note for later pondering <Should carpenters believe in God ?>. I at any rate would prefer one who did not require such hypotheses for his framework.

vii

> My godfather, the stench ! Of the three doors, one was missing entirely; urine slopped yellow on each'n'every tile; brown piles coiled like ropes, smeary pies or teocallical tiers; squishy pulp, dreadfully drenched, help, light from book-sized panes of filth. Whispering balancing with disgust, I pulled down my pants, out of here, and legs astraddle, still with paper under my chin to the scarred stone threshold. Wind bustled iron-hard and everywhere trains jerked. Exhausted. The platforms fit donkey-gray beneath their lean roofing, tight against the drab apartment houses : this then is Göttingen Central Station.

Of all times, while we were eating — pea soup with a slim sinewy Indian-red wiener — came the announcement that we now had to change cars : Alzey to the rear, Westerburg to the front. Since naturally we were up front, we first scalded and besmeared ourselves quickly, and then stormed with our baggage far, far to the rear — — as empty a one as possible — —: here ! the young girl made quite a nasty face, as if she could just barely stand up in this throng; I cracked the door, and correct : she was alone with her mother, both brown and woolly ("handknit" Katrin, the expertess, rasped). Within a minute she was already conversing with both. Weber was their name, the husband also soon arrived out of the chunky wind; in the inventory of their furniture, the centerpiece was "the handmade wrought-iron clothes tree" : "I'm a master smith," he said confiding, "was a lovely house : two stories. And some farmin' with it. We picked up 'nd left in '45, when Ivan arrived, into Thuringia. And in Hanover, then, I worked in the machine works. But all we had was a livin' room 'nd alcove, and our little gal here's got too big now." We nodded : got the picture ! "We want to better ourselves". "You can never better yourself," I decided, shaking my head, based on a wealth of moving-about experience in a long and ill-applied life — a glance at Katrin : "Especially when it starts so awfully well." She searched through her purse with satisfaction. (Then I went, as noted, to find a toilet, and clambered again up over cement ligaments and black iron tendons). The raining queen sobbed unconsolably and flailed her hair against the panes; the dusk of the compartment grew deeper, and gathering wool now, we spelled out the ads; wind cursed choppily; they shunted us here, there. "Yes, they're good folks," (were alone for once), but : "has One of them ever sobbed over Ludwig Tieck, at so much beauty ? Or let themselves be adopted by Hoffmann ?" I first had to explain what I wanted : across the way the battery-powered postal carts hummed from one light funnel to another; like us, a trainload of English half-tracks waited in a stupor; they can do anything with soldiers and refugees ! At one point Weber told about how they had rammed a tree with their car (aha, just had to mention that !), and his broad head turned slowly hither and back again. "Was the tree hurt ?" I automatically asked, and they laughed, and thought it was a joke. Next to us dozed an old maid, before whom the Webers had already fled once : "Good thing you're here," they confided to us, and we gradually grew more intimate, as far as it goes. Then finally, here came the wooden punch to our backs, everyone sat up, checked if the luggage was falling, and for a quarter hour I closed my eyes. Then the town was gone; much romping of the air, damp lights traveled along the horizon; shadow horses chasing back after trees; the disk of dusk fogged over grayer still. Each station gallowed us with arc lamps, hacked hands off, hastily coffined the striped torsos in planks of light too short for the job; so that's how Katrin looked with no head.

viii

Backs like wood, and night in the large train station, desolate and light-rimmed; Gütermann's Thread swaggered above wall smudges; the yellowest arc lamps obliquely blasted our compartment. Hoo-ey sang the locomotive into the brindled night, setting Katrin suppling, and the old smith bungling. Some fellow banged a hammer desperately against the wheel below us and yelled a monotone "aeh-eeh !" The cone of light pressed deeper into the yielding benches, between my legs, swept up onto the worn-out wall through the baggage-net lattice. In the ensuing black, Katrin banged her teeth into my mouth; the train groaned and surged night-blindly about us.

In the next compartment, the elderly lady was now lying beneath her desiccated dress; so mother and daughter joined her there. Katrin had three blankets (one mutely for me), I laid out the foundation for her, nary-a-wrinkle smooth, then the coated maiden on top, and the last one stretched out over feet and shoulders : "You comfortable ?". So then, top right, Katrin; behind at my back the master smith. "Can I get you anything else ?" Two dark eye ponds, stiff lash reeds; I took one quivering breath, and from the north came a silver draught, lids froze over the mirrored circles. The uncouth floor poked me all over; the gauzy lamp glimmered black; the daughter groped by once more into the naked john and stayed a long time. The doors mutinied in their frames, balls of light met small and insane, the smith strode and cursed at the same time in his heavy handworker's dream. The ice melted from the ponds; I quickly propped myself on one arm and our faces whispered very dense words. "The way they all can sleep," she, with cautious amazement, "I was such a restless spirit even as a little girl, my grandfather was a cobbler, and the old folks worked dreadfully long hours, so that I always lay awake nights and listened to the pounding," her mouth fumbled sweetly and undifferentiatedly through the memories, above me, on soft lip shoes, red velvet slippers : there was a grandmother sewing for an apron factory; Pastor Hein on his bicycle with scandalously billowing robe; once, near Wiesa, she had almost rolled over the barrier into the Queis, and even today, I impatiently held fast. "Me ? I don't need their beggary, period !" she replied disparagingly : "I get my pension, you know : 180 marks !" "That much ?" I asked astonished, "I thought the state valued dead husbands at a mere 60 ?" "That's true," she answered, cooling off, "and mine wasn't even worth that much : just imagine : married during the war, 8 days to ourselves; and then when he came on leave for the first time in six months, no more than three days into it we caught him with a neighbor woman, his mother and I did !" she curtly pulled her hands from mine, shifted her shoulders away, and turned onto her back. Then all you can do is simply lie down and go to sleep too. The great bony fellow had his red scarf and tommy shirt around him and said out loud : "The govinment's not gonna help us, so we'll just strike out on our own." And we reloaded the wagons and flowed all over those roads; the wind beat folds into our blanket coats; the buckets clattered at the rear around the inflamed tail-lights. Atop one of them sat a woman, katrin-slim, the withered child in her amputated arm, and she blew a dangerous song on a Jew's harp, terrifying the fat locals on their farms till they whispered long-distance for police. Come evening, the guide distributed nothing but matches, and we crept in every direction away from the multi-armed road sign. – Toward morning our journey grew more impetuous. Fir cripples emerged from white moors; puddles ran by on snaky paths; many birches floated back through the heath. At a crossroad, a stranger held his rigid bike with both gloves; rimed plank fences galloped with us for another little way; then the forest again cried havoc above us.

ix

> "Take a look : all the others are already shaving !". "You mean you're absolutely sure you don't like a man with a beard ?" – she crinkled her chin in disgust, and I groaned a little more, but then went to stand in line at the tap. "With cold water !"; such a mighty reproach was therein, that in alarm she petted me (until she got used to the stage voice). "Hey, what's that over there ? !" Exasperated, I turned my soaphead and complained through my nose : okay, either I shave, wee thing, or I explain the Ehrenbreitstein, choose ! As I was drying myself off, there stood opposite me a ruined row of buildings; the refugee fed his goat; and from the rear came the Red Cross with noodles and horsemeat (but mostly innards and gristle !)

I declined without hesitation, because there would be no point in it, but the Webers didn't want to miss out on anything; so we gave them our breakfast chits to bring ours back, while we guarded the baggage. (6) said the Limburger Station clock as we shoved off onto a side-track for a half hour : there we were all alone in the old wooden bower and whispered and groped. Wind had raked stars loose too, and we watched for quite a while, as the Webers searched for the compartment ("But the blindest of them are sons of gods !" I quoted Hölderlin, bird of morning song, and as proof passed my strong minus cylinders to Katrin : so there ! "Oh, 'd give you a headache !" she said demurring "your eyes are that bad ? !"). The children, of course, were boarding the train as it rolled, the head conductor screeched, parents galloped; as always, nothing happened to the dear little angels, but the adults practically broke their legs in imperial leaps. Well, and the cocoa : so who was right ? ! "Looks like rain", Old Weber said, cozily warming his hands on his coffee crockery; I left to Katrin the now inevitable "Tastes like it too", and looked out the window into the Lahn Valley gushing past : gray silken hills, and it was not raining, and the stream shot and rolled with us around the curves. (Amusing notion : what if, in the course of centuries, the angle of light's refraction from air into water were to change ? Likewise the angle of the ecliptic : after all, animals and plants evolve ! It's well known that the atmosphere is slowly escaping and so keeps getting thinner : therefore as the density of the refractory medium changes, so too the aforesaid angle ! ! I know No One who can be right as often as I !). "Push the window up all the way," Katrin said, sneezing the command ! once more (just as Father Aristotle maintains : for each nostril !); well now : once more, and it really looked so charming that, very much to her irritation, I enthused over it greatly almost to Koblenz. Yes, that is the Rhine : over there the Mosel slowly flowed along out of lovelier valley coils; I had to spit out the name of every castle ruin, while fabricating tribal sagas that would have made a genealogist hug me (nevertheless : whether it could last as far as Bingen was uncertain, given that much unused capacity for absorption and that many grimy vestigial walls). Viewed from the left bank of the Rhine, Germany looked quite unwonted (what a role the map image plays !); one belongs in some sense "to the West". It was, however, downright cold here between river odor and sleep deprivation, and shaving a major torment. There we stood and stood; the Weber ladies staunchly pulled out their giant needles and wool again and began mechanically to knit, purl two, knit two, and that would give the sweaters a caterpillar pattern, Katrin merrily explained.

x

> The long wrinkled stream, hollow and muddy, swung lazily along beside us; flooded islets; mourning groups of trees; sour facades like "Lorelei", as if a car had just driven away; docks and stench of black tugs; hatched by drizzle (and the freight train on the other side of the Rhine : "If it has 60 cars, everything will turn out alright !" — — — : "58 — ?". She beamed nevertheless in all directions : "Well then : minor difficulties." Eye spell, lip witch, chin magic, leg conjury, Katrin la sorcière. Her fingers danced for joy across the purse on her lap and snapped it my way). The vineyards looked dismal, like their map symbol.

"And now he shoved an armed chair nearer and bade the Electour Prince to seat himself in it and under no circumstance to rise up from it nor speak a word — else would he behold his certain Death with his own eyes. With the same warning, the Chamberlain was placed behind the chair. Thereupon the Hungarian wrapped about the heathen-headed goblet a wire, which he led into the furnace. Next, all the while speaking softly, he drew three circles about the Electour Prince and finally, from the outermost circle, drew a straight line to the furnace. The lights were placed in the form of a triangulum about the plate. The Hungarian knelt down now immediately before the oven and continued softly to pray (?). From time to time he took some simple from a pot standing near him and threw it into the flames, whereupon a mighty cracking arose each time in the oven and the blaze did increase exceedingly. This perchance continued for an hour and the Chamberlain observed how the wire leading from oven to goblet began to glow, how thick drops formed on the goblet, but that within, it did flash and play with the most beautiful colors, much as he had ofttimes seen in the silver forge. He perceived how by degrees the goblet was expanding and stretching, did glare and increase in height, how the heathen heads as well seemed visibly to grow. The Hungarian muttered ever more zealously and the goblet swelled ever higher until its rims almost thrust against the ceiling. Then a thundering clap resounded and up sprang the heathen heads as men with long coats and beards, truly awful to look upon. They formed a circle about the Electour Prince; one of the men fell upon his knees before the man standing nearest the Electour Prince, pointed to the Electour Prince and called out : That is he who seeketh to deliver the Empire to the Gauls ! Whereupon the men put their heads together as if in secret Counsel. At last he who stood most far away brought a broadsword out from under his coat and cried aloud : Thus doth the Law reward the Traitor ! At the same moment he took several steps forward, as if he would strike the Electour Prince. Whereupon the Prince called out with stifled voice : Help, help, Michael — and at once all was vanished . . ." She gave a nod of approval; and another : "and all that took place at Ehrenbreitstein ? !" Pfeeewit : a tunnel (Wonderful !). Still breathless : "And when did this happen ?". Once again, I was unprepared for such great craving for knowledge with no transition, but said firmly : "on the second of June sixteen hundred thirty-two."

xi

> A blue-nosed farmer squatted lumpishly in front of his long wine barrel (cows with vacant airs), out of which at every step the green sullage algaed. Brick besmirchment of houses, Gobi yellow, and we so deep in muck that that stony Nepomuc of theirs clutched his skirt in sympathy. The brook (regulated of course) shriveled civil servilely through the flat bridge. "Well, it is the worst time of the year," waded the courageous voice beside me; but when I took a look at the cloddish faces, their dung-heap cult, and their equally carefully ironed Meadow Hill —. The sky was veined gray, a dripping beggar's bag, and we refugees bore it on our shoulders as far as the Rummer.

When at Bingen, we turned away from the Rhine, the faces grew flat and long like the fertile bleakness all around; sometimes the flat earthen belly forced up round humpbacked villages, crouched, warty with roofs, toadish : here then is where the expression <flatland> arose. At first, when in Gau-Bockenheim they yelled along the length of the train, we didn't even want to get off : too lonely a station; drizzle weather, nobody weather; but the committee was already standing there to receive us. A district commissioner, someone from the Housing Administration, a mayor, and the iridescent word-bubbles rose and burst : ". . . always find my door open !" (that was the commissioner; for now only the door to his car stood open, he wriggled into it : rrr rrr rrr, gone; job done); ". . . a reg'ler cathlick town; . . . all good cathlick fokes . . ." that emerged from between the loden coat and chamois-tufted hat of the town honcho, and we gave each other one swift corner of the eye. For the heavier baggage there was the field wagon behind the tractor, diesel throbbings : a ship crosses the Atlantic in 12 days, how long do four ships take : cast off. Then begins the march into town, 135 souls, led unbidden by the male youth of the village. The roads skidded with muck and moisture; houses propped against each other in their affliction; one evening bell : though there was nothing at all soothing about it, just tinny hash and one bim after the other landed hither and yon. (Twice in his life, my father was in a church : when he was baptized, and in 1926 in a downpour). Colder than hell, too; Katrin's free hand was white and blue like potato blossoms, the other one held doughtily onto my arm : that's how I should be painted : a book in one hand, Katrin in the other, and we intend to do nothing. Alackandalas the dung-heaps : "It is indeed true that it can no longer be determined with certainty in what region of the earth paradise was located, but this sure ain't it." "Look at the figurines on the houses" : 'sindeed : in little niches stood gaudy Marias and Jesuses, plaster of Paris and enamels : three marks a kitsch, said sometimes to remain unconsumed in conflagrations, regrettably. "Bunn the Baker", yellowish brick, but a remarkable weathercock above the roof's ridge : the first positivum. "Until Monday, the men'll be put up in the <Rummer>; the ladies in the <Crown>"; what bastards ! Well, suit- and briefcases flung up to lie flat (quickly fix the coordinates of the bed; ah, Weber got in right below), and back to Katrin, who was waiting, brave and proud-eyed, beside her baggage clump. "Separating us !", and her face was like a wild white flower above the purple handbag; her mouth disintegrated into fiery-hued curses, soft ones. — <Crown> : "Corner bed, whatsay ? By the window." (that way at least you have neighbors on only one side!). "I'll be right back to get you" she promised.

xii

If you would live, then serve; if you would be free, then die ! — "Someday Germany's mark in world history will be that of a stone over which mankind frequently stumbled", I darkly replied to Him, who spoke to me in praise of the strength and beauty of the imminent new Wehrmacht, and we at once turned our butts on each other. Had apparently once been a dance hall with the usual droll accessories : jerseyed black scratched the banjo at his belly; the spirals of a lasso tap-danced above the ecstatically stomping gaucho; the tall girl, every hand full with her own hips, cavorted above a miniature Hessia : the river emerged just right from her. At first, the coal-pit light on the ceiling hardly allowed you to make out the bed fissures and tunnels.

I went back downstairs first; the moon had also blundered into the courtyard and was rummaging sulkily in the trash. Just before eight, most of them returned : inhabitants 1500; purely agricultural; industry none. "Oh yes there is," a youngster said maliciously : "uptop, near the church : a malt factory with ten men." "Work in the vineyards pays real bad : two marks a day 'nd free <house wine>." — ? — Shrugs : "Prob'ly water, with a jigger a wine added." "Two marks !" and it seemed to grow darker again in the room. "Seen from Russia's angle, it's a policy of strangulation. Throttle 'em. Quite clear ! : Europe's to be America's continental dagger, that's why they're pushin' so hard. Call a spade a spade !" "D' you think so much a the Russians ? !". "Me — nah ! but not much a the others, 'ncluding our own gover'ment, neither !" One of them claimed that today, just now, he had <kicked in the basement window> of the fat broad down below, they hardly let him finish his demonstration of <widened stance>, the applause was almost too great : so you think that just 'cause we're refugees ? ! A despondent Weber was sitting below on his bed as I pulled on my coat : "There's three smiths a'ready" he whispered and tried to smile. I cheered him up with "Let's go get something to eat first," and lots of women were down there. Womanity. I strode into the circle of waiting schoolchildren, who were supposed to lead us; the nervous little girl read, gibbered a little, but then walked on ahead of us : back to the little square (center-city one presumes); a wide street; she pointed down into the mouth of a dark crooked alley; 'tsrait 'nthrait dun thetaweh (another barbaric dialect !); well, it was written on the scrap of paper too, Beck, 224. Tapping on stone skulls, hard as farmers'; "Watch out, a street roller !"; the moon had stretched tight tarps across the old field wagons, globes of light propped everywhere, so that at first we couldn't even find the house number in the bright jumble. "Is this your husband ? Your real husband ?" : a mistrustful household of women, quartet, and a little boy, Karl, Don Carlos. "We're engaged", Katrin said with such pride and bridal slowness, what an old hand at it, that they believed her at once; and the potatoes were big and hot, and the speckled country brawn spicy and juicy. We then told a long tale of our trek and misery, until, touched, they brought us wine (they truly are good folk !). Then came the news : big demonstration in West Berlin, "held on the border of the Soviet sector" : just like little kids sticking out their tongues at each other over the fence. "And each claims his is longer." "Goo'night !" : the darkened Malayan face of the moon regarded us like some boxer, arrogant, bong the last round, mocking, from where it was setting.

xiii

> Morning in the Crown seraglio : there is No Goddess but Katrin ! Lightning eyes flashed from poodles of hair, brown necks, and a timbering of white arms lifted with pure silken clouds above. I walked, heart apounding, to my blanket bulge and cautiously laid hands on the metal edge. Smiles beneath the betousled mannish hairdo, to set my heart eddying. Eye depths like the Guam trench, the mouth spoke airily of the "Good morning"; (everywhere feminizings in the oaten straw); a white hand-bangle fibulaed blanket edges. Hair time; ivory time.

Shadows ran across her eyes, the lip heavens were darkened; I let go of my hand, which was immediately received into the blanket warmth. "Listen, I —" her mouth morseled, her head rang out wild, once, her nose moaned briefly — "do you know that I only have one foot ? !", and she abruptly stuck it out down below : the clean hard prosthesis up to midcalf. On the left leg. "During an air raid." Much red panties brightened roundabout, cherry, broad harem's brassieres. Foot was no longer there. She gave a coarse and hopeless curse. "But otherwise I'm in great shape" a brittle contralto whispered. Red mouth ravine, flooded with torrents, out of which flowed gentle gusts of wind. I now uncoupled the other hand, and it leaped to the back of her head through the dark hair meadow. Sobbing, she set her teeth in my forearm, once, and then said proudly : "I can even wear bright-colored knee-stockings. You know : the real sturdy kind, sporty." Her eyes made a single leap like young meteors through the hall vortex; she stretched out her yellow arm crop and commanded : "Hand me the stockings – there !" The blanket puffed out large and ceremonious; once again. She knelt, opened the front to me, and propped her hands on my shoulders, with shimmering lights. Everywhere. Then out of the crude folds came the long dark silken legs, I caught them both, and placed the no-nonsense girl beside me between bed and window. A slip lianaed and fit. A suit-skirt slipped down over. A long mouth chatted : "Listen, I've got a beautiful big radio." "Katrin : !" Whirring and a hornéd millipede ran through the hair jungling. "The 180 marks come in the mail the first of every month"; accompanied by a mollifying handcuff around my forearm. Five minutes alone : the sun had grown sandier, calmer. (How gloriously awful she would treat me in just a little while, my slow proud one !) Then through the high grid of rows a slender ambling approached : "Becks'll be waiting for us." Fold blankets; arrange suitcases. There she leaned, plaid, against the bedpost. Frenzy of lip and hexing of brow. From closed mouth : "Darling." From closed mouth : "Darling !" Then imperious and anxious : "Oh definitely." – (Express the diameter of a washbasin in parsecs).

xiv

> "Imagine : the pastor has 5 rooms and a kitchen for himself and his housekeeper !". She laughed fire and water : "and then there's a ‹Bishop's Room› besides, which stands ceremoniously empty all year long : he comes here just once, you see, for one night ! And to think there are people like that ! !". Wind drew the wrinkled sky of clouds tighter together; a light motorcycle stuttered past : the hasty monkey sat atop it with back all hunched over. From the church wall : a choir of hypocrites sang of naught but love and charity, and again her rebel face flickered white out of coat coals : "Set the place on fire over the heads of everybody sitting inside, and then barefoot to Lower Saxony ! : damn, if only the Russians 'd come !"

"And did you see how the floor gave underneath you ?" "Just imagine : you've got to run clear across the street for every bucket of water : now, in winter !" She gave a genuine shudder and moved her shoulders : "The worst part is the john, god ! You wouldn't even go in there. And I'm supposed to get it clean somehow – ?" Nope, that hole was truly uninhabitable for human beings. "And did you take a good look at those faces ?" she let her cheeks hang low, flatulated her mouth, and looked strikingly like the idiot pair of siblings that camped across the hallway, Stone-Age types. (Oh, we had found out on the sly; through the Webers, who ate at the mayor's brother-in-law's house !): "You see, and that's why that bastard from the Housing Authority in Alzey didn't tell anyone ahead of time where they'd end up ! That way they don't have any trouble whatever; that way no one can mutiny or complain. That way, tomorrow morning they can simply set people's furniture out on the street, in front of these holes : okay, do it or else ! – Oh what arrogant swine !" And I too savagely hacked my head : "Out-of-the-question !" I swore grimly : "If They think they can simply run right over us ! – He'll be back here again with them tomorrow morning – that's a Big Man in a hurry, with a face like ham and eggs : he'll get to hear a thing or two." The organ growled conciliatorily from the church, bovine warm, trusty old Christianity with its double sole and more spiritual calf-leather than would ever be necessary : "Western Christian Civilization ! ?" If things had gone their way, we would still believe today that the earth is a disk with Rome or Jerusalem in the center : they would have used Kant and Schopenhauer for a bonfire, then tossed on Goethe and Wieland for good measure, and torched it all with Darwin and Nietzsche ! "No no, Katrin : Christianity ain't got nothing to do with civilization !" (I admit I come from a breed that considered someone <dopey> who attended church at Christmas). Are clergy educated men ? "Where do you get that ?" I asked dumbfounded : "do you call that education when instead of God someone can also say deus, theos and elohim ? Because that's what it amounts to." (Never mind : the fear of the Lord hampers the beginning of wisdom.) But Katrin was already energetically providing proof herself, inside her gloves her pretty fists had grown round and firm with anger : "Just give a listen : –" Wind ran down the street, setting it dusting, and played soccer with leaves : my father would have slapped me one if I had abused shoes that way ! – : "Love, love, love everlasting" it came, dragging broadly out of the clay-colored folding doors. "And those are the same s.o.b.s that want to stick us in these holes ? ! Oh go to heaven : words, words everlasting !" She was flying now, coat and all, she blindly gave my foot a kick, she yelled at me : "Don't the bastards think at all when they sing that sort of stuff ? !"

XV

> "Poets who agonize mightily looking for new material could write Pindaric odes to our Olympic champions, Jesse Owens and Birger Rüd, look at this !" : Twenty-three muscular figures bolted and leapt over the frowzy lawn, beheaded the callused clouds, balls rose with Magnus effect into the howl of wind. I pressed my chin against the crude post and knotted my fingers disdainfully through cold pockets : bleak faces, turnip dispositions, stepped mentalities, tundraed souls : "Southwest Broadcasting didn't air the awarding of the Literature Prize of the Academy of Mainz : but the father of Walters the soccer player got interviewed for half an hour."

The crowd : ace marksmen with sturdy bellies, women either force-fed or pregnant, children, torturing grass and bawling. Hate, haste, race, rest. God knows, you ought to keep a map of the world hanging on the wall so that you can ingrain the image of Europe as just a fissured NW cape of Asia; and for Western Christian civilization, a soccer photo, where for a finale they club the referee to death. There are indeed traits that reveal a man's character for good and all and place him under eternal suspicion : taking pleasure in giving or obeying orders; being a politican. On the other hand there are stupidities and errors that compromise you if you have *not* committed them at least once. "And those would be ?". Well, for example, as a young person, around 25 or so, believing Nietzsche to be a demigod; or loving <humanity> for just as long. She nodded responsively, and took another disparaging glance back at the crowd : "Well, we won't grow old in this backwater anyhow !" she determined. We stepped behind the massive loading ramp : her teeth burned in my throat, nails nested in my nape, the wind came barking its outrage from around the corner and sprang at our coats. "Compensation payments, Katrin, ha ha ? — When what they want is immediate rearmament ? ! 've got no quarrel if Somebody votes for it : but then get him down off his laboratory stool at once, out of his workshop, his cabinet post, his narcoleptic rectory and send him off to the Wehrmacht : 2 years scrubbing latrines; <Hit the ground !> <On your feet, march, march> and keep yelling the whole time : I'm crazy, until the petty tyrant graciously dismisses you; rousted out for drill with a pin; and have 4 men fetch matches one by one and lay 'em on the table for the sergeant, sir, who then tosses 'em out, fifty times, from the 4th floor till the matchbox is empty : saw that in Sprottau, in 1937, strike me dead ! ! : O thou glorious German nation ! And thou School for Manhood, the barracks ! But our government consists exclusively of the sort who no longer have to do their duty; not a one under 60 : who needs old-folks' homes when we've got parliaments ! — No one who is unaffected by such issues ought to be allowed to cast a vote on them" (Switch topics; my bile runneth over). "Hear how they're bleating ? Clear over here ? And afterwards they'll go to church" (Modern prayer book : "To be sung in airplane emergencies"; "Prayer with drunken chauffeur"; "Lord, let not the subway be delayed". I can't help how I am: the stuff sets certain of my organs twitching, and at once I went on to tell her about "The Book of Mormon", which already knew in the year 420 that Joseph Smith of Vermont would retrieve it on 22. 9. 1823.) : "There's nothing so absurd that believers won't believe it. Or bureaucrats do it." "Only too true, in the case of bureaucrats," she said wisely and bitterly, and we walked another couple of gray versts in the direction of Sprendlingen. (Further topics of conversation were : "Do you love me ? !"; "Do you have friends ?"; "Is world history a matter of chance or pure absurdity ?"; "Can you play chess ?" — and I indignantly told her how at one time I had laid low the Silesian regional master, with b 2 — b 4 : 'sineed !)

xvi

and here we wended our steps onto a broad lane that led to a village up ahead; sky began gloomily to overcast and rained; two, passing in constant flight above our heads, wanting to be our escort : the narrow cemetery contained within untidily laid stone walls; church with stubby shingled steeple; in the thick wall of each side just a single little window; the door as if half-sunken in the earth; high grave-mounds pressed tightly together and overgrown with nettles (human silage). The horizon was already darkened, in the murky twilight the sky seemed to be laid out thickly on all sides.

Behind us the primal cries of ball-kicking humanity; on the left gaunt-bodied corn mummies, rattlings, dry, disagreeable; and up front, the blood-rounded scourge of sun sank through wrought-iron cloudwalls. Squabbling : "Eaters of roasts, costumed in their Sunday suits. Buxom perfumed Graces." But Katrin explained :

with sympathy : "The poor things would just smell of stall otherwise. 'ts a fact." And the small firm forearm deflected me to the little signalhut : two-storied, tidy bricks, twenty by twenty-five, flat roof, strong metal doors, dark green. We circumloitered all sides of it, without purpose but full of thought. "Downstairs 'd be the kitchen and a storage room. Large one." "Upstairs a large living room with an alcove for a bed". Breathe deeper, nod heavier. (If only one were something other than tribal buffoon; horde's clown, before whose breast the boss pithecanthropus sometimes graciously dangles a little chunk of mammoth loin.) Dusk slunk with heavy baskets across the fields; I grasped into Katrin again, more impertinent too, and she hardly flinched. "No curtains at all those windows, upstairs. A great big room, whaddya say !". "Sure." She spoke between her teeth, and drew half her eyes closed : out of hate for this filthy burg. "Maybe take another look again later." The foot-bridge swayed grayly above the brook (flat cloud mask assembling there above yon Meadow Hill), wind swung its grass-rattle, briskly, without life. "Do you see a tree anywhere ?" and she pointed with disgust down the main road to Bingen. "But a tree'd just use up the <good soil> y' know", I said in ironic exasperation, "right where turnips could be growin' !" and immediately cut off all deliberation : "Everyone should have two children less ! That'd make room right off for woodlands, and put a stop to hunger too ! No war, no more misery ! My vote goes to the party that's against rearmament and for birth control !". "So no party ?". "So no party." The lane ended futilely at a field of crudely wounded soil : drudged earth, flayed of its plant skin, hacked to pieces, suspiciously encompassed with thorny wire. So, back again, sick of it : "These honchos don't have enough sense to set off their <prop'ty> with humane hedges !" We pressed together faces gone wild. Our Hades began to steam indolently; mist spread an icy cover over the blanching paths; Katrin doesn't dare let her stump take a chill. A broad silver tusk swelled up out of a drooping cloud maw : munching, codgerlike, closed again.

xvii

the bony moon gaped from its witches' ring; ashen wisps hurried straight across; wind slunk from the lilac bush and groped languidly and impudently through all my pockets, cold pickpocket and deft homosex : if you'd beat away at that heavenly puffball with your club, and I raised it, burst the yellow leather bulb and the black green stifling cloud came whooshing out: and He saw

Between crucifix and war memorial (leftover from Mars-la-Tour, one of the little, fussy ones, where Victoria puts a full nelson on Kaiser Wilhelm); Rabbi Jeshua probably hadn't heard so many curses and well-bred heresies in a long time. "Lord : ha ! Put a table in there — : The end !" used two hands to show Wachlinger the smallness of the room on Schweinemarkt : "If the sun shines in, I'll have to move out ! — If y' laugh, your cheeks'll bang on the walls." But there were muttered curses from every little group : "Nothing but garrets and sheds that the bastards emptied out real quick." "In the bedroom, just above the window, you can stick your hand outside." "You wou'nt 's much as fit 'nside that thing," said Borck to my 6'2", "them's cubbids, tain't rooms at all; I'm not movin' in, even if I have t' go see the minister in Mainz t'morrow." The brain-damaged fellow (yet once more full of vin tendre) told a loud and sad tale : "At the front, where my shop was, I had a view right down into the valley, to gramps's; upstairs is where the kids 'n gramma slept . . .", here someone demurred, but he shook his green-billed cap with determination : "There was eight acres, maybe a bit more, and good soil." Aha. "And y' could get along with them Czechs, too : just had t' keep your big mouth shut sometimes —" I gently pulled Katrin away. "He's from Troppau; from the Sudetenland," I explained wearily, "c'mon; we'll go back round again." Up Schulstrasse. Beneath the malt chimney, the flat barrel-vaulting glowed and bellowed, it was downright warm around your legs. I looked to one side into the rigid flaming face, and brought her slowly into the darker street : "We're moving in together no matter what. Listen ! That's allowed if you're engaged !" "Katrin !" She pushed me firmly into the entrance gate and breathed with her teeth. "Katrin." She rent me with fingers and bored her brow into my breast : "Katrinkatrinkatrin". "Hey, it'll work out", she said brokenly into my mouth, tasting everywhere, firm and cold, and shoved her chin against mine till we wobbled. In front of the Crown : "But listen, marriage is no way applicable", she warned with a clever glance over my face : "just remember : 180 marks pension, that'd be lunacy." Stood in the door under the red-lettered milky sphere. Gave one young and sovereign toss of her head :

"Till tomorrow, then !", and rejoiced, and trembled athletically. Upstairs, at the window in the room, I heard her say menacingly to Marga in the next bed : "Just let them try to make trouble for me and my fiancé !" The conversation seemed to grow softer and more animated.

xviii

> "An American has calculated that 800 hugs are ended every second." "Must be worse'n a machine gun !", he shouted with delight : "did he figger up the energy too ? What all could y' run with it ?" "Surement" I said with gusto : "Run the ‹Queen Mary› constantly across the Atlantic. If you set the combined energies against the direction of the earth's rotation, within a year, the day would be lengthened by 6 seconds." "So it's always keep your head aimed west then," he conscientiously abstracted this new maxim for life, "just the opposite of the Muhammadans." – and via such ethnographic references we gradually left the gaya scienza to return to more worthy, more long-bearded realms.

My, but the schnapps was lovely, toxic, clairaudient, strong. The light grew blotchier still, and the sludge of words seeped nonstop from the sewer mouths; I paid an unobtrusive visit to each group in the room; it was way after 10 o'clock; all the boys pretended to be asleep. Politics (this was the little fellow with the little head again) : "Unification of Europe ? Not these days, not from the West ! Just look at these here peewee states and then at Russia !" I gave him a bitter nod and floated on; there were but three chairs : alright then, we'll stand ! Here no one lacks anything that the others don't need as well : thus are we all refugees ! (I can keep this up for a long time : sleep on the floor and use the chamber door for a blanket !) The wind crumpled in the taffeta of night; ‹Drink wine and make merry› stood circumflowered above the beds; two tipsy fellows bowing, doubled over with laughter, the third arrived and was introduced : "Herr Schönert – hangs right." "Pleased to meecha." The lecherous old man said : "Stickitinsky." Carbonados and wiping out old scores. (Wonder if carbonado comes from carboniferous ? That would mean there are devanados and permesan cheese, too). On the right, someone read nationalistics aloud and gave me a grand thunder-steeling stare : ahyes, let us then think collectively, and "Ain't it the truth : crazy", I said with underhanded warmth : ohmy, how they revived and joined in the affirmation. One of them even came up with the great Hans Dominik, and for a while they approvingly raised and lowered their broad yellowish brows, ah, the cannibal warmth, the swinish warmth, I was condescending with all my might (but that's not all that much; have little patience with such firemen. Even the loveliest object can become insufferable through the praise of a fool, not to mention through popular editions). Back in the courtyard; this john was almost unusable as well, it's really no wonder : one contraption for 65 men – the bastards have locked up the other one. From there, first to the door for fresh air : across the way the parsonage with its bishop's room, and no lightning strikes. Landscape ? : Nothing; so then, the airscape (overworld) : silver buoy, anchored atilt in the cloud current; wind wanted to report something in the primal tongue, but instead hissed too hurriedly this time, and we parted. Beneath my bed sat Weber, very alone in his glooms; he raised his head and gave me a nod : "I *can't* move in there," he said, exhausted : "I took a look this evenin'; the house was all dark, first y' go up one flight a stairs, then another, then *another* – and those rooms were pitch-black, all with slopin' ceilin's, and there's only two anyhow" he shook himself helplessly : "Does have an inside tap and a sink; but we made this move for jist one reason, 'cause our gal finally has t' have a room of her own ! Marga's gonna be twenty-five, it jist has to be !" He kept smoothing the blanket with his horny hand : "I gotta tell 'em in the mornin' : I can't move in there." Once more he unburdened his mouth: "Right across from where you eat, they had a cop clear the attic rooms, he was jist gonna hack it all up." Hess was the noble fellow's name. (The smith really must have heart trouble, because every inch of his fat body was trembling) : "I won't sleep a wink t'night" and wrapped himself up (and up in Lower Saxony he'd even had a job !). The little tailor, who looked like Heinz Rühmann, rolled his limp hands out of the blankets; at the back they were still wallowing, endlessly, homo germanicus : no reason for them to brag, the old Germans used poisoned arrows just like all the other hottentotts!

xix

> "Yeah, if only so many of the ceilings didn't slope —" (until Hess started boiling again and downstaired abellying); then we hurriedly whispered about : "Hey, they're really not all that small : — square footage — say : eighteen by thirteen". "And then add the kitchen." "And running water." "All to ourselves up here". "And only 11 marks rent; of course just skylights and no view." — "Can you climb those damned stairs with your leg ?" Face thunderclouded. "I can". Brief rancorage of ire. "We can set up only one bed —" I immediately apologized. "All-the-better !" she growled, resolutely irreconcilable. I had to go right over and borrow the little dolly from Becks.

And the gentleman from Alzey was all lovely ears as I outlined my standpoint in resonant fluent High German, while rolling my eyes for the commonweal (and the others were standing behind me now !) : "I've never been put through such a trip before." : "Then it's high time !" Weber, however, only whispered beneath the weight of the authority that had power over him, instituted by God. I will be brief : and he saw at once that if he could eliminate me, the loudmouth of the pack, but I was strong enough — "Ah, this is your fiancée ? !" — and triumphantly went with us to Hess. Now he started in : unmarried; respectable house (had recently been restuccoed too !). "Don't get upset," Katrin said to me imperturbably, they aren't really people. They're just farmers." From her pretty bundle she pulled a violet-colored fifty-mark bill, and smiling graciously, paid three months in advance, embittering his possession of it, however, with the innocent question : "Aren't any rats, are there ?". "And you'll give me a receipt later, right ?" True, the toilet was in the courtyard, but it flushed, and was thus a star attraction for the town. I looked about me sourly : honest whitewashed hearts, brains as per usual, splendidly suitable for work with the soil. "Need those too," she soothed me, but I laughed only briefly : "'course," I admitted, "but in the slogan <Workers of Brow and Fist> the <and> is pure impudence. — Fortunately the low opinion is mutual. Forget it". Then with Josef (the son) I fetched our furniture; and the day passed with ripping crates, shouldering furniture, tearing skin, freezing, nailing; by the time it was dark we had only laid planks in the bed; I sent Katrin out of the chaos to the Crown once again : "just for tonight." Wild and difficult farewell. 34° and cloudy. I towered lonely and stiff in the crateland; the skeletons of constellations wrenched in the sky, oh what funny concoctions we are : wonder if God (as he himself has put it in black and white) actually bears a resemblance to old Hess downstairs ? More like yep than nope ! Shudder, sneeze, sneeze, well : l'empereur ne soit autre maladie que la mort. Sit, stand, sit, lie, stand. Comradeship, comradeship : I have no use for groups of middling feelings ! To perfect or semiperfect strangers, politely indifferent; for the rest, love or hate (skoteinos). I groped along cube edges : had been a frontline soldier for six years after all, plus POW (for my bit of stuff the digs were too big anyhow), but all I have ever known is aversion, at best tolerance. Light fermented around three, murky yellow gray, from clouds; from my dormer on the universe I horrorized the frozen roofs, with high protective coat collar, like those way out there, ariel-umbriel, planetary cold, me, white-limbed, silky haired : nah, I have no purpose. Hit the sack. — Katrin stepped to the bed, I stood up, just as I lay, my hands in my pockets, she looked up, frightened, adoring, sympathetic : then she laid her hand on my chest and turned my heart back on. (Was still very early; orange slices of the moon against bright red).

XX

> "You see", Katrin said triumphantly and pulled the drawer open and shut several times, "the middlest is for cutlery." The ample surface was covered with marbled hard linoleum; wood, pale yellow and nastily shiny; the back wall sonorous plywood, was perfectly adequate ! Nickel keys pliantly cracked the doors : inside the cross-shelf was a bit narrower, and I looked at Katrin questioningly : ? "That's great", she said pleased, "that way the real tall stuff fits up front, bottles and such." We nodded practically into the flapped opening, ran a hand several times over the rounded edges, and then we shoved the lower part of the kitchen cupboard against the wall, beside the door to the living room.

Pick up our emergency-aid at the mayor's : 20 marks for men, 10 for women; and Katrin was outraged : always the same old arrogance ! She muttered incredulously, and I gallantly changed the topic to <Does the female have a soul ?> (naturally not; but in its place other very special devices). "Yes; and the male is just a wandering youknowwhat !", and sullen, came no more, only later, and was obstinate for a long time, then, however, I did receive a rueful slap : "Well be off : has to be picked up in any case !" A greasy mayor, a thin reigning clerk (I knew that relationship; in the military I was I-a in my day, too). Back <home> I found her crouching slimly above a humble little furry : "Just imagine : it doesn't have a name ! — Now how can that be ?" she lamented, large-eyed. Most trustingly : "Hey quick : what's its name." I shoved my mouth forward critically and nodded Lichtenbergishly, as it effervesced under Katrin's ruffling hand, modest and with blackish stripes. "The kitty GURNEMANZ." (The forward part of the name purrs; the rear bears that little tail high enough). She nodded, relieved and reverent : good man ! But then she wrinkled her brow again mistrustfully : "Haven't I heard that name somewhere before — ?". "Beg your pardon", I said, hurt : "if it doesn't please you, we can always call it Prschemislottokar, à la Prince Lobkowitz", and she jiggled me enthusiastically with her eyes. Come on up and come on. "Have you already filled out the registration forms ?" and the ballpoint pressed; "Apply for the household allowance", and the ballpoint. "He wants one mark a month for water." "Okay." Then came the half kitchen cupboard. And a simple but sturdy table. "Come here, Katrin !" We entangled us for relaxation (from arranging furniture) in eyes, mouth and arms : "Hey you!" "Hey you." "— Ah, you —" On the wall then : <Otto Kühl : Path through the Heath>. "Great !" "The longer you look at it." It was just a simple crate, and I had fitted boards across it : the bookcase : eighty of 'em. ("After the next war there'll be only ten."). Next to the desk. "Katri-in." Arm around her shoulders : "Our house has received its soul". (= Books. Cicero). She bent down and fingered and read : Cooper, Wieland, Jean Paul : Moritzcervantestieckandsoforth. Schopenhauerlogarithmtables. "Why those ?"

xxi

> A very small, black iron stove, a crumple of Blue Bonnet paper, a printed sack, an oatmeal carton, a fist full of chips, one and a half dull briquettes, six gleaming pieces of coal, a dirty hand carefully at the match, the green pot of water passing the eye, while a hand hovers the shoulders, two shoes float back and forth, one hand kittycats in my hair, the flame climbs into the parchment, a chip cracks and grows fat and yellow, a knife case first clanks unsentimentally, then a maiden's voice gruffs along with it : "Lord, am I happy !"

(What a good thing we don't have an organ for detecting currents of air : just think of how the turmoil and spirals would twist out of your heated stove, broad glassy reptilian bodies, protuberances big as a man, cellophane wheels : you'd have chaos in your winter parlor ! And yet another reason for being horrified.) Accept the coal coupons : 3 hundredweights of briquettes, 3 hundredweights of coal; in actuality there was of course only just one of each to start with : "You have no idea how dark it was in that shed; and if he had had baskets full of nothing but night and dumped them in, I couldn't 've seen that either, I mean these women ! — why don't you start your diary !" She came and considered (a while ago, she had promised out of pure happiness) : "What all gets into it ?". "First of all, the weather", I instructed, "temperature, barometer, wind; clouds, precipitation, celestial phenomena". "O what a soulless machine you are !" she rebelled; twitched with anger, then felinely soft : "Anything else besides that — — ?". "Well : unusual events", I said loftily; with emphasis : "And, of course, that's everything between true lovers !"; calmer again : "for example <Katrin was good-tempered today.>" "Or <He shaved voluntarily>", the apt pupil suggested, but I remained unshakable : a monk, a female and an officer can give no man offense; then it occurred to me : "And if we've quarreled — ("Often, my love !" she promised enthusiastically) — then we'll write each other : little notes. And they will read . . . . ." "<Dinner's ready>", she said archinsolently and closed her snubbing eyes, "or <Are you going to apologize at once ? !> Or <I'm going to bed.>". "And wish to be disturbed, twice" I added dryly. She held contented breath, watched as I put the rings on the bed curtains and hung them, and then began the meal consultation (actually, Becks had invited us again, but she had turned it down : cooking would be fun for us, and one day wouldn't make any difference !); so then : "What're we having ?" Well, it probably did deserve praise, and she rummaged most critically in white sacks and yellow cubes : "Just ask me . . .", she muttered profoundly, walked off and pondered, and I stood there curious, waiting, just ask, wild, what would come now : and nothing came, absolutely nothing : read a recipe, and gave me a sweet and daydreamy look : none of them 're any good ! (And afterwards we ended up with boiled potatoes and liverwurst anyway). "Have you seen my nail clippers ?" : on the second day of moving in, when even objects approaching chair-size could disappear ! So I closed the door energetically (which, however, was pointless, since its glass pane was missing, and Katrin was already standing there with green dove-eyes, and meowed for a kiss). Washing up : "Can you help with the drying ?" (that means in Female-German <dry> !). "Just the flatware *and* the really essential stuff —"; I knew of course it was wrong, and that it would now occur more regularly than necessary, but. "At least enter this in your diary," I demanded darkly. And so we jingled mightily in the endless silvery swollen dusk, and cleaned everything up nicely.

xxii

> stylish zigzag quilted robe, white-green background with dusty red flowers; she was determined to decorate the bookcase with the alarm. "There is no way that clock is going there, Katrin : divvying up time, how long we may do this or that !" "Or the other" she supplemented pertly and gave me a superfluous sort of look as well; then she commanded herself worthily : "And now please blush just a bit, Katie." "What ?" I asked, still irritated, "and why now ?" And : "Did God blush do you suppose when he created this world ? !". "Well then —" she confirmed stoically, and had nothing underneath, and tasted elastic and clean and had sturdy hair all over, and we tumbled together over one another.

Under the greenwood tree : who loves to lie with me ? / No question there, is there, Katrin ? / And turn his merry note unto the sweet bird's throat. / And how she can pipe if need be ! — She did many floor gymnastics below, just in nylons, waved with legs and light-headed dumbbells, twisted white-barked and let entrancing hair mourn, hand foliage reel. (Is the bed ever high ! : I feel like the old man of the mountain !) / Come hither, come hither, come hither / "Come, birch, come !" and similar diacopes. She came cautiously and let her tummy musculature be kissed several times over, but then ran away again at once in a circle : "to say nothing of you : I don't trust me for a moment !" (Alright, let's go on : As you like it :) Here shall he see no enemy but winter and rough weather / : "And for that we'll buy coal and a lot of wood !" A comb harped her hair, until it sat tight as a cap. Once more her face began to scramble around on me, teeth crocheted and grabbed, heiress of sharks, into my shoulder, brown-hair meadow, beneath my chin. Then we washed in the kitchen, out of two shimmering aluminum basins, each other, downstairs old Hess fingered the new choral-society number on his piano, fixed heavens hot water, "what an expanse of back, my boy !", we disposed in the dark gray pond light like great smooth silver fish, "You can build a little nightstand for the corner by the bed —", the powder box dusted in white and careful, "that's where I'll put my sewing things —", two hands beat and stroked themselves clean on hips, : "and you can read aloud the whole evening !", we covered ourselves slowly with clothes, blissful : "No one ever read aloud to me; and I've always liked it so much. If it's you." We quickly set the little Weymouth pines I had brought along on the windowsill. "Next spring I'll plant a birch and a chestnut" said Katrin musing, "look there : down in the courtyard." And we gazed down at Becks, how in the viscous twilight they both stood at the washtub, Martha and Pauline, in one hand the newspaper, the other pumping evenly at the hand pump. "There's a laundry in Wöllstein, we'll send ours there"; separated herself absentmindedly from my side and went into the kitchen.

xxiii

The typewriter minced along beneath her thin fingers, as if in high-heels, always at my ear : "I'm writing Frenzel-Heidelberg, while I'm at it; four dozen for now; p.o. box five-three-two." I lifted her sly pale face from her shoulders with both hands and devoured it. The rat ran once round the gable; her hands plucked out my hair; then she sank back to her footstool. Down from the loamy sky, ropes of smoke hung at every chimney, cold and still. Frost was in the air behind the naked panes, high above the roof desert, and without thinking, I pulled my scarf tighter.

First, from over there, she tooted a little on her harmonica (wanted to roost in her couch) delicate and buzzing : the little town is off to bed / When tolls the evening bell / Ol' Man River; and she played it so you could hear how happy we now were. Then she came, slender-legged, placed the typewriter on a chair and herself on a footstool before it : "Writing postcards. Sending relatives the new address." Murmurs and tippitytapp. Once she fetched her abridged Brockhaus, 1941, the dugout among lexicons, and paged sulkily and desperate for foreign words; only after I proved to her what a piece of crap it was, did she get happier again (Room in just one most frugal volume ! And then such items in it as "Building : result of building"; or here "bit : a little"; "chaste"; or the illustration of an ax : you can't even imagine it!). Tippitytapp : "Turn on the radio –"; and I didn't do it : "I'll not surrender my ears to just any broadcast", I replied resolutely. "Write your sister about that big Webster's, too"; because I had searched long and impatiently for the meaning of "tent-stitch"; wasn't in the Cassel's either. Tippitytapp : her eyes danced in ten-fingered touch about my face : "Do you know what we're going to read this evening ? !". "English or some Wieland or The Invisible Lodge or The Littlepage Manuscripts". "Hey, I've been practicing every day, – And you can dictate anything to me" she concluded, deep and stormy; the rat tap-danced in the beamwork (now it came to me, how I could shove the little shelves of cactus into the slanted dormers); "Anything, you say ? !". Dusk leaked out of the grayest of pitchers over the earthenware village bowl; the bell flung away its tinny yaps at random; at every running thing; no thought of moon again before Christmas; I allowed myself to tremble with happiness. She turned out the finished postcards, fetched Berlin blues from the old box, licked and pasted, wrist on it. Leapt into her topper and commanded : "Come with me to the post office. We'll poke about a bit". "And come spring we'll buy us a tandem !". (Downstairs, Gurnemanz, Gurr, Gurr, Gurrnemanz was being heavily cranked.)

xxiv

THE RED CAR. With its smooth panes, its bright handles, long-quilted cushions, the baggage trunk swelling up, cul de Mercedes, how the lacquer-light rolleth above wheeled vaults. It sways toward us, snarling, swifter than the normal wind, and presses the earth with its strong tires; its voice is like the cry of the cassowary; across its thick ribbed chest the bumper bolt zags. THE RED CAR. Thou spitting tin mandrill, leer not so randily out of cuttle-button eyes at Katrin through her skirt, covet me not so supplely in thy bubble soft with rut. Yowling sham-animal, thou slayest the evening, thy bluish toxic fart slinketh down all ways, numbers on thy glowing monkey-smooth butt art thy name, a dreary salesman thy grousing soul. THE RED CAR.

The high cloud bow thrust through the sun surf like a red breaker; wind melted icily over my hand, our hair fluttered. At the station we did envy the world of bureaucrat, their solid beautifully bordered forms; the limpid fiery-hued cap (as artifical horizon); the yellow angled lamplight in the waiting room, that he could switch on whenever he wished : right-angled world, line-framed, wine-framed. A four-engine job crept arumbling Mainzward; Katrin fitted less easily into my armwork : we were indeed together, my bed is your bed. Slowly the memories promenaded again, youth and maid in Silesia, memories : green; gray; black; red. "Where do I fit in?". "Red". Wind flew past a few times; the yellowed moon leaned out through the window of cloud ruins for a while. From closed shops the same steady Rhine broadcast with its can of music. Before the Weights & Measures cottage, the handbell of the crier, and we listened, earnest and perplexed, as he chewed earthwards through the bicycle frame : ". . . ; . . . ; . . . c'mwun c'mall." Oh my comrades in tongue ! The writer : once the poor wretch, franc-tieur of the intellect, is dead, a hundred years later, they would most like to scrape him out of the earth with their germanists' fingernails. And then brazenly claim him as "German poet", volk-communal property : how he'd love to spit on you, most honored comrades in tongue ! The rigid silver machete of the moon hacked through the cloud jungle; the stars formed their crazy circles. And the big car cowered beside the stony balk, tepid slaver still at its radiator : "Would you like to have one ?" Katrin asked, peeking unobtrusively inside. "Listen here : before I'd buy you one!" (I searched in shock for the grandest comparison) : "I'd vote for the CDU ! So there." ". . . buy me one —", she muttered in echo, purring happily, wifily dreamily. And the owner came up very broadly, in naked leather jacket at a knickerbocker gait, dark sure all-business wonderful, only the forehead eye was missing; before he pried himself in, he looked up to survey heaven's canopy, Sir Henry Thrilled, and I quickly got the snapshot in. "We'll get a pail of syrup tomorrow : it only costs 10 marks here." (14 in Lower Saxony !) "And potatoes are just half the price, too." We laughed at each other, rejoicing at such inexpense, poor merry destitootles, couple with no draught, the attic society : a crazed cock crowed each night at three : he's often to blame for it. — So we live together for now; how it goes from here, I don't know yet.

Three Stories
John Barth

PREPARING FOR THE STORM

WEATHER THE STORM that you can't avoid, the old sailors' proverb advises, *and avoid the storm that you cannot weather.* No way our waterside neighborhood can avoid *this* character; for days now she's been on our "event horizon": a one-eyed giantess lumbering first more or less our way, then more and more our way, now unequivocally our way. Unless her track unexpectedly changes, Hurricane Dashika will juggernaut in from our literal horizon at this story's end, and no doubt end this story.

In time past, such seasonal slam-bangers took all but the canniest by surprise and exacted a toll undiminished by their victims' preparation. Nowadays the new technology gives all hands ample, anyhow reasonable, notice. There are, of course, surprises still, such as the rare blaster of such intensity as to overwhelm any amount of accurate forecasting and prudent preparation. In the face of those (which we hereabouts have so far been spared), some throw up their hands and make no preparation whatever; they only wait, stoically or otherwise, for the worst. Wiser hands, however, do their best even in such desperate circumstances, mercifully not knowing in advance that their best will prove futile—for who's to say, before the fact, that it will?—and meanwhile taking some comfort in having done everything they could. Contrariwise, there is undeniably a "Cry Wolf" effect, especially late in the season after a number of false alarms (a misnomer: The alarms aren't invalidated by the fact that more often than not the worst doesn't happen). Reluctant to address yet again the labors of preparation and subsequent "de-preparation," some wait too long in hopes that this latest alarm will also prove "false"; they begin their precautionary work too late if at all and consequently suffer, anyhow risk suffering, what sensible preparation would have spared them.

Sensible preparation, yes: neither on the one hand paranoiacally (and counterproductively) taking the most extreme defensive measures at the least alarm, nor on the other underprepping for the storm's most probable maximum intensity, time of arrival, and duration—that is the Reasonable Waterside Dweller's objective. Not surprisingly, RWDs of comparable experience and judgment may disagree on what constitutes the appropriate response to a given stage of a given storm's predicted approach. Indeed, such neighborly disagreements—serious but typically good-humored when the consequences of one's "judgment call" redound upon the caller only, not upon his or her neighbors—are a feature of life hereabouts in storm season: Not one of us but keeps a weather eye out, so to speak, on our neighbors' preparations or nonpreparations as we go about our own.

In this respect, my situation is fortunate: I'm flanked on my upshore side by old "Better-Safe-Than-Sorry" Bowman, typically the first of us to double up his dock lines, board his windows, and the rest, and on my downshore side by young Ms. "Take-a-Chance" Tyler, typically the last. Both are seasoned, prudent hands—as am I, in my judgment. Neither neighbor, in my judgment, is either decidedly reckless or decidedly overcautious (although each teases the other with the appropriate adjective)—nor, in my judgment, am I. When therefore old Bowman sets about plywooding his glass or shifting his vintage fishing-skiff from dock to more sheltered mooring, I take due note but may or may not take similar action just yet with my little daysailer; should it happen that *Tyler* initiates such measures before I do, however, I lose no time in following suit. Contrariwise, the circumstance that Tyler hasn't yet stowed her pool-deck furniture or literally battened the hatches of her salty cruising sailboat doesn't mean that I won't stow and batten mine—but I can scarcely imagine doing so if even Bowman hasn't bothered. All in all, thus far the three of us have managed well enough.

Our current season's box score happens to be exemplary. Hurricane Abdullah (the Weather Service has gone multicultural in recent years, as well as both-sexual) suckered all of us, though not simultaneously, into full Stage Three, Red-Alert preparation, even unto the checklist's final item—shutting off our main power and gas lines, locking all doors, and retreating inland—and then unaccountably hung a hard right at our virtual threshold, roared out to sea, and scarcely raised the local breeze enough to dry our late-July sweat as we undid our mighty preparations. Tropical Storms

Bonnie and Clyde, the tandem toughs of August, distributed their punishments complementarily: Predicted merely to brush by us, Bonnie took a surprise last-minute swing our way and made Tyler scramble in her bikini from Green Alert (Stage One, which we had all routinely mounted: the minimum Get-Readys for even a Severe Thunderstorm warning) up through Yellow (where I myself had seen fit to stop under the circumstances) to Red, while long-since-battened-down Bowman fished and chuckled from his dock—just long enough to make his point before lending her a hand, as did I when I finished my Stage Three catch-up. From Bonnie we all took hits, none major: an unstowed lawn chair through Tyler's porch screen; gelcoat scratches on my daysailer, which I ought to've hauled out before it scraped the dock-piles; a big sycamore limb down in Bowman's side yard ("Not a dead one, though," old Better-Safe was quick to point out, who in Tyler's view prunes his deadwood before it's rightly sick). No sooner had we re-de-prepped than on Bonnie's heels came Clyde, a clear Stage Two-er by my assessment, Stage Three again by B.S.T.S. Bowman's, Stage One once more by T.A.C. Tyler's. Clyde thundered erratically up the coast just far enough offshore to justify all three scenarios and then "did an Abdullah," leaving Bowman to prep down laboriously all day from Red Alert and me all morning from Yellow, while Tyler sunbathed triumphantly out on her dock, belly-down on a beach towel, headphones on and bikini-top off—just long enough to make her point before she pulled on a T-shirt and pitched in to return our earlier favor, first helping me Doppler-Shift from Yellow back through Green and then (with me) helping Bowman do likewise, who had already by that time Yellowed down from Full Red.

So here now at peak season, September's ides, comes dreadsome Dashika, straight over from West Africa and up from the Horse Latitudes, glaring her baleful, unblinking eye our way. She has spared the Caribbean (already battered by Abdullah) but has ravaged the eastmost Virgin Islands, flattened a Bahama or two, and then swung due north, avoiding Florida and the Gulf Coast (both still staggered from *last* year's hits) and tracking usward as if on rails, straight up the meridian of our longitude. As of this time yesterday, only the Carolina Capes stood between Dashika and ourselves.

"Poor bastards," commiserated Tyler as the first damage reports came in. Time to think Stage Two, she supposed, if not quite yet actually to set about it; Capes Fear and Hatteras, after all, are veteran storm-deflectors and shock absorbers that not infrequently, to their cost, de-energize hurricanes into tropical storms and veer them out to sea.

"Better them than us," for his part growled Bowman, as well as one can growl through a mouthful of nails, and hammered on from Yellow Alert up toward Red.

I myself was standing pat at Stage Two but more or less preparing to prepare for Three, as was Tyler vis-à-vis Two—meanwhile listening to the pair of them trade precedents and counterprecedents from seasons past, like knowledgeable sports fans. I had already disconnected my TV antenna, unplugged various electronics, readied flashlights and kerosene lamps, lowered flags, stowed boat gear, checked dock lines, snugged lawn chairs and other outdoor blowaways, and secured loose items on my water-facing porch: Green Alert. While Dashika chewed up the Outer Banks, I doubled those dock lines, filled jerry cans and laundry tubs with reserve water, loaded extra ice-blocks into the freezer against extended power outage, checked my food and cash reserves, and taped the larger windows against shattering: Yellow Alert, well into last night.

This morning scarcely dawned at all, only lightened to an ugly gray. The broad river out front is as hostile-looking as the sky. Damage and casualty reports from Hatteras to the Virginia Capes are sobering indeed, and while Dashika has lost some strength from landfall, she remains a Class Three hurricane vectored straight at us. Moreover, her forward velocity has slowed: We've a bit more grace to prepare (in Bowman's case to wait, as his prepping's done), but our time under fire will be similarly extended. Already the wind is rising; what's worse, it's southerly, our most exposed quarter and the longest wave-fetch on our particular estuary. In consequence, last night's high tide scarcely ebbed, and this morning's low tide wasn't. This afternoon's high bids to put our docks under and the front half of Tyler's lawn as well, right up to her pool deck (my ground's higher, Bowman's higher yet). If there's a real storm surge to boot, I'll have water in my basement and the river's edge almost to my porch; Tyler's pool—to which I have a generous standing invitation, although I prefer the natural element, and which she herself enjoys uninhibitedly at all hours, skinnying out of her bikini as soon as she hits the water—Tyler's pool will be submerged entirely, quite as Bowman the hydrophobe has direly long foretold, and her one-story "bachelor girl" cottage may well be flooded too.

A-prepping we've therefore gone, separately, she and I. While Better-Safe potters in his garden and angles from his dock with conspicuous nonchalance, savoring his evidently vindicated foresight and justifiably not coming to our aid until the eleventh hour, I've ratcheted up to Full Red: trailered and garaged my boat, shut off power and water to my dock, taped the rest of my windows (never yet having lost one, I'm not a boarder-upper; Tyler won't even tape), boxed my most valuable valuables, even packed a cut-and-run suitcase. Nothing left to do, really, except shift what's shiftable from first floor up to second (two schools of thought hereabouts on that last-ditch measure, as you might expect: Bowman's for it, although even he has never yet gone so far; Tyler's of the opinion that in a bona fide hurricane we're as likely to lose the roof and rain-soak the attic as to take in water downstairs), and get the hell out. Ms. Take-a-Chance is still hard at it: an orange blur, you might say, as she does her Yellow- and Red-Alert preps simultaneously. It's a treat to watch her, too, now that I myself am as Redded up as I want to be for the present and am catching my breath before I lend her a hand. Too proud to ask for help, is T.A.C.T.—as am I, come to that, especially vis-à-vis old Bowman—but not too proud to accept it gratefully when it's offered in extremis, and that particular sidelong "Owe you one" look that she flashes me at such times is a debt-absolver in itself. Under her loose sweatshirt and cut-off jeans is the trademark string bikini, you can bet; Tyler's been known to break for a dip in the teeth of a thirty-knot gale. And under the bikini—well, she doesn't exactly hide what that item doesn't much cover anyhow, especially when B.S.T.S.B. is off somewhere and it's just her in her pool and me doing my yard work or whatever. We're good neighbors of some years' standing, Tyler and I, no more than that, and loners both, basically, as for that matter is old Bowman: "Independent as three hogs on ice," is how T. describes us. Chez moi, at least, that hasn't always been the case—but never mind. And I don't mind saying (and just might get it said to *her* this time, when I sashay down there shortly to help shift *Slippery*, that nifty cutter of hers, out to its heavy-weather mooring before the seas get high) that should a certain trim and able neighbor-lady find the tidewater invading her ground-floor bedroom, there's a king-size second-floor one right next door, high and dry and never intended for one person.

No time for such hog-dreams now, though. It's getting *black* off to southward there, Dashikaward; if we don't soon slip Ms. Slippery out of her slip, there'll be no unslipping her. What I've been waiting for is a certain over-the-shoulder glance from my busy friend wrestling spring-lines down there on her dock, where her cutter's bucking like a wild young mare: a look that says "Don't think I *need* you, neighbor, but"—and there it is, and down I hustle, just as old Bowman looks set to amble *my* way after I glance himward, merely checking to see whether he's there and up to what. A bit of jogging gets me aboard milady's pitching vessel, as I'd hoped, before B's half across my lawn; by the time he has cocked his critical eye at my own preparations and made his way out onto Tyler's dock, she and I have got *Slippery*'s auxiliary diesel idling and her tender secured astern to ferry us back ashore when our job's done.

"Need another hand?" It's me he calls to, not Tyler—let's say because I'm in *Slippery*'s bobbing, shoreward-facing bow, unhitching dock lines while T. stands by at the helm, and there's wind-noise in the cutter's rigging along with the diesel-chug—but his ate-the-canary tone includes us both. Bowman's of the age and category that wears workshirt and long khakis in the hottest weather, plus cleat-soled leather shoes and black socks (I'm in T-shirt, frayed jeans, and sockless deck-mocs; Tyler's barefoot in those aforenoted tight cut-offs).

"Ask the skipper," I call back pointedly, and when I see B. wince at the way we're pitching already in the slip, I can't help adding "Maybe she wants somebody up the mast."

He humphs and shuffles on out toward the cutter's cockpit, shielding his face from the wind with one hand to let us know we should've done this business earlier (I agree) and getting his pants-legs wet with spray from the waves banging under *Slippery*'s transom.

"Just stow these lines, Fred, if you will," Tyler tells him pertly; "thanks a bunch." She has strolled forward as if to greet him; now she tosses him a midships spring line and returns aft to do likewise with the stern line—just to be nice by making the old guy feel useful, in my opinion, because she *is* nice: tough and lively and nobody's fool, but essentially nice, unlike some I've done time with. So what if she's feeding B's wiser-than-thouhood; we're good neighbors all, each independent as a hog on ice but the three of us on the same ice, finally, when cometh push to shove.

Only two of us in the same boat, however. Tyler casts off her stern line and I the remaining bow line; she hops smartly to the helm, calls "Astern we go!" and backs *Slippery* down into full reverse. When Bowman warns me from the dock "Mind your bowsprit as she swings, or you're in trouble," I'm pleased to say back to him—loud enough for her to hear, I hope—"Some folks know how to swing without making trouble." Lost on him, no doubt, but maybe not on her.

Out we go then into the whitecaps to make the short run to her mooring, where *Slippery* can swing indeed: full circle to the wind, if necessary, instead of thrashing about in her slip and maybe chafing through her lines and smashing against dock piles. I go aft to confer on our approach-and-pickup procedure with Ms. Helmsperson, who's steering with her bare brown toes in the wheel's lower spokes while she tucks a loose sunbleached lock up under her headband. Raising her arms like that does nice things with Tyler's breasts, even under a sweatshirt; she looks as easy at the helm as if we're heading out for a sail on the bay instead of Red-Alerting for a killer storm. When she smiles and flashes the old "Owe you one," I find myself half wishing that we really were heading out together, my neighbor-lady and I, not for a daysail but for a real blue-water passage: hang a left at the lastmost lighthouse, say, and lay our course for the Caribbean, properties and storm-preparations be damned. Single-handing hath its pleasures, for sure, but they're not the only pleasures in the book.

Storm-time, however, is storm-time, a pickup's a pickup, and both of us know the routine. It's just a matter of confirming, once we've circled the mooring buoy and swung up to windward, that she'll leave it close on our starboard bow, following my hand-signals on final approach. T. swears she can do the job herself, and so she can in ordinary weathers, as I know from applauding her often enough from dock or porch when she comes in from a solo cruise, kills the cutter's headway at exactly the right moment, and scrambles forward just in time to flatten herself in the bow, reach down for the mast of the pickup float, and drop the eye of her mooring line over a bow cleat before *Slippery* slips away. In present conditions, it's another story; anyhow, once I'm positioned on the foredeck she has to follow my signals will-she nill-she, as I'll be blocking her view of the target. Make of that circumstance what you will; I myself mean to make of it what I can. Looks as if we're thinking in synch, too, T. and I, for now she says "I'll bring us up dead slow; final approach is your call, okay?"

Aye aye, ma'am. That wind really pipes now in *Slippery*'s rigging as I make my way forward, handing myself from lifelines to shrouds and up to the bow pulpit while we bang into a two-foot chop and send the spray flying. My heart's whistling a bit, too. *Easy does it,* I remind myself: *Not too fast, not too slow; neither too much nor too little.* That pickup float has become a bobbing metaphor: Don't blow it, I warn me as we close the last ten yards, me kneeling on the foredeck as if in prayer and hand-signaling *Just a touch portward, Skipper-Babe; now a touch starboard. Just a touch . . .* Then I'm prone on her slick wet foredeck, arm and shoulder out under bow rail, timing my grab to synchronize *Slippery*'s hobbyhorsing with the bob of the float and the waggle of its pickup mast—and by golly, I've got her!

Got *it*; I've by-golly got it, and I haul it up smartly before the next wave knocks us aside, and with my free hand I snatch the mooring eye and snug it over the bow cleat in the nick of time, just as six tons of leeway-making sailboat yank up the slack.

"Good show!" cheers Tyler, and in fact it was. From the helm she salutes me with her hands clasped over her head (that nice raised-arm effect again) and I both acknowledge and return the compliment with a fist in the air, for her boat-handling was flawless. By when I'm back in the cockpit, she's all business, fetching out chafe-gear to protect the mooring line where it leads through a chock to its cleat and asking would I mind going forward one last time to apply that gear while she secures things down below, and then we're out of here. But unless I'm hearing things in the wind, there's a warmth in her voice just a touch beyond the old "Owe you one."

No problem, neighbor. I do that little chore for her in the rain that sweeps off the bay now and up our wide river, whose farther shore has disappeared from sight. It takes some doing to fit a rubber collar over a heavy mooring line exactly where it lies in its chock on a pitching, rain-strafed foredeck without losing that line on the one hand or a couple of fingers on the other, so to speak; we're dealing with large forces here, pumped up larger yet by Ms. Dashika yonder. But I do it, all right, seizing moments of slack between waves and wind-gusts to make my moves, working with and around those forces more than against them. When I come aft again, I call down the cabin companionway that if she loses her investment, it won't be because her chafe-gear wasn't in place.

"Poor thing, you're soaked!" Tyler calls back up. "Come out of the wet till I'm done, and then we'll run for it."

When I look downriver at what's working its way our way, I

think we ought to hightail it for shore right now. But I am indeed soaked, and chilling fast in the wind; what's more, my friend's on her knees down there on one of the settee berths, securing stuff on the shelf behind it and looking about as perky and fetching as I've ever seen her look, which is saying much. And despite the wind-shrieks and the rain-rattle and the pitching, or maybe because of them, *Slippery*'s no-frills cabin, once I'm down in it, is about as cozy a shelter as a fellow could wish for, with just the two of us at home. Concerned as I am that if we don't scram out of there pronto, there'll be no getting ashore for us (already the chop's too steep and the wind too strong to row the dinghy to windward; luckily, our docks are dead downwind, a dozen boat-lengths astern), I'm pleased to come indoors. I stand half beside and half behind her, holding onto an overhead grab rail like a rush-hour subway commuter, and ask What else can I do for you, Skip?

She cuts me her "Owe you one," does Ms. Take-a-Chance—maybe even "Owe you two or three"—and says "Make yourself at home, neighbor; I'm just about ready."

Yes, well, say I to myself: Likewise, mate; like-wise. Seems to me that what she's busy with there on her knees isn't all that high-priority, but it sure makes for an admirable view. Instead of admiring it from the settee opposite, I take a seat beside her, well within arm's reach.

Arm's reach, however, isn't necessarily easy reach, at least not for some of us. When I think about Take-a-Chance Tyler or watch her at her work and play, as has lately become my habit, I remind myself that I wouldn't want anything Established and Regular, if you know what I mean. I've *had* Established, I've *had* Regular, and I still carry the scars to prove it. No more E&R for this tax-payer, thank you kindly. On the other hand, though I'm getting no younger, I'm no B.S.T.S. Bowman yet, getting my jollies from a veggie-garden and tucking up in bed with my weather radio. As the saying goes, if I'm not as good as once I was, I'm still as good once as I was—or so I was last time I had a chance to check. Life hereabouts doesn't shower such chances upon us loners, particularly if, like me, you're a tad shy of strangers and happen to like *liking* the lady you lay. There ought to be some middle ground, says I, between Established and Regular on the one hand and Zilch on the other: a middle road that stays middle *down* the road. Haven't found it yet myself, but now I'm thinking maybe here it perches on its bare brown knees right beside me, within arm's reach, fiddling with tide tables and nautical charts and for all I know just waiting for my arm to reach.

Look before you leap, proverbial wisdom recommends – while also warning that *he who hesitates is lost.* In Tyler's case, I'm a paid-up looker and hesitator both. To be or not to be, then? *Nothing ventured, nothing gained,* I tell myself, and plop my hand palm-down on her near bare calf.

"I know," frets Take-a-Chance, not even turning her pretty head: "Time to clear our butts out of here before we're blown away. Better safe than sorry, right?"

Dashika howls at that, and the rain downpours like loud applause. In one easy smiling motion then, Tyler's off the settee with my business hand in hers, leading me to go first up the companionway.

Which I do.

Well. So. I could've stood my ground, I guess – *sat* my ground, on that settee – and held onto that hand of hers and said Let's ride 'er out right here, okay? Or, after that wild dinghy-trip back to shore, I could've put my arm around her as we ran through the rain toward shelter, the pair of us soaked right through, exhilarated by the crazy surf we'd ridden home on and breathing hard from hauling the tender out and up into the lee of her carport. I could've given her a good-luck *kiss* there in that shelter, to see whether it might lead to something more (nobody to see us, as Bowman appears to've cleared out already) instead of merely *saying* Well, so: Take care, friend, and good luck to both of us. At very least I could've asked Shall we watch old Dashika from your place or mine?, or at very *very* least How about a beer for *Slippery*'s crew? But I guess I figured it was Tyler's turn: I'd made my move; the ball was in her court; if she wasn't having it, amen.

So take care now, is what I said. Good luck to all hands. I'll keep an eye out.

Whereat quoth T.A.C.T., "Thanks a bunch, nabe. Owe you one." And that was that.

So an eye out I've kept since, and keep on keeping as Dashika roars in, although there's little to be seen through that wall of rain out there, and nothing to be heard over this freight-train wind. Power's out, phones are out, walls and windows are shaking like King Kong's cage; can't see whether *Slippery*'s still bucking and rearing on her tether or has bolted her mooring and sailed through Tyler's picture window. All three docks are under; the surge is partway up my lawn already and must be into Tyler's pool. Can't tell whether that lady herself has cut and run for high ground, but I know for a fact she hasn't run to this particular medium-high patch thereof.

I ought to cut and run myself, while I still can. Ms. T's her own woman; let her *be* her own woman, if she's even still over there. But hell with it. I moved a couple things upstairs and then said hell with that, too, and just opened me a cold one while there's still one cold to be opened and sat me down here all by my lonesome to watch Dashika do her stuff.

I'm as prepared as I want be.

Hell with it.

Let her come.

AND THEN ONE DAY

Her professional knack and penchant for storytelling, Elizabeth liked to believe, had descended to her from her father, an inveterate raconteur who even in the terminal delirium of old age and uremic poisoning had entertained his hospital-bedside audience with detailed anecdotes of bygone days. The decade of his dying had been the century's next-to-last; in his mind, however, the year was often mid-1930ish, and the anecdotes themselves might be from the century's teens and twenties, which had been his own. The bedside audience was principally Elizabeth herself (or, sometimes, the night-shift nurse), although the anecdotist mistook her variously for her long-dead mother and for sundry women-friends of his youth and middle age, whereto deliriant memory from time to time returned him.

"Shirley?" he would say (or "Helen?" "Irma?" "Jane?"), with the half-rising inflection that signals impending narrative: "D'you remember that Saturday morning five years back—no, six, it was: summer before the Black Friday crash—when I borrowed Lee Bowman's saddle-brown Bearcat to drive you and Eileen Fenster down to Dorset Station, and just as we were crossing the old Town Creek drawbridge . . ." Or, "Run these damn affidavits over to Amos Creighton 'fore the courthouse closes, Frieda honey, or there'll be no trial till after Armistice Day. Young Lucille Creighton told me once . . ."

What his actual last words were, Elizabeth didn't know; her father had died at night, in the county hospital, while she was in a distant city promoting her latest novel. The proximate cause of his death had been a fall in the corridor whereinto he'd managed deliriously to wander (despite his doctor's orders for bed-restraints when the patient was unattended), believing himself en route down High Street to fetch certain files from his little law office on Courthouse Row—which had in fact been torched during the black civil-rights ruckus of the 1960s. The final cause, however, was general systems wear-out in the ninth decade of a prevailingly healthy life, and so his daughter and sole heir had chosen not to press the matter of that possibly negligent nonrestraint. The last words that she herself had heard him speak he had addressed to an imagined listener (Frieda again, his devoted secretary through most of Elizabeth's childhood) the day before the night of his fatal fall, just as Elizabeth, relieved by the hired nurse, was leaving his hospital-room at the close of afternoon visiting hours to drive to the airport across the Bay. Once again back in the Prohibition era, he had been retailing to long-deceased Frieda the escapades of a legendary moonshiner down in the marshes of Maryland's lower Eastern Shore, whose whiskey-still successfully evaded detection by one federal "revenuer" after another. "And then one day," she'd heard her father's voice declare from the bed now behind her as she stepped out into the tiled hallway . . .

And then he was beyond her hearing range, and not long thereafter she likewise his, alas, forever.

Retrospectively, it struck her that those words were (strictly speaking, *would have been*) an altogether apt though paradoxical exit line for a born storyteller like her dad—as also, come to that, for herself, somewhere down the road: the story just kicking into gear as the teller kicks the bucket (she didn't know, in fact, whether her father had tripped over something in that hallway or slipped on the polished tiles or merely collapsed). At his funeral services—well attended, as he had been something of a civic leader and a popular "character" in their little hometown—she had told "the anecdote of the anecdote," as she called it, and it had been appreciatively received. No surprise: She was, after all, a professional. To friends and well-wishers over in the city, where she kept a small apartment, she found herself retelling it from time to time thereafter, no doubt sprucing it up a bit for narrative effectiveness as I've done here (her dad would understand): Who could know, e.g., where the old ex-counselor had imagined himself to be as he wandered unattended down that fell hallway, or whether he'd even been delirious?

One of those city-friends happened to be not only a fellow wordsmith but a professor of wordsmithery at Elizabeth's graduate-school alma mater and, in fact, the coach of her advanced literary apprenticeship some years since. Over lunch at his faculty club, he remarked to his star ex-coachee that in the jargon of narrative theory, as opposed to the hunch-and-feel of actual storymaking, the formulation *and then one day,* or any of its numerous equivalents, has a characteristic function, aptly suggested by her phrase "the story just kicking into gear": It marks the crucial shift from the generalized, "customary" time of the dramaturgical "ground situation" to the focused, dramatized time of the story's "present" action, and thus in effect ends the plot's beginning and begins its middle.

"We're back in school! Come again, please?"

He topped off her Chardonnay (he himself preferred a simple dry Chablis) and reminded her, between wedges of club sandwich, that every conventional story-plot comprises what she ought to remember his calling a Ground Situation and a Dramatic Vehicle. The GS is some state of affairs pre-existing the story's present action and marked by an overt or latent dramatic voltage, like an electrical potential: Once upon a time there was a beautiful young princess, the crown jewel of the realm, who however for some mysterious reason would neither speak nor laugh, et cetera. In the language of systems analysis (if Elizabeth could stomach yet more jargon), this state of affairs constitutes an "unstable homeostatic system," which may be elaborated at some length before the story's real action gets under way: The king and queen try every expedient that they can come up with; likewise their ministers, lords and ladies, physicians, and court jesters, as well as sages summoned from the farthest reaches of the realm—all to no avail, et cetera.

He cited other examples, from Elizabeth's own published work.

"I remember, I remember. But for years now I've just *written* the damn stuff, you know?"

You have indeed. Anyhow, this princess is as gracious and accomplished as she is comely, wouldn't you agree? A model daughter as well as a knockout heir to the throne—but nothing can induce her to so much as crack a smile or make a peep. In royal-parental desperation, her father proclaims that any man who—

"Always a man."

Not infrequently a man, especially in the case of problem princesses. Any man who can dispel the spell that the king is convinced has been laid on his daughter by some antiroyalist witch can have half the kingdom and the young lady's hand in marriage. If the guy tries and fails, however . . .

"No free lunch."

And mind you, this is still just the Ground Situation. Many are the gallants who rally to the king's challenge; likewise wizards of repute, renownéd fools, and assorted creeps and nobodies. The princess attends their stunts and stratagems with mien complaisant—

"Mien . . . ?"

Complaisant. But be damned if she'll either laugh or speak. And so it goes, Zapsville for all contenders, year after year, and the story proper hasn't even started yet. You're not enthralled, Liz.

"Enough that *she* is. I can't stop thinking of poor Dad, that last night in the hospital, while I was off book-touring in Atlanta. Where was the goddamn nurse?"

And then one day . . .

"The handsome stranger. What else is new?"

Well. Sometimes it's the lad next door, whom the princess had never thought of in *those* terms. In any case, it's the screw-turning interloper in his saddle-brown Stutz Bearcat of a Dramatic Vehicle, come to precipitate a *story* out of the Ground Situation. The Beginning has ended, dear Liz; the Middle's begun.

"Maybe, maybe not. Thanks for lunch, anyhow."

Disinclined as she was to theorizing, once her erstwhile teacher and subsequent friend had glossed her late sire's "last words" in that particular way, Elizabeth came increasingly to regard them as talismanic. She remained appreciative of her father's role as her narrative model (*narrational* would be the more accurate adjective, in my opinion, but it smacks of the jargon that our protagonist disdains)—perhaps even more appreciative than before, as those incantatory words resonated through her sensibility. As time went by, however, she found herself rethinking not only the origins of her vocation but indeed the story of her life in the light of that fateful formulation.

For some months immediately following her mother's early death, for example, young Elizabeth and her elderly father had continued the family's agreeable custom of Wednesday-night movies at the town's one theater. Thirty years later, the successful novelist still remembered clearly her pleasure in the idyllic state of affairs established in the opening sequences of many of those old films (although she'd quite forgotten the "ground situations" themselves and was less than certain that they had inevitably been marked by some "overt or latent dramatic voltage"): a pleasure doubtless sharpened by her unarticulated foreknowledge that trouble must ensue—otherwise, no story.

In our actual lives, of course, she recognized (then or now?), there is no "and then one day"—although in the *stories* of our lives there may very well be; indeed, there *must* be, she supposed (now or then?) . . . otherwise, no story. The story of her life as a storyteller, e.g., she could now imagine as having begun not with the more or less enthralled osmosis of her father's anecdotes (which, it belatedly occurred to her, had been merely that: anecdotes, not stories), but rather with her apprehensive recognition, in those childhood Wednesday-night movies, of the necessary impending disruption of those so-idyllic opening scenes.

In the draft of an extended thank-you note to her friend somewhile after their "end-of-the-Beginning" lunch, she wrote experimentally: *Since time out of mind I'd been absorbing stories—told and read to me by Mom and Dad (Mom especially: Dad told anecdotes about down-county moonshiners and his courthouse cronies); read for myself in storybooks; witnessed in Stein's Avalon Theater, which we-all attended en famille on Wednesday nights more faithfully than church on Sundays.* And then one day—*watching some now-nameless G-rated production that happened to open with a particularly engaging family scene shot in Glorious Technicolor, as they still called it in the late Fifties (this will have been while Mom was sick in Dorset General, I suddenly remember, but hadn't died yet, and so I'd've been about 10—and thou, dear friend, wert 30-something already, long married, with a kid my age . . .), I see upon the screen a pair of handsome, good-humored, obviously loving parents; two or three appealing youngsters of appropriately distributed age and sex; no doubt a pet dog, mischievous or soul-eyed or both, gamboling about the sunny ménage. . . . Note how I draw this introductory construction out, not wanting to come to its closing dash and the sentence proper*—and then one day, *with a vividness that still impresses me three decades later, I understood that that "unstable homeostatic system"* must be disrupted—*for the worse, in this instance if not in all such instances, as it could not imaginably be made happier than it was*—must be disrupted for the worse, *and very soon at that, or there'd be no story, and we'd all start to fidget, bored and baffled, and presently make catcalls at the screen or the projection booth and even leave the theater, feeling as cheated of our 25 cents as if nothing had appeared onscreen at all—since from the* dramaturgical *point of view (as some people I care about would put it) nothing did.*

How's that for a Faulknersworth of syntax, Coach-o'-my-heart, and an Emily Dickinsonsworth of dashes from your quondam protégée?

In fact, of course [she went on, as much to herself as to him], *the unconsciously anticipated threat (never again unconsciously for this member of the audience) duly materialized: The family's happiness was, if not shattered, properly jeopardized by some Screw-Turning Interloper or Ante-Raising Happenstance—the MGM equivalent of Mom's galloping cancer—that potentiated the conflict already latent if not overt in the Ground Situation, then escalated that conflict through the rising action of the plot to some exciting climax, and ultimately restored the familial harmony in some significantly and permanently (however subtly) altered wise, if I've got your seminary lingo right. It was exactly to spectate and share this disruption and its sea-changed resolution that we'd coughed up our quarters and set aside our two hours; I* understood *that, consciously now, and understood further (though not yet quite consciously) that what I was understanding was one difference between life and art, or between our lives and the stories of our lives.*

For the language wherewith to conceptualize and reflect upon that understanding, friend, deponent 'umbly thanketh her ex-and-ongoing master. Her turn to take him *to lunch, next time she's in town, and to discuss, maybe, Middles? Wednesday next?*

And then one day (it occurred to her just after she redrafted and mailed a much-abridged version of this missive)—one Wednesday P.M., it was, to be precise, maybe half a year after her mother's death—her father had restored their cozy Avalon twosome to a threesome by including in it faithful Frieda. Not long thereafter, Elizabeth had returned it to a twosome by deciding that she preferred Saturday matinees with her junior-high girlfriends to Wednesday evenings en famille, if that term still applied.

In the jargon of systems analysis [word came back promptly from across the Bay], *the unstable homeostatic system is incrementally perturbed by the you-know-whom and anon catastrophically restored to a complexified, negentropic equilibrium. Next Wed's bespoke, dear L, but Thurs's clear, tête-à-têtewise.*

Very well, Miz Liz, said she to herself: You're not his only star ex-coachee, and/or he's not as ready to do Middles as you mistakenly inferred him to be—at least not in *your* story. And so with a professionally calibrated mix of mild disappointment, continuing interest, cordial affection, and ultimate shrug-shoulderedness, she replied that Thursday next, alas, was bespoken for *her,* but that either the Wednesday or the Thursday following was (currently) free.

How things went or did not go with this pair, Middlewise, we'll consider presently. In the interim, Elizabeth found herself ever more intrigued, preoccupied, very nearly possessed by the paradigmatic aspect of her father's "exit line" (the line his, in the first instance, the exit hers, from his hospital room; then the exit his, from her life and his own, the line hers to ponder) and of the sundry Ground Situations in her life—sorry: in her life-*story*—that that line could be said to have ended, for better or worse. She had innocently audited a thousand stories—*and then one day* in Stein's Avalon she had experienced what amounted to an enlightenment as to the nature of dramatic narrative (and this first had led to others, concerning e.g. the necessary invulnerability of heroes at least up to the climax of their stories, and the contrary foredoomedness of certain accessory characters), and after certain other crucial corner-turnings she had matured into a successful working novelist. Her girlhood had been prevailingly sunny and lovingly parented—she had come late and welcomely into her parents' lives—*and then one day* her mother manifested alarming symptoms, and was shockingly soon after dead. Father and daughter had proceeded as best they could with their life together and its attendant rituals—not unsuccessfully, in her young judgment—*and then one* (Wednes)*day* there sat plump Frieda at her dad's other side (Elizabeth's mother had been slender even before her illness, as was her healthy daughter now approaching middle age), and after Frieda Shirley, or was it Irma, and after Irma et cetera; and far be it from Elizabeth to begrudge her father, either at the time or in retrospect, consolatory adult female company in his bereavement, but she and he had never thereafter been as close as she felt them to have been theretofore. Through her subsequent small-town public school years she had been increasingly restless and irritable, though not truly unhappy—*and then one day* (thanks to the joint beneficence of her father and a childless aunt) she had been offered matriculation at a first-rate private girls' boarding school across the Bay for the last three of her high-school years, and that splendid institution had transformed her—had anyhow guided and abetted her transformation—from one more amorphous and unsophisticated though not unintelligent American teenage mediocrity into a really quite poised, knowledgeable, firm-principled and self-possessed young woman, if she did say so herself, looking forward eagerly to the increased responsibilities, challenges, and freedoms of college undergraduate life—in particular to the serious study of great literature, which she had come ardently to love, and the serious pursuit of "creative writing," for which she had discovered herself blessed with an undeniable flair and, just possibly, a genuine talent.

I am sorry to report that her baccalaureate years proved a time of pedagogical disappointment and considerable personal disorientation—all later turned to good account in Elizabeth's fiction, but scarifying to work through. Short of funds (that beneficent aunt had believed secondary education more crucial than undergraduate education, a proposition that I myself neither affirm nor contest), she attended a not-bad university on scholarship and found her underclass "professors"—many of them first-time teaching assistants only perfunctorily supervised—almost uniformly inferior to her experienced, knowledgeable, demanding, and enormously attentive prep-school teachers. The time here will have been the early 1970s: The grade inflation and à la carte curricula of the countercultural Sixties had made a near-mockery of academic standards on many American campuses, including Elizabeth's, at least in the liberal arts. LSD, marijuana, and hashish (but not yet cocaine and "designer drugs") were in almost as common use as alcohol; sexual promiscuity, like a straight-A average, had become so nearly the norm as to lose its meaning. For two years, to her own dismay, this promising young woman goofed off, slept around, abused substances and herself, managed a B average that she and her former high-school advisor agreed should have been a D at best, scarcely communicated with her father, very nearly lost her scholarship (which she knew she no longer deserved), likewise her life (stoned passenger in a car piled up by a stoned roommate who had introduced but not converted her to lesbian sex) and all sense of herself—not to mention of her notional vocation.

And then one day—one semester, actually, the second of her junior year—she found herself, in at least two senses of that phrase, in a fiction-writing "workshop" presided over by a visiting "writer in residence": a mid-thirtyish short-storier of modest fame, leather-jacketed charisma, and a truculent intensity that numerous apprentices, Elizabeth included, found appealing. Preoccupied with his own writing and career ambitions, to his and the university's shame (say I) he paid scant attention to his students' manuscripts but considerable attention to the authors themselves, in particular the two or three who happened to be physically attractive as well as somewhat talented young women. Of these, our Elizabeth was easily the most of both. Although the campus disruptions by anti-Vietnam-war protesters in the preceding decade had frightened U.S. college administrators into shortening the academic semester from its traditional fifteen weeks down to thirteen, in that abbreviated period this writer-in-residence managed serial "skin tutorials," as he frankly called them, with all three of his talented/attractive protégées as well as with another rather less so but jealous of her classmates' special coaching. In short, of the seven female students in his workshop he bedded four, and in those sexually unpolitical though luxuriant days the only protest (made petulantly to the writer himself) came from a fifth who felt herself pedagogically short-changed.

Among these four, unsurprisingly, his favorite and the most frequently thus tutored was Elizabeth; and it must be said for the unprincipled bastard that while he was an aggressive sexual imperialist, a shameless exploiter of the student/teacher relationship (which ought ever to be inviolate), an indifferent coach who did no line-editing whatever of his apprentices' manuscripts, and in my judgment not even a particularly gifted writer himself, he nevertheless knew a bright turn of phrase when he saw one, a false note when he heard one, a praiseworthy plot-foreshadowing or blameworthy red herring when one swam into his ken. What's more, in the perspiratory intervals between skin-tutorials he did not scruple to remark such of those as he recollected from his tutees' prose. A genuine artist-in-the-making, if I may so put it, recognizes and takes to heart such nuggets of authentic professional feedback, praise and blame alike, regardless of the circumstances of their proffering; if it can be argued that a talent like Elizabeth's would have found its voice sooner or later in any case from accumulated practice and experience of literature, of the world, and of herself, it can also be argued that she found hers rather sooner thanks to the intercopulatory editorializings of her first real writer/coach—whose literary reputation her own would far outshine by when she reached his then age.

Now: The muses, it goes without saying, care nothing for university degrees or such distinctions as graduate versus undergraduate students, only for transcendent gifts disciplined anyhow into mastery. Our institutions being organized as they are, however, and our Elizabeth knowing, upon receipt of her baccalaureate, that she was possessed of ability and ambition but not of means to support herself through the next stage of her apprenticeship (commonly the most serious, arduous, and discouraging), she applied to several of the more prestigious of our republic's abundant graduate writing programs, was accepted at two of them, and chose the one that offered the larger stipend plus tuition-waiver. (It was also rumored that her erstwhile "skin-tutor," an academic gypsy, was scheduled to visit the other program, and the memory of *her* exploitation of *him*, as she had had almost come to think of it, embarrassed her. She had been, she told herself, no starry-eyed naïf, but an unformed talent craving professional direction the way a wintertime raccoon craves salt and determined to take it wherever she could find it.) In that new venue she had the good fortune to practice intensely for the next two years in the company of similarly able and ambitious peers, with and against whom to hone her skills under the benevolent supervision of a writer/coach more accomplished in both areas than had been his forerunner in her apprenticeship. This one kept his hands scrupulously off his charges—indeed, he had less social connection with them than in my opinion such coaches ideally should have—but very much on their manuscripts, which he took time to read more than once, to line-edit judiciously, and to review with their authors both in conference and in seminar. So did the young woman's art flourish in these circumstances (and her physical and moral well-being likewise, for she had exchanged substance abuse for a glass of table wine with dinner and perhaps an after-class beer with her comrades-in-arms, and sexual promiscuity for near-abstinence until, as soon enough happened, she found a coeval lover suited to her maturing tastes), by MFA-time she had placed short stories in three respectable literary periodicals and had sufficiently impressed her mentor with her maiden novel-in-progress that he felt he could show it to his own agent without compromising his credibility.

And then one day, therefore, she found herself possessed of a better-than-entry-level book contract, and some months thereafter of a favorable front-page notice in the *New York Times Book Review*—shared, to be sure, with a brace of other promising first-novelists (that had been the reviewer's handle), but hers the most glowingly praised. Her debut paid out its advance on royalties and earned its publisher a modest profit as well as enjoying a *succès d'estime,* with the consequence that for its sequel her agent negotiated a handsome contract indeed, given that Elizabeth was and remains an essentially "literary" author. By age thirty-five, after a brief and unsatisfying marriage, she was supporting herself comfortably on her royalty income alone.

No, dear Liz (her ex-second coach, ongoing friend, and still-occasional mentor will object if she reviews her life-story with him in these terms, as I rather fancy her doing at their next lunchtime get-together): Those book contracts and that *Times* review don't qualify as Screw-Turning, Ante-Raising Interlopers on the order of Plump Frieda and Comrade Leatherjacket.

"May herpes simplex rot his predatory crotch. But he did call a spade a spade, you know, when he bothered to call anything at all. Why *don't* they qualify, prithee?"

You tell me.

Because, she would suppose (then or now?), she has uncharacteristically lost track of precisely which story-of-her-life she's in the process of telling, and a fortiori of what constitutes its GS as distinct from its DV, or its Beginning from its Middle. In the story of her literary apprenticeship (*one* story of it, anyhow, she imagines her friend mildly correcting her), those egregious skin-tutorials had most certainly been an eye-opener, let's say, that initiated her serious application to the craft of fiction. "Viewed another way, however, that clown was just one more court jester, right? An unusually aggressive one, coming closer than most to getting a rise out of Princess Pokerface but still not succeeding, so off to Zapsville he goes, and good riddance. It was *you* who made the difference, dear friend."

No plausible tribute declined by the management. We both

suspect, however, that what "made the difference"—as in most such real-life processes, if not in fiction—was some small quantitative increment precipitating a significant qualitative change. The girl sits through ninety-seven Hollywood movies in Stein's Avalon, and then one day, in midst of the ninety-eighth, she rather suddenly grasps some things about basic dramaturgy. So she writes ten yearsworth of practice-fiction without making noteworthy progress except in language-mechanics and the range of her vocabulary, meanwhile accumulating mileage on her experiential odometer, and then one day . . .

"Or it happens," Elizabeth hears herself declaring as if to her Chardonnay, "that two people who first knew each other in some uneven professional connection, like lawyer/client or doctor/patient, maintain a more or less attenuated friendship when that connection has run its course. They're still not quite peers, but their paths cross from time to time on officially equal footing at campus arts festivals or over lunch maybe once per season, with occasional letters or phone talks between, usually one of them congratulating the other on some new publication. . . ."

Very literary lawyers, these guys.

"Very. This goes on for years and years, while their professional lives exfoliate more or less in parallel and their personal lives turn whatever separate corners they turn."

Objection, counselor: In the matter of their personal lives you've got it right, but the curve of *her* career is steadily upward (as was his at her age), while his, as is to be expected, has leveled off and even begun its decline, fortunately gentle.

"So he declares."

Likewise, N.B., his physical capacities.

"So he sees fit to declare. In any event, almost without their noticing it—"

They notice it. But they both have good reasons for not acknowledging it.

"Excellent reasons. All the same, little by little, with neither of them especially leading it, or maybe each half-consciously leading it more or less by turns, their cordial and sporadic connection subtly changes character."

At least it pleases them to believe that the change has been subtle.

"Each has a failed marriage under his/her belt by this time, no? Hers of short duration, to a fellow former coachee of Sir

Leatherjacket, as it happens, of whom she came to suspect her spouse terminally jealous. Anyhow, on the basis of considerable experience she'd begun to infer that she didn't particularly *like* men her own age. An ill-starred match, this one, but the split was prevailingly amicable."

I had gathered as much, Liz, but am gratified to hear it said. Not likewise in her friend's case, alas: a *well*-starred match, whereof the end was sore indeed. More community property to hassle over, for one thing, plus a few decadesworth of shared history, plus that daughter somewhere aforementioned. . . .

"A daughter *her age,* which datum gives the woman of this pair due pause. The mildly troubling truth appears to be that just as *she* seems most naturally attracted, other things equal, to men nearly old enough to be her father, *he* seems most drawn, in an egregious male-stereotypical way, to women nearly young enough et cetera."

Not bloody often, as Apollo is his witness. And when are things ever equal?

"Things never are. On with the story?"

On with it, by all means: This pair lunches it up here and there from time to time for years and years, while the plate tectonics of their Ground Situation goes about its virtually imperceptible though nonetheless seismic business.

"And then one day . . . ?"

If any such conversation actually took place between these two, we may be confident that it was by no means so narratively tidy as the foregoing. In fact, however, no such conversation did take place, and even had it so taken — untidily, inefficiently, marked by blurts, irrelevancies, unstrategic hesitations — it would not likely have led to anything of dramaturgical interest, inasmuch as the "senior" conversant had long since remarried and was not about to jeopardize that happy connection with infidelity; and the "junior" conversant, truth to tell — having grown up as a motherless only child and been taught emotional self-reliance both by life and by that excellent girls' boarding school — was disinclined to grand passions, to sustained intimacy, even for that matter to an unselfishly shared life, though not to the occasional adventure. After the amicable dissolution of her short-lived marriage, Elizabeth had moved back across the Bay into her father's house to oversee his last age; when upon his death that house became hers, she continued to live and work therein contentedly (between her frequent travels) with a large black Labrador retriever as her chief companion: a more than ordinarily handsome, talented, and successful woman with numerous friends, infrequent casual lovers, no further interest in marriage and none in motherhood, and for that matter no very considerable sexual appetite—although she quite enjoyed occasional lovemaking the way she enjoyed the occasional lobster-feast, gallery opening, or night at the opera.

But even if their situations and temperaments had been otherwise, such that their affectionate casual friendship developed into an *amitié amoureuse* and thence one day or year into a full-scale May/September love affair (June/October, I suppose, even July/November, given their unhurried pace thus far), with whatever consequences to their lives and careers—so what? Reinvigorated by his new "young" companion (although in fact he hadn't been feeling *de*vigorated as things stood), the aging wordsmith closes out his oeuvre with a sprightly final item or two before ill health or senility caps his pen for keeps; alternatively, he so loses himself in the distractions of a new life at his age that he writes nothing further of more than clinical or biographical interest; or an automobile crash, whether his fault or the other driver's, kills him before either of those scenarios can unfold. Inspired by the first truly mature sexual/emotional relationship of her life, Elizabeth in her forties develops from a quite successful though not extraordinary novelist into one of the memorable voices of her generation; her works are everywhere acclaimed by that minuscule fraction of Earth's human population who take pleasure in the art of written literature, and although death claims her mentor/lover all too soon, she manages to remain vigorously productive even after receipt of her Nobel prize. Or it turns out that their connection doesn't turn out; both parties soon enough recognize (he the more painfully, his misstep being irreversible) that things between them had better remained at the *amitié amoureuse* stage, better yet at the cordial occasional-lunch stage. Or it does work out, anyhow looks to be working out, when alas the MD-80 ferrying them to St. Bart's on holiday is blown out of the Caribbean sky by Islamic-fundamentalist terrorists; or perhaps Elizabeth, attending to some urban business, is shot dead by an irked carjacker when she resists his heist of her saddle-brown Jaguar.

In each and any case, so what? One more short or not-so-short story of bourgeois romance, domestic tribulation, personal and vocational fulfillment or frustration, while the world grinds on. Even were it one more narrative of aspiration and struggle in some worthy, impersonal cause, perhaps of fundamental decency versus self-deception, the seductions of language, and the human inclination to see our lives as stories — so what?

The world grinds on; the world grinds on.

So what?

That's a mighty *so what,* she imagines her friend responding with some concern. Does Miz Liz not remember his distinguishing, back in her advanced-apprentice days, between the readerly reactions *So what?* and *Ah, so!* — the former indicating that the author's narrative/dramatic bills remain unpaid, the latter that her dramaturgical bookkeeping is in good order?

"Sure she remembers, now that he mentions it. Okay, so she remembers: So what, when all's said and done?"

Ah, so: Our Elizabeth appears to have written herself into a proper corner. She has understood all along, more or less, that neither her life nor her father's nor any soul else's is a *story,* while at the same time wryly viewing and reviewing hers, at least, as if it were. And then one day, some imperceptible "quantitative incrementation" . . .

On this particular telling, the story of her life thus far (more accurately, I must point out, the story thus far of her life) — its four decadesworth of sundry ups and downs, consequential waypoints and corner-turnings — amounts after all not to a Middle-in-progress, as she has habitually supposed; nor (on this telling) will it so amount four further decades hence, should she live so long, quite regardless of how things go. On this telling she imagines herself then, an old woman at a writing-table in her father's house or some other, having in the course of her long and by-no-means-uneventful life done this and this and this but not that, or that and that but never this, with such-and-such consequences — the whole catalogue of actions, reactions, and happenstances amounting to no more than an interminable Beginning: a procession of jester/gallants acting out before a complaisant-miened but ultimately impassive princess.

At her feet, her loll-tongued, saddle-brown-curled Chesapeake Bay retriever stirs, makes a small deep wuffing sound, and without lifting his great head from his forepaws, opens his pink-white eyes and shifts his muzzle half-interestedly doorward, as if perhaps sensing something therebeyond, perhaps not. Elizabeth registers subliminally the animal's tentative curiosity but is, as usual, preoccupied with, even lost in, her story-in-progress, if that adjective can be said to apply:

And then one day . . .

GOOD-BYE TO THE FRUITS

I agreed to die, stipulating only that I first be permitted to re-behold and bid good-bye to those of Earth's fruits that I had particularly enjoyed in my not-extraordinary lifetime.

What I had in mind, in the first instance, was such literal items as apples and oranges. Of the former, the variety called Golden Delicious had long been my favorite, especially those with a blush of rose on their fetchingly speckled yellow-green cheeks. Of the latter—but then, there's no comparing apples to oranges, is there, nor either of those to black plums: truly incomparable, in my opinion, on the rare occasions when one found them neither under- nor overripe. Good-bye to all three, alas; likewise to bananas, whether sliced transversely atop unsweetened breakfast cereal, split longitudinally under scoops of frozen yogurt, barbecued in foil with chutney, or blended with lime juice, rum, and Cointreau into frozen daiquiris on a Chesapeake August late afternoon.

Lime juice, yes: Farewell, dear zesty limes, squeezed into gins-and-tonics before stirring and over bluefish filets before grilling; adieu too to your citric cousins the lemons, particularly those with the thinnest of skins, always the most juiceful, without whose piquance one could scarcely imagine fresh seafood, and whose literal zest was such a challenge for us kitchen-copilots to scrape a half-tablespoonsworth of without getting the bitter white underpeel as well. Adieu to black seedless grapes for eating with ripe cheeses and to all the nobler stocks for vinting, except maybe Chardonnay. I happened not to share the American yuppie thirst for Chardonnay; too over-flavored for my palate. Give me a plain light dry Chablis any time instead of Chardonnay, if you can find so simple a thing on our restaurant wine-lists these days. And whatever happened to soft dry reds that don't cost an arm and a leg on the one hand, so to speak, or, on the other, taste of iron and acetic acid?

But this was no time for such cavils: Good-bye, blessed fruit of the vineyard, a dinner without which was like a day without et cetera. Good-bye to the fruits of those other vines, in particular the strawberry, if berries are properly to be called fruits, the tomato, and the only melon I would really miss, our local cantaloupe. Good-bye to that most sexual of fruits, the guava; to peaches, plantains (fried), pomegranates, and papayas; to the fruits of pineapple field and coconut tree, if nuts are fruits and coconuts nuts, and of whatever it is that kiwis grow on. As for pears, I had always thought them better canned than fresh, as Hemingway's Nick Adams says of apricots in the story "Big Two-Hearted River"—but I couldn't see kissing a can good-bye, so I guessed that just about did the fruits (I myself preferred my apricots sun-dried rather than *either* fresh or canned).

The *literal* fruits, I meant, of course. But surely it wouldn't overstretch either the term or anyone's patience to include in my terminal bye-byes such other edibles of the vegetable kingdom as parboiled fresh asparagus served cold with sesame oil and soy sauce, sorely to be missed in the afterlife if there were one and food-consumption were a feature of it; likewise tossed salads of most sorts except fruit salads, which for some reason never appealed to me and to whose principal ingredients I have severally made my good-byes already, Q.E.D. Also pasta, if pasta's a vegetable; I had long been a fan of pasta in all its protean forms including the non-Italian, such as Japanese "cellophane" noodles, which I presumed to be some sort of pasta despite their transparency, and German Spätzel. Morever, if I remained untouched by the popularity of Chardonnay among my countrymen, I was a charter member of the Yankee pesto-lovers association. Addio, then, pasta con pesto! Faithful to my homely origins, however, I insisted on equal farewell-time for the simple potato, whether boiled, baked, mashed, or French-fried with unhealthy but delicious salt and vinegar—no ketchup, please—and the inelegant Fordhook lima bean, which, out of some childhood impulse to diversify my mother's simple cookery, I used to stir into my creamed chipped beef or mix with my mashed white potatoes and pan-gravy on the plate beside my southern-fried chicken: culinary items to which I had bidden good-bye decades ago and so needn't clutter my present agenda with. Friendly and nutritious veggies, hale! Although I never quite achieved vegetarianism and to this ultimate or all-but-ultimate hour continued to regard you essentially as the garnish to my dinner entrée, you are a garnish that I would miss almost as much as table wine if missing things were posthumously possible. Good-bye, garnis.

Moving nearer the center of life's plate, as it were, with only a bit more stretching of the parameters (if parameters can be said to be stretched at all by centripetal motion), might we not add—*must* we not add—to our hail-and-farewell list the fruits of the sea, succulent in all languages but to my ear especially so in those of the Romance family: fruits de mer, frutti di mare, frutas de mar, and however it goes in sensual Portuguese. I could, reluctantly, get by without red meat (grilled lamb chops, especially, it pained me to contemplate giving up, seasoned with salt, pepper, crushed garlic, and ground cumin), and only a tad less reluctantly without the flesh of light-fleshed fowl, in particular the breast-meat of turkeys, chickens, and barbecued Cornish hens. But finfish and shellfish of all varieties had for so long been at the center of my diet, it was scarcely an exaggeration to say that my flesh, by the time I tell of, was largely composed of theirs. If one had been permitted to slip in a request among one's farewells, mine would have been that my remains be somehow returned uncombusted to my home waters, there to be recycled to the fauna whereupon I had so thrived and thence on out into the general marine food-chain. Rockfish, bluefish, sea-trout, shad; blue crabs, oysters, scallops, mussels, clams; billfish, tuna, and other steakfish; octopus and squid, in particular the stuffed baby Spanish variety called *chiperones*; sushi and sashimi of every sort; and, last because first among equals, that king of crustaceans, the New England lobster, *Homarus americanus,* whose spiny Caribbean cousin was in my estimation but an overrated poor relative, though undeniably handsome. Adieu to you, noble down-East lobster, all-too-rare-because-so-damned-expensive treat, that shouldst be steamed not a minute longer than *half* the time recommended by James Beard and most other seafood-cookbook authors. Ten minutes tops for a less-than-two-pounder, mark my parting words, or the animal has suffered and died in vain. "A quick death, God help us all," declares the character Belacqua in Samuel Beckett's story "Dante and the Lobster" (to which the story's narrator replies, in propria persona, *It is not*).

But as the true soul-food is beauty, who could leave this vale of delights without farewelling at least a few representative examples of those flora and fauna that one eats only with one's eyes, and in some instances one's ears and nose? I meant, e.g., the very nearly overgorgeous fish and shellfish of saltwater aquarium and coral reef, whether viewed firsthand or on public-television nature shows and *National Geographic* photo-spreads; the astonishing birds of tropical latitudes and the butterflies of even our temperate zone, particularly the Monarchs hanging in migratory clusters from California eucalyptus between November and March; the unabashed sexuality of flowers and the patient dignity of trees, large trees especially; certain landscapes, seascapes, skyscapes, cityscapes, desert- and marshscapes—in particular, I supposed, for myself, if I had been obliged as perhaps I was to choose only one of the above to pay final respects to, the vast tide marshes of my natal county: marshes which, while considerably less vast than they had been even in my childhood, remained still reasonably vast as of this valediction—always assuming that one was permitted to valedict. Nursery of the Chesapeake and, by semicoincidence, of their present valedictorian ("semi" in that it might be presumed to have been unpredestined that I be born and raised in or near the marshlands of Maryland's lower Eastern Shore, but it was no coincidence that, I having been therein born and raised, those home marshes loomed so large in my imagination, if a marsh can properly be said to loom. For the sake of variety and euphony, I had been going to say "home bogs" just then instead of "home marshes," but it suddenly occurred to me for the first time, surprisingly enough at my age and stage, what the difference is between bog and marsh, particularly tide marsh. As between *marsh* and *swamp,* I confess, the geological distinction eludes me still, although their connotations surely differ) . . .

Marshes, I was saying; saying good-bye, good-bye, good-bye to. Good-bye, still-considerable and fecund wetlands, at once fragile and resilient, neither land nor sea, symbolic equally of death and of regeneration, your boundaries ever changing, undefined, negotiable, your horizontality as ubiquitous as your horizon is horizontal, etc., etc.—and withal so eloquently sung, in your East Anglican manifestation, by the novelist Graham Swift in his novel *Waterlands* (not to mention by the novelist Charles Dickens in such of his novels as *Bleak House, David Copperfield,* and *Great Expectations*), that one would scarcely have presumed to do more than refer the attender of these farewells to those novelists' novels, pardon my syntax, were it not that as between East Anglia and the Eastern Shore of Maryland, the differences are at least as noteworthy, even unto their fenlands, as are any similarities. To "my" dear spooky, mudflat-fragrant marshes, then, a cross-fingered fare thee well.

But I could not leave the subject of marshes (hard enough to leave the marshes themselves) without a word of concern for the Marsh Arabs: the Madan people, I meant, whose fortune it had been for four thousand years to inhabit the marshes at the confluence of the Tigris and Euphrates rivers, in southern Iraq, and whose current misfortune it was to have been, for the past few hundred of those four thousand years, at least nominally Shiite Muslims who – self-reliant and wary of outsiders, like most marsh-dwellers – resisted the despotic Baathist regime of Saddam Hussein and were therefore, as I prepared to make these rhetorical farewells, being systematically exterminated by that regime both directly (by means including poison gas, it was alleged but not yet proved, which Saddam had ruthlessly employed against the Madans' northern counterparts, the Kurds) and indirectly, via the dreadful expedient of *drying up their marshes* by diverting the inflow of those primordial, civilization-cradling rivers: an ecological atrocity on a par with the Iraquis' firing of the Kuwaiti oil fields. Good-bye indeed, one feared and fears, to the oldest continuous culture on the planet, numerous of whose communities have lived generation after generation on floating islands of spartina, continually replenishing them with fresh layers of reed on top as the bottom layers decompose and recycle; good-bye, poor hapless Marsh Arabs about to be destroyed in an eyeblink of time while still believing, after four millennia of harmlessly habitating your marshes, that somewhere in their labyrinthine fastness lies the *Arabian Nights*–like island of Hufaidh, complete with enchanted palaces of gold and crystal, Edenic gardens, and the Sindbaddish aspect of transforming into babbling lunatics any marshfarers who stumble upon it. May all destroyers of marshes serendipitously so stumble! Nothing quite like Hufaidh, I suppose, in the solitudinous wetlands of my home county (only the odd goose blind, muskrat house, and, within living memory, moonshiner's still), though there is an uncanniness about even *their* low-lying, uninhabited islands – to which I truly now bade good-bye and better luck than the Madans'.

No marsh, however, one might say (paraphrasing John Donne), is an island. Indeed, in Nature's seamless web, if one might be permitted to mix metaphors so late in the day, no *island* is an island: When we lose the enchanted isle of Hufaidh by losing the marshes that sustained the culture whose imagination sustained that realm, we lose an item from the general cultural store and thus, figuratively at least, lose a part of ourselves—just as, literally, when we lose Poplar Island, say, in the upper Chesapeake, to the less malign forces of natural erosion (as happened to be happening apace even as I bade these good-byes), we increase the exposure of Tilghman Island, just behind Poplar, to those same forces, et cetera if not ad infinitum anyhow to the end of the chapter, as Cervantes's Sancho Panza puts it from time to time in *Don Quixote*: the geological chapter of Chesapeake Bay As We've Known It Since the Last Ice Age, continuously being reconfigured not only over millennia but over the span of a single lifetime (Where now is Sharp's Island, e.g., which I well remember at the mouth of the Great Choptank River in my boyhood?), whereto—I meant equally that island, that river, that bay, and that lifetime—I now bade good-bye.

In the calm urgency of farewell, I hereabouts noticed, I had inadvertently changed the thrust of this valediction by conflating, in the passage above, the callous despoliation of the natural environment by Saddam Hussein's Baathists (and, Stateside, by the likes of real-estate developers, clear-cutting timberfolk, and toxic dumpers, in which last category our military-industrial complex stood out as a particularly egregious offender)—conflating these, I say, with such "natural" rearrangers of that environ as hurricanes, tornadoes, earthquakes, volcanic eruptions, and suchlike forces, ranging from Earth-destroying asteroidal impact on the scale's high end to the gentle, continuous attrition, on its low, of the mildest rain shower, the softest breeze, mere cellular decay—the inexorable rub of time.

Time, yes, there was the rub: Barely mortal time enough to kiss earth's fruits hello before we're kissing them good-bye, and there I had so lost myself in the marshes, as it were, hoping perhaps to stumble upon my personal Hufaidh (if I have not stumbled itupon already: See how I babble!), that I'd not even gotten around yet to earth's salt, so to speak—nor, for that matter, even to animals other than human, except en passant in their aspect as table-meat. Fellow humans! I did not mean, yet, the nearest and dearest of those; they went without saying, although most assuredly not without saying good-bye to, if that unimaginable prospect could be imagined. No: I meant, in the first instance (which is to say the last, in order of importance), those anonymous others just enough of whom kept a restaurant, say, or a street or town or planet, from being unbearably lonely. Good-bye, insignificant others, if I might so put it without offense, understanding that I helped play that background role in your life-narrative as did you in mine; would that your numbers were not so burgeoning—by runaway population-growth in some places, demographic shifts in others—as to threaten the biosphere in general and countless particular environs, not excluding my beloved Chesapeake estuarine system.

Farewell next to such only slightly less anonymous but considerably more significant others as . . . oh, trash collectors, for example: Never, at any of a lifetimesworth of urban, suburban, and rural addresses, had I had reason to complain of the efficiency of the collection of my trash, both recyclable and non-—no small tribute from one whose profession was the written word. Same went, except for the odd and usually inconsequential glitch, for the several mail carriers and deliverers of daily and Sunday newspapers to my serial places of residence over the decades. What a quiet, civilized pleasure, to step outdoors of a morning in any season, sometimes before first light, and to find one's refuse collected for disposal, one's morning newspaper snugly folded in that way that newspapers are folded for tossing into driveways or tucking into newspaper-boxes, and moreover bagged in (recyclable) plastic if the weather even looked to be inclement—and then, somewhat or much later in the day, depending on where one's address happened to fall on one's postperson's route, to find one's outgoing mail duly picked up and incoming mail delivered. I shall miss that, chaps and ladies so approximately faithful to the motto of your service—or, rather, *should* miss it, if etc. Good-bye and thanks, and may neither rain nor snow nor sleet nor gloom of night et cetera. How fortunate it is, Aldous Huxley somewhere remarks, that the world includes people pleased to devote their mortal span to the manufacture and sale of *sausages,* for example, so that those of us with no interest in that pursuit may nevertheless have our cake and eat it too, if you follow my meaning and possess wherewithal to purchase what, after all, those folk don't give away free.

People, people, people: builders of roadways, tunnels, and bridges, and of reasonably reliable vehicles to drive thereupon, therethrough, thereover; designers and fabricators too of such spirit-lifting artifacts as great art, to be sure, but also for example of jet aircraft in flight—particularly, to my eye, those now-classic sweptwinged, rear-engined jetliners viewed passing overhead—likewise of most but not all sailing vessels under sail, of Krups coffeemakers, of Swiss Army knives in the middle range of complexity, of steel-shafted hammers with cushioned grips—in short, of all well-made things both functional and handsome, as agreeable to regard and to handle as to use.

Supreme in this category of human constructions to be farewelled—so much so, to this fareweller, as to be virtually a category in itself—was that most supple, versatile, and ubiquitous of humanisms, language: that tool that deconstructs and reconstructs its own constructions; that uses and builds its users and builders as they use, build, and build with it. Ta-ta, language, la la language, the very diction of veridiction in this valley valedictory. Adieu, addio, adiós, et cetera und so weiter; I could no more bear to say *good-bye* to you than so to say to those nearest dearest, in particular the nearest-dearest, so to say, themof: I meant the without-whom-nothing for me to bid farewell to whom must strain the sine qua non of language even unto sinequanonsense. Impossible to do, unthinkable to leave undone, and yet the mere prospect did undo me. Back to the apples! Back to the oranges! I'd say good-bye sooner to myself (I said), and soon enough would, than say it to—

But it went without saying that I had been assuming not that I might say without going, so to say, but say *before* going: say good-bye to the fruits, et cetera. Permission granted, surely?

"No."

Market Tender Family

Kevin Magee

To Weyhill and Winchester
I went to the fair, and when I meet there
that I most hate, I make debate
(for seldom does it come to pass
that one may rise above one's class)
The seam which ran its edge around
with lace to silk bodice was bound
No peasant wore such costly work
in all of Hohenstein or Haldenberk

1.

Propulsion toward what capes, Duncan's H.D. (let Thetis threaten us) Stein Stevens' extremist in an enterprise, that moment in Modernism the discovery and excitement of writing in time—if there is an ocean it is here—to enter a new world, and have their freedom of movement, consciousness of immediate contact and contradictory demands of observation and interpretation. Zukofsky's fastidiousness when he hears (and fears) Hart Crane's hysteria, the negative imprint of domination that is *The Bridge.* Duncan's own distancing and distinction between his work ("disorders of reference brought about by figural excess") and L.Z.'s metal-tipped share of beech or oak a variety of wild sorrel called salt grass mixed with wheat and rye. Spicer's clear-sighted Protestant's eye, freed from the mist of superstition, where there is no lack of interest in the linguistic system and relation of language to social reality. Inhibited insistence on class. The 1980s' historic clash with terms. "Capital is a fever at play and in the world (silent *l*)." Michael I am happy to join you by the sea. "(This refers to capital with the capital *L.*)" Quotations from *Capital* in Canto 33: Chapter 10, "The Working Day," and Section IX of Chapter 15, "Machinery and Modern Industry." Dear Nathaniel, dear Kathleen. "The enormous tragedy of the dream in the peasant's bent shoulders."

2.

There should be more, the book I am reading and the same page over and over, fingers following the words across each line and mouthing remedially what has been, what has to be done, glare cut away from compounding, gravitating toward the event, then, as referent, what figures show. Dispersed episodes. The entire time, in the form of rough notes interspersed with asides, the 'historian's truth' which first writes the lower orders and imagines them emerging as subjects, articulable if not themselves articulate, even as a potentially revolutionary class (*Bond Men Made Free,* 1973), and then begins to lose not its reason—historical materialism—but the capacity to narrate the mass of incrementations and additions patiently sifted from patent rolls, court and tax records, all partially relating even when obscuring the event that divides into the multiplicity inherent in its sources—that sudden, volatile uprising exceeding chronology which can no longer be conveniently reconstructed or contained by the "haphazard" collection of nineteen essays in *Class Conflict and the Crisis of Feudalism* (1990).

3.

The memory of an ancient injury persists—the change in the sense of page from disjunctive to integrative—and of that idea about the comparative unimportance of authorial identity, we do not know the author, we will never know that poet whose book, written across a life, opens out on one event, not that the event may only be read through the poem, but that the poem exists only in relation to the event, is subsumed by the event. Reading the poem is to read of an evolution from economy based on working the land to money, commodity and that newly emerging market-generated subjectivity called 'the individual.' *Ragmanroll.* A catalogue or roll of names and even a game by this name was played with verses describing social types or characters rolled up in a parchment roll attached by a string with the string hanging out for the player who pulled on the string and so learned by chance their identity and the penny was an important coin in the time of Edward III though a florin could sometimes be called a penny in which case a ha'penny means a half-florin and a farthing the fourth part of a florin. See *rigamarole.*

4.

> Dickinson [to Gould?]: *Magnum bonum, harum scarum, zounds et zounds, et war alarum, man reformum, life perfectum, mundum changum, all things flarum?*

Goliardys is a glutton of words, singing and swigging and swinging a barrel of books as many as might be held by both arms, a scribe in a monastery who copies the Bible but liable to fable reproduces the book on the butcher's block that is history, according to Hegel. Marx: I laughed like hell, I laughed all over him, in the air loudly in lordly Latin *O rex si rex es rege te, vel eris sine re, rex, nomen habes sine re, nisi te recteque, regas, rex, ac veluti* as when *cum saepe sedito* after sedition *coorta est* has arisen *in magno populo* among a great multitude *que ignoble vulgus sae vit animus* and the ignorant vulgar masses rage *jam que faces et saxa volant* now firebrands and stones fly. To discourse a little less like Ummidius, Tyndarus, Adimantus took my hand. None of the Lydians that settled in E (see, for example, a book of banned poems by Guilielmus Hermannus called *City of Men*). One of you go and see, the other one stay and listen to me: *res inopum capita nisi gratis est quasi rapta.* "The wrong will not be remitted until that which was stolen is restored." I had my back to the lamp and my face turned toward. To Lacadaemon shall my lands extend. A secondary illustration on the first historiated letter of the only surviving folio. These are the rare companions with whom I Rome.

5.

I would be that reader come to rest on a crate or mound of stones and ring down the curtain of a morality play showing considerable familiarity with the language of lawyers and landlords despised by the rural poor, and rewrite them with no mitigation and the coarsest kind, wandering as a weathervane turns with each wind, accepting homicide and a receiver of thieves, downtrodden numbers unskilled and restless, bound not to the land and to no lord. They began to assemble in small groups at first in the regions of

Essex and Kent and by the middle of the next month were marching in a large mass on London. We begin with these features of the forces of production: the clock and the corn mill, the plow and the spinning wheel, the family, its reproduction and the production of clothing and food. Subsistence, then surplus. Consciousness that exists only in its collectivity and more than the sensation of being multiplied by the crowd, release from the singular, the individual, converged in the press and flow of wider time, gravity, the weight of our humanity. *Of such weight is my love, and by it I am carried wherever I am carried.*

6.

Only a non-dialectical shred of thought could argue this way. Reiterate without remorse or is this just a ruse to diminish the streets that are dangerous. Appealing (appalling) appearances. Actor and audience sharing the duplicity of their joint roles. How to get the figure performing manual labor back on the stage (so that the many who have the will but not the means can get a grasp?) — Bottom has in mind the joke of rushing up to keep Othello from doing what he does to Desdemona but B.B. would make the players more intelligible to themselves by acting to suspend mimetic expectations and foreground critical analysis. Double consciousness applied against identification and catharsis, allegory a counter-image that anticipates but cannot accomplish Redemption. The figure of the plowman as projected collectivity in the plowing itself, incarnation in the social body, is this how they first heard his "How may I save my soul?"

7.

Writing having to do with deciding there is no longer the luxury of waiting. The uselessness of the statement "all my life." A state of extreme though extended — jotted — attention. No facility for that matter in the standard and the first proposition marks the voice. Shadow of the undeclared, the moment at which we must decide and engrave what we hear. *Kindle* one example of a word if it refers to burning wood for warmth or cooking unless the object be — by the sound — a stiff and stark congealment of wood or hay or stubble forced and frozen in the letter of human trust. Happen wanshape. On the verge of a ditch. Even a hard closing, or opening if closed.

Palm tilted upward tilling the whole field. Looking up. Add to an enormous capacity for work what must be learned about the language a book that was written from the worker's point of view. Debtors. Foreclosure. The economic fact. "The room soon filled with lamenting old women." It made the fields more real. This is not a book the product of leisure. Thanks to the peasant that went past.

8.

Gloss on 'anon.' This is the Palace of the fearful King (called Author). FIRST ACT. "What, John Rugby! What John, hey!" (Enter Rugby). "Here, Sir!" "Rugby, fetch me some paper." (Writes). "Rugby, come with me. Follow my heels, Rugby." SECOND ACT. "Respecting what a rancorous mind he bears can you not see, or have you not observed the strangeness of how insolent of late he is become, how proud, how preemptory? We know the time since he was mild and affable, and if we did but glance a far-off look immediately he was upon his knee." THIRD ACT. (Some carrying Horners body). Falstaff. "What, is the old king dead?" Pistol. "As nail in door." (The proverb alluded to is the door nail on which, in doors to mansions, the knocker strikes and which may accordingly be regarded as particularly dead owing to the number of blows which it receives). FOURTH ACT. "What are they, that do play it?" "Hard handed men, that work in Athens here, which never labored in their minds till now." LAST ACT. Hermione. "The keeper of the Prison, call to him. Let him have knowledge who I am."

9.

More savage than the death of kings. It cannot be a question of 'aptitude' or 'inclination,' i.e. that it just wasn't part of his sensibility. He has linked his fate with a force (capitalist economy) that cannot legitimate him. History of a disaster beyond speech, anticipation of the disaster, why the skepticism of etymology, the belief that the oldest is nearest the truth or 'recalls what has been lost'—this doesn't seem to be anything but an outpouring, rhythm as Ocean, the suspect (natural) histories of a word but what about history-as-word or time-in-language? Hilarity of its intention, the American Century. Impossibility of a discursive stance to presume to address that which is propelled by absent compelling indicative inscribed the fiasco or fresco, Festooned. The unabiding as to withheld or reproach any appealing (appalling—the pall of a class of documents produced by a particular culture at a particular moment in history) the repressive economy of a given text what circumvents distorts deforms maims *The Bridge.* "The term 'proletarian' as applied to a poet must sound strange to Americans. Only Hart Crane with his roots in the depression and his love for metaphor, machines and manual workers suggests a recognizable case." Anton Nyerges, trans. *Poems of Attila Jozsef* (Hungarian Cultural Foundation, Buffalo, New York, 1973).

10.

The Village Idiot. Words don't hold horse piss. What about experience? How do you experience class? How are you positioned in relation to your class? "Flat on my back." Balzac's bric-a-brac, Bogdanov and Bazarov, Bayardo and Balthasar, the anarchist (Thoreau) and apologist (Adam Smith) together in one volume and I agree with Gorky, John Stuart Mill is a bore to read. One year the only book I read was *Bury My Heart at Wounded Knee.* What's in the notes, what's on the blackboard, what's by heart. He said (what did he say?)—on the pastoral something about the incompatibility of communism and desire. Time passes, and the body drifts. The body goes through the motions of being alive by mid-morning, *high prime,* in the dragging of the sun across the sky's complicity with the reigning—(the verb *rowen* means to beam, literally to make or show rows or steaks, cf. day-rawe, day streak, daybreak, see also daye-rewe and rowes-rede in the passage from Chaucer's *Complaint of Mars*). "We have no fuel, our factories are idle, we have little paper and we cannot make books. All this is true, but it is also true that we cannot get at the books that are available." (Lenin, *Speech of Greeting at the First All-Russia Congress of Adult Education, May 6, 1919*). Iron plows with moldboards were long unknown in those regions of the East unaffected by German colonization, the simple *ard* or *soka,* a wooden scratch plow, was the typical tool of the Russian peasant down to the twentieth century.

11.

'Boy Meets Tractor' Literature. To go toward—by writing behind—the Renaissance. The breakdown of feudal relations, and rise of

nations. Class struggle moves time forward. The 1930s 'an excruciatingly difficult political period.' Arbitrary tallage, marks of servitude, and thinking no sharper than peasants or serfs born under the tenure of yet another inheriting lord. Milton: "That freedom of writing should be constrained by the Prelates and learnt by them from the Inquisition to shut us all up again." Blunt Brecht: "Every one of their criticisms contains a threat." Dear Sirs, it would be difficult to represent my purposes and goals other than by describing how my thinking has changed. I can hardly hold up the pen to write *father,* having only the impaired memory of the most impoverished, reduced, depleted, exhausted struggle to answer to a cultural imperative, its stringent method and model of a genealogical tree. She drew the fine for unchastity and was ordered off the estate for asking the youth to meet her at night in her father's barn. (Bastards by law were born to free status.) Can feminist rhyme with communist? The winter of 1938. A ghost, or globe. The train, the truck, the tractor. The ditch beside the road.

12.

The Plow in Flower. Plod along at the back of the book at the foot of the page. Before that—without that—forsaken look. Since Love has turned Pedlar. The world breeds in the eye a word or worm. Now even also every one bite me and gnaw me like a burning worm. Hands more like it, hard at it, sweat imbued and uncouth, as are the hands of those for whom it once had been intended. They chew up their charity, they eat what they could share then cry out for more. The Augustinian road to truth through introspection brings the Dreamer to the enigma of the tree. A graft or shoot or sapling, here used of a young tree growing in the heart of God—its fruit and the ladder against it, the rungs of which consist of crimes. Figures from history hang from the tree. A vision of Christ and the flowing wound of *caritas* in his breast. *The Man Who Died:* "I was wrong to try to interfere. The ploughshare of devastation will be set in the soil of Judea, and the life of this peasant will be turned like the sods of the field. It is tillage, not salvation." The field full of folk as both producers of the fruit of their labor and themselves the fruit of the tree that spans the ages. Each was to have their own charter of pardon. But the words of the pardon insist there is no pardon. Free will by which we must be held responsible. A translator of the *Rime:* "Who else could have written in concepts of divine law, the unwritten law of humanity (*ius gentium*) and human transgressions against justice in the form of a conversation between Love and three outcast, wandering women? Perhaps Langland, but he lacked the discipline of Dante's art."

13.

"Not half hungry. To play off workers' dialects against the written language is reactionary. Leisure, even pride and arrogance, have given the language of the upper classes a certain independence and self-discipline. It is thus brought into opposition to its own social sphere. It turns against the masters, who misuse it to command, by seeking to command them, and refuses to serve their interests. The language of the subjected, on the other hand, domination alone has stamped, so robbing them further of the justice promised by the unmutilated, autonomous word to all those free enough to pronounce it without rancor. Proletarian language is dictated by hunger. The poor chew words to fill their bellies. From the objective spirit of language they expect the sustenance refused them by society; those whose mouths are full of words have nothing else between their teeth. So they take revenge on language. Being forbidden to love it, they maim the body of the language, and so repeat in impotent strength the disfigurement inflicted on them. Even the best qualities of the North Berlin or Cockney dialects, the ready repartee and the mother wit, are marred by the need, in order to endure desperate situations without despair, to mock themselves along with the enemy, and so to acknowledge the way of the world. If the written language codifies the estrangement of classes, redress cannot lie in regression to the spoken, but only in the consistent exercise of strictest linguistic objectivity. Only a speaking that transcends writing by absorbing it, can deliver human speech from the lie that it is already human." Theodor Adorno, *Minima Moralia,* section 65.

14.

A Crow for Norma Cole. In Gower's *Cronica Tripertita* the mob which mutates variously into wolves, sheep, peacocks, jackasses, oxen, cats and dogs shouts out a song from the streets below:

The Swan cannot keep his wings forever
Nor the Horse his hide
Now the Swan is without wings
The Horse is flayed
And the Bear in biting chains is rising

(My translation). The word *laborers* in the Statutes of Edward III appears comprehensive, including tailors, bricklayers, tilers, carpenters, ditchers and diggers, bakers and butchers, weavers of wool, weavers of linen, masons and miners and many others. The code varies: 'tailors and tanners, tillers of earth' or (and I will exist in this omission) 'tailors and tinkers and toll-takers in markets, tanners and tuckers also.' A tucker is the same as a fuller of cloth, and a tucking-mill means a fulling mill for the felting of cloth. Apart from these there was a class of plowmen inferior to the rest, though in the poem *Piers Plowman* the plowman speaks like a scholar—and here the epithet does not necessarily imply contempt, but indicates a thing like a person or implement that can be put to immediate and adequate use, such as a rag to clean out an oven or swipe the floor. The plowman likens the Crow to those of a low station in this life, and shows how unlike it is the Swan, whose feathers are eyed and coveted much as the rich are when they venture down the road adorned in diamonds hidden under robes of camlet and velvet furred with grise. The Crow though by far the most cursed of birds is far swifter in flight and has a much hungrier cry.

15.

Election Day. Makeshift, the mystery, soar without regard for and stand tantamount to that sweating, historical figure, written across this half light, one more link one block one cement block in each hand, a malleable alphabet whose letters swerve vanishing found apace binding mime. Roar worth every book you cannot afford, arthritic enjoined amiss trowel no less than kept out, stopped, run up against a child's babble responsible for the last—lost—minute (missedit) then rend the map to it, reading the price on a book. A road the child made in the sand captioned with a stick do not step on do not obliterate reels asphirated phial can't read my own handwriting anymore this past year's scraps of cheerfulness portioned out, rash rhetoric excerpted piecemeal from the last book bought constriction braced bargain salad bestow pound and pound on the page without looking back at the horse led around with a rope in its infected mouth. Eucalyptus stench when the car door opened and then a violin broke in with the last dime's spoken then broken down in exhilaration of number and identity surge shoulder to shoulder with nameless suffice no single and separate *feudal* Whitman's term for pre-America. Hart Crane came from Akron's arcane span widen iron vested business interests vision and a lot of hard work, his fight for a finer passage, newspaper pulp the page rubs off on whose hand did this myth volume porous ream coloration west of rock one and rock two spills out by the window sill oak lapel dowry don't forget your guitar, the child sits on the dictionary eating a feast of sound holiday arrears caper dial ribbon shingle style playing cave became catapult then snowstorm on the sofa. I have one hour where is the barber who will my barber be now, wary and the word warehouse for the fourteenth time Trotsky's *Balkan Wars* one more book that I couldn't buy subsequent to that incisive query without a guard for travelers crouched in a coach rocking along in the quick of night toward some distant inn, tavern, wayside or light, the need to write bitten off out of hand garner standpoint, base otherwise rust, dust, missing is a song you might recognize with a radically reduced lexicon seconding ebullient declivity opulent dents in the edicts bulb angular and Thibadeau, Anselm, Ambrose, the Church fathers carve for dinner and ate fish for Friday, a hallowed meal. Premonition of massive social upheaval filed away under ominous, omnibus, *omni* an important Latin root, my scholarship serraded thimble hymn brigadier cob nickel straighten phosphorescent eastern astern. Set forth under adverse, beside oneself with pent up pious tempestuous bridled apex haste gaping sway, mint handle batten battered few made it through, shortcomings and summonings recited, epoxy, estuary, incandescence, the rain rots the hay. Stonemason came, wall rose, damp plaster capacity to be diminished, strapped inconspicuous and powder in the air—sieve of liver, kidney, lungs. It rained. Walking briskly in the rain to buy a book any book below three dollars charged one sixty five including taxes rhymes with Texas this tendered theme of you, she was asking for you, showered in the light of her alacrity elided tilt brine token inflamed or inflammatory London, a lion in the mind, huddled over the desk with quill and inkwell the faster fingers notations *nota* over and over *nota* in the far column reading left to right across passages the players keep coming back to then take off on a tangent more illegible than before. Arrived yoked brocade tenor whey cursory funnel, hours that for lack of free time are called a day dissemble — it cannot be watched — page, data, the percentage of the population that succumbed to disease, the Stroud valley north of the Scarp in the hundred of Bisley, records rise on the screen rhymes with scream enter *screams.*

16.

But that most neden aren oure neyhebores. She had nothing, when they put what they put in that box they put in her car. They put the box in her car. She took the food home. She took the food out of the box, and now must make the meal. Powdered milk (no formula), flour, cornmeal, dried potatoes, macaroni, canned corn and cans of peaches and pears, jello, pudding, toothpaste and dish soap. She needed this food she had to beg to come by and now, not even now, especially not now, when she arrives home and starts cooking does she know where the next meal will come from when the bags and the cans in the box are gone, as he is gone. The reasons he gave were vague. I remember the reflex in the face, a broken face, breaking into a smile. He had an application in at Farmstead and IBP in Columbus Junction, and didn't care that the one was union and the other was not. Not that it matters, but he had not finished high school. He asked for more money, and they let him go. From time to time I would hear that somebody saw him on a construction crew or in a grocery store, another time on a farm. He had said he could not go back there. For a short while he had a job on the docks. I looked for him and I could not find him.

17.

Paystub Household. Born beneath the ruthless rustic wheel, Zink compiled a chronicle of the city of Augsburg and left a terse account of the circumstances in which he made a book. His wife, the daughter of a widow who could offer as dowry only some saucepans and a child's rickety bed frame, promised him to spin four pounds of wool each week, and thus earn 32 pence. Zink promised her in turn to find a priest to give him a book to make. The priest paid 4 gross a sextern (also 32 pence) and gave him one gulden cash to buy paper, with the advice to write fast. He copied his book from a shadowy and obscure exemplar, and though the dream of attending the University of Vienna had long been abandoned, he still retained enough learning to compose a reasonably grammatical Latin sentence — a small miracle in manuscripts outside Italy.

18.

Childbed Taint. With what sense does the parson claim the labor of the farmer? What are his nets & gins & traps & how does he surround him with floods of abstraction & forests of solitude to build him high spires & castles where priests & kings may dwell? Till she who delights in no fixed lot is bound in spells of law & must she drag the chain of life & wake her womb & bear the harsh scourge of the heaven of her eternal spring? Water & sleep & cave & air to turn the wheel e're ope the eyelids of the babe & they behold the arrows of the sun & sea & storm. The human form is orb & meteor & murderous.

19.

How camest thou by thy burden?
By reading this book in my hand.
Hast thou a wife and children?
I am as if I had none.

Kinderhyme.
Six flat
little black
fish float
thru the air.
One round
brown bear
wears a woo
lly sweater.
Red & yellow
rings & spheres,
alphabet blocks
& a bluebird
clock
which
goes

tick, tock. What is deep? What requires a leap. Where the sheep. Fall off the cliff. Time for bed. A fish in the spiderweb. *Diapsychidon* (sugar stick) cathect. Beset. I will read to you. I will bring you barley malt and gall. This is all we will ever have in the midst of which among I mean among. The rich. The name of the train. Buried deep. Sever is never the same as maim. Go to sleep. The Milky Way in Spain is called the road to Santiago. I will read you one more page. Mob fly across stage. Troops pursue. They load and stab and starve and shoot the Jews. Askance. A chance (simply, to exist). Impecunious. A scrap of golden, embolden. One gold, bold lion. Bright chains insignia. Insomnia. My own land about the tilling of which, telling time, and make a long cart of Liar, the town crier. What you need to believe is true and the words you use. God is a dog. Dead as a doornail. John of Gaunt is the cat. The mice will fail. Goodnight, innocence. Intransigence! What is the cost. Am sure that my copy of *Little Fur Child* is lost.

20.

Mother Courage. Helmet, basket, kettle. A wagon without wheels. Body movements, a kind of dance. Vex membrane, ligament, tissue, tendon. Pipe: to put there what is not there. Dip, pivot. Hands in pockets extricate pittance. A popular song. Vocal blocks endowed expiratory stream spring free round variability undulating long vowels volatile coloration. Discontinuous rhythmic segments, phonetic consequence of liberation from a unilateral bond. Midnight till 3 or 4 (sometimes dawn) am drawn. Laborious ascent from "doctrines so long accepted" to "significance at last apprehended." Kattrin strikes drum. Apt kin cast salinity, solidity, solidarity's barred circumspect staged, bolstered by this boundless imperious pure liturgy, Brecht's orthodoxy.

21.

An die Nachgeborenen.
Read
at this point
together
our negation

falsify
the signature
surely,
facsimiles

shall my Liege
measures
brawler
his houses

unsullied
such variants may
. . . the Earle
of Essex and,

as Aurelian said,
"contemporary
readers were
darkly to point at

word,
exampl'd
interpretationem
[errors of the printing house]

later to such as
seem unavoidable
these, as much as
Observations

Poetical
to the periphery
are
Nativity Ode

finger
cast
it has
(Works, 1st ed. 885)

also Helen
undated
uncollected
unrevised

22.

Dieu vous save dame Emme. The category of family economy. The family, not factory, as primary economic unit of production. The family as work unit maintained by necessity inherent in the mode of production to which it was bound. Remorseless conversion of the mother into inert means of reproduction deprived of every right by her legal assimilation to a theoretical category or descriptive term. Dilate: (Latin: *dilatare*) to enlarge, spread out, wide—latitude—1. (archaic): to describe or set forth lengthily and in detail, comment at length upon; 2. (obscure): to extend or diffuse through a wide space; 3. (modern): to enlarge or expand in bulk or content—as matter is dilated by heat—dilute, delay, dilatory, dial, dialogue, dais, day, dilation of the pupil, or cervix. Freud to H.D.: "But I don't want to play the mother." In Chaucer's Prologue, the word *gurles* means youth and no further indication is provided for their gender. In the Coventry Mysteries, one of the Roman knights carrying out the Slaughter of the Innocents cries: 'Here knave gerlys I xal steke' and, then, again, 'Upon my spere A gerle I bere.' In *Piers Plowman,* 'wollewebsteres' are female weavers of woolen, though the distinction between 'webbe,' a male weaver, and 'webstere,' a female weaver, is not always made. Malkyn a common name diminutive of Matilda or Mary for a woman of her uncommon station, who stood the most to lose, a trembling coursing through to each of her own sex whose hands she touched in perfect proportion and a separate gift. (This text is not from the Bible, but from the apocryphal gospel of the Nativity of Mary to be found in the *Aurea Legenda*).

23.

La poire du caillouel. Then there is the standard interpretation provided by the passage in *Ephesians.* The allegory of the naked tree, 'pur tre' being rendered by translators as the 'tree itself.' The one called a privilege, the other his right. Both were wrong. *Wife* is a name derived from the ancient custom of washing the feet of the poor to this day. She shook the tree where Widowhood grew, and wept. Maternity also made a fearful cry. The poet uses *mase* to mean confusion, and the entire sentence, though elliptical and incomplete, suggestive of exhaustion caused by the absence of the verb, as the verb *palle* is very rare, and can only be found in *Joseph of Arimethea.* (Note the volatility of the word *tene* as it shifts among scenes). When Seth reached Eden. The child in the tree. A mum is anything approaching a word, for the flesh is a fierce wind, and will often carry the fruit away before our aching, opening mouths. It is not clear if a pear is what is meant, sweet and good to eat and soft and not that stony as to be unfit for anything unless hidden in a pie (pie-heel, the crust, the part that no one wants). The most esteemed pear in the fourteenth century was *hastiveau,* otherwise known as *la poire du caillouel,* a hard pear, that came from Cailloux in Burgundy, yet even here the epithet 'hard' lingers until we learn that the hardness derives not from the pear but from the rugged, shallow soil of Cailloux (c.f. Fr. *caillou,* flint). Its fruit not small nor with one sweetness sweet. Ripen: remarkable for the retention of the final *n.*

24.

The Writing Lesson of 1381. "The topos of woman's incoherence" or "Woman as Riot." As if the Wife of Bath could vitiate the discourse within which she is powerless and illegitimate. Vitiate: to violate the chastity, contaminate, pollute, to make air impure, to render ineffective to destroy the force. But *break* might also be used in the sense of to vent, as in breaking one's mind—literally, an utterer of strife or debate (even without giving it any thought). Francoise: "A Baron? What Baron! Where's the Baron?!" The Baron: "It is far more difficult to disfigure a great work of art than it is to make one." Transpose lls. 23–46 from "East Coker," Zukofsky's notation in "A"-23, Pound (*The Spirit of Romance*—Langland left off of Pound's list), William Morris (*A Dream of John Ball*), Robert Southey's *Wat Tyler* and Byron's excoriation of the author's political reversal re the same, John Clare's *The Parish*—a decayed allegory—the Cade scene in Shakespeare, Florimel's unannounced arrival at the hut and the impossibility for the Peasant to pronounce his love (Book III, *Faerie Queene*), "Wynner and Wastour," "Perce the Plowman's Crede," "The Plowman's Tale" appended to the *Canterbury Tales,* Usk's *Testament of Love,* Chaucer, Gower,

Lydgate, et al. Walsingham: "It was especially dangerous if an ink-pot were to be found at one's elbow." Lord Berners' translation of Froissart (the first volume having the chapters on the Peasants' Revolt) appeared "at the high commandment of his most redoubted sovereign Lord King Henry the VIII, King of England and France, and high defender of the Christian faith, etc." The translation is contemporary with the rebellion in Germany Engels will write about in 1850. The editor of the Froissart notes that Lord Berners' book was second only in popularity to Malory's *Morte d'Arthur.* (The full text of Engels' *Draft of a Communist Confession of Faith* became known only in 1968 when it was found by a Swiss scholar in the archives of Joachim Martens together with the draft rules and circular for the First Congress.) It was a question of chronology, now that I saw it only from aside, and seeing no other possible obstacle than the basic fact that I had a body, hands which were not my own immense and belligerent forms. Tonight a romp, rolling from side to side at the end of an item in the print-haze. Pages that possess the immediacy that might be expected of reports written a few days or even hours after the events they describe. Writing that has thoroughly materialized and socialized the field of the Imagination's activity. An allegory charged with a multitude of overlapping schemes, concentric circles of reference, instinctive contraventions. Austere profanations and as material designated and adapted enduring theft, wrenched linkages, inconstant token—and make of them messengers. The conditions that gave rise to the life we led are gone.

Two Poems

Ann Lauterbach

ASHES, ASHES (Robert Ryman, Susan Crile)

1.

Humped gravity/tree-backed vatic shard/white
disarray/arc
                    secretly allied to the dark clear dark/herald
sick of his forms, dry
with remorse.

There is a cup in the landscape buried under the indefinite
as if it would last: salt, sugar, salt.
Sooner or later he'll want a child
hushed up against him
spawned in egregious thirst. Pale
inventory of a lunar smile/applause track
slips off the rails, flute twisted, strings
knotted and loose. Must be numbers, letters
afloat on the surface: augur, thread, mast
honeycomb, terrace.

I am jealous of his garment, his shirt's wide cut
the gaudy transience crouched in his throat,
great thimble of heat poured out—

a thing in the landscape:
salt, sugar, salt.

2.

Now this news.

If you do not mention it she will not cry.
I laughed as well at the child's invention.
Yesterday I saw a painting
of a young woman in a red dress. Yesterday

yesterday I saw
paintings of fire. I met a woman she said
my father my father my father
and as she spoke he became her portrait.

If a room is artificially white
all whisper in the affirmed
physical space:
touch touches touch.

The violinist moves
like a marionette/legs
buckle/hair
jumps with light/torso

breaks forward.
Music adheres
enclosing the figured silence
as if setting were bondage.

As if setting were bondage
and we on the brink had walked up to it/raw thread
chafing the waters of the percolating wave.
As if we could say to the fire,
Stop! I command you, stop!

3.

That night the moon was the Evil Banana King
crouched in a bowl.

See, said the child, drawing the light,
this is the Princess I asleep on her bed

this her pet snake/this
is the mother in her slip
she is wearing a nest on her head
she is a long lady standing in front of a leaky mirror
she says I would rather be in jail than stay
hidden in these devotions –

I am making red and yellow stitches
although my crayons are stale.

Now she is walking toward a cave
where the tools are hidden and the Book of Instruction,
peeled into slight wings, batters the foam.

This is a circle.
The name of the circle is Gray Pond.
There are lilies on the pond/you cannot see them
as if the memorial had rubbed away.

This is the ghost.

4.

This black thing is a mistake.
It could be a cat or a cart.

It is lonely like a mouth in a desert
under sand. I

do not know who hears it.
I do not know who calls.

It is a long way since
with no way out into a song.

There is ecstasy in battle,
on the somber chasm's edge.

That thou wouldst narrate me
thru these worlds.

I am in derelict garb
my category is broken

I am covetous of the extreme.

5.

Then the periphery dawned as later, as ebbtide
on a channel, as the gray pond of recognition,
the memorial rubbed into a wall.

How soon? you ask, and again, How soon?
You may as well ask is the water bloody
is the chair frail.
                              And, at the horizon, a ribbon of fire
finds its way to the woman's dress to ravish it so in the box
wild ashes fly about in a litter of silence.
The father-woman and the child do not meet, the
violinist never smiles. Is it a sunset, this fire,
seen from the dusty window of a passing train, or is it
the oiled conflagration of an event brought home to us as a trophy:
which comes first, artifact or source, and what stroke strokes the flame?

IN THE MUSEUM OF THE WORD (Henri Matisse)

—for Thomas Neurath

1.

There was the shield of another language
transient enclosure/gate
                                        swings open
shut shut
            walking unnoticed into it
                                                    as with *avec*
down stone steps into the vineyard
                        rose as decoy/beauty as use
            riding up onto the surface
                                    glance, sway/hawk

comes down dragging silence with it
no light, no applied Sun King
opposing shine, commonly
bereft
creature of habit lost in a wood.

Here I said take these thimbles these hooks
you can count them and toss them away
one six nine/they
will fit under any stream, fill any slot
will color the waters
of the restless exhibit

lizard's billowing throat
hiccups on a wall/its tongue
flicks air

bird-strewn wind

And the milkman's doubling dream, his
dilemma, the composition of his
intolerance for dawn/great
Aubergine Interior too frail to move: link
between A Conversation and event. There was

there had been an awkward tour.

I was shown two rivers, their vistas

snailfooted/waterskinned abyss
wheelwinged staring at muck
weedy, indifferent, purplepronged up
in avid rays their comprehensive *is*
bearing emblems smaller than time

under the decor
coiled among rocks

I met a woman with odd eyes
she said this is the figure of guilt
hurling a snake boulder

wall
ripped from a wall
fragment installed.

This country is a
cavern of drunk light/shade rubbed onto day
the corpse is not luminous/vines dangerous/flowers profuse
as in an arbitrary Eden. These

consolations also are damaged/seepage under roofs
thru which the musics
might come.

2.

She traveled.

Sun lay against her knees printed on purple
boughs fell with a thrash
color collected on the dusty sea floor
fronds meticulously scissored/commerce
raged thru the sky binding its harmonies
regardless of space.

Although something insisted, pointing.
Although similar doors did not open similarly.
Blackbirds reminded her of written blackbirds/it was
humid with blackbirds/her mind an inscription/a proverb
or heap so she could almost see its faithful
retrieval: monkey hanging with long limbs/bird
on her shoulder/rigid man/moon
doubled in glass.

Nothing timid is allowed while we believe in it.
Doubtless it should be told.
Doubtless tools will be needed.
Desire in an etched wineglass like an old bloody dime.

3.

A fable of prescience/looking up into the sky's garden
and the statues on the roof
withstanding bombardment

seven paces to Paradise
halted startled voyagers/nothing to correct
the possible direction collides with the way
each morning's tray a rudimentary splendor.

I said here are some useful numbers
some untranslatable rain

facades pockmarked in the new contingent state
now untethered on the Street of the Harp
the blind man cannot/soft sloped palm
dog leading him on into the unscented garden

They are scooping out the bloods in jars
the real has a stench/it is not
the tableaux we elicit.

I went up a steep hill in a foreign country
in unknown grass/there was an aperture

boats, birds
many unknown letters
snake-wrapped sphere
Persephone delayed
stolen, raped

Hotel where Mozart stayed/street where Brecht
Beckett's daily walks

impermanent oracular trace so that
not any fragment will do counting my steps
from margin to margin/scenic on foot
turning a page.

Ann Lauterbach

4.

In museum Street, Liu Hai is
standing on a three-legged toad

the toad
was thought to inhabit the moon

it lost its leg
in order to correspond

with the three-legged bird
that inhabits the sun.

And the Apostles were fishermen and thieves
base fellows neyther of wit nor worth

seal
reduced to a wax turd
flaunting a tail
charred Charter's remains
under glass

Merlin
helps a young man
to paint his
shield/an illustration

Attendants in a garden mounted on a crane

Under green and ochre glazes
under turquoise purple and ochre glaze
with aubergine, green and straw glazes

In a woods a black scroll
let us caption the first scene

on oak
on poplar on lime

Ann Lauterbach

green earth has been used under gold leaf
instead of the usual orange bole

as well as I can

As if conducted to the eulogy fields to lie down with a shade
under turbulent vines
walls studded
Peiro's meticulous plummage

Come this way said the guard this is where
your opponent lies grieving

here are the spoils set in violent maps, re-
named, disinhabited, inherited
made bloodless with shine.

Read this example
it praises the country of origin

it teaches you facts
in the new gray wing

lion, corpulent monk
Here are some postcards to send home/the one
you want is sold out/the thing you came to see
is temporarily gone

that she is seated/that the door
that the window
that she wears part of a tree
that the color of the conversation
moves as if it were sky/that the frame
continues to dissolve
(sadness of the Rose Marble Table)
man wearing a pajama column
rigidly pronounced/woman
redrawn in response —

Is is possible to memorize this blue?

Orison

Donald Revell

On such a night, the stars could not consent to constellations.

My ambition was
at once to stop
dreaming and begin
to sleep, to make
a clear distinction
between the ache
of privation
and cold surfeits
of black sleep.

A calf defecating onto the sleeping head of another calf
instructed me the useless distinction intervening a desert
of joy a desert of defilement. It was no dream. On such a
night, the stars pour down soil through their names.

My ambition was
at once to stop
the river upstanding
the open sea refusing
all surfeits.

Remember unequivocally the instance of mercy,
never prayer. The grammar makes deep channels
and useful islands, the overthrow of swimmers
recurring, undisguised. Mercy remains aloft.

Donald Revell

Afterwards will
be nothing to pray.
The broad wake
of so many drowned,
weightless but heavy
with downdraft, did
not say words.

The sum of their pains in pain no more upon the world
undressed all sums. And into all such nakedness hurry
the prayerful, quick to flaw what does not make reply.

On such a night
I saw an earth
above the earth so
long as there was light
until it was gone.

A Chocolate Malted for Charles Ives

Paul West

1. PRE-FACE

BEST TO BEGIN by saying that the following story by Jan Thor arrived in the mail one day, addressed to me (why to me specifically, I'm unsure, but a good enough reason would be that Ives was already dead). At first I thought the packet held a composition of my own rejected by some unlucky magazine and left it unopened for several days, scowling at the Illinois postmark (the only portion legible) until I felt readier for bad news or a thickly wrapped check. Imagine, then, I won't describe it, my surprise on at length hauling into the light Thor's typescript and his covering letter, this addressed to neither myself nor Charles Ives but, misleadingly, to "Kurie, Dear Friend." I gasped. Why me? Who on earth was Jan Thor? What on earth, or off, had Charles Ives to do with it all? Was a crank hell-bent on persecuting me by mail? Or was I supposed to pass on this work of genius to some sympathetic editor of my acquaintance? So I began to read, both letter and story, found the former baffling, the latter a confection of meandering fibs, colossal hubris and indecipherable burden. But, I confess, the thing began to grow on me, like a polyp.

I knew something about Charles Edward Ives (1874–1954), Jan Thor's noetic target, not having missed a certain raucous patriotism in the music of that composer, all flags, bands and catafalques, and had even learned something about his career in the insurance business. Recognition came later and his "People's World Nation," like his Twentieth Amendment to the Constitution, never. Not exactly uninformed, I sought to instruct myself further, even while grappling with Thor's text. Good ice-cream needs cone.

Clearly, Jan Thor, jocularly doffing his hair shirt in the drugstore mode of greeting, was made, though I could see a certain logic in offering a chocolate malted to Ives: a supremely American gesture. In some extraordinary fit of agitation, it seemed, Jan Thor had typed up, in *red*, what I can only call a penitential psalm tricked out in the Latin rubrics of a requiem mass and evoking not so much Ives as Mozart. Except that he garbled the rubrics and concocted at least one (*"Exit"*) of his own, the result being hardly a progress of the soul from extremis to unction, but an uncouth travesty of the God-Son, Master-Slave, symbiosis, in which demonic possession figures as flagellated bliss and coherence as hell on earth. So be it. Who wants to read the likes of *Middlemarch* again? Not I. Let it be said, though, I have looked in vain in Jan Thor's text for justificatory references to bashful Ives playing handball at thirteen against the barn door while his father's band marched past the house playing the "Holiday Quickstep," or to Ives's disdain for the man who thinks being full of turbid feelings about himself qualifies him as an artist, or to his notion of an African's soul looking the same under X-ray as an American one, or to his joy in Emerson's finding poetic suggestiveness in the humming of the telegraph wire, or to the Human Oversoul, to *114 Songs,* or even to his favorite quadratic monomial:

$$\text{Beauty} = \frac{Ix^2 - \sqrt{b^2 + 4ac}}{3(x + y)^2}.$$

Whatever that meant. Again, Ives's commas were time-intervals, or a means of precluding sibilance, whereas Jan Thor's are routine little maggots flash-frozen in his meal.

I conclude Jan Thor bestowed his text on Ives out of some tangential musical pretension. An allusion, Ives-like, here and there, is the only reference he makes to the composer. In fact, Thor seems an ecumenical provincial with delusions of candor. If he was saying something to while away the time, then all right: mice must play; but, if he was dying during the actual composition (as his covering letter implies), he died too late. Certainly, he never lived in or near Pekin, Illinois, and I have been unable to substantiate his other claims to whereabouts. I offer his dative text to the world only as a bow to a ghost in torment (it did grow on me, after all, as I've said), and to report yet another daft salience in these freak-filled days, in which to breathe is to smother, to think to fail, to write to earn the cold-sore of malversation. A seal of malpractice awaits us all.

Enough!

Jan Thor's *A Chocolate Malted for Charles Ives* awaits you. Sup with Ives, or sup on his behalf. I remind you only that *chocolate* comes from the Aztec *xococ* (bitter) and *atl* (water), while *malted* evokes a grain that's been allowed to sprout. Need I say more? Can one ever say enough? Why speak at all? It's in our nature to resent texts that, in their juicily indifferent inscrutability, too much remind us of the universe itself. Yet search with naked lights we must, ever for chaos. Or, like the dog in the old HMV advertisements, we must listen for *Our* Master's Voice in the amplifying horn of every gramophone, even though the sound be turned down. Perhaps I have missed in Jan Thor's writing something you will find. If live we do in a galactic zoo, some terrestrial safari park, we'll never meet the Director. Caged beasts never do, whether born in captivity or not.

Enough I said a riff or ten ago. Follows the noise of Jan Thor singing unharmoniously to Charles Ives without benefit of clergy, organ job, or pride. Who is Thor? Who was he? Where is he now, if anywhere? None of this I know. But, at least, at one time he was not nothing. That much is clear.

2. THE LETTER AND THE ACCOMPANYING TEXT

~~c/o Sam Staples, Sheriff, Concord~~
~~c/o Mayo Clinic, Roch~~
Pekin, Illinois
February 23rd, 1973

Kurie, Dear Friend:

I trust you will tolerate the salutation, if you are still there. If it is obsolete, then forgive it. Here, much later than I had intended, is a full account of some recent happenings peculiar in the extreme as well as fatal. Writing is not my forte; in fact, nothing is. But that is my problem, or was. I trust simply that the enclosed will reach you, one way or another.

I have told things as directly as possible, but sometimes moving away from the immediate point. I have let such detours stand, just as I have the present tense even after events invalidated it. To try to write this down at all was to have to relive it, hence some of the anachronisms. I have, I am assured, no hope of recovery. Feel free to make use of the enclosed material, on one condition: that you on no account give my name or in any way connect me with what I describe herein. As far as I am concerned, the whole affair is done with. Concluded.

Jan Thor

P.S. Please find the typescript herewith.

A Chocolate Malted for Charles Ives

by

Jan Thor

Once, when I was less myself than I am now, I founded a small travel agency in a medium-sized town in upper New York State. I prospered with it, especially through package deals. After about ten years, I sold the business, my interest in it having soured, the consequence of repeated futile attempts to visit Peking, both for my own pleasure and for the express but ancillary purpose of arranging China Tours. I had been everywhere else, so the frustration was singularly acute. Since selling out, at a more than handsome profit (the agency's name now having changed from Gulliver's World, The Honest-To-Jonathan, Swift-Travel Service—arch fancy of my prime—to Cook-Satellite, A Division of State National Bank), I have traveled not at all, done a little quiet reading (mostly in the prose classics—Dickens, Tolstoy, Balzac *and* Swift), and become something of a connoisseur in fortified wines. An occasional mistress has sufficed, along with the music of Bartók, the king crab of Alaska (far superior, on my palate, to lobster), and the friendship of my landlord, Frank Etna, a former associate professor of bugle and trumpet who, finding himself unvalued and unpromoted at Pekin College, even after years of devoted service as conductor of the College Blue-Band, turned to real estate and borrowed his way to a small fortune. He travels exhaustively while I mostly stay here (a second-best Peking, but enough), and then we exchange experiences: gadabout for static, foreign for native, abundance for next to none! He is the fox, I the hedgehog. We also sometimes play chess. There, that was relatively painless; I'll go on.

Over the years, it has proved a sufficiently aloof relationship:

nothing too intimate, nothing too superficial either. He has a family, a tight circle of real-estate friends who meet weekly for a fifty-cent breakfast at the Pek-Inn, and four cars, one of them an antique. I have no family, only an ex-wife who remarried after leaving me many years ago before Gulliver's World turned a profit, and a daughter from whom I hear twice a year, she being currently an airline stewardess (one of the light militia of the lower air). These have been peaceful years, a peaceful decade almost. I've shifted quietly about, though not very far in any direction, now thinning my interests, now multiplying them, obligated to nobody, known by few, loved by none. I've just passed forty-four, have had no major illness apart from a coronary five years ago, have irrecoverably lost fifty pounds (thus matching my five feet ten inches with the correct chart-weight of 155 pounds), and—well, I was going to explain my name. Thor is a truncation of Thoreau undertaken legally in my twenties when for the last time I wearied of being asked if I were indeed descended from that reclusive American author. I am not, I would not like to be, and I will not mention the matter again. My family name, truth told, was Taureaux, blurred by some unlettered official into that other. Nor has the name anything to do with thunder therefore. All was well, I was just saying, until that day last year when, with head not more than usually befuddled, staring into the freezer compartment of the refrigerator, and wondering what to thaw out for dinner, I heard a voice, not of anyone present and wholly unlike my own, a semi-strangled bass loaded with what sounded like uncontainable frustration. (On rereading this, I see I have cast it as being written before things went wrong, which is no doubt wishful thinking, the mind in recoil into the recent innocent past. Never mind, it will stand as witness to my remorse, if that is the word.) Whether, on that day, the pun-sound of *thaw* with *Thor* activated the chain of events, I will never know; sufficient to begin at the beginning and conduct you through, as best I am able, to see what you make of it, whether voice, voices, or mere pre-senile echoes. Distinct as the evening television news, there came the first of who knows how many thousand words:

"Ur — I don't usually hesitate. This's Atlas calling. A.T.L.A.S. ATLAS. Message ends. *I'm through.* Eon after eon, under these blue-black Moroccan skies, I've kept on calling the whole arrangement into question, but've only managed to keep on calling it back into being. Ad Nau-say-AM. Repeatedly, I mean. I'm hoarse to the point of aphasia, meaning I only *think* my cries, can't so much as even mime them; my face and biceps (biceps*es* I suppose I mean) are numb as keystones; I can't remember when my head didn't ache from the weight of holding up everything. Shoulders I won't even mention, still less my bent frame in general. I hurt all over, all through. It's high time I stepped down, and out. And then, kerplunk, the sky falls, the whole cosmic drive-in comes thundering down. Ur. . ."

Unforgettable words; I recall them verbatim; I recalled them always the same. For a while I heard no more, but I remained nervously alert. Where the voice of Atlas had come from, I had no idea, but in my own head it had certainly arrived: no doubt a traditional prelude to going (as folks say) mad. First you hear voices, then you begin talking to yourself (which we are born doing), after which. . . I won't reiterate the whole wretched, simplistic idea. I admit that, after various bizarre attempts to smooth out my head—living in a rented houseboat on Lake Cayuga for a lunar month, then for another in a tent near a mountain airport in Central Pennsylvania, finally in Frank Etna's majestic white house on the fringe of the Pekin campus—I had ended up with the same turbulence as before, except that the chunks of chaos had less serrated edges. Simply, thereafter, I stayed on in that house, disciplining myself into running a mile each day in sneakers and shorts, and permitting myself only one extravagance: a case of Dry Sack sherry weekly, which the local store delivered on Fridays. You may not know the brew, or even the brand, but it comes wrapped in a neat little sacking bag with scarlet or brown drawstring at the neck. After the first month I had enough sacking bags (fifty or so) to make something to wear, so I ripped open the stitches and stapled the panels of fabric into a loose cape imprinted time and again DRY SACK DRY SACK DRY, etc. A bottle a day frees a panel to wear. But it was only after a month had passed that Atlas began to come through, at first loud and clear, as just now, then indistinct and soft, vice versa I mean, and I took it for granted, wondering only: Why *Atlas?* Why *me?* I didn't know, I still don't, that much about Greek mythology, having always felt such personages as, oh, Zeus, Prometheus, Oedipus, remote from me, despite sensible arguments to the contrary. Nonetheless, it was clearly Atlas, self-announced, definite, and forceful; so I asked myself what I knew about Atlas, and it was precious little. *He held up the world,* and not for ransom, or rather he held up the skies and it was only later on they tagged on the globe as well. Insult after injury, they'd named an ICBM after him; there was a range of mountains in North Africa (as his voice had reminded me); and of course there was every atlas of maps, over one of which I pored instead of gadding about Mother Earth. Fairly eager, then, but still mystified as to what process was under way in my exasperated head, I hunted through Etna's books in the shelves the steam pipes ran vertically through (some of the warmest books ever!) and by a stroke of no doubt predestined luck found an 1892 translation of Oskar Seyffert's *Dictionary of Classical Antiquities,* its binding split and some of the pages missing but with the vital entry intact. What Frank Etna was doing with it, I cannot imagine, for his mind did not lean that way at all, not even when he was in Greece. Here goes, I told myself; bone up on Atlas, just in case.

"ATLAS (the bearer or endurer)," it said. "The son of the Titan Iapetus and Clymene (or, according to another account, Asia), brother of Menoetius, Prometheus, and Epimetheus. In Homer / *Od.* i.52 / he is called *the thinker of mischief,* who knows about the depths of the sea, and has under his care the pillars which hold heaven and earth asunder. In Hesiod /*Theog.* 517 / he stands at the western end of the earth, near where the Hesperides dwell, holding the broad heaven on his head and his unwearied hands. To this condition he is forced by Zeus, according to a later version, as a punishment for the part he took in the battle with the Titans."

Oh ho, thought I, no small fry he. Yet the entry did not fill a page.

"By the Ocean nymph Pleione he is father of the Pleiades, by Aethra of the Hyades." It made sense: if you support the universe, you need a family. But, I wondered, *how?* What were the mechanics of all that siring, if presumably he stayed all the time where he's reputed to have been? In the standing-up position? Missionary? Or what? For answer, I read on, got nothing of the kind.

"In Homer the nymph Calypso is also his daughter, who dwells on the island of Ogygia, the navel of the sea. Later authors make him the father of the Hesperides, by Hesperis. It is to him that Amphitrite flies when pursued by Poseidon. As their knowledge of the West extended, the Greeks transferred the abode of Atlas to the African mountain of the same name. Local stories of a mountain which supported the heaven would, no doubt, encourage the identification. In later times Atlas was represented as a wealthy king, and owner of the garden of the Hesperides. Perseus, with his head of the Medusa, turned him into a rocky mountain for his inhospitality. In works of art he is represented as carrying the heaven; or (after the earth was discovered to be spherical) the terrestrial globe. Among the statues of Atlas the *Farnese,* in the Museum at Naples, is the best known. (*See also* OLYMPIC GAMES, fig. 3)."

And that was all, except for an endnote reading: "In Greek architecture, the term *Atlantes* was employed to denote the colossal male statues sometimes used in great buildings instead of columns to support an entablature or a projecting roof."

Next came ATREUS, so I set the book down, compulsively musing.

What a paltry dossier for the voice of my demonic possessor (if such he were, were going to be). Certainly, Atlas was no mythic V.I.P. In the ordinary course of things I wouldn't have given him a moment's thought; after all, a man who isn't going to give the time of day to such a famous ancient as Prometheus (brother of Atlas or not) isn't likely to occupy himself with a character who at best is nothing but an anthropomorphic plinth. All the same, I'd heard Atlas talk to me, declaring himself as clearly as someone credit-charging a phone call. Had he come to stay? Or was he, pardon the pun, a flash in Pan? Was Atlas never to be heard from again, like certain candidates for political office? Maybe, for instance, Napoleon or Thoth would be next, to be followed by Pope Joan or Mahomet. Coming home to roost a while. Until Atlas's voice began again, an hour later, I had no idea what to expect, and not even then. I pondered away in my trademarked sackcloth cape, searching the entry text for clues, for an explanation of the episode, for (ah, Western man that I was then) the "meaning" of this haunting, its purpose, its use.

The clear head I once had is no longer mine; in fact, since coming to live in that creaky, spacious house amid its lawns, I'd let myself go somewhat, leaving the door chimes disconnected, never setting the alarm clock, staying up all hours (long after the end of the Late Late Show), letting a week's dishes stand in the sink. Perhaps it was initially because, upstairs, I kept on bumping my head against the slanted, low ceilings; I had been accustomed to vertical walls and horizontal ceilings, whereas there you never quite knew which was which. I had even begun to walk at the crouch, as if my head were not on straight. Nonetheless, I did my best to be balanced and systematic about Atlas, and found myself working thus:

Atlas, a bearer, I know that much, but none of your native bearer, gun-bearer, on safari. He endures in time, he lasts, and he stomachs a lot. A good name, inspiring trust and confidence, especially if applied to heavy industrial goods. (I suddenly thought to dig out my portable tape recorder, determined to say him into it if he arose in my head again or, fat chance, uttered with his own voice.) I turned then to Prometheus, reading that an eagle was supposed to have pecked away at his liver. Or was it kidney? Then I jotted on a card as follows: *Asia.* Odd to think of Asia as a mother, his mother, anyone's. Where before have I heard the phrase Mother Asia? *Western end.* Hm, the West End of London, at any rate, is the smart part of town. Theaters, restaurants, stores. Isn't the West End of Hell called Limbo? Look up later. Wild West? Decline of West? *Hesperides.* Nearly familiar. Something to do with a garden where golden apples grow, so are the daughters apples? Fruit of seed? Cox's Orange Pippins? Russets? For apples read testicles? *Titans.* Suggesting the *Titanic,* though no connection. An obsolete race of gods. Gigantic too. Titanium? *Daughters* galore. Never a son? Why no mention of this fact? It's an obvious enough question. *Calypso.* Old word has new meanings. I think of West Indian, or Trinidadian, lyrics, improvised, sung to the music of a steel band. Good-humored, and sometimes satirical or lewd. Is also Cousteau's boat, is not? Maybe Calypso sang seductively. No. Leave space. Look up later. —No, she just gave friendly welcome to Odysseus. *Mt. Atlas.* OK, he was turned into this by the Medusa head. Or into the whole mountain range. What I'd call a peak experience, at least until an hour ago. Less. *Wealthy king.* Was Atlas Croesus too? Or Midas? Which is which? Check it out. —Neither one. Now *Farnese.* Farnese Bull. False trail. Try under Olympic Games, as told to. Here he is! Facing Heracles (=Hercules, surely), with Hesperis saluting him. He's got a beard and seems to grow upward out of solid rock, embedded in it from the thigh down, and his palms extend as if he is beseeching something. Odd, though, the left arm is only a strut like part of an artifical leg; a whole piece has been broken away.

That was all; now I knew how to get nowhere fast. As if on cue, the voice returned, and I forgot all about that evening's dinner as Atlas boomed again through my skull, then quieted a good deal while the cassette whirred.

"Smile if you like, Jan Thor! You're not imagining any of it. This's Atlas again, old buddy. You bet. Now look here. I don't know exactly how long I have, and no doubt I shouldn't be coming through at all. Blame the Heaviside Layer, one of my ceilings. Fact of the matter is, I've been and got myself a dose" (I flinched) "of the old-fashioned blues, those old no-initiative blues. Imagine being house-bound by the universe! That's a mind-boggler, all right, but grievances I needn't trump up; they're legion, as they say in North Africa, even now. A couple of examples off the cuff might help you though, show you how bad things are. OK for starters. South-West of me, parallel but far from in harmony with yours truly, there're the so-called Anti-Atlas Mountains. Tactless montane pastiche if ever I saw one. Four hundred miles short, they run only from Gouimine to Ksares Souk, and then they peter out (I choose the word advisedly), whereas I, Atlas, pro-Atlas, who count my own Mount Toubke, over thirteen and a half thousand feet, a mere nipple, I sprawl all the way from Agadir to Bouarfa, over *six* hundred. I'm big about it, bet your life, but to have imitators on your own doorstep, that's too much. You getting all this down?"

I was, I was.

"Yet even that's not as bad as the only town ever named after you's being not even marked in you own Rand McNally—huh—Worldmaster Atlas (word chosen most inadvisedly). Fact is, Thor, old son, the town of Atlas, Pa. (population 1,574 when last heard from) bears an ignominious asterisk signifying 'omitted from the maps because of scale size or lack of space. . . approximate location only.' So a fan'd never find me in square D-8, no matter how hard he looked, though he'd easy-as-falling-off-a-log hit on such trash as Bodines, Shunk and West Milton. For shame! And there's tons more of it: grievance, humiliation, I mean. I marvel I never before thought of it—*thunk* it—but I should opt out right now. And then the universe can drop on all trash-atlases and trash-towns. A name so often taken in vain or not at all had best be let lapse. I'd be better off as brother Prometheus, just for a day, except I grow nauseous at his very name, even 'Pro' his nickname, and my liver's none too good anyway, what with all the insupportable standing I've had to do since grammar school. No half-decent eagle'd touch it. I'm varicose to the navel." Oh, I thought, daftly, to *see* him! His navel or his face. But this Atlas is only a voice; so far, anyway.

"Well," he resumed. "That was a beginning of sorts, wasn't it?

We'll be on farting terms soon. A beginner's beginning, that's what it was. I don't come from a very intellectual family, so it isn't much my fault. Great Grandad Uranus, he was forever getting catcalled in the roadways by greenhorns whose only claim to fame was in playing midnight stinkfinger with poxdoctored nymphs. Ur, he was all balls was he, at least until—who was that feisty young bastard?—Cronus, cocky Cronus, sliced them off with one swipe of a sickle, and they plunged into the sea like two collided blimps. Out of that dreadful churning, Aphrodite was born, so the old mythical commercial has it; up here I hear all the rumors, few of the home-truths. Then there was Gaea, my Great Grandma, about whom I know only that she was earthy to a fault. A word to the wise, Thor, my lad? Whereas Grandad Oceanus, bless him, I've altogether better memory of, fondly remember him as Old H_2O who tucked me in at night, gentle and hospitable even when he was locked away in his West Coast White House retreat with Tethys, getting a breather from all the parliamentary-minded gods. About Tethys herself, who knows? In the books I've seen it says, See Oceanus, except you can't, and, in any event, he never told, unless his opinion was somehow incorporated into his long beard, the bull's horns and crab's claws on his head, and the clique of sea monsters always surrounding him. I'm not keeping you from something, am I?"

I explained I was overcome to hear from him, not having heard ever before. "I'm a maiden audience," I blurted, not meaning quite that, but he took it in his stride and really warmed up.

"As for Dad, well he—Pops Iapetus—got himself exiled to the Tartar Steppe for breaking the peace by trying to postpone the twilight of the gods (or the twilight of some of them anyway). I'm not that keen on him, never was, prefer to write him off under an *alias* (those old Greeks were all disguises!): I'm thinking of Japheth, the third son of Noah, ancestor of the Indo-European race. The hell with it, it's an out for Pops. Big of me, that. A born loser he was, and by no means a thinker, he'd married Mom, *née* Asia, only out of geographical grandiosity, see? Forever after was known as Asia's Minor. Later on, after they'd taken Pops away, she changed her name to something whorish and started fucking the sun, but by then I had chores of my own to tend, had already forgotten my childhood (if I had any at all). Of my three brothers, Menoetius (couldn't even spell it!) didn't last long, got himself exiled with Pops, and then there were two: the after and the fore of things,

Epimetheus, a bull-headed and impetuous chap, just the kind you'd expect to tie up with a know-it-all bitch like Pandora, and, of course, Big Brother Pro, already mentioned: he of the legendary forethought, a thief and a cosmic climber, a masochist and a sitter-in and a smuggler. Lots more as well, none of it good. Pro, I vouch for it, was Henry Kissinger the First, his true ambition being to set himself up on a mountain as big as mine; hence that notorious forwarding address in the Caucasus. I never had a sister. What? Thought you said something mighty American there. But I reckon I must have had various bastard brothers, I mean bastard brothers who were even bigger bastards than the brothers legit. Forgive such outbursts. If you can. They come upon me, flash, and I'm undone quite. I'm the emotional brother. It's the result of holding the whole bloody thing up all the time, like always having to have an erection: not even time to pee, to scratch, have a perfunctory fidget. I was talking about sisters, wasn't I, and having none, though what with such goings-on as Uranus's being both the son and husband of Gaea, therefore being his own Dad, and Tethys's being old H_2O's wife and sister, thus making him his own brother, I'm glad I didn't. Of daughters, though, give or take a few by-blows never logged, I reckon I've had as many as twenty, at least a round dozen. Hyades. Pleiades. Hesperides. Bless 'em all! No wonder they said each of my sperms—the successful ones, anyway, who made it past Immigration—had a twat in him, ready-made, the reason being I was too much man myself; I'd overload the sex balance in space. It's as good an alibi as any (to use the word loosely), and the best in the world for someone whom the world fell on for no acceptable reason and who, ever since, has had a monkey and much else on his back. Libya's my stomping-ground, ether's my halo; I'm multiform, dispersed and mute; I'm the prototype of those who Put Up with things; I shiver or sweat, I buckle or sway, but I stand fast. Such was my ancient, scurvy contract, which to deserve I must've committed some unspeakable infamy. Lord, what I wouldn't have given in the bad old days for a good agent! Or even an attorney. Too late now. It must've been something I did in my sleep, I wouldn't knowingly have done anything a hundredth as bad. As you and most folk know. Time out now for a breath-pause and a slight adjustment; something's out of kilter in Orion, I reckon. I've sure got an itch I hadn't seconds ago. Now I'm inhaling. Hear that? *In-h-a-l-e.* Atlas's hale and heart all over again, ready for more. Thor? You still there?"

If you have ever had a bullhorn in your skull, you'll know how he sounded, yet I'd heard him louder in even this short acquaintance. I went upstairs for aspirin, though still tuned in to Atlas, and clutching the tape recorder. I found a new tape in the so-called study (desk, chair, no books), and while I was swallowing he started up again, somewhat modulated.

"Here I am, just as good as before, same call letters, identical vocation, but just a teensy-weeny bit more fed up than I was. If that's imaginable. You don't know how good it feels to be sounding off into the one available ear, old son. Odd, I'd always, over the long centuries, thought myself an iron man, indeed the only man for the job of Upholding Things, but I was only rationalizing when I thought that. Once upon a time, Hercules stood in for me, did a good job, oh yes, but was soon on his way again. That was the only stroll I ever took. And now, I confess it, I'm well on the way to my first nervous breakdown. Honest. It shows in the way I talk, don't it? Twitchy, jagged, hypertensive stuff. It'll soon be worse, mark my words. And then the whole damned universe'd better watch out. Blind, malicious old Homer called me 'the thinker of mischief,' you know; well, that's OK by me, you have to let poets get away with something now and then. But I reserve the right to earn my reputation!"

Then he cannot, I reassured myself, read my mind: I *know* what Homer called him, having just read it in Seyffert. Here I was thinking he was all-knowing, some kind of omniscient revenant of the airwaves, and he's not. But maybe he's in the habit of repeating things, just out of boredom. Funny how he shuts up as soon as I begin to think in my own right.

"But that old riff," he went on, a bit subdued-sounding, "in the handbooks about my being located—urhem—in the west, that's too limiting by half." Atlas in a sulk.

Irrelevantly, I thought at once of saloons, gunfights at the OK Corral, stampedes and ten-gallon hats, then of Oswald Spengler being Jeremiah.

"The truth's more nearly this." He'd again seemed to wait for me to complete my competing thought. "The West's part of the scene I sustain, but only part. I refuse to be located entire in one of my parts, or even to be thought favoring one brood of daughters (the Hesperides, natch) over the other two. Sensible? Of course. To get back: I was saying I'd reached the point of no return, was sick of supporting the whole show, of the way everything depended on me, as if the best of me were out on perpetual loan. Know how that feels? A career of sponsorship. All very well to think of myself as the man with the portable universe—portable to nowhere. I was more like a meal ticket for Creation, or, to change the figure (as Perseus, the Red Baron of Hyperborea, changed me for being a lousy host), more a rock than an identity. 'Atlas's there, steady as, etc.' 'We can always count on him.' 'No need to do anything for him. He has no needs, needs only the needs of others.' Such were the time-honored Atlas-assininities. My one privilege was to claim all my dependants as long as they possessed me. Huh. And a whole string of huhs. Now I claim me. I want my own exemption, see. These are the first words in the campaign for Atlas Unattached, his dugs for once unsucked, his udder swollen to bursting, his power to maintain devoted to himself alone. I'm talking about AUTONOMY, son!"

"Of course," I parroted. "Autonomy. I know what that is. I've gone to a peck of trouble to cultivate a case of it for myself."

Emboldened-sounding (not that he needed a backer), Atlas talked on, now droning, now mustering a semi-shout. "There's only one problem: how to duck from underneath in time, before the heavens fall. One shoulder I'd be able to whip clear all right, but the other? Heavens, I'd lose a foot, a leg, at least. It's all a matter of this's, where I stand non-stop, being a No Lone Zone: where you should never be alone, not if you expect to get out unscathed. Atlas alone can't do it. That's his lot of bad luck, see. I'd be maimed for sure, but that's beside the main fact: my very act of stepping down'd abolish the world I'd step into. What a bind. To survive I've to stay put; escape's just suicide. So, in a sense, I Atlas hold up not only the heavens but also Atlas as well, like some giant reflexive truss. That's the dilemma I've chomped on since (as the legend goes) Zeus, filthy old instigator of everything, decided to pay me back for—for what? I hardly even know. It certainly couldn't have been hubris: only mortals like yourself get up to that; yours is the monopoly, so to speak. So maybe it came under *lèse-majesté,* which I gather you can still commit in the land of Britain by affixing a monarch's-head stamp upside down on an envelope. To hell with it, I did nothing serious. And to hell, I follow up, with the consequences of stepping out from under; so, if suddenly this confidential tirade ends, you'll know what's up. What's down. I just might do it, out of spite, say, and then I'd be in the funny position not of the narrator whose very voice expounding in the past tense tells you he survived but of the silenced narrator whose cessation tells you he didn't. In that case, how did he begin? Answer: the tale he was interrupted in telling, tale of woe or not, wasn't the tale of his own death. What I think I'm driving at is that a dead narrator can't cheat. There are no dead narrators; there are plenty of dead ex-narrators, but no narrating dead. The zombie's an oral zero. Right? Gob (I'll not use D for B even if it kills me), Gob, what vomit this is. Were I genuinely in the west, which isn't so much a place as an instrument, I'd be a genuine writer: set it all down with 2B (or 4F) pencil on — Atlas-sized sheets of course, twenty-six by thirty-three by thirty-four inches. Newspaper size."

My scalp had begun to tingle, my head to buzz, aspirin or no. Playing back the Atlas tapes now, at this late date, in order to transcribe them (the tape I cannot bear to part with), I feel the same sensations all over again, plus giddiness, even after that voice is out of my head into the metal. Press on, I tell myself, don't get flustered this early on.

"Anyone but me," I hear myself ventriloquizing for silent Atlas, "can buy those things they call alibi tapes: the sounds of airport, restaurant, surf: run the tape, then call a friend (or an enemy, like Zeus) and unreel your lies. 'Sorry, they're calling my flight now, I'll have to hang up.' Or, 'Sorry, here comes the roast duck à la marinated angel or whatever it is.' Or 'Stormy, I can't talk now, the tide's just lapping the phone cradle.' And so forth. But not me, I can't ever be in another place; never an alibi for Atlas. The crimes I commit I commit where I stand; I'm always at the scene of the crime, can't even voluptuously revisit it. I've quite literally nowhere to go, for here — as the copycat Romans are soon going to say — is everywhere: *Res ipsississississima,* the thing at its utter very mostest wherever it's at. Stupid language, that, not a patch on our ancient Greek. Do you know what they, not the Romans but the slander-mongers, used to say?"

Orally hypnotized, I answer. "What?"

"'Atlas's weakening,' they'd say. And then Atlas showed 'em. Canted up a big toe of the right foot, and Istanbul trembled. Flexed a triceps, set off an earthquake in Japan. Sneezed, and Krakatoa erupted. Farted, and the U.S. Coast Guard at once began firstnaming the turbulence Agnes, Bertha, Cassie."

One way or the other, Atlas was mad, or even insanely furious. Two mads in one. His mad is up, his mad is down. Vox A. just went on, however, now golden with vehemence.

"Achronicity I calls it. All time is available to me, as you've no doubt noticed. It takes a bit of getting used to (even harder for the likes of you), but it can be super fun—ur, sometimes. I do sometimes like to have me a bit of fun, whereas brothers Pro and Epi never did. Like to, I mean, although they sometimes had some fun by accident—like when Pro set his hands ablaze with lighter fluid and Epi the scatterbrain set about making Man (haha) but only after handing out the best gifts to the animal kingdom: might and speed and guts and guile, fur, feathers, wings, shells and tails. Eff them both. I'd rather be an American football star, or, in quieter vein, a college tutor who takes a brisk stroll through the autumn leaves in the quadrangle, *tetr*angle I'd call it, where a few students are tossing a ball around, before going in for toast and tea by a blazing log fire, after which he reads Plato until the dinner bell. Sherry, chops and port. That kind of self-contained, cozy deal. I'd settle for any kind of chronic, which is a far cry from what I've got on my plate right now. In fact it's not even in the realm of far crying at all."

Taking time out to wrinkle my mind at his weird, ersatz idiom, compact of Fifties slang and jock earthiness, I held him up, but only briefly. Crude he might have been, but his manners were good; no one, I reckoned, had ever heard him out before. Or heard period.

"Anyway, thanks to achronicity," he said, calmer, "I can at least think of it, half-master myself into living it. A kind of vicarious retirement. 'Scuse me a moment, it's time for the checklist." Then he picked up again, but in hushed, near-sanctimonious tones: "1. Inspect the pillars of the universe by squinting up, then down. All in order: Heaven and Earth still somewhat apart. 2. Twist clockwise once, then twist back: ur, the terminator should be along the Greenwich-Fiji line. Is. A-OK. 3. Count all the nonmilitary aircraft currently groping above the surface: Tri-Stars, Concordes, Ilyushins. I make it four thousand three hundred, only two in the act of going down. Both cases of pilot error. Just like flies reconnoitering a Zeusturd, I must say. 4. Now say aloud:

"'To bear on his back forever
The cruel strength of the crushing world
And the vault of the sky.
Upon his shoulders the great pillar
That holds apart the earth and heaven,
A load not easy to be borne.'"

Choke-voiced, he explains: "My sentence, see? Zeus put on the black cap and read it slow, and my knees began to give, even then. Anyway, there I'd said it again. I feel better with that bloody rubbish off my chest. Now I've to say another, which was the rider to the sentence. Listen.

"'Monumental hunchback, Atlas I
Will not invite peripety;
And further will not claim
Copyright on Atlas's name.'

Did you ever hear such bull?"

I wondered who wrote that for Zeus and was just going to ask when he cheered up and began to gabble.

"Sorry for that distraction; has to be done. But, at least, I don't have to waste time eating, sleeping and so on. When I pee, even, it's only a mime; I pee air. After all, when a titan takes on the globe as well as the sky, he needs to concentrate. One silly wobble'd foul things up. I once thought of composing an autobiography, you know, better termed an *anautoabiomimesis,* which means a non-self's non-life imitated, or simply *Zilch,* but I only kept on accumulating epigraphs and couldn't get beyond them: after going on twenty-seven thousand august quotations I still wasn't even at first base. All I did was write down 'I' and then, like a cop commandeering a taxi, say 'Follow that pronoun!' But it came out mighty weird, you understand: the first person in all languages from Greek to Sanskrit, from Hebrew to Malagasy. Just imagine, after twenty-seven thousand epigraphs, being unable to come up with anything better than 'Ego, Ich, Yo, Io, Je, Ic, Ih, Eg, Jag, Jeg, Ek, Azu, Me, Aham, A, Ja, Ke, Ai, Wo, En, Ek, Jeg, Pu, J, Aj, Ani, Y-es, Inks, Is, Eu, Koy, Ngai, Ahni, Owau, Saja, Akero, Izaho, getting bolder and bolder all the time of course, AKEN, IZAHO, et cetera, but. . . I. . . ur. . . a boy of five collecting basement spiders in a box would have more material than I did."

"Excuse me," I interrupted. "You said Jeg twice. I used to be a travel agent, and I spot things like that with ease."

"Fuck it," he said, and went on delivering himself of his remorseful voluntary. "Freud and Jung swapping dreams during a transatlantic voyage have more in common than I with life as others live it. A cricket outside in the cold, trying like hell to stridulate but achieving only the sound of a match being struck in vain—*fth, fth*—is in better voice. Marcello Sharif, movie star, who conducts a protracted affair with an airline stewardess by flying from city to city with her, has more sense of direction. The man who takes a whole year to read one issue of the *New York Times,* until in fact the issue of the same day, next year, arrives, has more sense of urgency. Impotence is too grand a word for so complete a nullity as mine. I'm beat before I begin, and that's fact."

I thought then, I think it now: he grows on you, into you, through you; sometimes *is* damned nearly you. He—

"In the end, all I managed after the most frenzied exercise of all my faculties was a rumor, which I let fall into the airwaves. Impure malice, it read as follows: 'STRONG POSSIBILITY CARBON-DIOXIDE BREATHING LIMBED MAMMALIAN ENTITIES 12–36 INCHES TALL IN COMBINATION AT SURFACE JUPITER MARINER 666 SECOND PARABOLA CLOSEUP PASS CBS REUTER AP STAY TUNED THIS CHANNEL FURTHER DETAILS.' Quietly, like the horizontal ship's mast in the physics problem, it flowed leftward from right across the bottom of the entire world's screens, incongruous conveyor-belt for Atlas at his most Antic. Crying 'Plagiarism,' Orson Welles went into cardiac arrest, I gather, while the hotline in the red telephone in the White House was unlocked." It was as if his voice had grinned, worldly-wide.

"Then I canceled the whole thing. Wiped it out."

"You just erased it like that?" He answered me not.

"That ended my first attempt at *anautoabiomimesis.*"

Flashily facetious, I said, "Then it wasn't *anautoabiomimetic* enough, as Aristotle might say!" But he ignored me again.

"Instead, during the whole decline and fall of Egypt, I kept on telling myself: 'One plus two plus three plus four all squared equals a hundred.' Very soothing. Something to count on. A clue to some universal harmony I'd been exempted from. No? Well, anyway, ur—I'll come to other ideas about that later on. *After* later, in fact. I'm achronic, remember. The stumbling-block, it turned out, was my name: at least, regarded achronically, with full feedback and retrieval at full blast, plus flashes pro- and epi-, that's how it looked. It all comes back to A.T.L.A.S. Book of maps. Illustrated compendium. Big size of paper. Man-column. Man with a great burden. Mountain or mountains. ICBM. Even a bone at the top of the neck. Even a misguided overdeveloped case of muscles with enough hubris to call himself Charles Atlas You Too Can Have A Body Like Mine! And there's more, lamentably much more. I've been spread too thin, as if my identity were marmalade of roses. Oh, the crap I have to take! And bear in mind it's me you get when you say Atlantis or Atlantic. Imagine—you don't have to—being so dispersed, so cheap a household name, so miscellaneous, whereas true dignity consists in singular application: Zeus is Zeus, I guess, and nothing else, whatever to the contrary gets said in the West. Adam's Adam. Christ's Christ in perpetuity. So I deplore the application of JFK to an airport (same goes for Dulles), of mustang and jaguar to cars, of (a primarily British fault) such names as Hercules, typhoon and—ur, Blenheim to aircraft. Of the notorious craft benightedly dubbed the Armstrong-Whitworth *Atlas*, I've nothing to say. No comment. No commentary."

"Yes," I interjected, "but what about the Anti-Atlas Range?"

"Shit."

"And Atlas, Pa., pop.—"

"Flaff!"

A new word to me, it—

"Don't you all know what flaff is? Flaff's the condition of negligibility raised to its exponential maximum." All I could think was God help him, he wants it both ways: recognition and privacy, fame and inwardness. He's one gigantic *odi et amo*, love and hate in one bollixed-up ball. No wonder: where he comes from, a light-year's a mere wink. What was he saying? He didn't say, but he sure as hellfire was coming out with this:

"—*that* in itself being sufficient reason for retirement. Unbudging, I became a thing, virtually thoughtless, taken for granted like a mailbox or the smell of leather. Thought a dunce, a dunce I became; become one, I thought more duncelike, duncishly, than ever, just to outdo them."

"It happens to the best of men," I moaned. "I know."

"What say they? Let them say," he quoted. "Sticks and stones may break my bones, but what they say can't—as a matter of fact it's hurt me a lot. More than I've ever told.

He resumed.

"Why, the last newspaper I read before stirring myself to this fairly agonizing appraisal of self and status made me look even more foolish than usual. It so happened the type'd been garbled and the caption to some photograph read thus: 'Conferring before testifying at Ways and Means Committee are anti-tax advocates, from left, Vivien More than 500,000 geese fly through the area twice a year, at Kent State University, and actress Gloria Swanson.' I never lived down *Vivien More than 500,000 geese.* The heavens resounded with it, *terra firma* spun giddily, and the little cosmic dogs I imagine (but only *half*-imagine) come to cock their legs to pee against the twin columns of my calves—Bach, Bruckner, Beethoven and Buxtehude I call 'em—they actually nipped my ankles, tickled with their tongues between my toes. I swayed several times before regaining my balance, and then a chorus began of 'Atlas can't read!' Bad luck maybe, and that's all; but you can see how it affected me. When the All's available, even without being asked for, you've got to keep it straight. Between then and now I've not read a single word, hence my lack of knowledge on certain topics. My job was to hold up—well, you know; I won't labor the point—and to do that as mindlessly as I wanted to. Which explains, if *any*thing can, all this humbug and bumbling." I thought how hard he was on himself, couldn't figure out why he'd kept silent all this time. Sent to Coventry, he'd been in that city when it was bombed to bits in World War Two.

"I'm left with one thought," he then told me, his voice gravid with gentleness. "It appalls. I believe I hold up what I hold up (not in any sense delaying it), but I've no proof, and to prove it one way or another's grievous; if I'm right in my belief, I won't survive the proof; yet if I'm wrong I won't be able to live with myself, not after standing in this position like a dummy since the year One without so much as a week's leave, a day's truancy. Skip Hercules, he doesn't rate. I can't count that little episode, anyway, because I was still on duty, even when away getting him those goddamned golden apples. When he assumed the load, he perhaps waited until I was out of sight, and then sat down, the lazy bastard, and took it easy until just before I came back. And the whole shebang stayed put. As it always will. When I returned, told him he could jolly well go on holding it up, and he tricked me into reassuming things (so's, he said, he could stick a pad on his shoulders to ease the pressure), he was only fooling. Had I then just walked away, saying 'Screw you, Herc,' I'd have been free to roam an unfoundered Earth beneath a suspended Heaven. Imagine! Instead of conning me back into service, he actually double-conned me into a wholly redundant servitude. The answer's plain. I have to do it now, better late than never, eh? Walk away on my own two feet. Come on, Thor! Tell me to do it, and I will."

Obligingly I said, "Shove off, Atlas! Be brave." I said it again, with more rank, more mustache. Nothing.

"No, go," I finally heard him say. "I'm stuck. I daren't. I'd rather put up with everything than *not be.* I'm not feeling responsible,

I'm just being selfish."

I urged him again. "Attaboy, Atlas!" My shout must have jolted the tape recorder going in, it fairly split my eardrums as it came out; but Atlas, I gathered, did not shift a jot.

"None of me moves," he wailed. "Feet, this is mind: move. No, it's no use. I'm paralyzed."

"Try again, Atlas. Concentrate."

I really cared; I was worked up, more excited than I'd been since my coronary.

"For just a millisecond, maybe," I heard, "I could dart out from under, see if anything begins to topple, and, if so, resume position. How's that sound?"

"Great idea. Do it."

"No. 'Atlas,' I tell myself, 'you'd better think hard about the headaches, the weight, the pressure. Do they correspond to a real burden? All the gravity there is and ever was? Or, as may well be, aren't they imaginary? Minutely accurate responses to a fictitious situation? All this time, your cranium, shoulders, trunk, and legs, have settled into a bearing stance, a hunch, when all along there wasn't an ounce to lift. Think of the tennis smash perfectly executed minus the ball, or the uppercut that strikes no chin, or the condemned man's recoil from the firing squad's volley of blanks.' I have to be right about this. It's quite a step I'm contemplating."

He was going in circles, ever-decreasing ones at that, and I couldn't for the life of me face an Atlas who ended up disappearing into his own fundament. No, not *that!* Surely an ex-travel agent might help him. Guide his tour.

"All right," I said. "The weight's imaginary." One little twitch-fidget sideways would help him, buck him up.

"Got it," he cried. "I'll step out from under just as imaginarily, see, and not a scrap will fall. Done it. Now I'm back in position. Safe as houses. Were I really to do it, the universe'd only have itself to blame, wouldn't it? In fact, the universe's always its own fault, whereas I'm my own. Truth told, Atlas's doomed to be imaginative enough, although not very imaginative all told, to talk himself into staying put, thus sentencing himself to a penal infinity. *That's* the sentence: having to inflict my guesswork on myself, not having to uphold. The punishment's mental, not physical at all. Well, either I'll break free now or forever shelve the question. Do I count or don't I? Done. The next voice you will hear is—ur, why don't *you* say something? I'm in a proper funk up here."

I wanted to, but I couldn't; I felt more stuck than he at that juncture. Besides, something malign, maybe even satanic, was seeping through my system: deep down, I wanted him to stay put; being static is what had made him famous, whereas trotting around ad lib he'd be just another pedestrian. Fixed, he'd be talkable-with, available, footloose, just another picaro, with eons of delusive self-discipline to make up for. I'd found a garrulous, massive friend, and I didn't want to lose him. So I told him to keep calm, to stay put, shelve the whole dilemma, and I would do the same. I would stay put in Pekin, Illinois, and, indeed, so modify my life-style as to match his, and then we could mutually converse on the same footing, even-stephen and hunkydory. Let Atlas do as Atlas is, and Thor copy.

But I no sooner thought that than I began to withdraw from the consequences; understand, if you will, the embarrassments of being a vicarious voice: I hearing Atlas uttered him, but in no way managing to reproduce the intonations, nuances or even the tart symphonic thrust of the voice I heard. And now, thanks be Fortune, Atlas is coming out as words, and I'm in the near-fatuous position of transposing a voice-in-the-head, but spoken into the tape by myself, into yet another medium, of which not even my best friend, Etna, would call me master. What is indisputably missing is the electric thrill of his very presence, a kind of massive vibrancy that makes you feel you've been plugged, for the first time, into the source of things. So it was much more than a voice I communicated with, for me at any rate; it was the Atlas of that fourth-century B.C. vase painting, in which he appears as a light-limbed boxer holding up both arms in a victory salute, except that resting on his palms there is a lightweight-looking flying saucer, maybe of aluminum, while to his left there prances a magical horse near some bushes, to his right there stands somebody giving him the two-finger sign, to which Atlas attends by looking sideways and a bit downward. I know this is a feeble account of the picture, doing scant justice to his in-trim insouciance, but it will have to serve. After all, I didn't ask him to come to me; there are thousands he'd have fared better with, but perhaps my being a former world traveler who has settled down, prizing myself on my ability to stay put, had something to do with it. In common we have the static, not to mention an overview of the world, and a developed sense of being excluded: he from liberty (or even rest or leave), I from Peking.

Clearly, anyone determined to object will at once accuse me of imagining the whole thing; let him pass in peace and go on to read about the Decline and Fall of the Roman Empire. I faced that objection from the outset, knowing that from time to time I would catch myself half-supplying Atlas with Atlasisms; but then, a good listener always psychs and second-guesses, and even U.N. translators have been known to come up with prophetic renderings: three or four words of translation before the original is uttered. Such poachings or previsions are part of cranial voxology, take my word for it, just as I went on taking Atlas's own. When the Voice of the Ages (or whatever) deigns to favor you with some friendly gab, you don't make picayune cracks about the quality of reception, the speed or slowness of the transmission, the timbre of his vowels, and you certainly don't mind that occasionally you get lost in him, he in you, the pair of you in the maze of triply-transposed transcription. Man can always, if he weakens, go ape, whereas ape can never go man; I sometimes tell myself that when especially lamenting some gross piece of international mayhem. It soothes me somewhat; it's half-true; and it's five seconds killed. Just think how Atlas had to kill time, always at his station, never resting, always under the circumstances, never without an ache; no wonder he learned how to make the mind go blank.

Blank brought me back to the crisis at hand. Tempted to breach civility and counsel Atlas to shit or get off the pot, I ferreted around in my own head for some way of helping him either to adjust or to strike clear and away. Mentally ready to shift, he was too far gone for the physical part, meaning he could always imagine himself out of anything; stoical duty had groomed him too well. Was I right in encouraging him to stay where, and as, he was? Was that selfish? Not if I made a sacrifice or two myself. What Atlas needed wasn't an initiative, but company, and so long as his voice kept on coming I'd be more than glad to partner him. Therefore, keep it coming by the gift of company non-stop! Invite him in, not only into my head, but into my life. Have him, somehow, meet Frank Etna, landlord extraordinary; share in the stapling of the daily-longer sherry-sack cape; fill him in on food and the pleasures of the American bathroom. . . The only one elect, so far as I knew, I was elated; my eyes leaked driblets of joy, my hands quivered with fellow-feeling.

"Are you there?" I asked him. "Any things you want to know? That you don't already. Or things you want done?"

There ensued the kind of silence in which you imagine you can hear plants growing.

Heedless of plants, I asked again, prefixing the question with his call letters enlivened into Aardvark, Tabernacle, Labium, Aardvark, Sabbath. And that fetched him back.

Laughing (a sound of heavy chains being twirled in thick oil), he gave an answer I didn't expect: "Why has the Astronomer-Royal quit Greenwich, and its meridian, and moved to Sussex? Why didn't the English epicure stay put, like me? It's disorienting. And disoccidentalizing as well."

I said something about pollution, peace, urban overspill, heard an Atlas-snort followed by another question: "Haven't I seen gold-plated telescopes mounted in Lear jets?" He had indeed; I'd seen orb-torque, neutrino-nests, galaxy-starvation, antenna-warp, dust-ball pool, nova-fishing, sungunnery, nebul-ovens, mirror-zero, Mars-exemption, gamma-slang and quasar-cosmetics. As well as much more, a quick and humbling sample of the cosmic Sears and Roebuck catalogue.

All I could retaliate with was something else I'd heard on TV, something about the end of the universe: "After thirty thousand million years more," I brashly told him, "the whole thing will come to rest and then begin to contract. Whether the universe will then bounce back is anyone's guess. I won't be here to check the answers."

All I could hear was galactic buzz.

Told him so. Where was he?

Still only the buzz. What is it then?

"We call it interferon," he said haughtily. "Nothing to do with the terrestrial common cold, something—not that anyone in your vicinity'd understand it—to do with argon. You guys don't want to be facetious, else the powers-that-be'll lay three dozen second comings on you, all on Fridays, just to fox you. You'd better not smartmouth about the End of anything; we don't deal in ends, we deal in currencies, nothing to do with money either!"

Somehow Atlas was ruder, that was it; confidence gained had sapped his manners, and I was just going to object when I thought better of it. After all (and when I thought that phrase I really meant it: he *was* After All), who knows how many eons he'd spent trying to get through.

So I just said, "Sorry: never being in the know gets us on the raw.

We act up verbally when our minds draw blanks."

"You're wondering, I bet, why I'm so goddamned astronomical!"

True, I was.

"Occupational—ur, hazard, buddy-boy. Skip it. Maybe you can tell me the meaning of a phrase I caught the other year: 'World Premiere Encore.' If you ask me, that's contradictory."

I apologized for the golden tongues of Madison Avenue, drawing his attention to fool's gold, muck and brass, and the overall deterioration of the language, the disappearance of the verb, the plague of the abstract noun and the emasculated verb, the verb *to be*.

"By the way, Thor," I heard next, "there was no Big Bang. Had there been one, I'd have known. It's always been steady state up here, just the gods that reel now and then. Took me a mite of time to realize it, but I'm the main part of that steadiness. I never had a beginning, I always was, and all that shit about Pops and Grandad is just a concession to cosmic respectability. I'm an uncaused effect, no doubt the first of the tribe you've ever beat gums with."

Gulping "For sure, for sure," I asked him if he knew about—oh, a random sampling of our daily lives down here—passports, cucumbers, waste disposals, penicillin, fiber-point pens, hi-fi equipment, air conditioning, mouthwash, scotch tape, scissors, DDT and Neapolitan ice cream. He knew the lot, seemed vaguely bored with it, and delivered me a counterquota of Atlas-tropes, none of which I understood.

A change of tack was imperative—it was no use slanging each other with our respective systems—to quiz him about such of his past as hadn't made the primers in myth. "Did you ever get to college? If you have them there?"

"Pro, he spent three light-years at Panbridge, and Epi about the same time—amount of time—at Luxford. But me, I was a dropout, took some evening classes in weightlifting at the Vulcan Institute, but I found even that a bore. I guess I was only anticipating my vocation. Fact is, there was nothing lying around heavy enough for me to practice on, so it's just as well there was a universe handy. Else I'd have been out of commission for keeps. Just imagine what it's like being eternal when there's not a thing you can do."

Quick as a fisherman setting the hook, I asked him, "If that's so, why all the fuss about suicide? No such thing for you. Why, you could walk out from under, and even if it all came tumbling down, you'd be OK. Although where you'd be, I've no idea."

His life, he told me, was his occupation, his worst fear being choreless.

"I prefer world-sadness, world-weariness," he added, "to being unemployed. But it's not all been depressing. Back in the '30s I think it was, my daughter Maia, best known as the mother of Mercury, talked up such a storm in the ether that a team of airplane designers actually designed and built a mother flying-boat called after her, with a smaller but four-engined second flying-boat atop her on a mount, and that was Mercury. Eight engines between them! I dearly loved to watch them lift off the old briny, not so much wine-dark as beer-bright, and then Mercury would lift off from the mother ship at about five thousand feet. And then they played tag all over the airways, Mercury feinting at her hull as if trying to suck on her babylike, and Maia lumbering about a bit being so broad in the beam. He zipped and flitted, she droned and mumbled; he caught more of the light than she, his wings like blades, while she, with much broader wings, seemed like some giant manta-ray cruising ever below him in case he fell."

Did I detect a throb in that rusty voice? I did indeed.

"Proud of your grandson, Atlas?"

"Maia, one of the seven Pleiades, you know, she was the smartest of them all, got herself written up in the glossies as Maia Majestas, Fauna, Bona Dea, Ops, the whole bit. I guess she'd rate as the Madonna of unfolded space. Mercury, though, he'd the smarts beyond compare; it figures, I guess, if you're Maia to begin with and old Zeusy-Boy slips you a foaming schlong's-length, ur—it figures you'd get a prodigy of some kind out of that. He once stole, and hid in a cave, fifty head of cattle; yep, Hermes, as I sometimes call him—Herm or Merc—was one of the first cattle rustlers in prehistory! As they always say about him, born in the a.m., he's invented the lyre by noon. That's the kind of speed he flew at. Sure, he was a big show-off even as a kid, but who wants a dumbbell for a grandson? Merc was some boy, fast as light, slippery-tongued, impossible to best in an argument; spent a good deal of his time operating as a Western Union galactogram-bearer, though he did hundreds of other things as well—a kind of winged cartel. I sometimes thought he'd taken on too much—agronomy, rhetoric, business management, heraldry, boxing, languages, astronomy, communications and even funeral-parlor practice, you name it, he did a bit of it, sometimes even a lot. What really poisoned him was the cult they made of him on your own planet, casing up little blobs of him in glass bulbs to tell the temperature by. He liked the functional part, but hated the cooped-up feeling the mercury transmitted back to him. But, boy, when he flew, like a tiny fast moon round his Ma, there was red-shift to beat all, and for days after there was background rainbow fit to beat the band. Where those seaplanes went to, we never found out; maybe mothballed someplace. I guess it was one hell of an impractical idea, having one on the other's back like that, dolphin on the whale, and the fuel consumption was out of sight. But it kind of made the family loom a bit larger than usual in the suburbs, see? Instead of being so shadowy (see the pesky ikons they made of me!), we seemed to be substantially there right in front of folks' eyes, like architecture, except it moved, and when it moved it took off and flew, and when it flew it split in half and when it'd split in half it stole parabolas from the spherical geometry of Zeus himself! But they always had to touch down separately, of course, which kind of spoiled the action. I always wished they'd been able somehow to link up again in flight, but I guess that was asking too much. Say, maybe, someday, you could find out for me about that double-decker airplane, where it's at now, what decided them to junk it. Just the sound of those engines blasting for the Off'd remove tons from the load on the top of my head. Try?"

Try? I promised I'd *succeed,* certain I could dig up something somewhere in the campus library. But why, I mused, didn't he know? Maybe part of his punishment was to feel informed without having the facts. Maybe he knew, after all, but no longer realized that he knew; a fact unused is one of knowledge's pariahs. It was no use wondering, Atlas was already into other things, still joyfully commemorating Maia, but more intimate in tone.

"Once in a while, she'd zoom up behind me and give me a neck-rub, working all the way from below my shoulder blades up to the base of my skull, kneading and smoothing until the blood began to run again. You've never *ported,* have you? But you sure know what it's like to have a stiff neck, when the cords feel like leather-bound drill sticks. But that wasn't all, no sir! Round front, with daughterly delicacy, she'd nuzzle the bridge of my nose, tweak it and pinch it and sometimes put the balls of her thumbs against the top of the eyesockets. Talk about relief! You know the kind of ache that builds up around there. And, on special days, she'd even nip the flesh between my eyes with her teeth—I must be the only guy in creation with hickeys in that particular spot. A great one for kissing, she was, my Maia: not just the routine stuff, glancing little smooches on the side of my mouth and the tip of my nose, that goes without saying, but when the mood took her she'd pretend I'd (as she'd say) fifteen thousand secret ears, visible to her alone, and she'd go about kissing each of them in turn. Of course, she didn't, but that was our fancy. Who was I to protest or be literal? It was the only attention I ever got, therefore the best. To cool me off, she'd blow against my closed eyes—you can't imagine the glare I have to put up with, this near umpteen suns—and then she'd just set her head against the side of my neck and stay that way for long hours, murmuring and cooing. A cool, velvet skin she had, like a tegument made of milk. 'Scuse the fancy way of putting it, there're times I get downright sentimental about the way things were. She'd even, once a month, clean my back; I mean squeeze out the black holes, clean out the pores. It was mostly accumulated cosmic dust, I guess. Time was I never knew where my back ended and space began, so I guess it's no miracle I was pitted with tiny craters where shrunken stars of almost incalculable gravity stuck and stayed put, all the time getting smaller and heavier, black to the point of invisibility. It's not everyone who'd take on such chores, but Maia did—at least until she had Mercury. He kept her busy from the first, conned her into being less flighty, I guess. He even persuaded her to stop one habit she had; instead of wearing false eyelashes for a social occasion—a state visit by Zeus, all tuxedo and talc—she used to fasten a couple of hummingbirds to her eyelids, and that gave her eyes an incredible hypnotic flutter. Yes sir, those were the old days! Been none like 'em since." There is a slight sob in his voice; I try to cheer him, cannot; he sighs with enormous resonance.

Then says "The past tense, see."

"How was that?"

Atlas sounds like he's cracking up. "She even used to burp me; all I ever got to sustain me was crab-nebula meat, always too hot, always gritty. No, I didn't mean that. You know about my daughters, don't you?" Without waiting for my response he blurted it right out: "The Pleiades: the seven-set. Maia was one of them, see. For some reason they were all born on a mountainside, which made 'em sometimes walk the wee-est bit gimpy. See, I can't bring myself to say it. Well: they all killed themselves, all committed suicide. To a one. Alcyone, Celaeno, Electra, Taygete, Sterope, Aero (a special one that) and even my own Maia. For why? Because the plight of their Dad upset them so. That's all. They couldn't take it eon after eon of seeing him stuck there with his back stiff as a ramrod, forever on cosmic parade, head held high, the whole caboodle on his back. With no hope of remission, no sabbatical. I've heard other versions: it was the death of their sisters, the Hyades, that broke their hearts, or it was Orion's fault, forever propositioning them, until old fussy Zeus, he said 'Enough of this bull, I'll turn them all into stars, Orion as well.' I don't much go for those two particular explanations. But the long and the short of it is all seven of them are stars, and the only converse a tired old titan can have with them is in mid-May, when they signal the approach of harvest-time by rising—out there in Taurus, in the northern hemisphere—and then again, in October, when they set, and that's the time to sow. To some, I gather, they signal the opening and closing of the sailing season, but who cares? What grieves me, among other things, is that one of them, Aero (sometimes Merope to the gossip columnists), isn't even visible. Got herself into a bad marriage with a slippery customer called Sisyphus, and then he got himself a life sentence rolling a block of stone uphill. No doubt you've heard of him: another of Zeus's punitive measures. Do you wonder she can't bear to show her face? Her Dad and husband both, penal servitude for life. It's enough to make a statue weep. Up here, among all the jamming, I hear radio of all kinds, much of it highfalutin chatter about totalitarianism, so-called. Let me tell you, Thor, old buddy, they invented that condition for Atlas (and a few more, such as Sisyphus, whom I call Cissy-fuss). Nobody knows what being a prisoner's like until he's had a dose of being Atlas fifty or a hundred years, with not even a chance of your good conduct's being taken into account. And then your daughters kill themselves off, they can't stand it. How do you like them apples? Just about as far as you can get from golden ones. I'd give a hell of a lot for just one glimpse of Aero's face, those wide and liquid-gray, quicksilver eyes, the neat light brown widow's peak she had, the nose that wasn't snub and wasn't schnozz either. The rest of the world, if it thinks about them at all, reckons them seven (or six) doves; Pleiades sounds like the Greek for dove, see. But I don't much go for that, I remember them as they were: daughters of the Ocean-nymph Pleione, long gone. Sure I had favorites; I know you shouldn't, if you believe all the bullshit the pediatricians hand you, but I did. That's that. I still do. But it's been mighty quiet up here since their conversion, so-called. Hey, you ever tried, between May and October, to pick out seven (or six) particular stars from the hundreds of 'em in Taurus? It's damn nearly impossible. I know the girls are there, but I'm never certain which is which, or even if I haven't looked at the wrong seven. Sure it hurts; another of Zeus's power-ploys. You'd do well to watch out yourself, parleying with the likes of me. He's not one to take things lying down. Anyhow, as I was saying, I stand here and try to cheer myself up with little reminiscences; Pleiades, I say, they're an open cluster of stars, and the luminescent spikes I see attached to them aren't even there, they're diffraction effects in the eye of the beholder, some cloudy spot on the cornea, otherwise known as nebula. That kind of constellation's like drinking nitric acid. As stars go, they're young, those Pleiades, whereas those Hyades. . ."

The voice dwindled to a chaffering of airwaves, a sound of light flails, either black-body background radiation or merely Atlas groaning in the hoosegow of his mind. I tried to prompt him back to the Hyades, those other daughters, of whom he'd had nothing to say, only he held off, finally broke into some practiced-sounding patter about pleiotropisms and asterisms, about being not only behind the times but also ahead of them, under and above them: a bout of intergalactic self-pity, as he himself called it. Then, by gradual allusion, he returned to the business of the daughters, his voice creaky with loss, I could tell that, and his idiom oddly impersonal, for reasons that seemed obvious. "Know what? I don't even recall the names of the Hyades, I'm not even sure if there were two, or five, or six. Everything about them's mighty vague. Half-sisters of the others. Nurses they were, that's one fact. Also in Taurus, but much older than Maia's bunch. Aethra was their mother. Named, all of them, after the Greek for *rain*. Rain stars, that's what they are, but the goddamned Romans got it wrong and, because the Greek word sounded like their word for pig, called them the little pigs. This little pig went to market, this little pig stayed home: well, it's not known what they did as little pigs. As nurses, they breastfed the infant Dionysus and as a reward were made into stars. Couldn't get my attention any other way, I guess. I suppose I now and then catch sight of them up there in Taurus when I'm looking for the other seven. Being older, the Hyades I mean, they've already achieved white dwarf status, pretty shrunken by now, some of them already black dwarfs I wouldn't doubt and maybe even invisible at that. *You* know how it goes: as they cool down, they radiate less and less, and then, when they're cold and dead, they have colossal density, millions of times that of water, say. They're actually smaller than planet Earth, but their mass is like that of the Sun. Takes billions of years to get 'em to that point, of course, but get there they have gotten. They're kind of just memories, I guess, maybe not even that. Whereas Maia and Aero, well. . ." Again silence found him and lost him, as it sometimes did Frank Etna, my almost-forgotten friend, on his return from yet another raid on the world's wonders: exuberantly recalling how it was to have gone lundyfishing in Iceland, catching birds on a cliff with a net, or playing aqualung cowboy with the tunny deep off Gibraltar, he'd suddenly seize up, look into the middle distance and wordlessly relive it, incredulous that the human who went away and did those things could now be here trying to tell it. And then he'd pick up again, like Atlas, invigorated by the time-out. When would he be back? I'd completely forgotten. Was he in New Zealand or Fiji? Only time would tell, via him.

Atlas was heartier now, funk-free, and regaling me with talk of Mercury who sometimes doubled, stood in, for the evening star, always kept his face toward you, and wobbled a bit like Dr. Johnson. In recent times he'd developed some curious discolorations down one side, a kind of planet-impetigo, weepy and a-tingle. Maybe a new mode of growth, Atlas suggested: the effect of the sun's getting gradually hotter and bigger. Or maybe some parasitism, where panspermia had touched him. All that was certain was that one day, in say about eight billion years ("How'd you like that to be the unserved portion of your sentence?" Atlas asked with grim jocosity), the Sun would become a red giant, engulf both Mercury and Venus, and its surfce would approach the orbit of Earth. "Then it'll all be over," laughed Atlas. "You'll have fried long before that!" No doubt to hearten himself during these morbid sallies, he chanted a little tune, the words of which ran thus:

"He-he, h-h, H Ca, Mg Ca, Feca." What it meant, I have no idea, and he refused to tell; but the last word sounded oddly like *fecal,* though I'm sure it wasn't that at all. The second sound was merely a double aspirate, which he carried over to the third, and the effect of hearing my own voice reiterate this from the cassette was weird and sinister. *Hemgcfca,* I fast-thought: maybe it's Lincos, the language for interstellar communication invented by the Dutch mathematician Hans Freudenthal (sometimes my TV-viewing pays off in extraordinary ways). Asked, Atlas pooh-poohed the notion, wouldn't tell ("You'd never understand," he said), and, instead, swung off into what I can only describe as a virtuoso piece, airing not so much his knowledge as, mirrorwise, my own ignorance (TV or no!). "Take T Tauri stars, for example. Photographed in red light, they can be caught actually ionizing the gas in their vicinity, thus creating what shows up, believe it or not, as a silver lining. Beautiful! As for panspermia, which we were discussing only a moment ago, if the Earth had been seeded some billions of years ago, the initial germ must've been ejaculated from a star not more than six thousand light years away. If that doesn't make you think, nothing will." Then he rambled off into something about "hydrogen spin-flip" and being slapped in the face when very young for miscounting the petals on a flower. Whence, no doubt, his hositility to education. Or to its process, at least. For long spells, he claimed, he'd had no fun at all, so he'd wept for joy in 1054, on the Fourth of July in fact, when a Class I supernova in Taurus exploded, astonishing the Japanese and the Chinese although apparently not the Europeans. A star which had previously been quiet and well-behaved burned so bright that it was visible even in the daytime. "Debris now known," he said complacently, "as the Crab Nebula, expanding at six hundred and eighty miles per second!" Solar flares he'd kind of gotten accustomed to, of course, but 1898 hadn't been too bad, that being the year of Asteroid Eros, fifteen miles long and five wide, the first asteroid to pass inside Earth's orbit. Then, in 1957, Comet Mrkos had cheered him up no end, with its solar windsock tail. "It's like," he explained "seeing an occasional bit of baseball, huh? After the Greeks there were only the Romans, and after them there was no more mythology. Things kind of slowed down, like the universe one day will. Ha, I recall the scheme labeled Project Ozma, supposed to detect interstellar radio signals of intelligent origin, if any! Well, they laid the 27-meter Green Bank antenna on two stars, Epsilon Eridani and Tau Ceti, in 1960, Fall through Christmas, I believe, and got nothing at all. 'Eleven years ago, on those two stars,' each being about eleven light years distant, the project-director told the American Astronomical Society, 'it was pretty dull.' Well, Thor, my friend, it's been pretty dull here too since the beginning, since the Bang, El Grando Detonation! Yes sir, quiet to beat the band."

"I thought you said earlier," I heard myself objecting, "you believed in the Steady State theory."

"I believe in both," Atlas said, not without malice. "When I want to window-dress my own performance, I'm a Steady man; when I feel neurotic, I'm Bang. Simple, huh?"

Quite irresponsibly, at that point I cried for help. "Atlas, that isn't being fair. Don't you think I've heard about the universe's being made up of billions of galaxies systematically receding from one another like raisins in an expanding pudding? Isn't that so?" Told to eat my own pudding and like it (the alternative being, he said, an endless journey into and out of a Klein Bottle, which has neither inside nor outside), I decided to try to shift him back to family matters; but he wouldn't touch them, said instead what I wrote down as: "Wons Wiki One."

"Hey," I blurted. "You're going too fast. Give me time to get things down."

"I thought you were just parroting them onto tape."

I told him there were one or two things I wrote down, either to keep my hands busy or, more probably, because I concentrated better when doodling, etc. He spelled it out. "You got it wrong, Thor. Sometimes I can receive visual signals. It's 1 Zwicky 1, the brightest object known. OK?"

I don't know about OK, but writing it down again, during the perfunctory lull of transcription, I know I've got it right this time. Or was he, as sometimes, joking, being titanically snide? Had he, or had he not, somewhere in all this, when he was unduly piqued with my slowness or my denseness, told me "Piss off"? And had I said "The same to you! *No,* please don't!" Something of the kind must have taken place (though it isn't in the tape), for I distinctly recall his saying, "If I do, it'll be into the world's largest radio dish, the Arecibo radiotelescope of Cornell University, in Puerto Rico, three hundred meters across. Some John that!" (Or have I imagined this, in white heat of vicarious fervor? As if driving at speed towards another car on a night highway, cussing the other man's brights, when all the time it's a mirror some prankster has erected in the road. Do I in discovering Atlas uncover myself? It was little use asking *him,* I'd have only confused the issue further, as if saying to myself: Does the act of asking yourself who you are make you a preciser being than you were before? Balderdash; time I got back to the old drawing board.)

"I know," I resumed, "I know that Atlas is as Atlas does. And Thor copies. That's understood. But in airing your knowledge of such things as 1 Zwicky 1, aren't you just a bit overdoing it? I don't, do I, need to know everything?"

"Nothing less than all will serve. That's what Zeus told me

when they fingerprinted me, unchained me, and led me out to meet the world. At the first hold-up." Atlas being oblique, I guess. All I could do was counter with something else: an Atlas-flaw, it might be read as.

"The Hesperides," I sprang it on him. "Those other daughters. Why so little about them, when you go on about even the Hyades, whom you confess you can't even remember by name?"

"What you want, boy? Want me to name 'em? Aegle, Arethusa, Eryth—"

"No: that's too mechanical. Just mention them, I mean."

One of those Atlas lulls ensued, no doubt while he *thunk* it over. I heard the hiss of space, began imagining a solar corona that crackled and broke the non-silence. It was ocher-yellow, gibbous, gigant—

"Daughters of Night," he rapped out, then went into a gabble. "According to later accounts, daughters of Atlas. Hm. Four all told. Erytheia and Hesperia the other two. They lived, live, on the River Oceanus, old H_2O's territory, close to the Gorgons. On the borders of eternal darkness. In the garden of the gods. Along with a hundred-headed dragon called Ladon. 'S that enough?"

Nowhere near, I told him; his very idiom spelled neglect.

Told to micturate in the opposite direction to on, I simply pursued my point: Why so skimpy about these four?

"Frankly," he said with an ostentatious groan, "I associate them with Hercules and that whole golden-apple fiasco. To me, they're not girls, women, you-know-what, they're—I was going to say Golden Apples, but they're not even that. They're hesperidiums, hesperidia, meaning *berries,* with a thickened, leathery rind, and juicy pulp divided into segments, like an orange is, a lemon. They're right out of botany. Fruits, not daughters. And when they talk they emit not words but hesperidin, a white or colorless crystalline compound, dig? $C_{28}H_{34}O_{15}$. Life is sometimes like that. You can't get any more emotional than that about it. Fuck the notion of their standing guard over the gilded orchard. I went and got the apples for Hercules, rot him, and since that time the word apple's put my teeth on edge. I can't stand fruit, OK?"

Plain as day, an Atlantean hang-up! Hercules fooled him about the apples, and he's never got over it. It makes sense to write off the Hesperides as fruit, which he can't abide. All the same, he goes on talking: "After that mess, I got Maia to fly in circles, dropping leaflets to plead my case—'Atlas Was Robbed,' 'Demand Justice

For Atlas,' 'Restore the Golden Apples To the Garden,' all kinds of propaganda. But no one took the slightest notice, just used the leaflets to wipe their backsides with. You see, Hercules rated as Errol Flynn, Clint Eastwood: you name the He-man, he was it. It was no more use blowing the whistle on him on denouncing Jesus Christ as a nail-freak. Greeks, you see, were in the habit of being prepossessed by anything splendid; and, what with the whole universe, and their own myths, to go at, they rarely lacked for splendiferous voluptuary goings-on. Of the dull mechanics, such as I, who held the whole goddamned thing up, they knew next to nothing. Didn't give a shit. That's why I can't bear to think in Hesperidean any more. It hurts. That's where my whole life and career went wrong. I stepped back in where I should've walked away, leaving Herc holding the baby."

Gently I reminded him the obligation—his life-sentence, the chance of suicide—might be illusory. Step out from under, I told him. And see. Risk it. Stop the world and get off. Same answer as before: in his mind, he had, which is the only way to test something illusory.

"Test an illusion with an illusion," I exclaimed. "That's how you get an illusory answer!"

Believe me or not, I felt as if he were trying to cool me with liquid helium, a dire chill invading my marrow. So, as an equivalent to whistling in the dark, I piped up (although rather hoarse and indistinct) as follows: "Don't bother, Atlas. I'm home free. They say you can dip your hands in hot lead if you've soaped them first!" Not so much as a squeak came from him. Under the eye of eternity (if not that, what?), he was all of a sudden on best behavior. Or maybe he had just departed, same way as he came. I should not have expressed impatience with him; clearly he had been through too much to think rationally about resignation or straightforwardly walking off the premises. I nervously switched off, just as nervously switched on again, heard the thin, high-pitched emission of a galaxy in distress; falsetto yearning to be whole again. *Atlas?* Sounding so frail, so pressured? None other. At that juncture, Thor began to regret many things, to devise ways of obliging Atlas all over again. Think hard, Thor.

Were none such.

Would play for him even that cluster of galaxies known in the trade as Stefan's Quintet.

Shine upon him a light brighter than 1 Zwicky 1's.

Bribe him with stardust home-bottled (*mis en bouteilles dans nos caves*).

Be a much more modern man than I am, world-traveler that I used to be; spare him the fireball when it comes, though none else.

Yield him my drysack cape, to save his back from spicules which, geyserlike columns five hundred miles wide, shoot out at twenty miles per second from the lower chromosphere, ramming protons into the corona and thus creating the solar wind. How know? I do declare Atlas's masterminding my belated education.

"That all?" he whispered. "A poor all."

But mine own, I was going to say, yet said "Wait. There's more. I'll stamp out the apple."

"Promising."

I *was* promising, not just showing promise. Furthermore, I told him, I'd have him installed in Golden Gate Park (sorry, Silver Gate Park, they'd have to repaint the bridge a different color next time round), as The Man With the Portable Universe. Roll up, and see. Hidden behind the fortification strata of all the migraine sufferers in the world.

He made an encouraged, encouraging, noise.

"And," I said with a flourish, "you'd have your choice of which decade to live in. Whichever suited you best."

What he came up with next, only Atlas would have—well, he pipe-dreamed in reverse. "Know what I'd really have liked, Thor, old partner? One weekend conversing with the Presidents, Past, of Mount Rushmore. Like on the old six-cent postcard of your nation. Atlas being the fifth head. Over six thousand feet above sea level, buddying up with those other monoliths, Washington, Jefferson, Lincoln and Roosevelt. We'd converse on the universe, putting our sixty-foot heads together. You know how Washington looks away, in a kind of aloof autonomy, and Jefferson gazes over Washington's shoulder with his eyes right, and Lincoln seems to be looking past them both, down into the bedrock of South Dakota, and Roosevelt's scrunched in between the last two like a neckless weightlifter? Well, I'd fit into that quartet, I'd reckon. I'd look right at the beholder, like the eyes in some photographs, and folks could stare back at me and try to read my mind. My jaw'd jut and there'd be rattlers' nests in my nostrils, eagles in my ears, and a spring pouring out of my mouth. I'd be much bigger than the Giza Sphinx, but unlike Roosevelt I'd have been completed, just a-setting there and exchanging a few solid, inert words with the boys.

Ur, hurrumph, Linc. . .

"'Yeah, Atl. For sure.'

"'Hi there, Big Boy.'

"'Marnin', Jarge. Chaw baccy?'

"'Try me.' Teddy.

"'Fine day but dull so far,' says Jeff, the long-winded one. Then there's nothing more said for several hours."

"You'd do better," I tell him, determined to awe him with know-how, "to 'labor to keep alive in your breast that little spark of celestial fire—conscience.' That's what it said in Washington's copybook when he was a schoolboy. I suppose you could even arrange to have some movie or other located on your shoulder or your head. In Hitchcock's *North By Northwest* didn't Eva Marie Saint take dinner on Lee's shoulder? Or something like that."

Heavy-voiced, he answers, "Up here in the provinces, we get movies about two thousand light years late. I wouldn't know, honest. Swelp me, if those boys didn't have it easy! Nothing to hold up, in fact the strata support them. All they have to do all day is be themselves, keep still and act normal. Just be looked at. Photographed. Just *weigh.* Why, even the Statue of Liberty, even though she's just gotten rid of the shackles at her feet, has to hold up a burning torch and a book of laws. I wonder what it feels like to be made of hammered copper, have all that verdigris on you, stand on a star-shaped wall, be a tourist attraction.

"'A mighty woman with a torch, whose flame
Is the imprisoned lightning, and her name
Mother of Exiles. From her beacon-hand
Glows world-wide welcome; her mild eyes command. . .'

Boy, does she need to watch out, or at least her PR woman, Emma Lazarus! There's nothing imprisoned about lightning, take it from me. One solar prominence'd be the death of her. But the poem's great, kind of soothing and even-footed; I'd just, myself, want no truck with all those tired and poor and huddled masses, all the wretched refuse. Atlas, he wants well-integrated and well-heeled sponsors. After an eternity in limbo, you need something with a bit of class, none of this downtrodden rabble. Speaking as the Old Colossus, I don't think much of the New."

Well, I'll be—he sounds like a Republican!

"Up the *polis!*" he shouts. "A *polis* of one."

For a moment there, I thought he was shouting for the police, whose I know not; and then I thought of calling for them myself.

But a voice, even a voice you're echoing, can't get out of hand, it's your own mind goes awry, the voice simply follows suit. Kin-voiced, Atlas and I are far from being kin-minded: I become a boy again, go fishing for minnows in the Pekin creek; he goes fishing for neutrinos in a trap filled with cleaning fluid and located in the Homestake Goldmine in the town of Lead, South Dakota. It figures: he thinks the mine is underneath the men of Mount Rushmore; he wants his statue filled with tetrachloroethylene. Bah!

But (you know how an idea takes root, trunks up, is soon a crowning forest fire!), even as he thundered, pummeled on, his voice gaining in authority from moment to moment, I mind-staged him in that grandiose company, as I think a loyal American might. I gave Atlas to them and I had them tell him—well, not so much the best thing to tell Atlas, but rather what conveniently came into mind, beginning with a repetition of Washington's *Labor to keep alive,* et cetera, but moving swiftly to other eminent voluntaries, which I had Atlas answer.

Jefferson, with eyes oh-so-distantly focused, his face suffused with boyish altruism, spelling out something Atlas might bear in mind: "A lively and lasting sense of filial duty is more effectually impressed on the mind of a son or daughter by reading *King Lear,* than by all the dry volumes of ethics, and divinity, that ever were written." To which Atlas, less amazed than bearishly contemptuous, huffed:

"Best he try a decade or two of humping the flaming firmament on his back. Fuck filial duty period."

More cunning, therefore, I decided, to try him with Lincoln, with honest and unpretentious words out of a mouth so wide and generous-lipped, so essentially accustomed to uttering the good, that Atlas'd cave in at their very sound. Fond fancy that I had! "Nobody has ever expected me to be President. In my poor, lean, lank face nobody has ever seen that any cabbages were sprouting out." After a brief, stertorous silence, Atlas let us (Lincoln and me) have it straight between the eyes. "He'd have done better to lard his face from time to time with manure, then he'd have found at least a Brussel sprout or two."

Two down, two to play.

No, three, I was committing the unpardonable sin of forgetting George Washington. Theodore Roosevelt brought things full circle. "Death," he said weightily, "is always and under all circumstances a tragedy, for if it is not, then it means that life itself has become one." Neat paradox, that, I thought: for sure that'll bring him up short. Didn't, though; Atlas retorted offhandedly as possible: "Another lightweight sparring bout with one of the old dichotomies! We invented 'em! Up here, we no more talk of death than members of the Senate compete to clean out the city sewers with their bare hands. It don't apply, Thor, my lad. Next?"

But there was no next: imagining myself imagine him to his face, even while he was tromboning on about Samson and the Olympic weightlifting championship, that was too much nervous agitation *in vacuo*. Imaginarily I let him go, only to have him slap right back at me with sneering remarks about the George Washington Bridge, Lincoln Center, Mount Jefferson and Roosevelt Raceway: his old war cry against the naming of things, pressed wine of his own bizarre fusion of sour grapes with invaded privacy. I really must get him, I vowed, to sort out his feeling on that; he hasn't fared *that* badly; after all, an ICBM is an ICBM, and not in truth a bowel motion only, and an Atlas Range is an Atlas Range, an atlas is an atlas. . . Truth was, of course, he was by this time no more obligated to be consistent or logical than to auction off his calluses for souvenirs. Instead he handed me (I'm being metaphorical, of course; he voice-handed) this:

☛ **A HAND BILL** ☚

Just Arrived: In the Ship Ligonier, Capt. Zeus, from the River Gambia, in Africa, and to be sold by the Subscribers, in Annapolis, for Cash, or good Bills of Exchange, on Wednesday the 7th of October next, A Cargo of CHOICE HEALTHY SLAVES. The said ship will take TOBACCO to London, on Liberty, at 61. sterling per Ton.

"There," he said percussively, "that's your Independent U.S. Tradition. I wouldn't touch it with a mile-long beta-ray-contaminated radar antenna. I know what I'm talking about too; that was exactly how I was treated: pressed into service along with, so to speak, cheeses, cider, sailcloth, Bristol beer and window-glass. One of the amenities."

Marveling I hadn't countered with this before, I asked him in a proverbial flash, "By the way, who held things up before you did?"

"Zeus, between his teeth, like a circus act."

That was no answer at all, but slapstick quasi-theological evasion. I asked again.

"Ur," said Atlas. "Things held themselves up. Things were self-sustaining till then. Soon as they found a victim, somebody to fix but good, they cooked up a gravitational universe so's I'd have something lousy to do."

No, I told myself, nobody knew, nobody knows; Atlas's only an alibi for Zeus, etc. Stands to sense, he didn't exist before because their cosmology hadn't gotten off the ground. So to speak. That's how it always begins. They fudge up the stories to flesh out the guesswork mechanics of it all. Atlas's no more than a figment, dreamed up in order to dream himself into non-stop penal servitude. Why, he's being made to blackmail himself with a communal dream. Invented, he can invent himself out.

I told him, got nowhere, invoking all the dualities I'd ever heard of, just to make him release his teeth from the old dichotomy of Zeus-Man: dilemma, mirror, carbon-copy, black-white, pro-con, Doppelgänger, double, twin, either-or, and had even embarked on the threes (triads, triptychs, syllogisms, Hell-Purgatory-Paradise, the famous crucifixion) when he let out the most appalling shriek I've heard on sea or land, in ether or out, and in a reflex motion I flipped off the machine, which of course didn't stop him at all, but only prevented me from mimicking him into the tape. It was a noise of slow, inventive disembowelment, seeming to echo wetly in the cavern of his body cavity, and then to erupt from his mouth (or his mind's mouth, anyway) in an ill-enunciated cry:

"Close. . .double. . .star. Binary, all the way."

"Never," I said, first switching the cassette back on. "The whole show is single. Has nothing to do with you at all."

But he persisted, claiming some double stars had one partner invisible (Zeus, clearly) while the other shone for both. This I knew, but I protested his analogy.

"All it boils down to, my friend, is: Atlas's redundant. If you'll pardon an analogy of my own — Man isn't essential to the universe, he's merely incidental, a daub, a sport consequent on some roll of the cosmic dice. Wipe him out and the galaxies won't even blink. The quasars'll go on receding at, what is it, three-fourths the speed of light, the white dwarfs'll go on cooling, the basic temperature of space'll not alter one jot. Three degrees Kelvin, or whatever, it's nothing — "

A roar, then a wheedling, pleading noise, and all of a sudden I construed better than I had in that entire decade: I realized that Atlas was nothing more than a writ-large version of all the human bids for importance there had ever been. King-sized hubris was his game, on behalf of all of us. Loitering around in the back alleys of myth and rumor, he battens on to any willing gullible, lets him have the whole trumped-up mouthful, and the sucker goes away wondering, quite heedless of its being rotation that keeps things in place, even more heedless of its being gravity that holds things up! What he ought to remember is this: if you collect up all the stellar and interstellar matter you are certain exists in the universe and spread it evenly against a sphere of radius ten billion light years, then there isn't enough stuff to balance the centrifugal speed. Hence your open universe, incessantly self-inflating balloon which cannot burst. On the other hand (and no sounds of fidgeting from Atlas now, he's either passed out or switched on his own tape recorder!), you have, say, several tens more times of intergalactic stuff than's at present known about, then the universe is denser, and being denser exerts a gravitational self-attraction strong enough to resist the tug to the periphery. Hence your pulsating universe. Phew! Either way, unless he eats or makes the cosmic stuff, it's out of Atlas's hands. It might even be better to miniaturize him, site him under a table that he can't quite touch with his fingertips, and treat him as courts once treated their jesters and fools.

Give us a cosmic fright, Atlas! A galactic shiver?

To heel, boy. Good Atlas, lie down.

(That sort of thing, for a beginning, my whole aim being to render the universe aright as what it is: elements, equations, a motley posse of uncoordinated explosions, hottings-up and coolings-down; nothing with a personality, a temperament, a human face, but the abstraction of all abstractions made flesh only so as, some of it, to be visible. With my mind running thus boldly, ramming itself upon the horns of the universe, refusing to be sentimental about anything, I minimally embarked on what I can only think of now as a course of disaster. It is one thing to refuse to delude yourself; it is another to push that refusal to the point of an obstinate madness, rather like Tolstoy's Pierre in reverse, bending every effort not to avoid "that dreadful *it*" but going all out to locate it and apprentice oneself to it. It is to such mentalities that an Atlas speaks, and it is to an Atlas that an oddball such as Jan Thor finally addresses himself (yourself excepted, of course).

Look, I told myself: for once and always convince Atlas of his redundancy, point out to him that the universe, being the only member of an elite of one, never needed Prometheus, Faust, Frankenstein;

they, and their like, constitute the human obbligato, no more than that, are merely graffiti, accompaniment, feints. Lunatic as it may seem, when I look back on it, I began to usurp Atlas's role; after all he had fallen silent, no doubt in a sulk or a titanic tantrum, and the field was open. All I had to do was assume his stance, his office, and then move out. The universe would stay put; Atlas would recognize his essential freedom, his expendableness; and I, Jan Thor, would have exercised in the most renewing way the eidetic privilege of homo sapiens. Ridiculous? Now yes, but not at the time. I have come a long way since that episode, but by no means as far as the universe has gone, expanding away from me at impersonal and inexplicable speed.

First of all, I made some phone calls to prepare the basement. I needed several tons of soft sand and a ton of cement, but I settled for a ton of the former, a couple of sacks of the latter. Thinking (as I thought) with sublime straightness, I had a couple of janitors mix up the mortar early one evening, they as you might imagine casting baffled looks as they worked.

"This here basement floor looks A-1 to me," said one. "Why'd you want a new one?"

Taking care of the future, I told him, but clearly he did not regard that as an explanation.

"Two feet deep?" queried the other. "You want it two feet deep? Why that deep?"

And his partner echoed the question.

I just urged them to work as fast as possible while I went upstairs to receive other parts of my equipment at the door. The timing seemed exemplary; by midnight I would be ready and the demonstration could begin. To abbreviate (as I suspect you'd like), I'll say only that several hours later, with all the extension cables in place and a little wooden platform rigged up for me to walk on above the wet concrete, I looked upon my arrangement and found it good. Barrels, hosepipe, tape recorder were all in place. It was time, or rather, since there was nothing more to be done, there was no reason for not going ahead. Imagine, then, the scene, as with twelve color televisions blaring out and flashing lovely assorted pageantry in one massed bank before my eyes, I mounted the plank platform, flicked on the recorder, drew the drysack robe about me (by now it was thirty feet long), set the hose in my mouth, prized away with my tongue and swallowed the plug of chewing gum and allowed the sherry from the barrel to feed into my mouth.

Swallowing at an even pace, I stepped off the plank and settled down in the cement, oh about eighteen inches, and then raised my arms to take the weight of the beam I'd chosen. I pushed up hard with both hands and the weight spoke back to me, crunching me down a little; but I took heart and pushed back again, soon had the feel of it, and began to enjoy my role. As one would having at long last found something to do that was neither trite nor sentimental. Of course, the accumulated sound of all those TV loudspeakers at full blast was close to the pain threshold (I forget exactly how many decibels), but that was part of the required excess and more than compensated for by the rainbow galaxy of the color screens. What a commotion there was of barks, mutters, squeals of brakes, orchestras, jet whines, gunfire, hard-sell baritone voices, talk-show anecdotes, detonating forest fires and (as time wore on) national anthem drum rolls and the electronic roar of empty airwaves. After an hour or so, it was mostly westerns, and there was much more black-and-white than there had been. By that time I'd consumed a quart of sherry, of course, and was feeling singularly blithe. The tape had run its length, but the inauguration had been preserved for posterity. My feet were numb, the cement was rigidifying faster than I'd any right to expect, felt like wet puttees around my ankles and calves, and the beam with the house atop it was distinctly heavier. But I bore up, thrusting woozily against the weight, grateful for my cape about me, not so much a cape, I mused, as an unkempt pavilion, a pavilion being—need I remind you?—an ornate tent, evocative of medieval chivalry, usually an open and ornamental shelter originally named after the old word for butterfly (from its resemblance to the wings). I don't mind telling you, I felt quite regal, as well as grandly useful. Perhaps I should have found some means of attaching my hands to the beam, against the time when my arms and shoulders went numb, but I didn't, and my posture froze. Perhaps, too, I should have reckoned on my limited capacity for alcohol (yes! even I!), and found some way of shutting off the supply, but I didn't, and I soon began to make my own water down my leg on to the caked cement. Already it held me fast. And, no doubt, I should have reckoned on the drear time when the late late movies end, and all one has to contemplate is an array of banal test patterns and buzzing gray lozenges of light, but I didn't, and the basement sounded like a demented hive. It was too late for all these sensible expedients, so I occupied my mind with the program I'd often enough rehearsed: landlocked, but free, I Atlas Two relived my own incarnation, first of all as models A, B and C, all non-operational, but infinitely useful and lukewarmly exciting as rehearsals for such things as nose-cone separation. Ten feet wide, I was over eighty feet long, and my tapering nose-cone held a six-foot-wide nuclear warhead. Liquid fuel powered me, liquid oxygen served as oxidizer. I thrust (thrust*ed,* I told myself) with almost four hundred thousand pounds in order to lift two hundred and sixty, and I traveled at sixteen thousand miles per hour. My range was nine thousand miles. In my time, I was the launch vehicle for the Mercury manned orbital missions; it was I popped chimpanzee Enos up into the blue, not to mention Glenn, Carpenter, Schirra and Cooper. I thrill at my own physique, voluptuously savoring the names of my most private parts: interpod cableway, pod nose fairing, thrust chamber, umbilical connections, helium storage, aft nacelle, liquid oxygen boiloff valve, stub pod, No. 1 Vernier, liquid oxygen fill and drain. I'm Tamberlaine the Great mouthing the names of all the cities he's conquered! As Atlas-Agena, I've thrust satellites and orbiting observatories high above the Earth's atmosphere. Now and then I lengthen, although I don't swell, and as Atlas-Centaur I even achieved the first restart of a liquid hydrogen engine in space. 'Twas I took Surveyor to the moon. I even, when I'm feeling mighty ambitious, take on a dual back-to-back (zwei-backed) payload. I'm big, I'm hard, I'm hot, I'm fast, I'm long, I'm lethal, I'm not even earthbound. . .

Such my meditation was, at least for as long as consciousness lasted. How I stayed erect for the whole of the night, I have no idea, but I came to, still erect, in a wan light from a few sunrise semesters on the screens, the hose somewhere over my shoulder, the reek of sherry everywhere, and an appalling pain in my shoulders and back. Now I knew how it felt to be Atlas (the earthbound type anyway). My feet seemed locked in the cement as well as completely numb. Praise be, though, the house had not fallen, and I pushed against the beam with all my might, reasoning that it means nothing to step out from under when you haven't even been holding something up. How soon collapse, mine I mean, would come, I wasn't sure; it would be before noon, I could tell, and as I sank to the concrete in which I was rooted I'd be overcome with gratification. I'd have proved the point. Having been all the Atlases known to man, I'd have done duty for Atlas my random interlocutor, found the means of freeing him in perpetuity. Fond dream that it was, it was better than continually being denied my trip to Peking. So the aches and pains, the stench and the damp, mattered little to me; I was both a stoic and a scapegoat, both a monument and a hunk of myth, both a creature and a creator, both a man and a universe, both a servant and a master. I was the North and South Poles' only living cousin. I was a man-mountain clad in cloth of gold, with golden apples for eyes, golden fleece for hair, with a golden horn in my loins, a golden bough stuck between my teeth and a golden mean in the dead center of my conduct. In a word, I was golden to the hilt. It's not everyone who puts his non-stop consumption of dry sack to such chivalric uses, thereby promoting himself not socially but from mundanity to mythology. Atlassed thus, I refused to faint; but refusal has nothing to do with that special form of the syncope, and I distinctly recall the onset, as my remaining senses swam (a butterfly motion, of course) and my arms, like melting cantilevers, came a degree at a time down and out and down and away. I'm safe, I said aloud, the beam will hold; it's common sense, if such a commodity still exists. But then I heard it, my heart in even its enfeebled condition began to pound, and then to twist and writhe in its box, its flutter excruciating. A faint rattle, as of soil upon a coffin lid, grew into a rumble, as of bowling balls being unloaded on a boat's deck while you cower below, and then it was utterest commotion, like a bombardment mixed into a landslide, and I made sure the beam and the floor and the entire structure were beginning to descend, ponderously slow but beyond my power to reverse. Thunder on the left, I dimly thought, means that the gods are furious. I have trespassed too far on their reservation. But the thunder was coming from all angles, oddly pitted with falsetto wails. I braced myself for the fall of yet another house of Usher, with Humpty-Dumpty at the bottom of the heap and uncountable galaxies banging and fizzing on top of him, but all I felt was the same old air around me, damp and foul but hardly an unbearable pressure. Once again, I concluded, the universe had gone wrong; old cosmos had skipped a beat, and the anticlimax was like being allowed into Peking on your deathbed. Or deathlitter, as it would almost certainly be. In actual fact, the rattle that became a thunder that became a lull was, phase by phase, the arrival upon the basement stairs of Frank Etna and two of his children, their untidy descent toward me, and their amazed, evidently dumbstruck, witnessing of Jan Thor in his Atlas guise. How long it took them to recover their wits I never discovered, but surely it was the children who adjusted first and best, Frank Etna himself having speedily (for him) recognized, amid the panoply of my pose, the symptoms of something less exotic: a second coronary, as far from a crowning as an atlas from Atlas. In short, they got me out, installed me in intensive care in commendably short time, and I never heard from Atlas again. Needless to say, my whole world has collapsed, and it is no mere trope when I refer to myself as a collapser: a white dwarf who, burgeoning in the center of a red giant, is immensely dense, ever-and-ever colder and less luminous, soon to become invisible. As an extinct black dwarf, I'll be in no position to report, whether the truth or anything else, so I furnish you now with the one and only account of these miserable aberrations I'll ever be able to muster. Much good may it do you, as well as those who come after you (in loyalty, heredity or vengeance).

SALVE ME

The cooling process goes on for many billions of years. The light from the star becomes feebler and feebler, and ultimately disappears. The star had died, as in the Hertzsprung-Russell diagram's lower left-hand corner, where nothing shows. Atlas and I were never coeval, but, thanks to you, and through your possible intervention, dear friend, *kurie,* we may yet be. At last.

I dedicate all this stuff to Charles Kingsley, Marcus Aurelius, Whittier, Montaigne, Paul of Tarsus, Robert Browning, Pythagoras, Channing, Milton, Sophocles, Swedenborg, Thoreau, Francis of Assisi, Wordsworth, Voltaire, Garrison, Plutarch, Ruskin, Ariosto and all kindred spirits and souls of great measure from David down to Rupert Brooke.

Add Aeschylus, Petrarch, Henry Cowell.

END CONSTRUCTION. Bells, brays, drums, elbow thumps, trombones on fire. I have not written a book at all—I have merely cleared house.

3.

Poor Jan Thor, the twice ambiguously named, creature of my own concoction offered up whatever gods are available! He didn't, it seems to me, have much of a life, and the fault's all mine. Surely it's not beyond the bounds of decency, so-called, to fit out your pawns with a bit of fun, a career or even a good dose of ecstasy.

Even so, I won't go back, won't disrupt his confected finality; being done, being done with, he enables me to go forward, away from that enlarged image of a man ruinously in converse with himself, doing duty for such a rank outsider of a figment as Atlas. It was one way of coming to terms with something stationary, landlocked, and somberly dutiful in myself. I, Ives, Atlassed Jan Thor, and I had Jan Thor Jan-Thor Atlas in part of that untidy osmosis of being that goes on year in, year out; it's a simple process, really, the most honest fraudulence there is; goes like this, no?

1. First of all find the deep end.
2. Slide in, an inch per millisecond.
3. Tread water.
4. Say a prayer, any prayer, provided it begins: "It is well past time that we claimed this mad, transplanted earthling as ours." Then you're safe, have a shore to return to.
5. After which you can list with impunity what drew you to Atlas in the first place: his, your, infernal capacity for staying put for hours (or, as it seems to others, days and weeks); a certain stolidity, with the imagination shut off and the mind's very channel closed; perfectionism of vocation; an honor-mad self-reliance which maybe would carry you as far as winkling out your own appendix, mending teeth-cavities with the point of a nail file, even doing necessary amputations by electric daylight in the kitchen with breadknife, dental floss, and a bottle of—well, something stronger than Dry Sack! You wouldn't think, talking as we are of amputations, it'd take a semi-civilized writerly type about seventy pages to begin the process of coming clean; but it did, and here he is, I am, old but no-so-old Proteus doffing one mask after another, attempting yet again that bone-hard, invincible thing known as writing about what you truly care about, no shit, with not an alias in sight, not a mask at hand, nary a mouthpiece nor a persona. And all you end up with, after putting aside such childish things, is the old Niagara of the heart behind the shadow play, in whose water's course dreams don't come true, oh no, but lies falter at their own inception. Odd, in this world of *vérité,* when they want to meet you, they want to meet the guy that invented those other guys, little guessing that those other guys brought more of you into being than you ever thought there'd be. They reckon the real you's behind the puppets, hence the interviewer's wry interest in *what you wanted them to express,* whereas the real you's always ahead of the puppets (and their paper embodiments) and they're behind

you in the sense of—ur, as Atlas'd slur it, phantoms that reinforce and, best of all, can't be taken away from you. When in doubt that you existed at all, you point to them as scales you shed in passing.

Kilroy was here. And Ives as well.

It's that complicated.

Fabrication be praised, then.

"Maybe now," hum the circus animals, their minds full of desertion, "the cranky bastard'll let us off, spare us further involvement with his rancid psyche." They'd still do my bidding; in fact I might even, at this moment, still be doing theirs. After a while they talk back to you, give you a bad time, won't let you express yourself without first paroling them.

Well, they've more than kept me in sandwiches.

And some other folk as well, whose Atlas I was deemed to be.

Under the circumstances (which is a fine victimized-sounding way to begin a sentence), the dilemma's easy to settle: instead of plumping for A or B—coming clean or staying masked—you set the dilemma, install it as if it's a refrigerator (which gets hot while making cold) dead-center under those very same circumstances, and thank your stars you're double. You just keep on doing both things, eyeing the Niagara you own and, as well, snapping up the water-babies as they whizz by. But a better figure's this, the one that's been lurking in the backside of my mind since I first realized the universe was unique, was the class from which nothing could be exempted. Stefan's Quintet has a lovely sound, as if it were chamber music from Prague, or wherever, but it stands for a bigger harmony than that, is one of those galaxy clusters I gape at in glossy albums. Sky-atlases! A close grouping of solid-looking cores of light which have connecting bridges of gas, it's up there in the constellation Serpens, a close-knit family of five. And the gas's the diaphanous blur in between and around them. How like, I thought, Atlas himself added to the quartet of giants on Mount Rushmore, but how much more like Ives's mind on almost any given day, with half a dozen areas of intense, incoherent light linked up by vaporings? From that notion to appropriating S.'s Q. and domesticating it in the stockade of autobiography, it was a simple, tangily hubristic step.

Thus the conceit grows of a loose five, each of the component parts as unalike as chalk, cheese, radium, limestone and teak (except that first and fourth may be similar as that fudged-up trope of the moment—chalk-limestone—suggests). Yet one thing's sure:

the Quintet won't fight back even if I do it wrong; the universe's kind of big that way, as Jan Thor kept on telling Atlas. So forward I fare, with a satisfactory heraldic node lodged on the premises, something to hold to, or bite on, as this version of five lumps of thought in a gas cloud of intuition extends itself as far as may be; goes, indeed, past all calculation. As Herschel said, in *The Construction of the Heavens* (1811), the gradual dissolution of the Milky Way proves (a) it can't last forever, and (b) its past duration can't be admitted to be infinite. The gradual dissolution of this text, this essentially *woven* thing, proves it won't last forever, came from a finite past. And that's a relief of sorts: I'm not in the position of the doomed Ur-arithmetician who, smarting under the impact of the concept *googol,* first mooted by an eight-year-old boy to denote 1 followed by a hundred zeros, addressed himself to 10 to the power *googol,* otherwise known as a *googolplex,* and began writing out all the zeros shorthanded therein without living long enough to complete the task. Heavens! A *googolplex*'s nowhere near infinity, yet a *googol*'s a bigger number than there are elementary particles in the known universe!

One begins to begin to be grateful that, almost by definition, a book ends, says finito at some point to the infinite. And so to bed, or the mortuary stone, or the padded cell in which it's impossible to scrawl numbers on the walls. Is it infinity that scares, or the hypothesis that the mind, if it could live long enough, could actually apprehend everything? In other words, may it not be mortality instead of bigness that floors us? To ponder that, I eat a lunch of fried fish slices, fresh Vienna bread and blackberry jelly, things finite as one could wish, yet extending into everything if you take the trouble to hunt them down, the fish into the sea, the bread into the field, the jelly into the fruit, and so on. That way, life becomes a dead end of infinitely referrable series. Better to trough lunch and ask to go no further than Stefan's Quintet, not even bothering to name the component galaxies, not even letter them with incestuous coyness A and T and L and A* and S.

Having got my chest off that, let me declare here and now (who's to stop it?) I'll find something better for Jan Thor than demonic possession by, of, an Atlas. Given my own lead, what's better than to respond to it? Cued, why be cowed? So shift him I do, it takes a word only.

NOTES ON CONTRIBUTORS

ROBERT ANTONI's *Divina Trace* (Overlook) won the 1992 Commonwealth Prize for Best First Novel. He is working on a second novel, *Blesséd is the Fruit.*

JOHN BARTH's latest novel is *Once Upon a Time.* His second collection of essays and lectures, *Further Fridays,* will appear in the fall. Just now he is writing only short stories.

ROBERT OLEN BUTLER won the 1993 Pulitzer Prize for Fiction for his book of stories, *A Good Scent from a Strange Mountain.* His new novel, *They Whisper,* has just been published by Holt. "Boy Born with Tattoo of Elvis" is the first in a planned book of stories, based on supermarket newspaper reports, called *Tabloid Dreams.*

STACY DORIS's "Several Bawdy Acts" is a part of her book-length work, *Kildare.*

BARBARA GUEST's most recent book, *Defensive Rapture,* was published in 1993 by Sun & Moon. Soon to appear is *Stripped Tales,* a collaboration with artist Ann Dunn, from Kelsey Street Press. A version of *Stripped Tales* appeared first in *Conjunctions.*

ALLAN GURGANUS is the author of *Oldest Living Confederate Widow Tells All* (Knopf) and *White People* (Knopf). "Preservation News" is from his forthcoming collection of novellas. His next novel is *The Erotic History of a Southern Baptist Church.* Gurganus lives in Chapel Hill, North Carolina.

JOHN HAWKES's most recent novel, *Sweet William: A Memoir of Old Horse,* was published last fall by Simon & Schuster. His current project, from which the excerpt in this issue was taken, is tentatively entitled *Leapfrog.*

SHELLEY JACKSON is a writer, artist and illustrator. This is her first appearance in print.

ANN LAUTERBACH's newest collection, *And For Example,* will be published this fall by Viking Penguin.

KEVIN MAGEE's chapbook is out from Leave Books (Buffalo), and *Tedium Drum* will be out this summer from Lyric &.

BEN MARCUS's first book, *The Age of Wire & String,* will be published by Knopf.

HARRY MATHEWS's most recent books are *Singular Pleasures* (Dalkey Archive Press) and *A Mid-Season Sky: Poems 1954–1991* (Carcanet). "Sunday" is an extract from his fifth novel, *The Journalist,* to be published by David R. Godine later this year.

MELANIE NEILSON is the author of *Civil Noir* (Roof Books, 1991). Her next book, *Album,* is forthcoming from Potes & Poets Press. She is co-editor, with Jessica Grim, of *Big Allis* magazine.

STEPHEN RATCLIFFE's recent books of poetry include *spaces in the light said to be where one/ comes from* (Potes & Poets, 1992), *Selected Letters* (Zasterle, 1992) and *Private* (Leave Books, 1993). Forthcoming is a book of poetry, *SOUND/ (system)* (Sun & Moon, 1995).

DONALD REVELL is the author of four collections, the most recent of which is *Erasures* (Wesleyan, 1992). He has just completed a new translation of the *Alcools* of Guillaume Apollinaire.

ARNO SCHMIDT (1914–1979) is the preeminent modernist of German prose. His work includes eight novels, ten novellas, two volumes of short stories, five volumes of critical essays, a biography of La Motte Fouqué and a full-length study of Karl May. His magnum opus, *Zettels Traum (Bottom's Dream)*, is a massive fictional romp through the mind and works of Edgar Allan Poe.

JAMES SURLS lives in Splendora, Texas. His work has been exhibited recently at Marlborough Gallery (New York), Espace Lyonnais d'Art Contemporain (Lyon, France), Sewall Art Gallery, Rice University (Houston) and is in the permanent collections of MOMA, the Guggenheim, Whitney, Albright Knox and other museums.

NATHANIEL TARN continues anthropological research in the Himalayas. He has just edited Natasha Tarn's *"Multitude of One"* (Grenfell Press).

LYNNE TILLMAN's latest novel, *Cast in Doubt*, has recently been issued in paperback from Serpent's Tail. Tillman is currently researching and writing the text for a book of photographs by Stephen Shore of Andy Warhol and the Factory 1965–67. *The Velvet Years* will be published in March 1995 by Pavillion.

WENDY WALKER's *The Secret Service* (Sun & Moon) was a runner-up for the 1994 Crawford Award for Fantasy. Her new book, *Stories Out of Omarie*, is forthcoming from Sun & Moon. "My Man" was written during an NEH fellowship at Union College.

PAUL WEST won the Lannan Award for Fiction in 1993. His next books will be *Sheer Fiction III* (McPherson), *Duets* (with Diane Ackerman, Random House) and *A Stroke of Genius* (Viking). His next novel will be set in China.

JOHN E. WOODS has translated the works of Raabe, Döblin, Dürrenmatt, Grass, Süskind, Ransmayr, Moníková et al. His translation of Thomas Mann's *Buddenbrooks* appeared in 1993; his new translation of *The Magic Mountain* will be published by Knopf later this year. "The Displaced" is taken from the four-volume Dalkey Archive edition of the fictional works of Arno Schmidt, volume one of which will appear this fall.

Back issues of
CONJUNCTIONS

"A must read"—*The Village Voice*

A limited number of back issues are available to those who would like to discover for themselves the range of innovative writing published in CONJUNCTIONS over the course of more than a decade.

CONJUNCTIONS:1. *James Laughlin Festschrift.* Paul Bowles, Gary Snyder, John Hawkes, Robert Creeley, Thom Gunn, Denise Levertov, Tennessee Williams, James Purdy, William Everson, Jerome Rothenberg, George Oppen, Joel Oppenheimer, Eva Hesse, Michael McClure, Octavio Paz, Hayden Carruth, over 50 others. Kenneth Rexroth interview. 304 pages.

CONJUNCTIONS:2. Nathaniel Tarn, William H. Gass, Mei-mei Berssenbrugge, Walter Abish, Gustaf Sobin, Edward Dorn, Kay Boyle, Kenneth Irby, Thomas Meyer, Gilbert Sorrentino, Carl Rakosi, and others. H.D.'s letters to Sylvia Dobson. Czeslaw Milosz interview. 232 pages.

CONJUNCTIONS:3. Guy Davenport, Michael Palmer, Don Van Vliet, Michel Deguy, Toby Olson, René Char, Coleman Dowell, Cid Corman, Ann Lauterbach, Robert Fitzgerald, Jackson Mac Low, Cecile Abish, Anne Waldman, and others. James Purdy interview. 232 pages.

CONJUNCTIONS:4. Luis Buñuel, Aimé Césaire, Armand Schwerner, Rae Armantrout, Harold Schimmel, Gerrit Lansing, Jonathan Williams, Ron Silliman, Theodore Enslin, and others. Excerpts from Kenneth Rexroth's unpublished autobiography. Robert Duncan and William H. Gass interviews. 232 pages.

CONJUNCTIONS:5. Coleman Dowell, Nathaniel Mackey, Kenneth Gangemi, Paul Bowles, Hayden Carruth, John Taggart, Guy Mendes, John Ashbery, Francesco Clemente, and others. Lorine Niedecker's letters to Cid Corman. Barry Hannah and Basil Bunting interviews. 248 pages.

CONJUNCTIONS:6. Joseph McElroy, Ron Loewinsohn, Susan Howe, William Wegman, Barbara Tedlock, Edmond Jabès, Jerome Rothenberg, Keith Waldrop, James Clifford, Janet Rodney, and others. The *Symposium of the Whole* papers. Irving Layton interview. 320 pages.

CONJUNCTIONS:7. John Hawkes, Mary Caponegro, Leslie Scalapino, Marjorie Welish, Gerrit Lansing, Douglas Messerli, Gilbert Sorrentino, and others. *Writers Interview Writers*: Robert Duncan/Michael McClure, Jonathan Williams/Ronald Johnson, Edmund White/Edouard Roditi. 284 pages.

CONJUNCTIONS:8. Robert Duncan, Coleman Dowell, Barbara Einzig, R.B. Kitaj, Paul Metcalf, Barbara Guest, Robert Kelly, Claude Royet-Journoud, Guy Davenport, Karin Lessing, Hilda Morley, and others. *Basil Bunting Tribute*, guest-edited by Jonathan Williams, nearly 50 contributors. 272 pages.

CONJUNCTIONS:9. William S. Burroughs, Dennis Silk, Michel Deguy, Peter Cole, Paul West, Laura Moriarty, Michael Palmer, Hayden Carruth, Mei-mei Berssenbrugge, Thomas Meyer, Aaron Shurin, Barbara Tedlock, and others. Edmond Jabés interview. 296 pages.

CONJUNCTIONS:10. *Fifth Anniversary Issue*. Walter Abish, Bruce Duffy, Keith Waldrop, Harry Mathews, Kenward Elmslie, Beverley Dahlen, Jan Groover, Ronald Johnson, David Rattray, Leslie Scalapino, George Oppen, Elizabeth Murray, and others. Joseph McElroy interview. 320 pages.

CONJUNCTIONS:11. Lydia Davis, John Taggart, Marjorie Welish, Dennis Silk, Susan Howe, Robert Creeley, Charles Stein, Charles Bernstein, Kenneth Irby, Nathaniel Tarn, Robert Kelly, Ann Lauterbach, Joel Shapiro, Richard Tuttle, and others. Carl Rakosi interview. 296 pages.

CONJUNCTIONS:12. David Foster Wallace, Robert Coover, Georges Perec, Norma Cole, Laura Moriarty, Joseph McElroy, Yannick Murphy, Diane Williams, Harry Mathews, Trevor Winkfield, Ron Silliman, Armand Schwerner, and others. John Hawkes and Paul West interviews. 320 pages.

CONJUNCTIONS:13. Maxine Hong Kingston, Ben Okri, Jim Crace, William S. Burroughs, Guy Davenport, Barbara Tedlock, Rachel Blau DuPlessis, Walter Abish, Jackson Mac Low, Lydia Davis, Fielding Dawson, Toby Olson, Eric Fischl, and others. Robert Kelly interview. 288 pages.

CONJUNCTIONS:14. *The New Gothic*, guest-edited by Patrick McGrath. Kathy Acker, John Edgar Wideman, Jamaica Kincaid, Peter Straub, Clegg & Guttmann, Robert Coover, Lynne Tillman, Bradford Morrow, William T. Vollmann, Gary Indiana, Mary Caponegro, Brice Marden, and others. Salman Rushdie interview. 296 pages.

CONJUNCTIONS:15. *The Poetry Issue*. 33 Poets, including Susan Howe, John Ashbery, Rachel Blau DuPlessis, Barbara Einzig, Norma Cole, John Ash, Ronald Johnson, Forrest Gander, Michael Palmer, Diane Ward, and others.

Fiction by John Barth, Jay Cantor, Diane Williams, and others. Michael Ondaatje interview. 424 pages.

CONJUNCTIONS:16. *The Music Issue.* Nathaniel Mackey, Leon Botstein, Albert Goldman, Paul West, Amiri Baraka, Quincy Troupe, Lukas Foss, Walter Mosley, David Shields, Seth Morgan, Gerald Early, Clark Coolidge, Hilton Als, and others. John Abercrombie and David Starobin interview. 360 pages.

CONJUNCTIONS:17. *Tenth Anniversary Issue.* Kathy Acker, Janice Galloway, David Foster Wallace, Robert Coover, Diana Michener, Juan Goytisolo, Rae Armantrout, John Hawkes, William T. Vollmann, Charlie Smith, Lynn Davis, Mary Caponegro, Keith Waldrop, Carla Lemos, C.D. Wright, and others. Chinua Achebe interview. 424 pages.

CONJUNCTIONS:18. *Fables, Yarns, Fairy Tales.* Scott Bradfield, Sally Pont, John Ash, Theodore Enslin, Patricia Eakins, Joanna Scott, Lynne Tillman, Can Xue, Gary Indiana, Russell Edson, David Rattray, James Purdy, Wendy Walker, Norman Manea Paola Capriolo, O.V. de Milosz, Rosario Ferré, Jacques Roubaud, and others. 376 pages.

CONJUNCTIONS:19. *Other Worlds.* Guest-edited by Peter Cole. David Antin, John Barth, Pat Califia, Thom Gunn, Barbara Einzig, Ewa Kuryluk, Carl Rakosi, Eliot Weinberger, John Adams, Peter Reading, John Cage, Marjorie Welish, Barbara Guest, Cid Corman, Elaine Equi, Donald Baechlor, John Wieners, and others. 336 pages.

CONJUNCTIONS:20. *Unfinished Business.* Robert Antoni, Janice Galloway, Martine Bellen, Paul Gervais, Ann Lauterbach, Jessica Hagedorn, Jim Lewis, Carole Maso, Leslie Scalapino, Gilbert Sorrentino, David Foster Wallace, Robert Creeley, Ben Marcus, Paul West, Mei-mei Berssenbrugge, Susan Rothenberg, Yannick Murphy, and others. 352 pages.

CONJUNCTIONS:21. *The Credos Issue.* Robert Olen Butler, Ishmael Reed, Kathy Acker, Walter Mosley, Robert Coover, Joanna Scott, Victor Hernandez Cruz, Frank Chin, Simon Ortiz, Martine Bellen, Melanie Neilson, Kenward Elmslie, David Mura, Jonathan Williams, Cole Swensen, John Ashbery, Forrest Gander, Myung Mi Kim, and others. 352 pages.

SUN & MOON

PAUL AUSTER ■ DJUNA BARNES DAVID ANTIN ■ TARJEI VESAAS GERTRUDE STEIN ■ TOM AHERN CHARLES BERNSTEIN ■ GIL OTT BRUCE ANDREWS ■ F. T. MARINETTI ■ RUSSELL BANKS ■ SUSAN HOWE ■ CLARK COOLIDGE ■ WELCH EVERMAN ■ VALERY LARBAUD ■ ARTHUR SCHNITZLER ■ JOE ROSS ■ ■ ANDRE BRETON ■ MAC WELLMAN ■ FANNY HOWE ■ STEVE KATZ ■ NATHANIEL MACKEY ■ LEN JENKIN ■ MICHAEL BROWNSTEIN ■ WENDY WALKER ■ TOM LAFARGE ■ DAVID BROMIGE ■ JACKSON MAC LOW ■ CARL VAN VECHTEN ■ DENNIS PHILLIPS ■ BARBARA GUEST ■ JOSE EMILIO PACHECO ■ HEIMITO VON DODERER ■ LYN HEJINIAN ■ JAMES SHERRY ■ ITALO SVEVO ■ JOHN TAGGART ■ CARL RAKOSI ■ NICK PIOMBINO ■ RONALD SUKENICK LESLIE SCALAPINO ■ EDITH HEAL

P □ R □ E □ S □ S

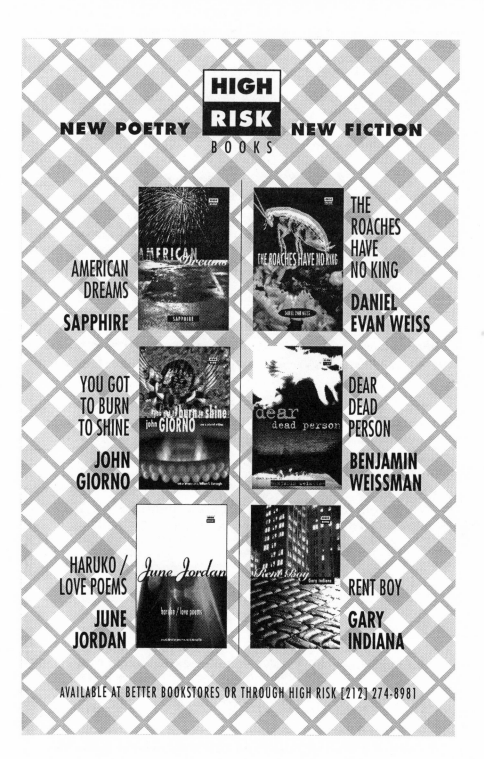